W9-BUQ-020

GUIDE TO PORTFOLIO MANAGEMENT

McGraw-Hill Finance Guide Series

Consulting Editor
Charles A. D'Ambrosio, *University of Washington*

Bowlin, Martin, and Scott: *Guide to Financial Analysis*
Farrell: *Guide to Portfolio Management*
Gup: *Guide to Strategic Planning*
Riley and Montgomery: *Guide to Computer-Assisted Investment Analysis*
Smith: *Guide to Working Capital Management*
Weston and Sorge: *Guide to International Finance*

McGraw-Hill Series in Finance

Consulting Editor
Charles A. D'Ambrosio, *University of Washington*

Brealey and Myers: *Principles of Corporate Finance*
Campbell: *Financial Institutions, Markets, and Economic Activity*
Christy and Clendenin: *Introduction to Investments*
Coates: *Investment Strategy*
Edmister: *Financial Institutions: Markets and Management*
Francis: *Investments: Analysis and Management*
Francis: *Management of Investments*
Garbade: *Securities Markets*
Haley and Schall: *The Theory of Financial Decisions*
Hastings and Mietus: *Personal Finance*
Henning, Pigott, and Scott: *International Finance Management*
Lang and Gillespie: *Strategy for Personal Finance*
Levi: *International Finance: Financial Management and the International Economy*
Martin, Petty, and Klock: *Personal Financial Management*
Robinson and Wrightsman: *Financial Markets: The Accumulation and Allocation of Wealth*
Schall and Haley: *Introduction to Financial Management*
Sharpe: *Portfolio Theory and Capital Markets*
Stevenson: *Fundamentals of Finance*
Troelstrup and Hall: *The Consumer in American Society: Personal and Family Finance*

GUIDE TO PORTFOLIO MANAGEMENT

James L. Farrell, Jr.
Chairman, MPT Associates
Adjunct Professor
New York University

McGraw-Hill Book Company

New York   St. Louis   San Francisco   Auckland   Bogotá   Hamburg
Johannesburg   London   Madrid   Mexico   Montreal   New Delhi
Panama   Paris   São Paulo   Singapore   Sydney   Tokyo   Toronto

This book was set in Times Roman by Beacon Graphics Corporation.
The editors were Bonnie E. Lieberman and James B. Armstrong;
the production supervisor was John Mancia.
The drawings were done by ANCO/Boston.
Halliday Lithograph Corporation was printer and binder.

GUIDE TO PORTFOLIO MANAGEMENT

Copyright © 1983 by McGraw-Hill, Inc. All rights reserved. Printed in the United States of America. Except as permitted under the United States Copyright Act of 1976, no part of this publication may be reproduced or distributed in any form or by any means, or stored in a data base or retrieval system, without the prior written permission of the publisher.

4 5 6 7 8 9 0 HALHAL 8 9 8 7 6 5 4

ISBN 0-07-019970-1

Library of Congress Cataloging in Publication Data

Farrell, James L.
    Guide to portfolio management.

    (McGraw-Hill finance guide series)
    Includes index.
    1. Portfolio management. I. Title. II. Series.
HG4529.5.F37   1983   332.6   82-12673
ISBN 0-07-019970-1

To my wife, Cyrille

and our children, Barbara, Catherine, and Jimmy

CONTENTS

Part 1   Underlying Theory

Part 2 Managing the Equity Portfolio

Part 3   Managing the Fixed-Income Portfolio and the Use of Options

PREFACE

Portfolio management can be generally described as consisting of three major activities: (1) asset allocation, (2) weighting shifts across major asset classes, and (3) security selection within asset classes. Over the years, there have evolved many analytical techniques with enormous potential for improving all three phases of the process of portfolio management. Many of these analytical techniques are described extensively in the academic literature, but for many practitioners and students they remain an abstruse body of knowledge with little practical relevance. Still other techniques that are more directly applicable are available only from relatively obscure and scattered sources.

The purpose of this book is to provide a comprehensive description of the practice of portfolio management and to show how the evolving analytical techniques can be applied to improve the process. While the book is analytical and of necessity quantitative in some parts, it is written with an emphasis on the economic intuition behind the theories and analytical techniques. Furthermore, it emphasizes application of the techniques by way of examples and problems as well as descriptions of actual applications. The book should appeal to experienced practitioners interested in the potential of these techniques for portfolio management as well as to students concerned with developing greater insight into the relevancy of this body of knowledge for practical application.

Chapter 1 describes the various asset classes, assesses the risk-return relationship among asset classes, and comments on the competitive nature of the capital markets. The next four chapters (2–5) describe methods for explicitly estimating returns for stocks and bonds as well as the theoretical framework for explicitly considering risk and return. The following four chapters (6–9) provide the framework for formally deriving an asset allocation; for measuring the quality of analytical judgments about stocks, groups, and the general market; and for developing active-passive strategies of portfolio management in both the domestic and international equity markets. Chapter 10 gives insight into active-passive strategies of fixed-income management, while Chapter 11 provides the formal framework for option evaluation and insight into uses of option strategies as a means of altering the risk-return characteristics of a portfolio. Chapter 12 provides the framework for assessing the manager's capability in the three components of portfolio management: (1) asset allocation, (2) asset class weighting, and (3) security selection within asset classes.

I would like to acknowledge the many people who have helped with the preparation of this book. I especially appreciate the efforts of Charles D'Ambrosio, McGraw-Hill series editor, who provided initial motivation, critical review, and constant encouragement. Bill Sharpe of Stanford University provided encouragement, commented on the initial outline, and reviewed several chapters. Peter Dietz of Frank Russell Company provided an excellent review of the complete manuscript, and Gifford Fong of Gifford Fong Associates reviewed the chapter on bond management. James Greenleaf of Lehigh University reviewed several chapters and was especially helpful in providing insights for the chapter on options. Madeline Keim of MPT Associates typed the manuscript and generally expedited completion of the project. Finally, my associates — Dave Baker, Mike Kantor, Mike Clare, Bill Brock, Gerry Goodwin, and George Peterson — were encouraging and helpful throughout the process, and I thank them for the support.

James L. Farrell, Jr.

ONE

INTRODUCTION TO PORTFOLIO MANAGEMENT

INTRODUCTION

Portfolio management consists of three major activities: (1) asset allocation, (2) weighting shifts across major asset classes, and (3) security selection within asset classes. Asset allocation can best be characterized as the blending together of major asset classes to obtain the highest long-run return at the lowest risk. Managers can make opportunistic shifts in asset class weightings in order to improve return prospects over the longer-term objective. For example, if the manager judges the outlook for equities to be considerably more favorable than for bonds over the forthcoming year, the manager may well desire to shift from bonds to equities. Finally, managers can also improve return prospects by selecting securities within the individual asset classes that have above-average return prospects.

Since the process of asset allocation should begin by defining the classes of assets available for inclusion in the portfolio, we'll begin the chapter by describing and comparing the basic characteristics of the major classes of securities. We'll also show market values as well as a total value for these major classes in order to provide some measure of the magnitude of the "market" and its components. We'll then describe the types of market indexes that are available and their uses in evaluating the behavior of the differing classes of securities.

Since understanding the differing return behavior and riskiness of asset classes is important, we'll describe methods of calculating the return on securities and ways of measuring risk. We'll then discuss the results of studies that have analyzed the behavior of returns on major security classes over time. We'll see that differing returns on asset classes have been in line with the differing riskiness of the classes, suggesting a risk-return trade-off in security markets. In this regard we'll discuss factors that have traditionally been associated with causing differences in the riskiness of assets. We'll conclude the chapter by describing the efficient-market hypothesis and indicating the way that it conditions our philosophy of portfolio management.

ASSET CLASS CHARACTERISTICS

By and large the portfolio manager has a choice of two major types of investments. First, there is the fixed-income class. This type is further subdivided into bonds and preferred stocks because the legal obligation of the corporation on bonds and on preferred stocks is substantially different. Nevertheless, both offer essentially the same investment opportunity—a fixed income. Second, there is the equity, or common-stock, security, which does not provide for any specific income in the investment contract.

Table 1-1 compares the characteristics of the different major asset classes. While technically they are fixed-income securities, short-term securities such as treasury bills and commercial paper are shown as a separate class of cash equivalents. Note that the fixed-income category includes three types of bonds—U. S. government, municipals, and corporate—as well as preferred stock. Common stocks are, of course, shown as the sole representative of that class. The columns show the major characteristics that are useful in distinguishing the different securities. These include maturity, form of return, certainty of return, and tax status.

Cash equivalents are short-term in nature, with maturities of a year or less, while bonds have longer maturities that typically range between 20 and 30 years at time of issuance. Preferred stocks generally and common stocks always have a perpetual maturity since, unlike bonds, they are issued with no set date for retirement or repayment.

Bond returns come in the form of coupon payments that are fixed at the time of issue and made periodically—generally every six months—over the life of the investment. At maturity the principal, or face value, of the bond is paid back. The certainty of these payments is generally high in the case of bonds, as they are specified by terms of a bond indenture giving the contractual obligations of the issuing governmental body or corporation. The prospect of payment on U. S. Government Bonds is certain, while on municipals and corporates it is generally high, depending on the credit standing of the issuing organization.

Preferred stocks provide returns in the form of dividend payments that are ordi-

Table 1-1 Asset class characteristics

Security class	Maturity of security	Form of return	Certainty of return	Tax status
Cash equivalents	Short	Discount	High	Fully taxable
Fixed income				
Bonds				
U. S. government	Long	Coupon	Certain	Fully taxable
Municipal	Long	Coupon	High	Not taxable
Corporate	Long	Coupon	High	Fully taxable
Preferred stock	Perpetual	Dividend	Moderately high	Partial exclusion
Common stock	Perpetual	Dividend and capital gain	Least certain	Some tax exclusion

narily set at the time of issuance. While these are fixed payments, they are not contractual obligations as in the case of bonds. Corporate directors can omit payment of dividends without incurring the severe consequences of failure to pay bond interest, where default can result in takeover of the corporation by the bondholders. As a result, the certainty of payment depends even more on the credit rating of the corporation than in the case of bonds.

Returns on common stock come in the form of dividend payments as well as in capital gains. Dividend payments are completely at the discretion of the corporate management; however, once a dividend level has been established, corporations are ordinarily reluctant to cut dividends unless operating conditions deteriorate severely. Capital gains are a function of corporate growth, the holding period of the investor, and the rate at which the market capitalizes the company's earnings at the end of the holding period. All these variables are uncertain, the last perhaps the least certain of all. While returns are essentially unlimited on the upside, common stocks are the least certain of the major asset classes.

Government bond and corporate bond interest is fully subject to income tax, while municipal bond interest is exempt.[1] For an investor fully subject to taxes, municipals are attractive for their after-tax return. Municipals tend to sell at even lower yields than governments, which are of higher credit quality because of this tax advantage. Preferred stocks are of lower quality than corporate bonds, but because the dividends are only partially taxable to other corporations, they tend to sell at a lower before-tax yield than high-grade corporates.

As previously noted, returns on common stock are in the form of dividends and capital gains. Dividends are fully taxable to individual investors but, as in the case of preferred stocks, only partially taxable to other corporations.[2] Organizations like casualty insurance companies have a preference for this kind of income. For individual investors capital gains are essentially subject to only half the tax rate that dividends are. Research is inconclusive, however, as to whether this tax preference leads to a preference on the part of investors for returns in the form of capital gains rather than dividends.

MARKET VALUES

Figure 1-1 shows the aggregate size and composition by asset class of a "world market" portfolio. The portfolio comprises cash equivalents, fixed-income securities,

[1] Municipals are classified as general obligation or revenue bonds. General obligations are bonds issued by state governments or municipal corporations chartered by the state under which all taxing powers are pledged for payment. Revenue bonds, however, do not have the taxing power of the state or local government to ensure payment. Interest and principal for these bonds must be met from the revenues of the project or service financed by the revenue bonds. Interest payments on both categories — general obligation and revenue — are free of taxes.

[2] Individuals can exclude $200 of dividend income from taxable income. Dividend income in excess of the exclusion is fully taxable to individuals. Corporations exclude 85 percent of dividend income from taxation; hence 15 percent is taxable and at a 50-percent tax rate the effective tax on this income would be 7.5 percent. As noted, dividend income is attractive to corporations, especially fire and casualty insurance companies.

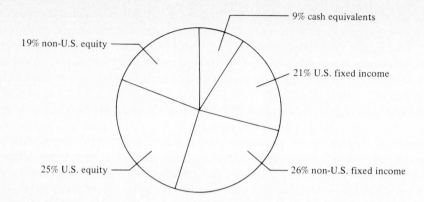

Figure 1-1 A world market portfolio of $5491 billion, December 31, 1980. (*Source: Gary Brinson and Jeffrey Diermeier, "A World Market Index," presentation to the Investment Technology Association, New York, Feb. 11, 1982.*)

and common stocks. It's a world portfolio since it includes foreign as well as domestic (U.S.) securities. With the exception of real estate, the assets represented include the major classes generally available for investment and are ones that we'll describe in some detail in later chapters of this book.

The world portfolio aggregated $5491 billion as of the end of 1980. Note that the cash equivalents represented a relatively minor portion of the portfolio. Fixed-income securities represented 47 percent of the portfolio, with foreign securities representing a somewhat greater portion than domestic securities. Common stocks comprised 44 percent of the total, with U.S. stocks representing a somewhat greater portion than foreign stocks. Foreign securities — both fixed income and common stock — represented 45 percent of the world portfolio, indicating that foreign investing should be an important consideration when undertaking an asset allocation.

Table 1-2 shows common stocks classified by trading markets: New York Stock Exchange (NYSE), American Stock Exchange (AMEX), and over-the-counter (OTC), which includes trading in all stocks not listed on one of the exchanges.[3] Note that NYSE securities represent 84.7 percent of the total, while OTC securities account for a larger proportion than the other listed market, AMEX. The table also shows the number of different stocks traded in each market. Note that there is a total of 5184 stocks that make up the universe of regularly traded stocks; the OTC has the largest number of different stocks, but the NYSE handles the stocks with the highest average value.

[3] We have included only those OTC stocks that are quoted on the NASDAQ system, an electronic quotation system that serves the OTC. (NASDAQ stands for National Association of Securities Dealers Automatic Quotations.) Inclusion in this system requires a certain minimum size and at least two active market makers in the stock. As noted in Table 1-3, there are 2983 companies that qualify for inclusion. There are, in addition, perhaps another 3000–4000 stocks actively traded on the OTC that are not quoted on the NASDAQ system. There may be another 10,000-plus issues on the OTC, but they are either quite small or inactively traded.

Table 1-2 Common stock classified by stock exchange
December 31, 1981

Exchange	Market value (billions)	% of total	Number of stocks	Average value (millions)
NYSE	$1077.0	84.7	1435	$750
AMEX	59.7	4.7	766	78
OTC	134.5	10.6	2983	45
Total	$1271.2	100.0	5184	

Source: Wilshire Associates, Santa Monica, Calif.

STOCK MARKET INDEXES

Stock market indexes provide summary measures of the behavior of the market and as such serve the following useful purposes. To begin, indexes allow comparison of movement in the market with such economic indicators as industrial production, changes in the money supply, and corporate profits. In addition, rates of return on the market itself can be a valuable benchmark for judging the performance of actual portfolios. Finally, as we'll see in Chapter 2, indexes of the market or groups of stocks are necessary inputs for the practical application of models of portfolio analysis.

Standard & Poor's Composite Index of 500 Stocks (known as the S&P 500) is a popular market value index that is usually taken to be representative of the market in general. As the name indicates, it comprises 500 stocks, mainly those listed on the New York Stock Exchange. It is a value-weighted index; that is, each stock is weighted in the index according to its market value. At the end of 1981 these 500 stocks had an aggregate market value of $860 billion. This represented 80 percent of the total value of NYSE stocks and 70 percent of the total value of all regularly traded stocks.

Table 1-3 shows the fifty largest companies in the S&P 500 and the weighting of each company in the index. Note that these companies represent approximately 50 percent of the weighting of the index; that is, 10 percent of the companies by number represent about 50 percent of the value weight. As a result, the index is probably most representative of the performance of large well-known companies like IBM, AT&T, Exxon, Shell, and General Motors. Correspondingly, it can at times give a deceiving picture of what is happening with smaller or more speculative securities.

An alternative method of index construction that helps alleviate this problem of overemphasizing large companies is that of equal weighting. This method is based on the assumption that equal dollar amounts are invested in each stock included in the index, so that if, for example, 1000 stocks are included in the index, each would receive a weight of one one-thousandth. An index constructed in this way would be more appropriate for indicating the movements in prices of typical or average stocks, whereas

Table 1-3 The fifty largest companies in the S&P 500
December 31, 1981

		Market value ($ millions)	% of S&P 500
1.	American Telephone & Telegraph	47,750.11	5.54
2.	International Business Machines	33,589.52	3.90
3.	Exxon	27,070.78	3.14
4.	Schlumberger	16,171.72	1.88
5.	Standard Oil of Indiana	15,378.26	1.78
6.	Standard Oil of California	14,667.92	1.70
7.	Shell Oil	13,593.80	1.58
8.	General Electric	13,073.41	1.52
9.	General Motors	11,589.77	1.34
10.	Eastman Kodak	11,479.29	1.33
11.	Atlantic Richfield	11,252.67	1.31
12.	Mobil	10,263.69	1.19
13.	Standard Oil of Ohio	10,200.57	1.18
14.	Royal Dutch Petroleum	9,347.82	1.08
15.	E. I. du Pont de Nemours	8,732.52	1.01
16.	Texaco	8,545.05	.99
17.	Johnson & Johnson	6,928.49	.80
18.	Gulf Oil	6,724.15	.78
19.	Procter & Gamble	6,650.39	.77
20.	Union Oil of California	6,532.19	.76
21.	Minnesota Mining & Manufacturing	6,400.75	.74
22.	Merck	6,272.85	.73
23.	Phillips Petroleum	6,163.33	.71
24.	Halliburton	6,142.98	.71
25.	Philip Morris	6,124.56	.71
26.	American Home Products	5,656.22	.66
27.	Sun	5,464.87	.63
28.	Getty Oil	5,309.20	.62
29.	General Telephone & Electronics	5,277.70	.61
30.	Sears Roebuck	5,089.34	.59
31.	Union Pacific	5,006.56	.58
32.	Dow Chemical	4,971.48	.58
33.	R. J. Reynolds	4,916.60	.57
34.	Caterpillar Tractor	4,859.96	.56
35.	Hewlett-Packard	4,834.25	.56
36.	Digital Equipment	4,707.85	.55
37.	Superior Oil	4,691.71	.54
38.	Smithkline	4,511.53	.52
39.	Tenneco	4,296.37	.50
40.	Coca-Cola	4,295.65	.50
41.	Lilly Eli	4,254.77	.49
42.	American Express	4,094.98	.48
43.	Pfizer	3,969.31	.46
44.	International Telephone & Telegraph	3,852.62	.45
45.	Cities Service	3,834.05	.44
46.	American International	3,705.71	.43
47.	Weyerhaeuser	3,699.62	.43
48.	Aetna Life & Casualty	3,534.92	.41
49.	Bristol Myers	3,509.76	.41
50.	Union Carbide	3,507.41	.41
Cumulative percent of value			50.16

Source: Greeley Securities, Inc., New York, New York.

a market-value-weighted index would be appropriate for indicating changes in the aggregate market value of stocks represented by the index.

Figure 1-2 shows the performance of two indexes: the S&P 500 and the Indicator Digest Average over the period 1964–1980. The S&P 500 is, as has been noted, a market-value-weighted index, while the Indicator Digest Average is an equally weighted index of NYSE stocks that is also widely quoted. Note that the indexes generally moved in tandem over the period. The correlation between the two indexes was in fact above 0.9, indicating that indexes will give essentially similar information regardless of the method of construction. The equally weighted index showed the most extreme fluctuations, reflecting the greater variability associated with smaller companies; it declined the most extensively in 1973 and 1974 and rose at the fastest rate from 1975 to 1980. The S&P 500 showed less extreme variation, reflecting the greater stability of the larger market-capitalization companies which dominate that index.

Each index thus provides some perspective that the others do not, and the usefulness of the particular index depends on the purpose for which it is intended. Value-weighted indexes that reflect changes in market value are more important for studies of relationships between stock prices and other indicators in the national economy. Value-weighted indexes also have the desirable property of "macroconsistency"; that is, it is possible for all investors to hold portfolios in which the individual stocks have a relative importance equal to the relative values of all outstanding shares. On the other hand, indexes based upon equal weighting are better indicators of the expected change in prices of securities selected at random.

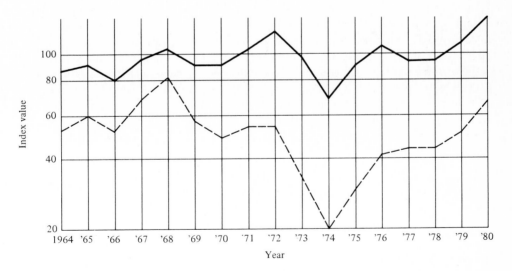

Figure 1-2 Index performance—equally weighted and market-value-weighted, 1964–1980. Solid line= S&P 500; dashed line=Indicator Digest Average. (*Sources: Standard & Poor's Corporation and Indicator Digest Average.*)

SECURITY VALUATION

Securities, whether fixed income or common stocks, derive value from the cash flow they are expected to generate. Since the cash flow will be received over future periods, there is need to discount these future flows to derive a present value or price for the security. Assuming that we are valuing the security over a single holding period, say, a year, we can illustrate the process of valuation with a particularly simple model:

$$P_0 = \frac{\text{cash flow} + P_1}{(1 + k)} \tag{1}$$

The model indicates that the present value or, alternatively, current price P_0 of the security is the cash flow (either dividends or coupons) received over the period plus the expected price at the end of period P_1, discounted back at the rate k. Note that the value of the security is positively related to the cash flow and expected future price of the security. That is, the current price will be higher as the cash flow and/or future price is expected to be higher, while the current price will be lower as the cash flow and/or future price is expected to be lower. On the other hand, the value of the security is inversely related to the discount rate k — so that the current price will be lower as the discount rate is higher and will be higher as the discount rate is lower.

The discount rate is alternatively referred to as a required return R and is composed of two elements: (1) a risk-free return R_f; and (2) a risk premium B. The risk-free return is, in turn, generally considered to comprise a real return component and an inflation premium. The real return R_r is the basic investment compensation that investors demand for forgoing current consumption, or, alternatively, the compensation for saving. Investors also require a premium to compensate for inflation and this premium I will be high when inflation is expected to be high and low when the inflation rate is expected to be low. Since the real return and inflation premium are a basic return demanded by all investors, the risk-free return is a return component that is required of all securities.

The risk premium is made up of the following elements: (1) interest rate risk, (2) purchasing power risk, (3) business risk, and (4) financial risk. We'll see in a later section of this chapter that securities differ in their exposure to these risk elements. As a result, the premium or return that investors require to compensate for risk will differ across securities as the perceived exposure to the risk elements is high or low for the security.

By rearranging the equation, we can solve directly for the discount rate k, and when in this form, it is usual to also think of the discount rate as a return expected by investors, that is, an expected return $E(R)$:

$$k = E(R) = \frac{\text{cash flow} + (P_1 - P_0)}{P_0} \tag{2}$$

Note that this equation indicates that expected return is directly related to cash flow and expected end-of-period price. When the cash flow and end-of-period price are expected to be high, the rate of return will be high as well, while a cash flow and end-of-period price that are expected to be low would result in a low expected rate of return. On the other hand, the equation indicates that the expected return is inversely related to the current price of the security. When the current price is low, the expected return will be high, while a high current price would result in a low expected return. Changes in security prices, when expected cash flow and end-of-period prices remain the same, thus provide a way that securities can adjust to provide returns required by investors.

We can also use Equation 2 for calculating the return earned on a security over a past period — realized return — only this time we would insert a realized value for the cash flow and an actual ending-period price rather than expected values of these variables.[4] In calculating the return for, say, a common stock, it's helpful to think of the realized return as consisting of a yield component — dividend divided by beginning-of-period price D/P_0 and a capital gain component which is the percentage change in price $(P_1 - P_0/P_0)$ over the period:

$$\text{Return} = \frac{D}{P_0} + \frac{P_1 - P_0}{P_0} \qquad (3)$$

As an example, we'll assume a stock was selling at $50 a share at the beginning of the period (P_0), paid a $4 dividend (D), and sold at $54 at the end of the period (P_1). We then calculate the return realized over the period, which we assume to be a year, as follows:

$$\text{Return} = \frac{\$4}{\$50} + \frac{\$54 - \$50}{\$50} = 16\%$$

The calculation shows that the realized return of the stock of 16 percent derived from an 8 percent yield component and from an 8 percent capital gain.

MEASURING RISK

In addition to determining the rate of return, it is also important to assess the risk or uncertainty that may be associated with earning the return. The variance of return and standard deviation of return are alternative statistical measures that are proxies for the uncertainty or risk of return. These statistics in effect measure the extent to which returns have varied around an average over time. Extensive variations around the average would indicate great uncertainty regarding the return to be expected.

Table 1-4 illustrates calculation of the variance and standard deviation for the returns realized over a three-year period for a hypothetical stock. The first column shows the year-by-year returns and the average return of 15 percent over the three-year period. The second column shows the deviations of the individual-year returns from the average, while the third column shows the squaring of these deviations. Squaring puts all the deviations in absolute (positive) terms and has other useful statistical properties

[4] We might note that the realized return and expected return will be the same when the realized cash flow and end-of-period price are the same as the expected value of these variables. While it would be unusual for these values to be the same over any single period, we might expect that over time realized returns and expected returns would tend to correspond. This is the basis for use of realized returns as proxies for expectations.

Table 1-4 Return, variance, and standard deviation

Year	Return R_1 % (1)	Deviation $R_1 - \bar{R}$ (2)	Deviation^2 $(R_1 - \bar{R})^2$ (3)
1	5	-10	100
2	15	0	0
3	25	$+10$	100

Average return $\bar{R} = \sum_{i=1}^{N} \dfrac{R_i}{N} = 15\%$

Variance of return $= \mathrm{Var}(R) = \sum_{i=1}^{N} \dfrac{(R_i - \bar{R})^2}{N} = 67\%^2$

Standard deviation of return $S = \sqrt{\mathrm{Var}(R)} = 8.2\%$

as well. The variance is merely the average of the squared deviations, as can be seen from the variance formula:

$$\mathrm{Var}(R) = \sum_{i=1}^{N} \frac{(R_i - \bar{R})^2}{N} = \frac{200}{3} = 67\%^2 \tag{4}$$

Note that the dimension of the calculated variance is the return squared, which is, of course, economically meaningless.[5] Hence we would normally take the square root of the variance to obtain the standard deviation S, which also measures the variability of the distribution and has the further advantage of being set out in terms of return. Despite the difference in dimensions both risk measures can be used interchangeably to rank the relative riskiness of securities; that is, if security A is riskier than security B in terms of variance, it will also be riskier in terms of standard deviation.

RISK IN A PORTFOLIO CONTEXT

While standard deviation and variance measure the riskiness of a security in an absolute sense, there is also need to consider the riskiness of a security within the context of an overall portfolio of securities. The riskiness of a security will thus depend on how it blends with the existing securities and contributes to the overall risk of a portfolio. The covariance is a statistic that measures the riskiness of a security relative to others in a portfolio of securities.

Table 1-5 illustrates the calculation of the covariance. The first column shows the year-by-year returns of the security used in Table 1-4 to illustrate the calculation of the variance and standard deviation, while the third column shows the returns of a second hypothetical security. Note that the pattern of returns for the second security is merely the reverse of the first, so that each will have the same average return and standard

---

[5]Technically the divisor in this formula should be $n-1$. This is to adjust for the loss of one degree of freedom in the calculation. For simplicity of exposition, we've avoided this adjustment here and in the other illustrations in this section.

Table 1-5 Calculating the covariance

Year	Return R_1 (1)	Deviation $R_{1i} - \bar{R}_1$ (2)	Return R_2 (3)	Deviation $R_{2i} - \bar{R}_2$ (4)	Product of deviations (2) × (4)	Combined returns (6)
1	5	−10	25	+10	−100	15
2	15	0	15	0		15
3	25	+10	5	−10	−100	15
	15		15		−200	15

$$\text{Covariance} = \text{Cov}(R_1R_2) = \sum_{i=1}^{N} \frac{(R_{1i} - \bar{R}_1)(R_{2i} - \bar{R}_2)}{N} = \frac{-200}{3} = -67\%^2$$

$$\text{Correlation} = \rho_{12} = \frac{\text{Cov}(R_1R_2)}{S_1 S_2} = \frac{-67\%}{(8.2)(8.2)} = -1$$

deviation of return. Columns 2 and 4 show the deviations of the returns of each security from the average return, and Column 5 shows the product of these deviations (Column 2 times Column 4). The average of the summation of the product of these deviations is the covariance of return $\text{Cov}(R_1R_2)$.

$$\text{Cov}(R_1R_2) = \frac{1}{N}\sum_{i=1}^{N}(R_{1i} - \bar{R}_1)(R_{2i} - \bar{R}_2) = \frac{-200}{3} = -67\%^2 \qquad (5)$$

Note that the calculated covariance is a large negative value. This is because the deviations of the two securities are consistently opposite; that is, the securities moved counter to each other consistently. In contrast, if the two securities had moved consistently in tandem, the deviations would have been in the same direction. In this case the calculated covariance would have been positive. An intermediate case would be where the securities moved in tandem in some periods and counter to each other in other periods. This pattern would result in a covariance of lower value as the varying directions of the deviations would be offsetting.

Note that like the variance the covariance is expressed as percent squared. For this and other reasons the covariance is difficult to interpret, at least for practical application. To facilitate interpretation it is therefore useful to standardize the covariance. Dividing the covariance between two securities by the product of the standard deviation of each security produces a variable with the same properties as the covariance but scaled to a range of −1 to +1. The measure is called the *correlation coefficient*. Letting ρ_{12} represent the correlation between securities 1 and 2, the correlation coefficient can be defined as

$$\rho_{12} = \frac{\text{Cov}(R_1R_2)}{S_1 S_2} = \frac{-67\%}{(8.2)(8.2)} = -1 \qquad (6)$$

In this instance the correlation coefficient is −1, which indicates that the two securities are perfectly negatively correlated, as might be expected owing to the fact that the two securities consistently moved opposite to each other. In general, negative correlation and hence negative covariance are desirable in a security, because such securities have great risk-reducing potential in a portfolio context; they are low risk in this sense. The last column in Table 1-5 illustrates this by showing that a combination of the two securities (equally weighted in a portfolio) would display constant year-by-year returns. Putting these negatively correlated securities together completely eliminates risk while maintaining the same level of return. The second security, while showing risk when viewed by itself, is a highly desirable risk-reducing (in this case risk-eliminating) security. We'll complete the analysis of the impact of differences in correlation between securities and portfolio risk in Chapter 2.

Meanwhile we should note that in this example the specific security — hypothetical stock 2 — had no risk when measured relative to the single-stock portfolio. This might bring to mind that one of the critical issues to resolve in assessing the risk of an individual security is determining what is an appropriate benchmark portfolio; that is, what securities and weightings of securities in the portfolio should be used for assessing the relative risk of individual securities. Intuitively it might seem that a portfolio including all securities — a market portfolio — would most appropriately serve the purpose of a benchmark portfolio. This is in fact the case, as we'll see when we discuss capital market theory in Chapter 3.

RISK-RETURN CHARACTERISTICS OF ASSET CLASSES

It's useful to calculate returns and measure risk for asset classes over various past intervals. First, this helps evaluate the behavior of the asset class over different economic episodes, such as the business cycle. Second, returns measured over sufficiently long periods may be taken as representative of the returns that investors may have expected to earn over the period. This may in turn be useful in establishing some benchmarks as to what returns investors might be expecting to earn in the future. Finally, availability of realized return and risk measures can be used to compare the relative performance behavior across asset classes.

Several researchers, most notably Ibbotson and Sinquefeld, have in fact calculated the realized return and standard deviation of return over past periods for four asset classes: common stocks, corporate bonds, treasury bills, and long-term government bonds. They not only wished to see how these securities performed over various time periods but also wanted to assess how the return on differing asset classes related to the relative riskiness of the asset class. Correspondingly, they wished to determine the real return earned on the various asset classes over the period.

To determine the real return on assets, Ibbotson and Sinquefeld obtained inflation rates and compared these with the nominal returns on assets.[6] A way to assess the risk-return relationship among assets is to establish a hierarchy of risk and return and compare across the various asset classes. For example, treasury bills would be considered the least risky of the asset classes, and we could compare the return earned on these assets with inflation to determine real return. Long-term government bonds entail greater risk than treasury bills, and we might characterize the added return to compensate for this risk as a *liquidity premium*. Long-term corporate bonds carry a credit risk not incurred by governments, and we might designate the extra return earned by corporates over government bonds as a *default premium*. Finally, common stocks can be compared with the least risky assets, treasury bills, to determine a risk premium for investing in this most risky of the asset classes.

Table 1-6 shows the rates of return and standard deviation of return for each of the asset classes, as well as the inflation rate over the fifty-three-year period 1926–1978. Note that common stocks provided the highest return over the period, and showed the highest standard deviation of return, while treasury bills earned the least return and exhibited the lowest variability, with government and corporate bonds showing inter-mediate risk-return character. Inflation averaged 2.5 percent over the period; using this rate to adjust the nominal rate of return would have resulted in a lower real return in all asset classes. The real return for stocks over the period was 6.4 percent, while the real return for treasury bills was virtually zero. The two long-term bond categories showed real returns of 0.7 and 1.5 percent over the period.

Comparing returns across classes, we can assess the differing premia earned for accepting risk over the period. Note that long-term government bonds earned 3.2 percent and treasury bills 2.5 percent, indicating a realized liquidity premium of 0.7 percent over the period. Long-term corporate bonds earned 4.0 percent compared

[6] The nominal return R on a security, conceived as real return R_r and compensation for inflation I, can be related as follows:

$$1 + R = (1 + R_r)(1 + I)$$

The real return can then be derived as

$$1 + R_r = \frac{1 + R}{1 + I}$$

By cross-multiplying this equation we obtain

$$R_r = R - I - R_r I$$

which reduces to the following analytically useful approximation when R_r and I are small:

$$R_r = R - I$$

Table 1-6 Realized return, inflation, real returns, and risk premiums
1926–1978

	Mean return, %	Real return, %	Liquidity premium	Default premium	Risk premium, %	Standard deviation of return, %
Common stock	8.9	6.4	—	—	6.4	22.2
Long-term corporate bonds	4.0	1.5	—	0.8	—	5.6
Long-term government bonds	3.2	0.7	0.7	—	—	5.7
Treasury bills	2.5	0	—	—	—	2.2
Consumer Price Index (inflation)	2.5	—	—	—	—	—

Source: Roger G. Ibbotson and Rex A. Sinquefeld, *Stocks, Bonds, Bills and Inflation: Historical Returns,* Financial Analysts Foundation, Charlottesville, Va., 1979, pp. 12, 23.

with the 3.2 percent return for governments, to provide a default premium of 0.8 percent over the period. Finally, common stocks earned 8.9 percent, to provide a risk premium of 6.4 percent for these riskiest of the assets compared with the least risky asset — treasury bills. As a matter of interest, comparing returns in this fashion is especially helpful when formally determining an asset allocation, as will be described in Chapter 7.

FUNDAMENTAL SOURCES OF RISK

While the previous section showed that returns vary over time and that there appears to be some sort of trade-off between risk and return, it did not indicate how these risks develop and impact assets. This section assesses four factors that have traditionally been considered important in determining the degree of risk associated with an asset: interest rate risk, purchasing power risk, business risk, and financial risk. This discussion should be helpful not only in understanding historical risk-return relationships but also in assessing the extent to which these factors will impact the risk and return of assets in the future. Furthermore, this discussion should help us understand the underlying fundamentals of more quantitative measures of risk.

Interest Rate Risk

Interest rate risk is the variability in return caused by changes in the level of interest rates. All market interest rates tend to move up or down together in the long run. These changes in interest rates affect all securities to an extent and tend to affect all of them in the same way, because the value of a security is the present value of the security income. Since the market rate of interest is a component of the discount rate used in calculating present values of securities, all security prices tend to move inversely with changes in the level of interest rates (refer back to Equation 1 to see this inverse relationship). Longer-term securities in turn show greater variability in price with respect to interest rate changes than shorter-term securities.

We can refer back to Table 1-1 for help in assessing the relative vulnerability of the different security classes to the interest rate risk. In particular, we would expect cash equivalents to be less vulnerable to the interest rate risk than long-term bonds. We would further expect long-term bonds to be less vulnerable than preferred stocks, which have a perpetual life compared with bonds, which might have a maturity of twenty years. Common stocks would be the most vulnerable to the interest rate risk because of their perpetual life as well as the presumed growth in dividends. In Chapter 4 we'll describe an analytical framework that allows a more precise characterization of exposure to the interest rate risk.

Purchasing Power Risk

Nominal returns contain both a real return component and an inflation premium to compensate for inflation anticipated over an investment holding period. Inflation rates vary over time, however, and investors do not always anticipate changes in the rate of inflation. This results in an additional factor that might be termed unanticipated inflation, which can cause the realized return of securities to diverge from that which was anticipated when the rate of inflation remained at the expected level. We can most directly illustrate this effect on security returns by restating our formula for calculating the expected return of a security:

$$\text{Expected return} = \frac{\text{cash flow} + (P_1 - P_0)}{P_0}$$

For fixed-income securities like bonds, where the cash flows (coupon payments) are fixed, the only way that the return can be adjusted to compensate for an increase in inflation is a decline in price. The decline in price reduces the denominator of the equation and hence increases the expected return on the security. Conversely, when there is an unanticipated decrease in the rate of inflation, we would expect returns to be lower. This would be accomplished by an increase in the price, thus raising the denominator and lowering the return expected in the future.

Bonds and other fixed-income securities, such as preferred stocks, are thus highly vulnerable to accelerating inflation — that is, purchasing power risk. On the other hand, fixed-income securities would be highly desirable investments during a deflationary period or a period of decelerating inflation. In fact, we'll see in Chapter 7 that the basic merits of fixed-income securities in an asset allocation scheme are as a hedge against deflation.

For securities like common stocks, where cash flows (dividends) are flexible, the price of the security does not necessarily need to adjust to compensate for unanticipated inflation. For stocks in particular the cash flow (dividend) term in the numerator could rise to offset an increase in the rate of inflation and thereby preclude any need for a price adjustment. Increasing cash flows presumes, in turn, an ability to price products accordingly and hold costs in line to increase the profitability necessary to generate the added growth. It is essentially an empirical question whether corporations have in fact been able to do this and thereby provide a hedge against inflation.

Table 1-7 provides some perspective on the success of corporations in offsetting inflation over longer and shorter intervals. It shows price, dividend, and earnings data from the S&P 500 as well as the Consumer Price Index (CPI) for selected dates from 1947 to 1980. It also gives the percentage changes in these variables at intervals over the period as an aid to evaluating the responsiveness of stocks to inflationary forces.

Note that during the 1947 – 1965 period the rate of increase in dividend income was on average considerably above the rate of increase in consumer prices. Stock prices also appreciated significantly and the total return on stocks over the period provided a good hedge against inflation. On the other hand, stocks did not provide a hedge against inflation during the 1965 – 1974 period. While dividend growth continued to be positive, it lagged the rate of increase in inflation, which had accelerated to the highest level of the postwar period. Stock prices also declined to provide a net return significantly below the inflation rate. More recently, dividend growth accelerated and stock prices appreciated; net return exceeded inflation, and stocks again provided a hedge against inflation.

Table 1-7 The Consumer Price Index versus the S&P 500
Selected years

Year	Consumer Price Index (1967 = 100)	S&P 500 (dollars)		
		Year-end price	Dividends	Earnings
1947	66.9	15.3	0.84	1.61
1950	72.1	20.4	1.47	2.84
1955	80.2	45.5	1.64	3.62
1960	88.7	58.1	1.95	3.27
1965	94.5	92.4	2.72	5.19
1970	116.3	92.1	3.14	5.13
1974	147.7	68.5	3.60	8.89
1980	225.8	135.8	6.16	14.79
		Percent change		
1947–1950	7.7	33.0	75.0	87.3
1950–1955	11.2	123.0	11.6	27.5
1955–1960	10.6	27.7	18.9	−9.7
1960–1965	6.5	59.1	39.5	58.7
1965–1970	23.2	−0.3	15.4	−1.1
1970–1974	26.7	−26.6	14.6	72.3
1974–1980	52.9	98.1	71.1	66.4

Source: Standard & Poor's Security Price Index Record.

These data, like those from the Ibbotson and Sinquefeld study, indicate that over longer periods corporations have been able to offset inflation and provide a significant real return to investors. Over shorter intervals, however, corporations have demonstrated ability to offset inflation as well as failure to cope with it adequately. On balance, then, it appears that stocks are exposed to purchasing power risk, but not nearly to the extent of long-term bonds or preferred stocks.

Business Risk

Business risk is the uncertainty of income flows caused by the nature of the firm's business and can be measured by the distribution of the firm's operating income over time; that is, the more variable the operating income, the greater the business risk, and the less variable, the lower the risk. Business risk is divided into two categories: internal and external. Internal business risk is associated with operating conditions that can be managed within the firm and is reflected in the operating efficiency of the firm. External business risk is associated with operating conditions imposed on the firm by circumstances beyond its control, such as the political and economic environment in which it operates.

The inclusion of business risk as a factor in the evaluation of securities recognizes the possibility that the stream of earnings expected by the investor will not materialize, which may adversely affect the value of the future stream of benefits that he expects to receive. In the case of common stock this would entail a capital loss when the investor went to sell his stock. In an extreme case it could mean bankruptcy and total loss to the shareholder. In the case of fixed-income securities the presence of business risk as measured by the deviation from expected earnings may impair the firm's ability to meet its interest or amortization payments. The more variability in operating income, the greater is the chance of bond default.

Common stocks as a class are subject to this risk much more extensively than bonds as a class. Of course, government bonds are not subject to this risk at all, while corporate bonds are subject to it only to a limited extent in all but the case of exceptionally low-quality bonds. We should then expect that stocks would carry significantly large premiums in their expected return to compensate for this greater risk as compared with bonds, which would generally have either no premium built into the expected return or only minor adjustment for this potential risk.

Within the equity market there can be varying degrees of exposure to business risk. Companies that are small, hold secondary positions within their industry, have heavy fixed costs and extensive operating leverage, are highly sensitive to the business cycle, and demonstrate significant variability in earnings are expected to have a high degree of business risk. Those that are large, are leading factors in their industry, have relatively low sensitivity to the business cycle, and show a stable pattern of earnings have a lesser degree of business risk. We would expect the former companies to offer higher returns than the latter to compensate for this risk.

Financial Risk

Financial risk arises from the introduction of debt into the capital structure of a corporation. It is usually measured by the percentage of debt as compared with equity in the capital structure — that is, the debt to equity ratio. Since the existence of debt means the obligation to pay fixed financing charges — interest payments — there is the risk that earnings may be insufficient to meet these obligations. This would, of course, have an unfavorable impact on bondholders, who would forgo the expected earnings (interest) on their investment, as well as on stockholders, who would suffer the consequences of default and possible complete loss of their investment. Furthermore, the increased variability of earnings associated with the presence of fixed charges increases the uncertainty that shareholders will receive the expected return on their investment.

Common stocks of companies that finance with debt would be subject to this risk, which would increase directly with the proportion of debt in the capital structure. This risk might also reflect back on the bonds of the corporation that finances too heavily with debt: the more extensive the debt, the lower the quality of the debt. Generally, however, corporate bonds would be subject to this risk to a rather limited extent, with government bonds again not subject to it at all. Common stocks of companies that finance with debt would be expected to offer the highest returns premium to compensate for this risk, while the premium required for corporate bonds would generally be rather limited.

EXPOSURE TO RISK COMPONENTS

It will be useful at this point to use the data shown in Table 1-8 to assess the extent of each of four major security classes exposure to the four sources of risk: interest rate, purchasing power, business, and financial. Note that the table shows four security classes: (1) treasury bills to represent a short-term security of the highest quality, (2) twenty-year government bonds to represent a long-term security of the highest quality, (3) thirty-year AAA corporate bonds to represent long-term corporates of high quality, and (4) common stocks.

The first four columns represent the four components of risk. Exposure to risk is rated on a scale of 5, where 1 means no exposure, 5 represents maximum exposure, and 3 represents average exposure. A rating of 2 indicates below-average exposure to a risk component, while a rating of 4 represents above-average exposure. The fifth column in the table shows the sum of the ratings in each row across, providing a measure of overall exposure to the risk components. This aggregation is merely an attempt to provide relative rankings of the securities with respect to risk exposure and should not be construed as a precise ordering.

Note that treasury bills are exposed only to the purchasing power risk, and even here only to a rather limited degree. Treasury bills are often used as proxies for risk-free securities, and their ranking as the least exposed to the components of risk provides some insight into why this is so. Long-term governments show a somewhat greater overall exposure to the risk components, mainly deriving from an average exposure to the interest rate risk and a maximum exposure to the purchasing power risk. AAA corporates are similarly exposed to the interest rate and purchasing power risks as long-term governments, but also exhibit a moderate degree of exposure to business and financial risk. Common stocks show maximum exposure to the interest rate and business risks, with some exposure to financial risk. Stocks, however, have a less extensive exposure to the purchasing power risk than the two classes of long-term bonds.

Table 1-8 Risk-return relationship

	Interest rate (1)	Purchasing power (2)	Business (3)	Financial (4)	Total risk (5)	Average risk (6)	Standard deviation, % (7)	Realized return, % (1926–1978)
Treasury bills	1	2	1	1	5	1.25	2.2	2.5
Long-term government bonds	3	5	1	1	10	2.50	5.7	3.2
AAA corporate bonds	3	5	2	2	12	3.00	5.6	4.0
Common stocks	5	3	5	3	16	4.00	22.2	8.9

Source: Roger G. Ibbotson and Rex A. Sinquefeld, *Stocks, Bonds, Bills and Inflation: Historical Returns,* Financial Analysts Foundation, Charlottesville, Va., 1979, p. 12.

   Overall, then, stocks show the most exposure to the components of risk, and treasury bills demonstrate the least exposure, with long-term bonds holding the intermediate position. Column 7 in Table 1-8 shows the standard deviation of return of the four asset classes and indicates that the risk ranking of the securities would be similar according to either statistical or fundamental measures. Both techniques are useful in providing perspective on the riskiness of securities and in this case resulted in essentially the same relative ordering.

   Given these underlying risk characteristics, we can depict the expected trade-off in return by means of the market line relationship illustrated in Figure 1-3. It is a risk-return diagram, where the vertical axis represents the return expected or, alternatively, required by investors, while the horizontal axis represents the risk associated with the asset. For the time being, it's useful to think of the risk as representing the exposure of the asset to the four fundamental sources of risk. In the next section, we'll describe an equivalent means of measuring of the risk of an asset.

   Note that the market line that has been drawn on the diagram is upward-sloping from the vertical axis, indicating that increasing levels of risk should be compensated by an increasing increment of return over the risk-free rate R_f. The four asset classes are plotted along the line to indicate the sort of return that should be expected given the fundamental risk of the class. Note that treasury bills are along the lower-left-hand part of the market line, indicating that we expect little added return from this asset class, while common stocks plot along the upper part of the line, indicating that we expect

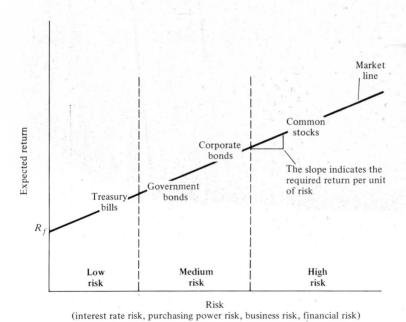

Figure 1-3 Relationship between risk and return.

a high return to compensate for their high risk. Bonds that plot at an intermediate level would be expected to provide an intermediate return.

While this is an expected relationship, we would expect that over longer periods the realized return and risk of assets would conform to it. In fact, the final column of Table 1-8 shows that over the fifty-three-year period 1926–1978 the realized returns on these asset classes were roughly in line with the expected risk-return relationship. In particular, common stocks provided the greatest returns, treasury bills the lowest, and long-term bonds an intermediate level.

SYSTEMATIC RISK

We have seen thus far that securities differ in their riskiness and that there is a trade-off between risk and return. There is thus a risk premium in security returns in addition to a risk-free component. We indicated that the fundamental sources of the risk premium are: (1) interest rate risk, (2) purchasing power risk, (3) business risk, and (4) financial risk.

In Chapters 2 and 3 we'll see that portfolio theory and capital-market theory assess risk within the context of a portfolio. This analysis indicates that the risk of a security is composed of two components: systematic risk and specific risk. Systematic risk is that risk which is common to all assets, at least to some extent. Specific risk is unique to the security, and we'll see in Chapter 2 that it can be eliminated by diversification. As a result, systematic risk is the component that should be rewarded; that is, it determines the risk premium.

While the portfolio and fundamental approaches to determining the risk premium on securities may appear to differ, they are in fact consistent with one another. In particular, the four sources of risk are fundamental and have an effect across all asset classes, and would be expected to have similar impact on securities within each of the asset classes. The commonality of this effect might be expected to provide the systematic force that causes securities within the class to move together. Also, the commonality of the effect across asset classes should lead to the systematic movement between asset classes. The four fundamental sources should thus be the factors underlying systematic risk; hence, the fundamental and portfolio approaches to assessing the risk premium should be equivalent.

PORTFOLIO MANAGEMENT

As noted in the chapter introduction, a prime task of portfolio management is to blend the various assets together to provide a portfolio that is best suited to meet the longer-term return goals of the fund at the least risk. For example, the fund's goal might be to earn a 4-percent real return (nominal return less inflation rate) over, say, a five-year planning period. The fund might find through a formal asset allocation procedure that a combination of, say, 55 percent domestic stocks, 15 percent international equities, 20 percent long-term bonds, and 10 percent short-term bonds will best meet its goal.

We further indicated that portfolio managers could attempt to increase returns over that expected from the basic asset allocation by (1) shifting weightings across the major asset classes and (2) selecting securities of above-average attractiveness within the asset class. Shifts across classes have a shorter-term orientation and would entail on, say, a year-by-year basis a weighting of assets different from that of longer-term asset allocation. For example, in a particular year the manager might determine that domestic equities are relatively more attractive than long-term bonds and increase the domestic equity portion of the portfolio to 65 percent and reduce the longer-term bond portion by 10 percent. The objective of security selection is to hold securities in the asset class that have the greatest promise of outperforming a market index representative of the general performance of securities in the class. For example, the manager of assets within the domestic equity class would endeavor to select securities with the best prospects of outperforming an equity index like the S&P 500.

While portfolio managers may attempt to construct portfolios that have the best chance of meeting longer-term goals and endeavor to improve returns by asset class shifts and security selection within classes, there is no guarantee that these efforts will be successful. The efficient-market hypothesis and related evidence provide some benchmarks as to the difficulty of successfully achieving the goals of portfolio management. Therefore, we'll review the efficient-market hypothesis and related research and then indicate the implications for portfolio management.

EFFICIENT-MARKET HYPOTHESIS

Capital markets, especially in the United States, fulfill many of the requisites of the traditional model of a highly competitive market. In particular, the markets are composed of many participants, no one of which has a dominant share. Information about the securities is generally available at reasonably low cost, and developing changes in the economic, political, and social structure are quickly disseminated. Transaction costs are low and markets are generally liquid, so that prices of securities can adjust to changes in the outlook. Finally, the institutional structure of the markets is well developed and existing regulation further ensures the smooth working of the markets.

Because of these underlying characteristics, we might expect the capital markets to be generally efficient; that is, we would expect the price of a security at any point to generally reflect the available information about that security. Correspondingly, we would expect the security to be fairly valued and provide a return commensurate with its risk. Furthermore, we would expect the price of the security to adjust quickly to new information so as to maintain its anticipated risk-return relationship.

The efficient-market hypothesis is a formal statement in three forms which relate to degree of market efficiency: (1) the weak form, (2) the semistrong form, and (3) the strong form. The weak form asserts that current prices fully reflect the information implied by the historical sequence of prices; in other words, an investor cannot enhance his ability to select stocks by knowing the history of successive prices and the results of analyzing them in all possible ways. The semistrong form of the hypothesis asserts that current prices fully reflect public knowledge about the underlying companies, and therefore efforts to acquire and analyze this knowledge cannot be expected to produce superior results. This data would include, for example, earnings, dividends, public announcements by management, and other widely reported statements. The strong form asserts that not even those with privileged information can often make use of it to secure superior investment results.

TESTS OF THE EFFICIENT-MARKET HYPOTHESIS

Since the weak form of the efficient-market hypothesis is concerned with the use of past prices to predict future security returns, tests have focused on determining whether there is any dependency in the prices of securities over time and whether specific trading rules can be used profitably in security trading. Results of these tests have shown little or no dependency in security prices and that trading rules cannot be used to earn profits over that of a buy-and-hold policy after adjusting for costs of trans-actions. Because this form of the hypothesis can be tested rather directly, and because the testing to date has been extensive, it is probably fair to conclude that the market is likely to be highly efficient at least in the weak sense of the hypothesis.

On the other hand, because of the variety and lack of regularity of the information involved, tests of the semistrong form of the hypothesis are not so unambiguous. Some examples of tests of this hypothesis are the effects on stock prices of secondary offerings, dividend announcements, reports of earnings, and changes in the discount rate of the Federal Reserve. Correspondingly, there have been tests of the use of valuation models like the Value Line timeliness ranking and of such strategies as the "low P/E" strategy for earning extra returns. These tests have provided mixed results, affirming the efficiency of the market and others, such as the Value Line timeliness ranking and quarterly earnings surprises, indicating opportunities for earning extraordinary profits. Because of the mixed results and the greater difficulty in testing this hypothesis in the first place, it is probably fair to say that the market is only moderately efficient with respect to all publicly available information.

The strong form of the efficient-market hypothesis makes the most extreme and perhaps least credible statement of the likely efficiency of the market, and it is at the same time the most difficult to verify. Tests of this hypothesis have taken two directions: (1) tests of whether any particular groups, such as corporate insiders or stock exchange specialists, might have privileged information which they could use to their advantage, and (2) tests of whether professional managers, such as those of mutual funds, might have a special capability for earning greater than average returns. Tests of the first groups have shown that both stock exchange specialists and corporate insiders are able to earn profits greater than might be expected in a perfectly efficient market, thereby providing evidence against the efficient-market hypothesis at least for these groups.

On the other hand, tests of the capability of professional fund managers have shown that funds in general have been unable to outperform the market over extended periods of time; however, this is not necessarily conclusive evidence in favor of the hypothesis. It is the author's opinion, from observation and analysis of the activities of large professionally managed funds, that much of the performance problem derives from three major deficiencies: (1) failure to explicitly establish performance goals in risk-return terms, (2) failure to analyze the investment process and assess the strengths and weaknesses of the organization, and (3) excessive turnover based on misassessment of return opportunities. These deficiencies are likely to overwhelm any superiority of analytical judgment within the fund organization relating to the three major phases of portfolio management: (1) asset allocation, (2) asset class weighting, and (3) security selection within asset classes.

CONCLUSION

Given the evidence we think that the market is likely to be generally efficient at least with respect to the weak form of the hypothesis and to a certain extent with respect to the semistrong form. This implies that simpleminded approaches, one-decision rules for selecting asset classes and individual securities, short-term trading strategies, and "black box" approaches to portfolio management are likely to be destined to failure. At the same time we do not find compelling evidence that the market is perfectly efficient and is, instead, likely to be only moderately efficient with respect to the strong form of the hypothesis. There is opportunity for managers to develop superior insights with the potential for above-average performance.

Since good judgment is only a necessary condition and not sufficient to assure successful performance, we think that it is critical for managers to consider and implement the following portfolio procedures. First, the organization needs a framework for establishing performance goals that explicitly consider risk as well as return. Furthermore, it needs tools for analyzing the components of the investment process. This is essential for assessing the strengths and weaknesses of the organization, so that strengths can be emphasized through active strategies and weaknesses hedged by passive strategies. Finally, it needs an objective method of evaluating the skill of the individual analysts and portfolio managers in making weighting decisions across the major asset classes and selecting securities within asset classes. The purpose here is to identify those individuals with superior insights and emphasize their use while reorienting the activities of others.

The rest of this book is in fact oriented to providing such a framework for enhancing the basic judgment of portfolio managers. Chapters 2–5 describe methods for explicitly estimating returns for stocks and bonds as well as the theoretical framework for explicitly considering risk and return. Chapters 6–9 provide the framework for formally deriving an asset allocation, for measuring the quality of analytical judgments about stocks, groups, and the general market, and for developing active-passive strategies of portfolio management in both the domestic and international equity markets. Chapter 10 offers insight into active-passive strategies of fixed-income management, and Chapter 11 gives the formal framework for option evaluation and insight into uses of option strategies as means of altering the risk-return characteristics of a portfolio. Chapter 12 provides the framework for assessing a manager's capability in the three components of portfolio management: (1) asset allocation, (2) asset class weighting, and (3) security selection within asset classes.

PROBLEMS

1 An investor is in a 70-percent tax bracket. What would the yield on corporate bonds need to be to make the investor indifferent to a municipal bond yielding 6 percent?

2 Assume that four stocks are representative of stocks in general. These stocks had the following market values at the beginning and end of the year:

Market value (in millions of dollars)

Stock	(12/31/79)	(12/31/80)
A	150	200
B	200	260
C	350	315
D	300	330

What would be the price change of a market-weighted index and an equally weighted index?

3 An investor purchased a stock at $30 per share at the beginning of the year and sold it at the end of the year for $36. The dividend received over the year was $2 per share. Calculate the realized return on the stock.

4 Assume that the same stock in the previous question declined in price over the next year from $36 to $26, while again paying a $2 dividend. What was the realized return in the second year, and what was the compound return over the two-year period?

5 Assume that the second stock in Table 1-5 had the same pattern of return as the first stock. Calculate the covariance of return and the correlation coefficient between the two stocks.

6 Moody's bond-rating service classifies corporate bonds into quality categories, in which AAA designates bonds of the highest quality and those rated BAA and below are considered speculative or of marginal quality. Comment on what factors would create differences in the quality categories. Also, where would BAAs fit into the risk-return array in Table 1-8?

7 A one-year treasury bill sells at 90, pays no coupon, and has a maturity value of 100. Inflation is projected at 8 percent for the year. Calculate the real return. Then using the calculated real return determine what the price of the bill should be if inflation accelerates to 12 percent and if it decelerates to 3 percent.

SELECTED REFERENCES

Cagan, Phillip: "Common Stock Values and Inflation—The Historical Record of Many Countries," National Bureau of Economic Research, report no. 13, March 1974.

Cohen, Jerome B., Edward D. Zinbarg, and Arthur Zeikel: *Investment Analysis and Portfolio Management*, Irwin, Homewood, Ill., 1973.

Cootner, Paul: *The Random Character of Stock Market Prices*, MIT Press, Cambridge, Mass., 1974.

Elton, Edwin, and Martin Gruber: *Modern Portfolio Theory and Investment Analysis*. Wiley, New York, 1981.

Fama, Eugene F.: "Efficient Capital Markets: A Review of Theory and Empirical Work," *Journal of Finance*, May 1970, pp. 383–417.

Fisher, Lawrence, and James H. Lorie: "Rates of Return on Investments in Common Stocks," *Journal of Business*, January 1964, pp. 1–21.

———: "Rates of Return on Investments in Common Stocks: The Year-by-Year Record, 1926–1965," *Journal of Business*, July 1968, pp. 291–316.

———: "Some Studies of Variability of Returns on Investment in Common Stocks," *Journal of Business*, April 1970, pp. 99–134.

Graham, Benjamin, David L. Dodd, and Sidney Cottle: *Security Analysis*, 4th ed., McGraw-Hill, New York, 1951.

Hagin, Robert: *Modern Portfolio Theory,* Dow-Jones-Irwin, New York, 1979.

Hayes, Douglas A., and Scott W. Bauman: *Investments: Analysis and Management,* Macmillan, New York, 1976.

Ibbotson, Roger G., and Carol Fall: "The United States Market Wealth Portfolio," *Journal of Portfolio Management,* Fall 1979.

Ibbotson, Roger G., and Rex A. Sinquefeld: "Stocks, Bonds, Bills, and Inflation: The Past (1926–1976) and the Future (1977–2000)," Financial Analysts Research Foundation, Charlottesville, Va., 1977.

————: "Stocks, Bonds, Bills, and Inflation: Historical Returns (1926–1978)," Financial Analysts Research Foundation, Charlottesville, Va., 1979.

Lintner, John: "Inflation and Common Stock Prices in a Cyclical Context," National Bureau of Economic Research, 53d Annual Report, September 1973.

Lorie, James H., and Mary T. Hamilton: *The Stock Market: Theories and Evidence,* Irwin, Homewood, Ill., 1974.

Malkiel, Burton G.: *A Random Walk Down Wall Street,* Norton, New York, 1975.

Reilly, Frank K.: *Investment Analysis and Portfolio Management,* Dryden Press, Hinsdale, Ill., 1979.

Sharpe, William F.: *Investments,* Prentice-Hall, Englewood Cliffs, N. J., 1978.

UNDERLYING THEORY

TWO

PORTFOLIO ANALYSIS

INTRODUCTION

Investment managers are concerned with blending securities together in such a way that the resultant portfolio provides the highest return at a given level of risk. Managers should thus be concerned with monitoring the risk and return characteristics of a portfolio over time and with utilizing techniques that facilitate the optimal blending of assets together into a portfolio. The basic analytical framework for such portfolio analysis is the Markowitz model. Index models are special cases of the Markowitz model that facilitate portfolio analysis by offering (1) a simpler framework, (2) fewer input requirements, and (3) fewer computational requirements.

Since the Markowitz model established the basic framework for portfolio analysis, we'll begin by outlining the key elements of that model. We'll then go on to discuss the notion of an efficient portfolio. After covering that important concept, we'll discuss the meaning of return, variance, and covariance in a portfolio context. These are essential concepts for understanding the meaning of portfolio risk and return. In the course of this discussion we'll illustrate the power of diversification as a method of reducing portfolio risk while maintaining the return of the portfolio at a constant level.

After covering these basic aspects of the portfolio analysis model, we'll discuss the practical problems of assessing the risk-return characteristics of a portfolio and of generating a set of efficient portfolios. In this regard we'll compare the Markowitz model with the single-index and multi-index simplifications of that model with respect to input requirements as well as facility in correctly generating the set of efficient portfolios. We'll see that the multi-index model best serves the purpose of simplifying the portfolio analysis process with the least sacrifice of explanatory power. It should be the preferred method of practical portfolio analysis.

MARKOWITZ MODEL

Markowitz' pioneering work on portfolio analysis is described in his 1952 *Journal of Finance* article and subsequent book in 1959. The fundamental assumption underlying the Markowitz approach to portfolio analysis is that investors are basically risk-averse. This means simply that investors must be compensated with higher return in order to accept higher risk. Consequently, given a choice, for example, between two securities with equal rates of return, an investor will select the security with the lower level of risk, thereby rejecting the higher-risk security. In more technical terms this assumption means that investors maximize expected utility rather than merely try to maximize expected return.

The assumption of investor risk-aversion seems reasonable and is bolstered by evidence. First is Markowitz' own observation that investors typically hold diversified portfolios. If investors weren't risk-averse, the logical course of action would be merely to hold the single security promising the highest return so as to maximize expected return. Further evidence that investors are risk-averse is the fact that they purchase various types of insurance, such as life, health and accident, and auto. Individuals who purchase insurance are willing to pay to avoid future uncertainty; that is, they want to avoid the risk of a potentially large future loss even if the cost (premium) exceeds the expected payoff of the insurance. Finally, as we showed in the last chapter, securities with different degrees of risk differ in their return realized over time, with higher risk accompanied by higher return. This is evidence that investors require a higher return in order to accept higher risk.

Presuming risk-aversion, Markowitz then developed a model of portfolio analysis that can be summarized as follows. First, the two relevant characteristics of a portfolio are its expected return and some measure of the dispersion of possible returns around the expected return, the variance being analytically the most tractable.[1] Second, rational investors will choose to hold efficient portfolios, which are those that maximize expected returns for a given degree of risk or, alternatively and equivalently, minimize risk for a given expected return. Third, it is theoretically possible to identify efficient portfolios by the proper analysis of information for each security on expected return, variance of return, and the interrelationship between the return for each security and that for every other security as measured by the covariance. Finally, a computer program can utilize these inputs to calculate the set of efficient portfolios. The program indicates the proportion of an investor's fund that should be allocated to each security in order to achieve efficiency — that is, the maximization of return for a given degree of risk or the minimization of risk for a given expected return.

CONCEPT OF EFFICIENCY

The notion of efficiency can be best illustrated by means of Figure 2-1. The vertical axis refers to expected return; the horizontal axis refers to risk as measured by the

---

[1] The Markowitz model of portfolio analysis is a mean-variance model indicating that the relevant characteristics of a security or portfolio are its expected return and riskiness as measured by the variance of return. Other aspects of a security or portfolio (tax status, marketability, etc.) are surely of importance, but for the purposes of this analysis they are excluded from consideration.

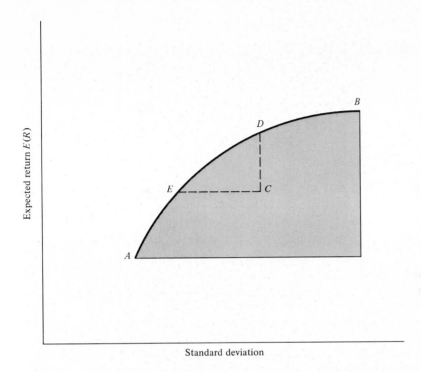

Figure 2-1 The portfolio possibility set.

standard deviation of return; and the shaded area represents the set of all the possible portfolios that could be obtained from a given group of securities. A certain level of return and a certain risk will be associated with each possible portfolio. Thus each portfolio is represented by a single point in the shaded area of the figure.

Note that the efficient set is represented by the upper left-hand boundary of the shaded area between points A and B. Portfolios along this efficient frontier dominate those below the line. Specifically, they offer higher return than those at an equivalent level of risk or, alternatively, entail less risk at an equivalent level of return. For example, note that portfolio C, which does not lie on the efficient boundary, is dominated by portfolios D and E, which do lie on the efficient boundary. Portfolio D offers greater return than portfolio C at the same level of risk, while portfolio E entails less risk than portfolio C at the same level of return.

Rational investors will thus prefer to hold efficient portfolios — that is, ones on the line and not those below it. The particular portfolio that an individual investor selects from the efficient frontier depends on that investor's degree of aversion to risk. An investor who is highly averse to risk will hold one on the lower left-hand segment of the frontier, while an investor who is not too risk-averse will hold one on the upper portion. In more technical terms the selection depends on the investor's risk-aversion, which might be characterized by the nature and shape of the investor's risk-return utility function.

PORTFOLIO RISK AND RETURN

As noted, an efficient portfolio (or any portfolio, for that matter) is described by the list of individual securities in the portfolio as well as by the weighting of each security in the portfolio. The estimated or expected return of the portfolio is, in turn, merely a weighted average of the expected returns of the individual securities of which the portfolio is comprised. Calculation of the expected return can be most easily illustrated for a two-security portfolio. Using X_i to represent the security's proportion of the portfolio and $E(R_i)$ the expected return, the expected return of the portfolio R_p is calculated as follows:

$$R_p = X_1 E(R_1) + X_2 E(R_2) = \sum_{i=1}^{2} X_i E(R_i) \tag{1}$$

While the expected return of a portfolio can be obtained directly, the variance (or risk) of a portfolio is not simply a weighted average of the variances of the individual securities in the portfolio. There is also need to consider the relationship between each security in the portfolio and every other security as measured by the covariance of return. The method of calculating the variance of a portfolio can again most easily be illustrated for a two-security portfolio. Using $\text{Var}(R_i)$ to represent the variance of each security, $\text{Cov}(R_1 R_2)$ to represent the covariance between the two securities, and again using X_i to represent the proportion that each security represents in the portfolio, the calculation of the portfolio variance $[\text{Var}(R_p)]$ is as follows:

$$\text{Var}(R_p) = X_1^2 \text{Var}(R_1) + X_2^2 \text{Var}(R_2) + 2X_1 X_2 \text{Cov}(R_1 R_2) \tag{2}$$

In words the variance of the portfolio is the weighted sum of the variances of the individual securities plus twice the covariance between the two securities.[2] We can, in turn, use this simple expression to begin to examine the effect on overall portfolio risk of adding securities with differing covariance characteristics. We'll then go on to examine the more general case of adding many securities to the portfolio and the effect on portfolio risk. This analysis should provide perspective on the effectiveness of diversification in controlling portfolio risk.

DIVERSIFICATION

To begin to understand the mechanism and power of diversification, it is important to consider first the impact of covariance more closely. We can do this most directly by redefining the covariance formulation in the following way:

$$\text{Cov}(R_i R_j) = \rho_{ij} S_i S_j$$

---

[2] As a matter of interest, although the formula refers to a portfolio of only two securities, it has great generality, since groups of securities can be considered a single security in analyzing the problems of portfolio management. For example, if we are interested in understanding what the addition of a security does to the variance of an existing portfolio, we can think of the existing portfolio as a single security. This simple formula therefore has great analytical power.

That is, the covariance is equal to the correlation coefficient between two securities times the standard deviation of each security. Holding standard deviation constant, this says that the higher the correlation between two securities, the higher the covariance added by two securities in a portfolio; conversely, the lower the correlation, the lower the covariance added by the two securities; hence the lower the correlation between securities, the lower will be the overall risk of the portfolio, while the higher the correlation, the higher will be the overall risk of the portfolio.

This has relevance to illustrating the power of diversification. Adding extra securities, especially those with a lower covariance, should be an objective in building portfolios. In order to see more specifically how different values of covariance or correlation can affect the variance of a portfolio, it will be useful to consider the data shown in Table 2-1.

Table 2-1 shows expected return, standard deviation, and variance data for two hypothetical stocks. Note that both stocks have expected returns of 10 percent and identical standard deviations S (and hence variances). Each stock has a weight of 50 percent in the portfolio to account for 100 percent of the portfolio weight; that is, the portfolio is fully invested. Given the data, the expected return of the portfolio R_p works out to 10 percent, as shown in the first line below the data. The next two lines show the variance formula along with the inserted values to illustrate the calculation. The final line shows that the variance of the portfolio depends on the value of the correlation coefficient.

Security Correlation and Portfolio Risk

The correlation coefficient measures the extent to which the two stocks move together and varies in value from $+1$ to -1 with a midpoint of zero. A correlation coefficient of $+1$, indicating perfectly positive correlation between the two stocks, is illustrated by the upward-sloping line in Figure 2-2a. For example, bearish new information concerning security A would result in lowered expectations for security B as

Table 2-1 Security covariance and portfolio variance

	Return	S	Variance
Stock 1	.10	.40	.16
Stock 2	.10	.40	.16

$$X_1 = .5 \quad X_2 = .5 \quad \sum_{i=1}^{2} X_i = 1.00$$

$$R_P = \tfrac{1}{2}(.10) + \tfrac{1}{2}(.10) = .10$$
$$\text{Var}(R_P) = X_1^2 \text{Var}(R_1) + X_2^2 \text{Var}(R_2) + 2X_1 X_2 \rho_{12} S_1 S_2$$
$$= (.25)(.16) + (.25)(.16)$$
$$\quad + 2(.5)(.5)\rho_{12}(.4)(.4)$$
$$= .08 + .08\rho_{12}$$

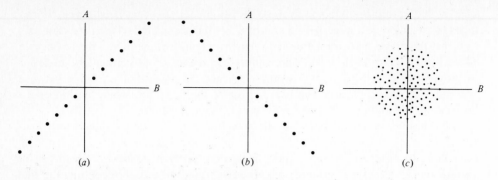

Figure 2-2 Correlation of returns between securities A and B.

well. The downward-sloping line in Figure 2-2b illustrates a correlation coefficient of −1 and indicates perfectly negative correlation between the two stocks. In this instance bearish new information about security A would increase expectations for security B. Finally, the random scatter of plots in Figure 2-2c illustrates a pattern of zero correlation, or independence, between the two stocks. New information on security A, whether bearish or bullish, would have no effect on security B.

Figure 2-3 illustrates the way that the returns of the two securities (A and B) might fluctuate over time when the correlation is perfectly positive and when it is perfectly negative. When the two securities are perfectly positively correlated, the dotted line representing the return pattern of security B would lie on top of the solid line representing the return of security A, as illustrated in part (a) of the figure. In this case, where securities move perfectly in tandem, ($\rho_{12} = +1$), the portfolio variance is .16[$\text{Var}(R_p) = .08 + .08(1) = .16$]. In this case the variance of the portfolio is a weighted average of the variances of the two securities and the same as the variance of an individual security. Diversification provides no risk reduction, only risk averaging, and is therefore not a productive activity when securities are perfectly positively correlated.

On the other hand, when the two securities are perfectly negatively correlated, the dotted line representing the return pattern of security B would move directly opposite to the solid line representing the return of security A, as illustrated in part (b) of the figure. In this case, where securities move counter to each other ($\rho_{12} = -1$), the variance of the portfolio is zero [$\text{Var}(R_p) = .08 + .08(-1) = 0$]. This is illustrated by the horizontal dashed line in part (b) that indicates an average return of 10 percent with no period-by-period fluctuations. Here diversification immediately eliminates risk and is a highly productive activity when securities are perfectly negatively correlated. Unfortunately, perfect negative correlation is rare; it is found only in certain arbitrage situations, such as the simultaneous purchase and short sale of a security traded in two different markets.[3]

[3] A similar instance is the simultaneous purchase of a convertible bond and a short sale of the common stock. Other arbitrage situations include the strategy of writing a put and simultaneously buying an equivalent call or having a long and short position in nearly identical futures contracts traded on two different exchanges. All such positions presume a temporary disequilibrium in prices which, corrected through convergence, will bring profit to the arbitrageur.

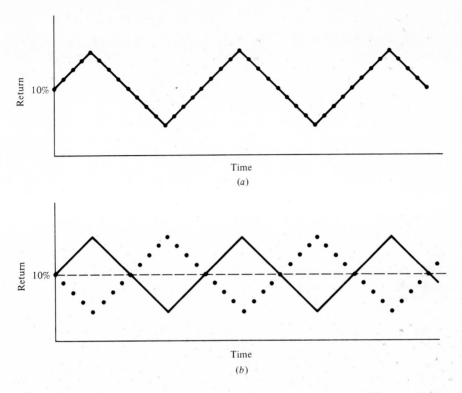

Figure 2-3 Security correlation and portfolio variance. *(a)* Perfectly positive correlation; *(b)* perfectly negative correlation.

If the correlation between the two stocks is zero ($\rho_{12} = 0$), the variance of the portfolio is $.08[\text{Var}(R_p) = .08 + .08(0) = .08]$. The portfolio variance in this case is less than that of a single security (.16). While Figure 2-3 does not illustrate this case specifically, we could visualize the resulting portfolio line, which would show fluctuation, but of a lesser amplitude than that of the line represented by a single security. Diversification reduces risk and is a productive activity when securities show no correlation.

Adding Securities to Eliminate Risk

This third case can further illustrate the power of diversification. First, note the gener formula for the variance of a portfolio:

$$\text{Var}(R_p) = \sum_{i=1}^{N} X_i^2 \, \text{Var}(R_i) + \sum_{\substack{i=1 \\ i \neq j}}^{N} \sum_{j=1}^{N} X_i X_j \text{Cov}(R_i R_j)$$

The formula says that the variance of a portfolio is a weighted average of the varian of the individual securities plus the covariance between each security and every of security in the portfolio.

If securities have zero correlation and hence zero covariance, the second term goes to zero and the expression reduces to

$$\text{Var}(R_p) = \sum_{i=1}^{N} X_i^2 \text{Var}(R_i)$$

Assume for purposes of illustration not only that securities with zero covariance are available but also that each has the same variance (as shown above) and equal amounts are invested in each.

$$\text{Var}(R_p) = \sum_{i=1}^{N} (1/N)^2 \text{Var}(R_i)$$

$$= N(1/N)^2 \text{Var}(R_i)$$

$$= 1/N \text{Var}(R_i)$$

$$S_p = \frac{S_i}{\sqrt{N}} \qquad (4)$$

Using this formula and assuming as in the example that the individual securities have standard deviations of 40 percent, the data in Table 2-2 show how the risk (standard deviation) of the portfolio declines as uncorrelated securities with identical standard deviations are added to the portfolio. Risk is reduced to less than 10 percent of that of a single-stock portfolio when 128 securities are in the portfolio and to less than 2 percent of the original risk when 510 are included. As the number of securities added becomes larger and larger (approaches infinity, in technical terms), the standard deviation of the portfolio approaches zero.

The principle here is that if there are sufficient numbers of securities with zero correlation (zero covariance), the portfolio analyst can make the portfolio risk arbitrarily small. This is the basis for insurance, which explains why insurance companies attempt to write many individual policies and spread their coverage so as to minimize overall risk. It also has direct relevance in providing a benchmark for assessing the

**Table 2-2 Portfolio risk
and number of securities
(uncorrelated securities)**

Number of securities	Standard deviation of portfolio return, %
1	40.0
2	28.3
8	14.1
16	10.0
32	7.1
128	3.5
510	1.8

extent to which diversification can be effective in reducing risks for equity investors. The next section discusses empirical evidence concerning the state of world with regard to the usefulness of diversification in reducing risk.

SYSTEMATIC AND DIVERSIFIABLE RISK

When dealing with U. S. stocks, however, eliminating risk entirely through diversification is not possible. Virtually no stocks show negative or even zero correlation. Typically, stocks show some positive correlation—above zero—but less than perfectly positive (+1). Empirically, it seems that the typical correlation coefficient for U. S. stocks is between .5 and .6; that is, if we sampled at random any two stocks out of the total stock universe, we would likely find that the correlation coefficient calculated for the two stocks was between .5 and .6. As a result, diversification (adding securities to a portfolio) results in some reduction in total portfolio variance but not in complete elimination of variance.

There have been several studies of the effectiveness of diversification in reducing portfolio risk. One by Fisher and Lorie provides perhaps the best illustration of the process. They looked at all listed stocks and randomly sampled from this list to build portfolios ranging from one stock to 500 stocks. Stocks within the portfolios were weighted equally. These simulations allowed Fisher and Lorie to see how the variance of a portfolio was reduced as stocks were added to the portfolio. Correspondingly, it also showed how quickly the effect of adding stocks exhausted the power of diversification.

Table 2-3 shows some representative statistics from the study. The first column shows the size of portfolios analyzed. These range from one-stock portfolios to portfolios of more than 100 stocks. Note that the one-stock portfolios on average provided a return of 9 percent; in other words, the average return for stocks was 9 percent. This average remained the same for all size portfolios. While the average return remained

Table 2-3 Portfolio size — risk and return

Portfolio size	Average return, %	Standard deviation, %	Diversifiable risk, %	Market-related risk, %
1	9	40.0	45	55
2	9	32.4	38	62
8	9	25.6	20	80
16	9	24.0	12	88
32	9	23.6	8	92
128	9	22.8	2	98
Index fund	9	22.0	0	100

Source: Lawrence Fisher, and James H. Lorie, "Some Studies of Variability of Returns on Investment in Common Stocks," *Journal of Business,* April 1970, pp. 99–134.

constant over all-size portfolios, the risk decreased with an increase in the size of portfolio; hence one can reduce risk and hold return constant through diversification. In particular, note that the standard deviation of a one-stock portfolio (or average standard deviation for an individual stock) was 40 percent, while the standard deviation of a large (128-stock) portfolio was 22.8 percent, or little more than half that of an individual stock.

We see, however, that the effects of diversification are exhausted fairly rapidly. Most of the reduction in standard deviation takes place by the time that the portfolio reaches 16 or 32 stocks. In sum, adding securities to a portfolio reduces risk, because securities are not perfectly correlated (+1). However, the effects of this process are exhausted quite rapidly, since securities are in fact rather highly correlated (.5 to .6). This is in contrast to the results in Table 2-2, which show the portfolio risk continuing to decline when securities are uncorrelated. There are benefits to diversification, but they are limited.

The fourth column in Table 2-3 indicates that one component of total risk (standard deviation) is market-related. This portion is in turn a function of the correlation of the portfolio with the overall market and is derived by multiplying the correlation coefficient of the portfolio with the market by the standard deviation of the portfolio, and then dividing this calculated value by the total risk of the portfolio. For example, an individual security with a correlation coefficient of .55 with the market and a standard deviation of 40 percent has a market-related risk of 22 percent. Dividing this calculated value by the total risk of the security of 40 percent results in a 55 percent market-related proportion of total risk. The table shows that market-related risk increases as a proportion of the portfolio as the size of the portfolio increases; large portfolios are more highly correlated with the market.

Because market-related risk impacts all securities and cannot be diversified "away," it is also referred to as *systematic risk*. Risk that is unexplained by the market is known as *diversifiable* or *unsystematic risk*. A small portfolio of, say, one or two stocks has a lot of diversifiable risk. A large portfolio has relatively little diversifiable risk. A perfectly diversified fund — an index fund — will reflect only market-related, or systematic, risk. The last column of Table 2-3 shows diversifiable risk decreasing with portfolio size.

These important concepts are illustrated in Figure 2-4. The chart shows total portfolio risk declining as number of holdings increases. Increasing diversification tends to result in only systematic or market-related risk. The remaining variability reflects the fact that the return on nearly every security depends to a degree on the overall performance of the market. Consequently, the return on a well-diversified portfolio is highly correlated with the market, and its variability or uncertainty is basically the uncertainty of the market as a whole. Investors are exposed to market uncertainty no matter how many stocks they hold.

The preceding analysis has implications both as to the sort of risk that should be rewarded in the marketplace as well as to the relevant measure of risk for securities and portfolios. In particular, since diversification provides a relatively easy way of eliminating a "deadweight loss" (diversifiable or unsystematic risk) from the portfolio, it seems reasonable that the marketplace is unlikely to reward it. It will only reward

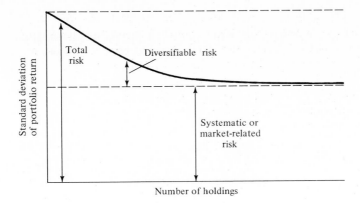

Figure 2-4 Diversification and systematic risk.

systematic risk, which investors cannot eliminate. Accordingly, this implies that the relevant measure of risk is systematic risk. (More on this in Chapter 3.)

SIMPLIFIED MODELS

In order to use the Markowitz full covariance model for a portfolio analysis, the investor must obtain estimates of the returns and the variances and covariances of returns for the securities in the universe of interest. To estimate the expected return and variance of a two-stock portfolio, five estimates are needed: expected return for each stock; variance of return for each stock; and covariance of return between the two stocks. Generalizing to the case of N stocks, there would be need not only for N return estimates and N variance estimates but also for a total of $N(N - 1)/2$ covariance estimates. For example, analyzing a set of 100 stocks would require 100 return estimates, 100 variance estimates, and 4950 covariance estimates, for a total of 5150 estimates. Note that the task of estimation is increased considerably by the need to consider explicitly the interrelationship among securities as represented by the covariance.

While the Markowitz model is the most comprehensive one, it has found relatively little use in solving practical problems of portfolio analysis, mainly because of the overwhelming burden of developing input estimates for the model. As noted, analysis of a universe of 100 stocks would require 5150 different estimates. The task of collecting the estimates for 5150 statistics is further complicated by the fact that few individuals are capable of estimating such sophisticated measures as variances and covariances. Also, the quantity of required data taxes the memory capacity of even the largest computers.

Furthermore, the coordination of this data-gathering procedure presents difficulties. Most securities research departments are organized so that specialists are assigned to the coverage of an individual industry or a small group of industries. In turn this specialization means that analytical personnel generally have little knowledge of the characteristics of industries other than their assigned industry; thus obtaining estimates of relationships across industries is difficult. For example, the electronics specialist is likely to find it difficult to assess the degree of co-movement between his assigned industry and others, such as the food or chemical industries.

Index models circumvent the difficulty of dealing with a great number of covariances by providing a simplified method of representing the relationships among securities. There are essentially two types of index models: single-index and multi-index. The single-index model is the simplest and might be thought of as being at one extreme point of a continuum, with the full covariance Markowitz model at the other. Multi-index models might be regarded as an intermediate point on this continuum. We'll first discuss the single-index model, as it was developed first historically, is in widespread use and provides useful perspective. We'll then cover the multi-index model, which has the greatest potential for practical portfolio analysis.

THE SINGLE-INDEX MODEL

The basic notion underlying the single-index model is that all stocks are affected by movements in the general market; that is, when the general market index is rising strongly, stocks in general will tend to rise in response to this market movement. Conversely, when the general market index is falling precipitously, stocks in general will tend to decline accordingly. Furthermore, this general market movement or market factor is assumed to be the only systematic force that impacts all stocks, while other effects are presumed to be specific or unique to the individual stock.

We can best illustrate this co-movement of stocks with a market index by referring to the scatter diagram in Figure 2-5. The vertical axis refers to the rate of return on the security or portfolio of interest. In this case we'll use a portfolio called the OMEGA Fund to illustrate the relationship. The horizontal axis shows the rate of return for the S&P 500, which is used here to represent the return on the market portfolio.

In preparing the diagram we first computed quarterly returns for the S&P 500 and the OMEGA Fund over the 1957–1976 period (seventy-two returns). We then plotted these returns on the diagram as follows. If for example, during one quarter OMEGA earned a 10 percent return and the S&P 500 earned 7 percent, we would move up the vertical axis to 10 percent and across the horizontal axis to 7 percent and plot a point. All seventy-two returns were plotted in this way, so that they lined up on the chart as shown in Figure 2-5.

The plots indicate a systematic relationship between the return on the OMEGA Fund and the return on the market. We described this relationship by fitting a line to these points, using the single-index model, also known as the market model. The model is a simple linear regression identifying return on a security, or portfolio in this case, as the dependent variable R_i and the S&P 500 return R_m, representing the market, as the independent variable. It is expressed as

$$R_i = a_i + B_i R_m + e_i \qquad (5)$$

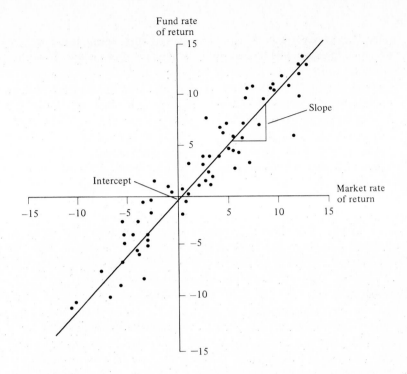

Figure 2-5 Scatter diagram. $R_p = a + BR_m + e$, where R_p = fund return, R_m = S&P 500 return, and B = market sensitivity.

The beta parameter B in the single-index model is the same as the slope of the fitted line in the scatter diagram in Figure 2-5. It measures the responsiveness of the security or fund to the general market and indicates how extensively the return of the portfolio or security will vary with changes in the market return.

In turn, the beta coefficient is defined as the ratio of the security's covariance of return with the market $[\text{Cov}(R_i R_m)]$ to the variance of the market $[\text{Var}(R_m)]$ and can be calculated as follows:

$$B_i = \frac{\text{Cov}(R_i R_m)}{\text{Var}(R_m)} = \frac{\rho_{im} S_i S_m}{S_m S_m} = \frac{\rho_{im} S_i}{S_m} \tag{6}$$

In this instance, the portfolio had a standard deviation of 21 percent and the market a standard deviation of 18 percent over the eighteen-year period. At the same time, the correlation between the two returns was +.94. The portfolio's beta can then be calculated with Equation 6.

$$B_p = \frac{(.94)(21\%)}{18\%} = 1.10$$

The calculated beta of 1.10 indicates that the fund is 10 percent more sensitive to the market than a fund with a beta of 1.00. For example, when the market goes up 10 percent, we can expect this fund to go up 11 percent, and when the market declines 10 percent, we can expect the fund to decline 11 percent.

The alpha parameter a is the intercept of the fitted line and indicates what the return of the security or portfolio would be when the market return is zero. For example, a security or portfolio with an alpha of $+2$ percent would earn 2 percent even when the market return was zero, and would earn an additional 2 percent at all levels of market return. Conversely, a security or portfolio with an alpha of -2 percent would lose 2 percent when the market return is zero, and would earn 2 percent less than expected at all levels of market return. The positive alpha thus represents a sort of bonus return and would be a highly desirable aspect of a portfolio or security, while a negative alpha represents a penalty to the investor and is an undesirable aspect of a portfolio or a security. In this case, the OMEGA Fund's intercept was virtually zero, indicating that the portfolio provided neither a bonus return nor a penalty for the investor. We'll see more clearly in the next chapter the significance of the alpha value, and in Chapters 5 and 6 we'll discuss ways of estimating alphas for individual securities.

The final term e in Equation 5 is the unexpected return resulting from influences not identified by the model. Frequently referred to as random or residual return, it may take on any value, but over a large number of observations it will average out to zero. It is further assumed that these residual returns are uncorrelated between securities; that is, once the market effect has been removed from the security there should be no significant correlation between securities. In other words, this assumption means that the only systematic effect influencing returns on stocks or portfolios is a general market effect.

Measuring Risk and Return

Using the single-index model specification, we can express the expected return of an individual security as

$$E(R_i) = a_i + B_i E(R_m) \tag{7}$$

The return of the security is thus a combination of two components: (1) a specific return component represented by the alpha of the security; and (2) a market-related return component represented by the term $B_i E(R_m)$. The residual return disappears from the expression as its average value is zero; that is, it has an expected value of zero.

Correspondingly, the risk of the security $[\mathrm{Var}(R_i)]$ becomes the sum of a market-related component and a component that is specific to the security, as illustrated by the following:

$$\mathrm{Var}(R_i) = B^2 \mathrm{Var}(R_m) + \mathrm{Var}(e)$$

$$\text{Total risk} = \text{market-related} + \text{specific risk} \tag{8}$$

The market-related component of risk is sometimes referred to as systematic risk as it is common to all securities; that is, it systematically impacts across all securities. The specific risk component is also referred to as diversifiable risk since it is unique to the security and can be reduced when securities are added to a portfolio.

In calculating risk and return of a portfolio we can use similar formulas and aggregate across the individual securities to measure those aspects of the portfolio. In particular, the expected return of the portfolio becomes a weighted average of the specific returns (alphas) of the individual securities plus a weighted average of the market-related returns $B_i E(R_m)$ of the individual securities. Defining $a_p = \sum_{i=1}^{N} X_i a_i$ as the portfolio alpha and $B_p = \sum_{i=1}^{N} X_i B_i$ as the portfolio beta, we can directly represent portfolio return as a portfolio alpha plus a portfolio beta times expected market return, as shown:

$$E(R_p) = a_p + B_p E(R_m) \tag{9}$$

Because of the assumption that securities are only related through a common market effect, the risk of a portfolio is also simply a weighted average of the market-related risk of individual securities plus a weighted average of the specific risk of individual securities in the portfolio. Again using $B_p = \sum_{i=1}^{N} X_i B_i$ to represent the portfolio beta, we can express portfolio risk as

$$\text{Var}(R_p) = B_p^2 \, \text{Var}(R_m) + \sum_{i=1}^{N} X_i^2 \, \text{Var}(e_i) \tag{10}$$

Note that the diversifiable risk component X_i^2 will become smaller as securities are added to the portfolio. This is because according to the single-index model these risks are uncorrelated. The reduction thus becomes similar to the example in Table 2-2, which illustrates how variance is reduced when securities are uncorrelated and securities have equal weight in a portfolio. The effect would be the same in this case, except that we are dealing with one component, diversifiable risk, rather than total risk. The market-related component in this case would remain unaffected by the addition of extra securities, as systematic risk is the component that cannot be reduced by diversification.

Applying the Single-Index Model

Table 2-4 illustrates use of the single-index model to calculate expected return and variance for a hypothetical portfolio of four securities: (1) Merck, a drug company, to represent a rapid-growth security; (2) Bethlehem Steel to represent a cyclically oriented security; (3) Kellogg, a food company, to represent a stable type of security; and (4) Standard Oil of California to represent an energy-oriented security. The table shows the weighting of these companies in the hypothetical portfolio; the weights sum to 1.00 to represent a portfolio fully invested in stocks. It also shows basic input data: alphas, betas, and residual variances for calculating portfolio return and variance.

The upper formulation in the table illustrates calculation of the portfolio return. Note that we've set the alpha values of the individual stocks at zero, as we're assuming no special information regarding the relative attractiveness of the individual stocks. (In Chapter 6 we'll discuss explicit ways of estimating alpha values for stocks.) In this case the weighted average alpha of the portfolio is simply zero. The betas of the individual

Table 2-4 Portfolio risk and return — single-index model

Security	Weighting	a_i	B_{im}	Var(e)
Merck	.25	0	1.20	446^2
Bethlehem Steel	.25	0	1.09	653
Kellogg	.25	0	.89	579
Standard Oil of California	.25	0	.89	310
Portfolio Value	1.00	0	1.02	124^2

1. $E(R_p) = a_p + B_p E(R_m)$
$$= 0 + 1.02(15\%)$$
$$= 15.3\%$$

2. $\text{Var}(R_p) = B_p^2 \text{Var}(R_m) + \sum_{i=1}^{4} X_i^2 \text{Var}(e)$
$$= (1.02)^2(324) + 124\%^2$$
$$= 337\%^2 + 124\%^2$$
$$= 461\%^2$$

Source: Terry Jenkins, I. T. S. Associates, Inc., Cambridge, Mass.

stocks have been estimated with historical data, while the projected market return is 15 percent, a reasonable approximation of the consensus of expectations at the end of 1980. The weighted average beta of the portfolio is 1.02, and using the projected market return of 15 percent results in a market-related return of 15.3 percent. With an expected alpha of zero the expected return of the portfolio is entirely market-related and is also projected at 15.3 percent.

The lower formulation in the table illustrates calculation of the portfolio variance. Since the standard deviation of the market over the 1952–1976 period was 18 percent or, alternatively, had a variance of 324 percent^2, we'll assume that this historical figure is appropriate for projection into the future. The specific risk estimates for each of the stocks are also historically derived. The bottom line shows the market-related risk calculated from the weighted portfolio beta and the projected market variance along with the weighted average of the specific risk of the individual stocks. Note that the specific risk of the portfolio is less than that of any of the individual stocks. This is, of course, consistent with the single-index model's assumption of being able to diversify specific risk by adding securities to the portfolio.

THE MULTI-INDEX MODEL

In applying the single-index model the assumption is that the general market factor is the only systematic effect operating across securities. There are, however, factors that impact across subclasses of securities and create correlation in addition to that of the general market — that is, extramarket correlation. For example, stocks that are expected to grow at above-average rates — growth stocks — tend to perform well or poorly as a group. Correspondingly, classes of cyclical, stable, and energy stocks tend to show similar group behavior. Finally, stocks classified into traditional industries, such as the steel or drug or food industry, tend to perform well or poorly as a group. We'll analyze this phenomenon of stocks performing as a group in more detail in Chapter 8.

Meanwhile, Table 2-5 shows the major sources of risk and the percentage of the total risk of a typical stock that can be explained by these factors. Note that there are four sources of risk rather than just the two, general market effect and a unique factor, which are assumed when using the single-index model. The additional two sources, a broad market sector effect and an industry effect combined, explain 25 percent of the total risk of a stock, or almost as much as that accounted for by the general market effect. Failure to account for these extra market sources of correlation can lead to errors in estimating the risks of individual securities as well as problems in generating truly efficient portfolios when undertaking portfolio analysis.

The most direct way to accommodate these extra factors is the multi-index model. The concept here simply augments the single-index model with additional indexes that account for these extramarket effects. For example, if we wished to account for group effects, we would construct indexes of growth, cyclical, stable, and energy stocks and incorporate these four indexes along with an index for the general market effect in a multi-index model. A multi-index model incorporating the market effect and the four extramarket effects takes the following form:

$$R_i = a_i + B_m R_m + B_g R_g + B_c R_c + B_s R_s + B_e R_e + e_i \qquad (11)$$

The model says that the return on the stock is a function of five factors: (1) general market factor R_m, (2) growth factor R_g, (3) cyclical factor R_c, (4) stable factor R_s, and (5) energy factor R_e. The alpha parameter has the same general meaning as in the single-index model: it is the return expected when the return on all five factors is zero. The beta coefficients attached to the five indexes have the same meaning as in the single-index model; that is, they indicate what a 1-percent change in the index will do to the return of the stock. For example, if the beta coefficient for the growth index were 2.0, this would indicate that a 1-percent increase in the growth index would result in a 2-percent increase in the stock's return. The residual term e has the same properties as in the single-index model; however, it is more likely to meet the specification of being uncorrelated with the residual of other stocks because the multi-index model ensures

Table 2-5 Sources of equity risk

Source	% of risk
General market	30
Market sector: growth, cyclical, stable, energy	15
Industry affiliation	10
Specific	45
Total	100

Source: James L. Farrell, Jr., "Analyzing Covariation of Return to Determine Homogeneous Stock Groupings," *Journal of Business,* April 1974, pp. 186–207.

that extramarket as well as general market sources of correlation are removed from the stock returns. As a result, once these factors are removed, we expect there to be no systematic effect impacting across securities and the residual returns to be uncorrelated.

A multi-index model of this type can be employed directly, but it is most easily used for computing risk and selecting optimal portfolios if the indexes are uncorrelated (independent). Generally, however, raw return indexes will contain a combination of factors. For example, an index representing growth-stock returns would contain an effect due to the general market as well as the growth-stock effect; that is, the general market factor impacts all stocks. Therefore, the general market factor should be removed from the growth-stock index so that it will be possible to focus exclusively on the impact of the growth effect on stocks.

Appendix A describes techniques of adjusting indexes for the general market factor to convert them into an independent form. Using these techniques of adjusting for the general market factor, a growth index, for example, becomes an index of the difference between the actual return on growth stocks and the return that would be expected given the rate of return on the stock market R_m. Similarly, B_g becomes a measure of the sensitivity of the return on the stock to this difference. Correspondingly, we can think of B_g as the sensitivity of the stock's return to a change in the return to growth stocks when the rate of return on the market is fixed at zero.

Measuring Risk and Return

Given these multi-index model specifications, we can express the expected return of an individual security $E(R_i)$ as

$$E(R_i) = a_i + B_m E(R_m) + B_g E(R_g) + B_c E(R_c) + B_s E(R_s) + B_e E(R_e) \qquad (12)$$

The return of the security is thus a combination of three components: (1) a specific return component represented by the alpha of the security, (2) a market-related component represented by the term $B_m E(R_m)$, and (3) four extramarket components as represented by the extramarket terms in the equation. The residual term again disappears from the expression (as in the single-index model) as its average value is zero; that is, it has an expected value of zero.

Correspondingly, the risk of the security $Var(R_i)$ becomes the sum of (1) a market-related component, (2) a component that is a combination of the four extramarket factors, and (3) a component that is specific to the security, as illustrated by the following formulation:

$$Var(R_i) = B_m^2 Var(R_m) + B_g^2 Var(R_g) + B_c^2 Var(R_c) + B_s^2 Var(R_s)$$
$$+ B_e^2 Var(R_e) + Var(e) \qquad (13)$$

In calculating the risk and return of a portfolio we can use similar formulas and aggregate across the individual securities to measure those aspects of the portfolio. In particular, the expected return of the portfolio becomes a weighted average of the specific returns (alphas) of the individual securities plus a weighted average of the market-related returns plus a weighted average of the extramarket-related returns. Defining $a_p = \Sigma_{i=1}^N a_i$ as the portfolio alpha, $B_{pm} = \Sigma_{i=1}^N B_{im}$ as the market beta of the portfolio, and $B_{pk} = \sum_{i=1}^{N} B_{ik}$ sector as the sector betas for the portfolio, we can represent portfolio return as a portfolio alpha plus the market and sector betas times their respective expected returns:

$$E(R_p) = a_p + B_{pm}E(R_m) + B_{pg}E(R_g) + B_{pc}E(R_c) + B_{ps}E(R_s) + B_{pe}E(R_e) \qquad (14)$$

Because we constructed the market and four extramarket indexes to be independent of one another, we can express portfolio risk as simply a weighted average of the market-related risk of individual securities plus a weighted average of the extramarket risk plus a weighted average of the specific risk of individual securities in the portfolio. Using $B_{pm} = \sum_{i=1}^{N} X_i B_{im}$ to represent the market beta of the portfolio and B_{pk} sector $= \sum_{i=1}^{N} X_i B_{ik}$ sector to represent the sector betas, we can express portfolio risk as

$$Var(R_p) = B_{pm}^2 \ Var(R_m) + B_{pg}^2 \ Var(R_g) + B_{pc}^2 \ Var(R_c) + B_{ps}^2 \ Var(R_s)$$
$$+ B_{pe}^2 \ Var(R_e) + \sum_{i=1}^{N} X_i^2 \ Var(e_i) \qquad (15)$$

Note that the diversifiable risk component becomes smaller as securities are added to the portfolio, while the extramarket risks do not. Since the single-index model incorporates these risks into the specific risk component, and this implicitly assumes that they are diversifiable, it will generally understate the magnitude of diversifiable risk in a portfolio. We'll be able to see this in the following example.

Applying the Multi-Index Model

Table 2-6 illustrates use of the multi-index model for calculating the expected return and variance for a hypothetical portfolio of the same securities used in the single-index example in Table 2-4. Recall that we used four representative securities: (1) Merck as a growth company; (2) Bethlehem Steel as a cyclically oriented company; (3) Kellogg as a stable company; and (4) Standard Oil of California as an energy-oriented company. The table shows the weighting of the stocks in this hypothetical portfolio. Note that the portfolio is heavily weighted in the growth sector (Merck) and the energy sector (Standard Oil of California), with only nominal weighting in the stable (Kellogg) and cyclical (Bethlehem Steel) sectors. The portfolio might be characterized as concentrated rather than diversified with respect to the market sectors.

The upper formulation in Table 2-6 illustrates calculation of the expected portfolio return. Note that we've again set the alpha values of the individual stocks at zero, so that the weighted average alpha of the portfolio is simply zero. The market betas of the stocks are the same used in the single-index example, as is the expected return of 15 percent for the market index. The weighted average beta of the portfolio is 1.04 and again, using the 15 percent return projection for the market, results in a market-related return of 15.6 percent for the portfolio.

The betas of the individual stocks with the nonmarket indexes were also estimated using historical data. Note that each of the four stocks has a significantly positive beta coefficient with respect to its assigned classification; that is, the beta coefficient is a

Table 2-6 Portfolio risk and return — multi-index model

Security	Weighting X_i	a_i	B_{im}	B_{ig}	B_{ic}	B_{is}	B_{ie}	Var(e), %
Merck	.45	0	1.20	.98	−.62	−.20	−.28	233^2
Bethlehem Steel	.05	0	1.09	−.26	.98	−.29	−.24	448
Kellogg	.10	0	.89	−.41	−.60	.74	−.58	385
Standard Oil of California	.40	0	.89	−.63	−.32	−.21	1.24	81
Portfolio value	1.00	0	1.04	.15	−.42	−.11	.30	65^2

1. $E(R_p) = a_p + B_{pm}E(R_m) + B_{pg}E(R_g) + B_{pc}E(R_c) + B_{ps}E(R_s) + B_{pe}E(R_e)$
   $= 0 + 1.04(15\%) + .15(1\%) + (-.42)(-2\%) + (.11)(-1\%) + .30(2\%)$
   $= 17.3\%$

2. $\text{Var}(R_p) = B_{pm}^2 \text{Var}(R_m) + B_{pg}^2 \text{Var}(R_g) + B_{pc}^2 \text{Var}(R_c) + B_{ps}^2 \text{Var}(R_s) + B_{pe}^2 \text{Var}(R_e) + \sum_{i=1}^{4} x_i^2 \text{Var}(e)$
   $= (1.04)^2(324) + (.15)^2(137) + (-.42)^2(193) + (-.11)^2(149) + (.30)^2(94) + 65\%^2$
   $= 347\%^2 + 48\%^2 + 65\%^2$
   $= 460\%^2$

Source: Terry Jenkins, I. T. S. Associates, Inc., Cambridge, Mass.

statistical criterion for classification to a group. For example, Merck's beta with the growth index is .98, Bethlehem Steel's beta with the cyclicals is .98, Kellogg's with the stable index is .74, and Standard Oil of California's with the energy group's index is 1.24. At the same time, note that the stocks are generally uncorrelated or negatively correlated with other indexes as indicated by low or negative beta values. We've assumed that the return on the nonmarket indexes for the period ahead will be 1 percent for the growth index, −2 percent for the cyclical index, −1 percent for the stable index, and 2 percent for the energy group's index. Given these return estimates and the portfolio betas for these indexes, the incremental return from these nonmarket sources would be 0.15 percent for growth, 0.84 percent for cyclical, −0.11 percent for stable, and 0.60 percent for energy. Thus nonmarket sources would add 1.7 percent in return and result in a total expected return of 17.3 percent for the portfolio.

The lower formulation in Table 2-6 illustrates calculation of the portfolio variance. Note that we've used the same estimate for the variance of the market as we used in the single-index example. The estimates of the variances of the nonmarket variances are historically derived. The residual variance estimates are also historically generated, but in this instance they reflect the removal of both market and group effects; hence they will be smaller than those shown for the single-index model. On the bottom line the market-related risk, nonmarket-related risk, and the weighted average specific risk of the portfolio aggregates to a total portfolio risk of 460 percent^2. The specific risk component can be reduced further by adding more securities to the portfolio, but the extramarket risk will remain if the weights of the portfolio in the four sectors remain the same.

Figure 2-6 is a chart similar to Figure 2-2 that illustrates this effect more clearly. In contrast to Figure 2-2, which shows two components of risk, this figure shows three: extramarket-related, market-related, and specific. These three risk components are shown for a portfolio of four stocks and another of twenty stocks. Both portfolios are constructed with the same weightings in the four market sectors (growth, cyclical, stable, and energy) as the example in Table 2-6.

Note that as in the previous illustration (Figure 2-2) the specific risk declines as securities are added to the portfolio — that is, as the portfolio increases from four to twenty securities. However, the extramarket risk remains, as will typically be the case with portfolios concentrated in the major sectors. For those portfolios that are weighted more evenly in the sectors, the nonmarket component of risk will be less. This is because these portfolios will be better hedged or diversified with respect to this risk component.[4]

ANALYZING PORTFOLIO RISK AND RETURN

Index models provide particularly useful insights into analyzing the risk-return characteristics of a portfolio, since they allow one to categorize the sources of risk and return into individual, identifiable components, as shown in Figure 2-7. The figure shows that the components of return can be considered as (1) market-related, (2) group-related, or (3) security-specific. Correspondingly, there are risks associated with each of these

[4] In a large diversified portfolio these extramarket effects tend to cancel out. In particular, a well-diversified fund can be characterized as one where the fund weighting in groupings of growth, cyclical, stable, and energy stocks, as well as of major industries, is generally in line with weightings of those groups and industries in the overall market. For example, if the energy group represented 20 percent of the overall market and the fund is weighted accordingly, then there will be no differential risk to the fund from that risk factor. In this example the extramarket effect tends to cancel out as the weighting of the groups are not too divergent from that of the market.

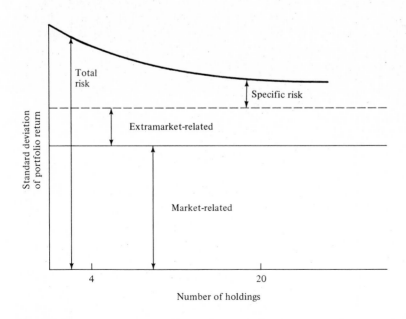

Figure 2-6 Market-related, extramarket-related, and specific risk.

return components, and we see that (1) the beta coefficient B_m is a general measure of exposure to market risk; (2) the relative weighting of the groups with respect to the market indicates exposure to group risk or, alternatively, extramarket covariance; and (3) residual risk Var(e) measures the uncertainty of earning the specific return.

Since the general market effect is a predominant source of return and risk for a portfolio, managers should be concerned with monitoring the exposure of the portfolio to this source to determine whether the portfolio positioning is consistent with longer-run policy targets or is appropriate for current market conditions. For example, if the outlook for the market were judged to be especially favorable, the manager might well desire to take advantage of this by raising the portfolio beta above its current level. Conversely, if the forecast were for a declining market, the appropriate strategy would be to lower the beta from its current level. Finally, if the manager were uncertain of the direction of the market and wished to hedge against this uncertainty, then the appropriate strategy would be to keep the portfolio beta in line with the market beta of 1.00 — that is, maintain a neutral posture toward the market. (We'll have more to say about this in Chapters 6 and 7.)

In addition, it's important that the manager evaluate the exposure of the portfolio to the group component to determine whether the positioning in growth, cyclical, stable, and energy stocks is appropriate for current market conditions. There may be periods when an individual group is judged to be particularly attractive, and the manager may desire to tilt the portfolio toward that grouping by weighting it more heavily in the portfolio. Conversely, a certain grouping may be deemed to be particularly unattractive, and the manager would then tilt away from the grouping by weighting it less heavily in the portfolio. When the manager has no opinion about the attractiveness of the groups, then the strategy would be to hedge against the risk of adverse group moves by weighting the groupings in line with their position in the overall market. (We'll illustrate this more specifically in the discussion of homogeneous stock groupings in Chapter 8.)

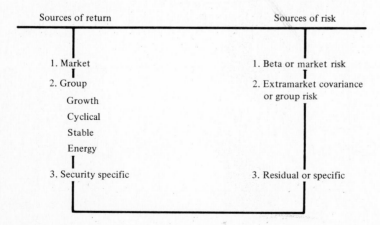

Figure 2-7 Components of risk and return.

Finally, index models indicate that the measure of security-specific return is the alpha value and that this is desirable when positive and undesirable when negative. Correspondingly, the measure of the uncertainty associated with earning the specific return is the variance of the residual; this will be large when the portfolio is poorly diversified and small when the portfolio is well-diversified. Portfolio managers should therefore endeavor to construct the portfolio in such a way that the resulting alpha is positive and large, but should also be aware of the amount of residual risk that is incurred in constructing such a portfolio. The lower the nonmarket risk, the greater the certainty of attaining the positive alpha; the greater the nonmarket risk, the lower the certainty of attaining the positive alpha.

As a result, the goal should be to construct a portfolio with a high positive alpha, while minimizing nonmarket risk, so as to develop a portfolio with high alpha per unit of risk. Portfolio optimization techniques, in fact, provide a way of formally determining from a security universe the combination and weighting of securities that provide the portfolio with optimal risk-return characteristics. We now turn to describing inputs needed to apply these techniques and outline the general method of generating such optimal portfolios.

GENERATING THE EFFICIENT FRONTIER

Index models not only provide insights into the sources of risk and return for a portfolio, they also facilitate the generation of a set of efficient portfolios. This is because both single- and multi-index models provide a simplified way of representing the covariance relationships among securities. This simplification, in turn, results in a substantial reduction in inputs compared to the number required when using the full covariance Markowitz portfolio selection model.[5]

Table 2-7 illustrates this data reduction by comparing the input requirements for the two index models to that for the Markowitz model. Note that the single-index model allows the most substantial reduction in inputs. This is because when using the single-index model for portfolio analysis there is need for only three estimates for each security to be analyzed: specific return a_i, measure of the responsiveness to market movements B_i, and variance of the residual term e_i. This is at the cost of two additional inputs: (1) an estimate of the market return $E(R_m)$ and (2) an estimate of the variance of the market $Var(R_M)$. In the general case of N securities, there would be need for $3N + 2$ estimates. For a universe of 100 stocks, there would be need for 302 estimates compared with the 5150 estimates required when using the Markowitz full covariance model.

[5] In an attempt to implement the Markowitz full covariance model, some have resorted to using historically derived data as inputs to the model. To begin with, calculating the historical data places a burden on computer capacity that becomes almost prohibitive when the universe becomes more sizeable, e. g., above 500 securities. More importantly, studies have shown that historically derived variance-covariance matrices contain substantial random variations that are not representative of the future behavior of securities under consideration. These errors of estimation can lead to a significant misrepresentation of the variance-covariance matrix and hence efficient frontier of portfolios. These errors have been shown to be severe enough that the full covariance model becomes inferior to the simplest alternative model.

Table 2-7 Data inputs for portfolio selection models

Model	Data inputs for 100 = security universe			
	Return	Variance	Covariance	Total
Markowitz	100	100	4950	5150
Single Index	101	101	100	302
Multi Index	105	105	500	710

Note that the multi-index model also provides for a substantial reduction in inputs, but less than that of the single-index model. This is because there is need for seven estimates for each security to be analyzed: specific return a_i; measure of responsiveness to the market B_m and to the four nonmarket factors B_g, B_c, B_s, and B_e; and the variance of the residual return Var(e). In addition, there would be need for estimates of the return of the market and four nonmarket indexes along with estimates of the variances of each of those indexes. In the general case of N securities, there will be need for $7N + 10$ estimates. The net requirement for an analysis of 100 securities is 710 estimates, or less than one-seventh of the 5150 required by the Markowitz model for analysis of the same size universe.

Given estimates of returns, variances, and covariances for the securities in the universe under consideration, the efficient set of portfolios is generated by means of a programming routine known as *quadratic programming*. A detailed description of the program is not essential and will only be summarized as follows. Essentially, the program is constructed to minimize the risk of a portfolio at a given level of return — that is, develop the efficient portfolio at a given return level (say, for example, at 5 percent, 10 percent, or 20 percent). The program develops minimum-risk portfolios at different levels of return, in each case specifying the securities and their weighting in the portfolio at that level of return.[6] Proceeding in this fashion, the program develops a series of portfolios differing in risk and return that trace out an efficient frontier similar to the one illustrated by the curve *AEDB* in Figure 2-1.[7]

Table 2-8 shows a portfolio generated in the course of a comparative study of the single- and multi-index portfolio selection models and is illustrative of the output from this process. Note that the table lists thirty-eight individual securities and their weightings in the portfolio. For example, American Home Products has a weight of 2.3 percent in the portfolio, while Sears has a weight of 7.1 percent and Eastman Kodak a weight of 7.2 percent. The weights total 100 percent, indicating that the portfolio is fully invested. The expected return for the portfolio is 14 percent and the

[6] Generally the maximum-return portfolios are generated at each risk level subject to the constraint that the portfolio be fully invested or, alternatively, that the weights of the individual securities in the portfolio sum to 1. The return, risk, and covariance inputs for the securities are constants and are not changed by the portfolio analysis. The weights of the securities are the variables which the portfolio analysis adjusts in order to obtain the optimum portfolios. By varying these weights the portfolio's expected return and risk are varied. However, as the weights are varied, the restriction that the portfolio be fully invested cannot be violated.

[7] We generally find portfolios increasing in number of securities as we move down the frontier from point *B* to point *A*. This is in line with the concept of diversification and variance reduction discussed in a previous section.

standard deviation 18 percent, as shown in the table subhead. The portfolio consists mainly of typical institutional-type names, for which different weightings have been determined so that the expected return is maximum for that level of risk.

TEST OF PORTFOLIO SELECTION MODELS

The usefulness of the portfolios generated by the quadratic programming routine will depend on the quality of the inputs to the process — on the quality of the estimated returns for the securities in the universe. (We'll have more to say about this in Chapters 4 and 5.) It also depends on the accuracy of the risk estimates, that is, the estimates of the variances and covariances of returns of securities in the universe of interest.

While index models are simplifications that facilitate the process of portfolio analysis, the trade-off in simplicity may be a less-than-adequate representation of the risk across the security universe. We've already seen that the single-index model omits consideration of nonmarket sources of risk, and omission of this significant source of additional risk could lead to serious misestimation of the frontier of efficient portfolios. The multi-index model allows incorporation of this additional source of risk and should result in a better representation of the efficient frontier while still economizing on the inputs to the model.

In order to evaluate the relative effectiveness of the single-index and multi-index models in generating an efficient set of portfolios, the author conducted an empirical test. A 100-stock universe was used and inputs were developed based on returns over the 1961–1969 period with both the single- and multi-index formulations. Once these inputs had been developed, two sets of efficient portfolios were generated: one based on single-index model inputs and the other based on multi-index model inputs.

Figure 2-8 charts the position of the full set of efficient portfolios generated by the two portfolio selection models: single- and multi-index.[8] Note that the efficient frontier for the multi-index model is above and to the left of the single-index model frontier for all but extremely high and low risk-return levels. The multi-index model provides higher return at the same level of risk and thus dominates the single-index model over a wide range of returns. This dominance of the multi-index model over the single-index model confirms the expected superiority of the multi-index model in generating efficient portfolios.

Evaluation of the performance of these portfolios over an ex post period (1970–1974) showed that the multi-index model portfolios were consistently superior to the single-index model portfolios. In particular, the multi-index model portfolios consistently provided higher returns than the single-index portfolios at equivalent levels of risk. In fact, the multi-index model portfolios outperformed standard market indexes and a sample of mutual funds over the same period. All tests seemed to verify that the multi-index model should be the preferred model for practical portfolio analysis.

---

[8] The efficient set is constructed of curves which are all convex toward the expected return axis. This is because securities have correlation coefficients between positive unity and negative unity. Only perfectly positively correlated securities will generate linear combinations of risk and return; and under no circumstances will a portfolio possibility locus curve away from the expected return axis.

Table 2-8 Portfolio composition
Expected return 14%; standard deviation 18%

Stock	Portfolio weight
Alcoa	1.5
American Can	2.9
American Home Products	2.3
Borg Warner	2.6
Burlington	2.2
Chesebrough Pond	1.2
Columbia Gas Systems	5.0
Campbell Soup	0.6
Deere	1.2
Eastman Kodak	7.2
Federated Department Stores	5.2
Gulf Oil	3.2
Georgia-Pacific	0.8
Gillette	1.3
Goodyear Tire & Rubber	3.7
Honeywell	1.6
International Business Machines	4.5
International Paper	3.4
International Telephone & Telegraph	1.0
Kellogg	0.3
Coca-Cola	2.6
Kraftco	1.0
Minnesota Mining & Manufacturing	3.1
Merck	5.6
National Cash Register	0.3
Nalco Chemical	2.1
Proctor & Gamble	3.2
R. J. Reynolds	1.1
Sears, Roebuck & Co.	7.1
Standard Oil of California	2.7
Sunbeam	0.5
Square D	0.1
Shell Oil	5.9
Timken	2.1
TRW	1.9
Texaco	6.3
Union Oil of California	1.7
Exxon	0.9
Total	100.0

Source: James L. Farrell, Jr., "The Multi-Index Model and Practical Portfolio Analysis," Occasional Paper no. 4, Financial Analysts Research Foundation, Charlottesville, Va., 1976, p. 43.

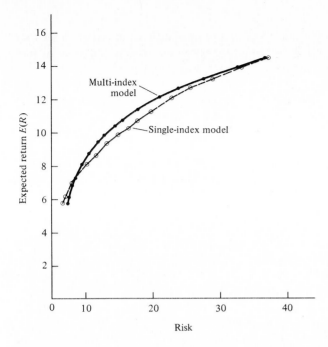

Figure 2-8 Ex ante efficient frontier: single-index and multi-index models. (*Source: James L. Farrell, Jr., "The Multi-Index Model and Practical Portfolio Analysis," Occasional Paper no. 4, Financial Analysts Research Foundation, Charlottesville, Va., 1976.*)

Before concluding, we should note that the quadratic programming routine for generating the efficient frontier is something of a "black box" approach. It's difficult to trace the inner workings of the programming routine and hence ascertain the reasons for the inclusion and weighting of a security in a portfolio. Recently Elton and Gruber developed techniques that enable one to understand the risk-return trade-offs that determine the suitability for inclusion of a security in an optimal portfolio.[9] Furthermore, these techniques are sufficiently simplified that the optimal weighting of securities in the portfolio can be easily calculated by means of a hand calculator. At the same time, the resulting portfolio composition is identical to that derived from the use of the more elaborate portfolio selection algorithms that require a large-scale computer for the solution. We illustrate the use of the simplified technique of determining an efficient portfolio in the appendix to Chapter 8.

CONCLUSION

The Markowitz model is a normative model; it shows how investors ought to behave but not necessarily how they will behave. Nevertheless, it is still possible to develop

[9] Edwin Elton, Martin Gruber, and Manfred Padbury, "Simple Criteria for Optimal Portfolio Selection," *Journal of Finance,* December 1976, pp. 1341–1357.

some implications for market and investor behavior from an informal analysis of the model. We illustrated this with the analysis, which indicated that the risk of a security could be regarded as being composed of two components, systematic and diversifiable, with the market likely to reward only the systematic component. In Chapter 3 we describe equilibrium models of investor behavior that derive from the underlying notions of portfolio selection models. These equilibrium models make more explicit and formal statements about investor and market behavior.

APPENDIX A CONVERSION OF CORRELATED INDEXES INTO UNCORRELATED (INDEPENDENT) INDEXES

This appendix outlines the method for converting correlated indexes into a set of uncorrelated (independent or orthogonal) indexes. We'll assume for purposes of illustration that there are two indexes: a general market index and an index of growth stocks. We would expect the growth-stock index to contain the general market effect as well as the growth-stock effect since the general market factor impacts all stocks. The intent in this case is to remove the general market factor and focus exclusively on the growth-stock effect. Defining R_m as the market return and R_g as the growth stock return, we can represent the return on a stock as

$$R_i = a + B_m R_m + B_g R_g + e$$

We can further assume that the return on the growth-stock index is linearly related to the return on the market and express it as follows:

$$R_g = c + DR_m + u$$

This can then be inserted into the prior expression:

$$R_i = a + B_m R_m + B_g(c + DR_m + u) + e$$

When we rearrange the expression, it becomes

$$R_i = (a + B_g c) + (B_m + B_g D)R_m + B_g u + e$$

The first parenthesized expression is a constant; the second, $B_m + B_g D$, indicates the impact of a change in the market return R_m on the security return; both the direct effect B_m and the indirect effect through the growth-stock return $B_g D$ are included. The term u is now an index of the difference between the return on growth stocks and that expected given the return on the market; that is, it represents incremental return. The combined term $B_g u$ indicates the effect of a deviation of the growth-stock return from its predicted relationship with the market R_m. The term e, as usual, measures the specific risk of the stock.

PROBLEMS

1 Refer to the data in Table 2-1. Calculate the expected return and variance of the portfolio, assuming that the portfolio weights are .75 for security 1 and .25 for security 2, that the expected return of security 1 is 18 percent and the standard deviation is .60, and that the correlation between the two securities is .5.

2 Refer to the data in Table 2-2. Calculate the standard deviation of the following portfolios: four stocks, nine stocks, twenty-five stocks, thirty-six stocks, and forty-nine stocks.

3 Determine the number of inputs needed to analyze a 250-stock universe and an 800-stock universe using the Markowitz full covariance model. Compare with inputs needed for a single-index and a five-index model.

4 Assume that the standard deviation for the market is 18 percent, and for an individual stock 40 percent, and that the correlation between the stock and market is .5. Calculate the beta of the stock.

5 Refer to the data in Table 2-5. Calculate the expected return and risk of the portfolio with the single-index model formulation using the following portfolio weights: Merck (.40), Bethlehem Steel (.15), Kellogg (.15), and Standard Oil of California (.30).

6 Refer now to Table 2-6. Weight each of securities equally (.25), and calculate the expected return and risk of the portfolio.

SELECTED REFERENCES

Brealey, Richard A.: *An Introduction to Risk and Return from Common Stock Prices,* M. I. T. Press, Cambridge, Mass., 1969.

Cohen, Kalman, and Jerry Pogue: "An Empirical Evaluation of Alternative Portfolio Selection Models," *Journal of Business,* April 1967, pp. 166–193.

Curley, A. J., and Robert M. Bear: *Investment Analysis and Management,* Harper & Row, New York, 1979.

Elton, Edwin J., and Martin J. Gruber: "Estimating the Dependence Structure of Share Prices — Implications for Portfolio Selection," *Journal of Finance,* December 1973, pp. 1203–1232.

————: *Modern Portfolio Theory and Investment Analysis,* John Wiley & Sons, New York, 1981.

Evans, John L., and Stephen H. Archer: "Diversification and the Reduction of Dispersion: An Empirical Analysis," *Journal of Finance,* December 1968, pp. 761–67.

Farrell, James L., Jr.: "Analyzing Covariation of Returns to Determine Homogeneous Stock Groupings," *Journal of Business,* April 1974, pp. 186–207.

————: "The Multi-Index Model and Practical Portfolio Analysis," Occasional Paper no. 4, Financial Analysts Research Foundation, Charlottesville, Va., 1976.

Fisher, Lawrence, and James H. Lorie: "Rates of Return on Investments in Common Stocks," *Journal of Business,* January 1964, pp. 1–21.

————: "Rates of Return on Investments in Common Stocks: The Year-by-Year Record, 1926–1965," *Journal of Business,* July 1968, pp. 291–316.

————: "Some Studies of Variability of Returns on Investment in Common Stocks," *Journal of Business,* April 1970, pp. 99–134.

Francis, Jack G.: *Investments,* McGraw-Hill, New York, 1980.

Ibbotson, Roger G., and Rex A. Sinquefeld: *Stocks, Bonds, Bills, and Inflation: The Past (1926–1976) and the Future (1977–2000),* Financial Analysts Research Foundation, Charlottesville, Va., 1977.

King, Benjamin: "Market and Industry Factors in Stock Price Behavior," *Journal of Business,* January 1966, pp. 139–190.

Lorie, James H., and Mary T. Hamilton: *The Stock Market: Theories and Evidence,* Richard D. Irwin, Homewood, Ill., 1974.

Markowitz, Harry: "Portfolio Selection," *Journal of Finance,* March 1952, pp. 77–91.

Markowitz, Harry: *Portfolio Selection: Efficient Diversification of Investments,* John Wiley & Sons, New York, 1959.

Modigliani, Franco, and Gerald Pogue: "An Introduction to Risk and Return," *Financial Analysts Journal,* March–April 1974, pp. 68–80.

Sharpe, William F: "A Simplified Model for Portfolio Analysis," *Management Science,* January 1963, pp. 277–293.

————: *Portfolio Theory and Capital Markets,* McGraw-Hill, New York, 1970.

————: "Risk, Market Sensitivity and Diversification," *Financial Analysts Journal,* January–February 1972, pp. 74–79.

————: *Investments,* Prentice-Hall, Englewood Cliffs, N. J., 1978.

THREE

CAPITAL MARKET THEORY

INTRODUCTION

As noted in Chapter 2, the Markowitz model is the foundation for portfolio analysis, while the capital-asset pricing model (CAPM) is the model for capital market theory. The Markowitz model is normative: it shows how investors ought to behave. On the other hand, capital market theory is positive. Given that investors behave in the fashion suggested by Markowitz, then there are implications for (1) the behavior of security prices, (2) the sort of risk-return relationship that one would expect, and (3) the appropriate measure of risk for securities. The section discussing diversification in the previous chapter attempted to develop some of those implications in an informal fashion. The CAPM is a general equilibrium model that attempts to provide more explicit answers for those implications.

This chapter begins by outlining the major assumptions underlying the CAPM. It then goes on to describe the two main components of the CAPM: (1) the capital market line (CML), and (2) the security market line (SML). We'll then discuss use of the SML in determining the appropriate expected return for stocks, along with its role as a benchmark for appraising the relative valuation of stocks. After describing these uses, we'll review the empirical evidence on the SML to see how well the model conforms to real-world market behavior.

We'll conclude the chapter by describing an alternative model for studying equilibrium in the market. It is known as arbitrage pricing theory (APT). While it differs in underlying assumptions and develops equilibrium in a different way from the CAPM, it has essentially the same implications for market behavior as the CAPM. Discussion of it should thus be useful not only for the additional perspective it offers in understanding equilibrium in the market but also for the further reinforcement it provides to an underlying risk-return relationship in the marketplace.

CAPM ASSUMPTIONS AND IMPLICATIONS

Table 3-1 lists the assumptions that are usually made in deriving the CAPM. Note that because the CAPM builds on the Markowitz model, it automatically makes the assumptions that are necessary for that model of portfolio analysis. In particular, it assumes that investors (1) are risk-averse, expected-utility maximizers, (2) choose their portfolios on the basis of the mean and variance of return, and (3) have a one-period time horizon that is the same for all investors. As noted before, the implications of these assumptions are that investors will diversify and will want to select portfolios from somewhere on the efficient frontier. The CAPM as a general equilibrium model with implications regarding the behavior of security prices, however, makes a stronger statement and hence needs other, stronger assumptions.

The bottom part of Table 3-1 lists those additional assumptions. Note that one of these is that a risk-free asset exists and that borrowing and lending at the risk-free rate is unrestricted. While treasury bills are risk-free in nominal terms and are usually taken as a proxy for a risk-free asset, there is question whether in an inflationary environment there is such a thing as a risk-free asset — that is, there will be uncertainty of real return. After developing the model on the assumption of a risk-free asset, we'll then examine the effect on the model of relaxing this particular premise.

Another assumption of the CAPM is that investors have homogeneous expectations regarding the means, variances, and covariances of security returns. This assumption suggests that every investor has an identical view of the prospects for each security. This, in turn, allows us to derive the model in a relatively straightforward fashion as well as to develop implications that are relatively unambiguous. Actually the model can be derived assuming only that there is a "considerable consensus" by investors regarding future prospects; however, the derivation then becomes more complex and the implications less clear than when homogeneous expectations are assumed.

The model's additional assumptions of no taxes and other market imperfections, such as transactions costs, are needed to make possible the arbitraging of "mispriced" securities, thus forcing an equilibrium price. When the assumption of no taxes is relaxed, the question arises as to whether high-dividend stocks offer higher pretax returns than low-dividend stocks of equivalent risk. This is currently a subject of considerable theoretical debate and empirical testing. Evidence to date indicates that the effect, if it exists at all, is likely to be small, perhaps 50 basis points or less. Correspondingly, the existence of transactions costs means that securities can potentially be

Table 3-1 Assumptions for the CAPM

Common to both the Markowitz model and the CAPM
1. Investors are risk-averse, expected-utility maximizers.
2. Investors choose portfolios on the basis of their expected mean and variance of return.
3. Investors have a single-period time horizon that is the same for all investors.

Additional assumptions
4. Unrestricted borrowing and lending at the risk-free rate
5. Homogeneous investor expectations regarding the means, variances, and covariances of security returns
6. No taxes and no market imperfections such as transactions costs

mispriced by an amount equal to transactions costs. This effect is also likely to be relatively minor, as transactions costs are small relative to the price of securities; that is, estimates for a typical common stock are on the order of 50 to 100 basis points.

The implications of these assumptions are that there is a CAPM consisting of a CML and an SML. The CML provides the framework for determining the relationship between expected return and risk for portfolios of securities. Correspondingly, it indicates the appropriate measure of risk for a portfolio. The SML provides the framework for determining the relationship between expected return and risk for individual securities as well as for portfolios. The SML also indicates the appropriate measure of risk for securities. It will be useful to cover the CML first, as it provides a foundation for better understanding of the SML, which in turn has broader application in understanding the risk-return trade-off in the marketplace.

LENDING AND BORROWING

The CML is usually derived on the assumption that there exists a riskless asset available for investment. It is further assumed that investors can borrow or lend as much as desired at the risk-free rate R_f. Given this opportunity, investors can then mix risk-free assets with a portfolio of risky assets M to obtain the desired risk-return combination. Letting X represent the proportion invested in risk-free assets and $1 - X$ the proportion invested in the risky asset, we can use a formula like the one in the previous chapter (see page 32) to calculate the expected return on the combination or portfolio R_p.

$$E(R_p) = XR_f + (1 - X)E(R_m) \tag{1}$$

The top panel of Table 3-2 uses this formula to calculate expected returns associated with three investor options: (1) mixing lending with risky assets, (2) investing only in the risky asset, and (3) mixing borrowing with risky assets. The lending example in the top panel of Table 3-2 assumes that the investor apportions half his funds to the risk-free asset ($X = .5$) and the other half to the risky asset. The leverage example assumes that the investor borrows (negative lending, or $X = -.5$) at the risk-free rate and invests half again as much in the risky asset. The intermediate example assumes exclusive investment ($X = 0$) in risky assets.

Note that lending provides the lowest return at 7.5 percent, borrowing the highest at 12.5 percent, and exclusive investment in the risky asset an intermediate return at 10 percent. While borrowing increases expected return and lending reduces expected return, there is a trade-off in increased and decreased risk. Intuitively, when one invests in risk-free *and* risky assets, the total risk of the portfolio is less than that of the risky set alone. Conversely, when one borrows to buy additional risky assets, the total risk of the portfolio increases over that of the risky set alone. The latter case is commonly known as *financial leverage*.

We can again use the formula in Chapter 2 (page 32) for calculating the variances of a portfolio to indicate the nature of the trade-off. In particular, if we let X represent the proportion of the portfolio in the risk-free asset and $1 - X$ the risky asset, the variance of the portfolio $[\text{Var}(R_p)]$ is

$$\text{Var}(R_p) = X^2 \text{Var}(R_f) + (1 - X)^2 \text{Var}(R_m) + 2X(1 - X)\rho S_f S_m$$

Table 3-2 Risk-return for differing combinations of borrowing and lending

		Return		
Proportion in risk-free asset X	Risk-free return R_f, %	Proportion in risky asset $1 - X$	Risky return R_m, %	Portfolio return R_p, %
.5	5	.5	10	7.5
0	5	1.0	10	10.0
− .5	5	1.5	10	12.5

	Risk	
Proportion in risky asset $1 - X$	Standard deviation of return S_m, %	Portfolio risk S_p, %
.5	20	10
1.0	20	20
1.5	20	30

		Risk-return trade-off		
Portfolio return R_p, %	Risk-free return R_f, %	Risk premium $R_p - R_f$, %	Portfolio risk S_p, %	Factor of porportionality $(R_p - R_f)/S_p$
7.5	5.0	2.5	10	.25
10.0	5.0	5.0	20	.25
12.5	5.0	7.5	30	.25

Note that only the second term of the equation $(1 - X)^2 \operatorname{Var}(R_m)$ has a positive value. The value of the first term is zero because the return on the riskless asset has zero variance; the third term has a value of zero because the return on the riskless asset has a standard deviation of zero. It is also true that the variance of the portfolio of risky assets is a given value. Thus the variance of the portfolio depends exclusively on the proportion which is invested in the risky asset or, equivalently, the proportion invested in the risk-free asset. The formula for determining the risk of a combined portfolio of risky and risk-free assets can be expressed as a standard deviation S_p, as in the following:

$$\sqrt{(\operatorname{Var}(R_p))} = S_p = (1 - X)S_m \tag{2}$$

Since the risk associated with the combination is directly proportional to the position in the risky asset, we have calculated in the middle panel of Table 3-2, the risk values associated with the three alternative versions of investing in the previous example. In particular, it shows the risk associated with (1) investing half the funds in a risk-free asset, (2) investing exclusively in risky assets, and (3) borrowing and investing half again as much in the risky portfolio. Note that the risk of 30 percent is greatest for the borrowing alternative with the greatest return and least, at 10 percent, for the lending alternative that had the lowest return. Investing exclusively in risky assets provided both intermediate risk and return.

In fact, returns are proportional to risk as illustrated by the calculation at the bottom of Table 3-2, which shows that the factor of proportionality is calculated by subtracting the risk-free rate from the return and dividing by the risk (standard deviation). Note that the factor of proportionality is .25, indicating that one unit of return is accompanied by four units of risk.

THE CAPITAL MARKET LINE

The possibility of lending and borrowing changes the original efficient frontier to the straight line $R_f MB$, as shown in Figure 3-1. This line rising from the interest rate R_f on the vertical axis and tangential to the curve at point M, sets out all the alternative combinations of the risky portfolio M with risk-free borrowing and lending.[1] The segment from point R_f to point M includes the mixed portfolios of risky and risk-free securities. Levered portfolios (combinations of M with risk-free loans) are represented by points along the line beyond point M.

Since, according to the CAPM, all investors have identical (homogeneous) expectations, they will all observe a risk-return diagram such as that illustrated in Figure 3-1. Accordingly, every investor will seek to construct a portfolio consisting of the risk-free asset and portfolio M. Because all investors hold the same risky portfolio, then, for equilibrium, it will include all risky securities in proportion to their market

[1] Note that the portfolio of risky assets represented by point M has the property of maximizing the angle formed when a straight line is drawn from point R_f to any point on the curve. Portfolio M is, therefore, the one that provides the maximum return per unit of risk (standard deviation).

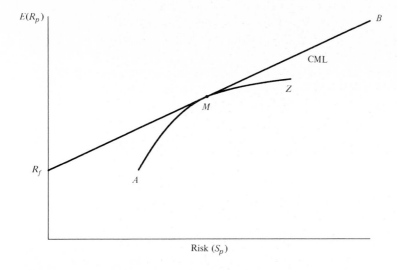

Figure 3-1 The capital market line.

value. If this were not true, prices would adjust until the value of the security was consistent with its proportion in portfolio M. This portfolio of all risky assets is referred to as the *market portfolio*.[2]

The investor can now attain any point along the line R_fMB by combining the portfolio of risky assets M with the risk-free asset R_f or by levering the portfolio M by borrowing and investing the funds in M. Portfolios on line R_fMB are preferred to portfolios between A and M and between M and Z, since they offer greater return for a given level of risk. These portfolios, except portfolio M, dominate those exclusively made up of risky assets.

The line R_fMB formed by the action of all investors mixing the market portfolio and the risk-free asset then becomes the capital market line (CML). Mathematically the CML can be described in terms of the risk-free rate and the return on the market portfolio:

$$E(R_p) - R_f = \frac{E(R_m) - R_f}{S_m} S_p \tag{3}$$

The equation says, in words, that for a portfolio on the CML the expected rate of return in excess of the risk-free rate is proportional to the standard deviation of that portfolio.[3] The slope of the CML has been called the price of risk. As the equation shows, it is the constant of proportionality and equals the difference between the expected return on the market portfolio and that on the risk-free security $[E(R_m) - R_f]$ divided by the difference in their risks $S_m - 0$. It is the additional expected return for each additional unit of risk, or the reward per unit of risk.

We can refer to data from the 1926–1978 period, described in Chapter 1, to develop a crude benchmark for what the price of risk might have been over that fifty-year period. In particular, the return on the market over that period was close to 9 percent, while the standard deviation of the market was approximately 21 percent. Using the approximately 2 percent return on treasury bills as a proxy for the risk-free rate and plugging these values into the formula would have indicated a slope of $1/3$. Investing in the market portfolio would provide a reward of 7 percent $(9.0 - 2.0)$ for bearing a risk corresponding to a standard deviation of 21 percent or a 1 percent return for every 3 percent of risk assumed over the period.

[2]The market portfolio is a critical notion underlying the CAPM. Recent work by Roll casts doubt not only on the possibility of identifying such a portfolio and of conducting valid tests of the explanatory capacity of the model but also on application of principles of the CAPM in practice. One of the merits of the alternative theory of asset pricing, the arbitrage pricing theory (APT), to be discussed later in the chapter, is that it does not depend on the existence or identifiability of a market portfolio.

[3]This formula can be derived by first rearranging the Equation 2 for the standard deviation of portfolio return from

$$S_p = (1 - X)S_m$$

to obtain $(1 - X) = S_p/S_m$ and $X = 1 - S_p/S_m$, and then substituting these expressions in Equation 1 for expected return:

$$R_p = XR_f + (1 - X)R_m$$

Simplifying, we obtain Equation 3.

The CML thus provides a risk-return relationship and measure of risk for efficient portfolios — that is, for those that plot on the line representing the efficient frontier. In particular, it indicates that the appropriate measure of risk for an efficient portfolio is the standard deviation of return of the portfolio S_p. It also indicates that there will be a linear relationship between the risk as measured by the standard deviation and the expected return for these efficient portfolios. The formulation for this risk-return relationship is given in Equation 3.

THE SECURITY MARKET LINE

While the CML shows the appropriate measure of risk and the risk-return relationship for efficient portfolios, it does not show those for inefficient portfolios or individual securities. Sharpe in his study shows that the analysis can be extended to a related but not identical measure of risk.[4] It is the familiar beta concept and a measure of risk that applies to all assets and portfolios whether efficient or inefficient. In addition, Sharpe provides the SML, which specifies the relationship between expected return and risk, again for all assets and portfolios, whether efficient or inefficient; however, his derivation is fairly complex, so we'll merely provide a more direct and intuitive derivation of the SML.

This can be done most effectively by referring back to the section on diversification in Chapter 2. Recall that we noted that the total risk of a security as measured by the standard deviation S_i is essentially composed of two components: systematic risk and diversifiable risk. We saw that the diversifiable component could be reduced as we added securities, or diversified the portfolio, thereby increasing the proportion of systematic risk in the portfolio. Correspondingly, we saw that when diversification increases, so does the correlation of the portfolio with the market. We concluded from this discussion that the systematic component is the relevant one both for measuring risk as well as for determining the risk-return relationship.

To measure the systematic risk of a security or portfolio, we simply multiply the correlation coefficient between the security or portfolio and the market portfolio by the standard deviation of the security or portfolio $\rho_{im}S_i$. For a portfolio that is perfectly diversified the systematic component will be equivalent to total risk, because the correlation between the portfolio and the market is perfectly positive ($\rho_{pm} = +1$), so that $\rho_{pm}S_p = S_p$. In this case the measure of risk is the standard deviation, and the CML, which employs the standard deviation, is the appropriate measure of the risk-return relationship.

For portfolios that are less than perfectly diversified or for individual securities, however, systematic risk and total risk will not be equivalent, because the portfolios and individual securities are less than perfectly correlated with the market. For example, the typical individual security will have a correlation coefficient with the market of .55. With a standard deviation of 40 percent the systematic risk of the typical security will be .55 × 40 percent = 22 percent, or little more than half the total risk. The SML,

[4]W. F. Sharpe, "Capital Asset Prices: A Theory of Market Equilibrium under Conditions of Risk," *Journal of Finance*, September 1964, pp. 425–442.

which uses systematic risk as its risk measure, is the appropriate risk-return relationship for securities and for portfolios that are less than perfectly diversified; that is

$$E(R_i) - R_f = \frac{E(R_m) - R_f}{S_m}\rho_{im}S_i \tag{4}$$

This relationship says that the expected return of a security in excess of the risk-free rate is proportional to the systematic risk of the stock. Note that the left-hand side of the equation is identical to the CML and that the factor of proportionality on the right-hand side is the price of risk. The SML and CML differ only in the measure of risk: systematic risk for the SML and total risk for the CML.

Using the definition of the correlation coefficient $\text{Cov}(R_iR_m)/(S_iS_m)$ and rearranging terms, the SML can be restated as

$$E(R_i) - R_f = \frac{\text{Cov}(R_iR_m)}{\text{Var}(R_m)}[E(R_m) - R_f]$$

Note that the first term on the right-hand side of the equation is the same as the beta of the stock, so that we can restate the equation in its more familiar form as

$$E(R_i) = R_f + B_i[E(R_m) - R_f] \tag{5}$$

It will be useful to note at this point that for all practical purposes the beta coefficient in the equation of the SML is the same as the beta of the market, or single-index, model. As a result, for application and testing of the relationship, researchers and practitioners ordinarily use the market model. Recall that in the last chapter we illustrated the way the market model can be used to calculate betas.

RISK-RETURN RELATIONSHIP

When the equation of the SML is plotted in expected-return beta coordinates, it yields a straight line as shown in Figure 3-2. Note that the vertical axis refers to expected return, while the horizontal axis uses beta rather than standard deviation as the measure of risk. The line is determined by the return on the risk-free asset, which has, by definition, a beta of zero and the expected return on the market, which has a beta of 1.00, also by definition. In equilibrium all securities and portfolios will plot along the SML, whether efficient or inefficient.

Since all securities are expected to plot along the SML, the line provides a direct and convenient way of determining the expected return on a security. In particular, each beta level might be regarded as representing a risk class, and all securities that fall in that risk class would be expected to earn a return appropriate for that class. Presuming that we know the beta of the security, we can directly use the SML formula to solve for the expected return or, alternatively, use the SML graph to generate an expected return for the security.

To illustrate this, Table 3-3 shows some market data along with data for two hypothetical securities A and D. Note that the risk-free rate is assumed to be 5 percent and the expected market return 12 percent, to provide an expected market-risk premium

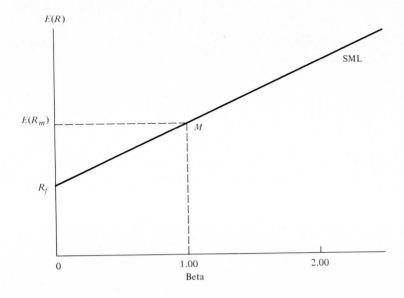

Figure 3-2 The security market line.

of 7 percent. Security A has a beta of 1.20, while security D has a beta of .80. Given market data and the beta for a security, the expected return can be calculated by means of the SML equation given in the body of the table, where security A has an expected return of 13.4 percent and security D an expected return of 10.6 percent.

Alternatively, one can derive an expected return for the security graphically, as illustrated in Figure 3-3, in which the SML is derived from the market data in Table 3-3. Once this and the beta values are known for the security, one can plot the securities and read off the expected return from the vertical axis. For example, security A with a beta of 1.20 has an expected return of 13.4 percent, while security D with a beta of .80 has an expected return of 10.6 percent. The expected returns are, of course, the same as those in Table 3-3 by formulation.

As a matter of interest, we might use the SML graph to classify securities. Those with betas greater than 1.00 and plotting on the upper part of the line, such as security

Table 3-3 Security market line (SML) data

	Expected return $E(R)$	Risk-free rate R_f	Beta B_i	Market-risk premium $[E(R_m) - R_f]$
Market	12.0	5	1.00	7
Security A	13.4	5	1.20	7
Security D	10.6	5	0.80	7

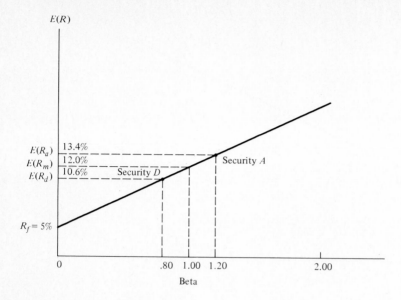

Figure 3-3 Security market line.

A, will be classified as aggressive, while those with betas less than 1.00 and plotting on the lower part of the line, such as security D, will be classified as defensive. Aggressive securities would be expected to earn above-average returns, while defensive securities would be expected to earn below-average returns, as can be seen in the SML graph.

UNDERVALUED AND OVERVALUED SECURITIES

The SML also provides a framework for evaluating the relative attractiveness of securities. In particular, high-risk stocks are expected to offer high returns because of their risk. The question is whether they are offering returns more or less than proportional to their risk. Conversely, low-risk stocks are expected to offer lower returns by virtue of a lower risk level. Again the question is whether they are offering returns more or less than proportional to their risk.

Figure 3-4 illustrates how the SML provides an explicit framework for this appraisal. The figure shows a hypothetical market line with nine securities plotted relative to it. Note that securities A, B, and C plot above the line, securities X, Y, and Z below the line, and securities M, N, and O on the line. At the same time, securities A, M, X plot at a beta level of .80, B, N, and Y plot at a beta of 1.00, and C, O, and Z at a beta of 1.20. Each of the three sets of securities is in the same risk class, of which there are three: high, low, and average.

In the market-line context, stocks that plot above the line presumably are undervalued (attractive) because they offer a higher expected return than stocks of similar

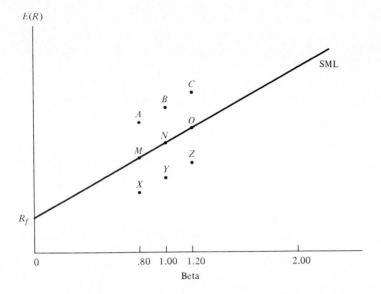

Figure 3-4 The market line and security valuation.

risk. Stocks *A, B,* and *C,* which plot above the line are undervalued relative to their beta class. The prices of these stocks are too low, and we can see from the simple rate of return formulation that they would have to rise — leading to above-average performance — to raise the denominator and lower the required return of the stock:

$$E(R_i) = \frac{E(P_1) - P_o + \text{dividend}}{P_o}$$

On the other hand, a stock is presumably overvalued (unattractive) when it is expected to produce a lower return than issues of comparable risk. Stocks *X, Y,* and *Z,* which plot below the line, are overvalued relative to their beta class. The prices of these stocks are too high, and in this case we can see from the rate of return formulation that they would have to fall — leading to below-average performance — to lower the denominator and thereby raise the return of the stocks.

Stocks *M, N,* and *O,* which plot on the line, are appropriately valued in the context of the market line. These stocks are offering returns in line with their riskiness. The prices of these stocks are "right," and one would expect average stock performance since they are neither undervalued nor overvalued.

Stocks plotting off the market line would thus be evidence of mispricing in the marketplace. There are, in turn, three major reasons for mispricing in the securities market. The first is transactions costs, which may reduce investors' incentive to correct minor deviations from the SML; the cost of adjustment may be greater or at least equal to the potential opportunity presented by the mispricing. Secondly, investors subject to taxes might be reluctant to sell an overvalued security with a capital gain and incur the tax. Finally, imperfect information can affect the valuation of a security. Some investors are less well-informed than others and may not observe mispricing and hence not act on these opportunities.

Figure 3-5 is an idealized illustration of how the SML would look when actual market conditions are as we just described. In this case all securities would not be expected to lie exactly on the SML. Therefore, in practice the SML is a band instead of a thin line. The width of this band varies directly with the imperfections in the market.

As may be surmised, the SML has practical implications as a means of identifying undervalued and overvalued securities. Chapter 5 will describe how this method has been implemented and the results of using this framework to identify relatively attractive stocks. The results demonstrate the usefulness of these techniques of portfolio management while also offering some evidence of the degree to which there may be mispricing in the market place.

EMPIRICAL TESTS

It will be useful at this point to describe how the SML Equation (5) has been tested empirically and thereby illustrate how well real market data has conformed to the risk-return relationship suggested by the CAPM. Also, it should provide perspective on which assumptions of the model are most severely compromised.

The risk-return relationship described by Equation 5 (the SML) is an expected, or ex ante, relationship. The returns referred to in the model are expected returns, while the beta to which it refers is derived from expected covariances and variances of returns;

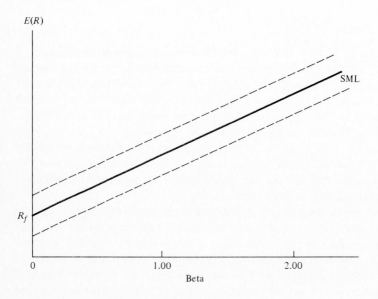

Figure 3-5 Security market line — presence of market imperfections.

that is, the relationship is forward-looking rather than backward-looking and should embody investors' expectations. Ideally then, in testing the relationship one would like to have data on expected returns and expected beta values for individual securities or portfolios of securities. Expectations, however, are difficult to observe, especially with respect to the risk attributes of securities and portfolios of securities.

In testing the relationship, researchers have thus relied on realized, or historical data. The assumption here is that if enough observations are available in a test, investors' expectations will be aligned with realizations — that is, realizations will be representative of expectations. For example, researchers would derive returns over, say, the most recent ten-year period and assume that these realized values were representative of expectations over that period.

After obtaining returns, researchers calculate betas by regressing the returns of individual securities or groups of securities against the returns of some market index, just as we described in the discussion of the single-index model in Chapter 2. Once the betas have been calculated, they can be plotted against the return of individual securities or groups of securities. For this purpose the average return of the security or group of securities realized over the period of the study is taken as representative of the return-beta relationship.

Figure 3-6 is a risk-return diagram illustrating this for a hypothetical set of, say, 100 securities. Note that the figure shows the plots of the beta-return values for each of the securities as well as a line fitted to the plotted points. The equation for fitting the line to the plots is the following:

$$\text{Return} = \gamma_0 + \gamma_1 \text{beta} + u \tag{6}$$

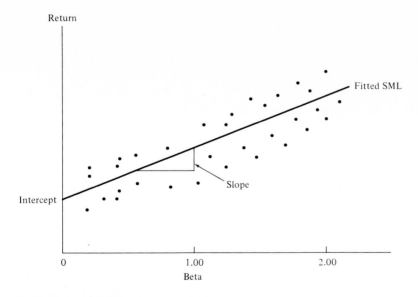

Figure 3-6 Empirical security market line.

In testing the risk-return relationship, researchers are concerned with assessing how well this fitted line conforms to the theoretical SML. If the fitted line conforms perfectly with the theoretical, it should show the following characteristics. First, the line should be upward-sloping, thereby verifying that securities or portfolios with higher systematic risk earned higher returns than those with lower risk, at least over longer periods of time. On average there should be a linear relationship between beta and return, verifying that other "nonsystematic" factors are not important in determining returns. Finally, the constant term, or intercept, in the equation (γ_0) would be expected to equal the risk-free rate (R_f). Correspondingly, the slope of the line (γ_1) would be expected to equal the average market-risk premium ($R_m - R_f$) during the period used.

AMENDED CAPM

As there have been numerous tests of the SML relationship along the lines just described, discussion of the various techniques of testing and results of the test would be interesting in itself; however, reporting such analyses and results would require considerable space and would not be appropriate to the intention of this book. For our purposes it is most useful to summarize and comment on the specific findings with regard to the three desired characteristics of the empirical SML just described. First, with regard to the anticipated positive risk-return relationship, researchers have generally found that it was upward-sloping when studied over longer periods of time. Over shorter intervals the relationship was not, however, necessarily upward-sloping. There were periods when the relationship was unclear as well as periods when it was in fact downward-sloping. The latter was generally found to be the case during bear-market periods, when the realized risk premium in the market was negative rather than the expected positive relationship which is more likely to be realized over longer periods. At the same time, tests of the linearity of the relationship showed that other factors were not important in explaining realized returns; the SML was in fact linear.

On the other hand, tests show that the line does not intercept the vertical axis at the risk-free rate and directly indicates a potential deficiency with respect to one of the main assumptions of the CAPM.[5] Specifically, it implies that the assumption of the existence of a risk-free asset and ability of investors to borrow and lend freely at this rate may not be a valid representation of the workings of the marketplace. Furthermore, it seems reasonable on the basis of casual observation that this may be one of the more questionable assumptions used in the model.

To begin with, investors generally cannot borrow and lend at the same rate. Financial intermediaries charge a higher rate than the rate at which they lend, to provide a spread that incorporates a profit margin and premium to compensate for the credit risks of the borrower. Borrowers thus pay a higher rate than they would receive for lending or investing funds.

Moreover, in an inflationary environment there is no such thing as a risk-free

---

[5] We should also note that the slope of the line has been shown to be flatter than it should be, implying that the realized risk premium for the market is lower than expected.

investment. Treasury bills have normally been cited as a reasonable proxy for a risk-free asset. These instruments are free of credit risk and because of their short-term nature are virtually free of the interest rate risk. Treasury bills are in fact essentially riskless in nominal terms but not in real terms. They are subject to the purchasing power risk, which becomes more severe as the rate of inflation becomes more intense.

Black, realizing this problem and observing empirical evidence, amended the CAPM to accommodate these violations of the risk-free asset assumption. His analysis indicated that it was possible to substitute for the risk-free asset an asset that he referred to as a zero-beta asset or portfolio. This is a portfolio which has a return that is designed to have no correlation with the market. The amended CAPM has a similar structure to the original, but now has the zero-beta factor (R_z) rather than the risk-free rate (R_f) in the equation:

$$E(R_i) = E(R_z) + B_i[E(R_m) - E(R_z)] \tag{7}$$

Figure 3-7 illustrates the modified SML, or CAPM. Note that the intercept of the line, designated R_z, would be at a higher level than the risk-free rate, designated R_f.[6] The fact that the intercept is higher in the amended model also means that the line will slope less than with a risk-free asset. We would also expect the slope of the line to vary over time as the return on the zero-beta factor fluctuated. All this is, of course, more in line with the previously discussed empirical results, implying that the Black zero-beta model offers a better explanation of the risk-return relationship than the pure version of the SML.

[6] The zero-beta factor, while not correlated with the market, would be expected to have some variance associated with it, unlike a risk-free asset, which would have no variance.

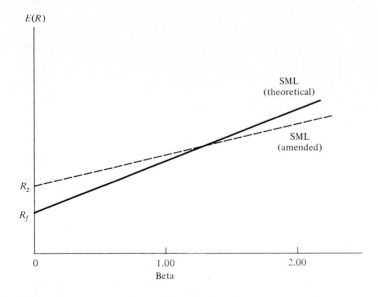

Figure 3-7 Security market line — theoretical and amended.

ROLE OF THE MARKET PORTFOLIO

While empirical results are generally consistent with some sort of a risk-return trade-off in the marketplace, Richard Roll has directed some fundamental criticism at the relevance of these tests in affirming the CAPM as the appropriate model for describing this trade-off. This criticism is aimed at one of the critical notions — the concept of a market portfolio — underlying the CAPM. Recall that the market portfolio is one that contains all the securities in the universe by their proper weights. This portfolio should, in turn, be an ex ante efficient portfolio — that is, offering the highest expected return at the expected risk level.

Although the necessity of the market portfolio being an efficient portfolio has been generally taken for granted by researchers, it becomes the crux of Roll's analysis. To begin with, Roll demonstrates that choice of the incorrect portfolio or index as proxy for the market can lead to misestimates of the systematic risk of individual securities and portfolios and hence result in an inappropriate estimate of the SML. Roll notes that this misestimation error is not of the usual statistical sort, but, rather, a basic bias that cannot be corrected by the use of more powerful statistical tools. It can only be avoided by properly identifying what the ex ante efficient market portfolio is.

Roll indicates, however, that identifying this portfolio is a highly difficult if not in fact impossible task, as it requires some mechanism or ability to capture investor expectations. We noted before the difficulty of assessing expectations, much less appropriately putting them into a proper framework. As a result, Roll contends that empirical tests that have been conducted are not, in fact, tests of the SML. Furthermore, because of the virtual impossibility of identifying the ex ante efficient market portfolio, Roll contends that it is unlikely that the CAPM can be tested empirically.

While Roll's observation that no unambiguous test can be achieved because of the difficulty of identifying the market portfolio exactly is technically correct, it's not so clear that the criticism is of practical significance. To begin with, the fact is that there have been many empirical studies of the relationship over differing time frames that have all virtually affirmed the risk-return relationship. Furthermore, even those studies that have used substantially different methodologies have also affirmed the relationship.

In view of this particular criticism there have recently been studies that have attempted to assess the sensitivity of the relationship to the use of differing market indexes. These studies have constructed market proxies using diverse asset classes, such as stocks, bonds, real estate, and durable goods, and combined these classes in varying proportions to construct differing indexes. We might note that these indexes, as is typical of almost any kind of broad index, are highly correlated, as we have already observed in Chapter 1. The results of these tests using the various market proxies have been virtually the same regardless of the market index and in line with previous empirical studies that affirmed the risk-return relationship. From these initial tests it appears that misestimation of the market proxy may have limited practical significance. Investors can obtain usable estimates of market-risk parameters (betas) and gauge the risk-return relationship by using a generally representative market index such as the S&P 500 or Wilshire 5000.

ARBITRAGE PRICING THEORY

Ross has developed an alternative model of equilibrium in the securities markets. Known as the arbitrage pricing theory (APT), it does not depend critically on the notion of an underlying market portfolio. Instead, it is a model that derives returns from the properties of the process generating stock returns and employs the APT to define equilibrium. Under certain circumstances it derives a risk-return relationship identical to the SML of the CAPM. We'll thus conclude this chapter by covering the APT, both for the additional perspective it offers in studying the equilibrium process as well as for the reinforcement it provides to the existence of a risk-return relationship in the marketplace.

It is useful to begin describing the APT by indicating the assumptions on which it is based and comparing these with the assumptions used in developing the CAPM. Like the CAPM, the APT assumes that (1) investors have homogeneous beliefs, (2) investors are risk-averse utility maximizers, and (3) markets are perfect, so that factors like transactions costs are not relevant. In contrast to the CAPM, the APT does not assume (1) a single-period investment horizon, (2) that there are no taxes, (3) that investors can freely borrow and lend at the risk-free rate, and (4) that investors select portfolios on the basis of the mean and variance of return.

The additional assumption that the APT makes and one that is basic to that model of equilibrium concerns the process generating security returns. In particular, the APT assumes that security returns are generated according to what is known as a *factor model*. This model takes the view that there are underlying factors which give rise to returns on stocks. Examples might include such factors as real economic growth, inflation, and market liquidity effects as well as the returns on a market portfolio. In fact, when returns are generated by a single factor, the general market effect, we'll see that the APT model produces a relationship like the SML of the CAPM. We should note, however, that the market portfolio plays no special role in the APT; that is, the market portfolio may or may not be one of the factors influencing security prices. The following equation illustrates the general form of the factor model, assuming that there are several underlying factors generating returns for the security:

$$R_i = \overline{R}_i + B_1(R_1 - \overline{R}_1) + B_2(R_2 - \overline{R}_2) + \cdots + B_k(R_k - \overline{R}_k) + e_i \qquad (8)$$

This equation says that the return on security R_i is a linear combination of its average return $\overline{R}_i$ plus a set of k factors.[7] The value of the factor is represented by the term R_k, which has a mean value of $\overline{R}_k$. The beta coefficient, as before, measures the responsiveness of the stock return to variations in the value of the factor from its average value. Note that when the actual values of the factors are the same as the average value ($R_k = \overline{R}_k$), they contribute nothing to the actual return. In this case the stock's realized return will be equal to its average return ($R_i = \overline{R}$). Differences of the factor values from their average will increase or decrease the realized return

[7] Note that this model resembles the single-index and multi-index models described in Chapter 2. There are, however, some differences that should be noted.

of the security. The error term e as before, represents the return not explained by the relationship.

APT Model

Assuming that the factor model is descriptive of the return-generating process, as well as making the three previously stated assumptions, Ross uses an arbitrage argument to develop a model of equilibrium pricing. Since illustration of this derivation would be excessively complex and would not serve our purposes, we'll omit it (those interested may refer to the Ross articles listed at the end of this chapter). Instead, we'll assume that the market portfolio is the single factor R_1 generating returns and only show the final form of the risk-return relationship derived from the APT and expressed in terms of the APT notation

$$E(R_i) = R_z + b_1\lambda \qquad (9)$$

Note that, like the SML, the APT risk-return relationship is linear. Since the APT does not assume an ability to borrow and lend freely at the risk-free rate, the R_z that is directly derived from this model could represent either a risk-free return (if available) or the zero-beta return that was derived by Black for the amended version of the CAPM. The λ term represents the risk premium associated with the factor, which in this case of a single factor would represent the risk premium associated with the market $E(R_m) - R_z$. The b coefficient measures the responsiveness of the stock to changes in the market factor and thus represents a measure of the systematic risk of the stock. As noted before, the expression is equivalent or at least empirically indistinguishable from the SML when the market is the sole factor.

Since there is only a single factor (the market), the APT pricing relationship is a straight line on a graph of expected return, $E(R_i)$, and systematic risk with respect to factor 1 (the market), as shown in Figure 3-8. Note that there are three plots: A, D, and U representing three portfolios with no diversifiable risk. Portfolio A has above-average risk ($B = 1.20$), while D has below-average risk ($B = .80$), and U has average risk ($B = 1.00$). Portfolios A and D are giving returns proportional to their risk — 13.4 and 10.6 percent, respectively — and are therefore fairly priced. Portfolio U is offering a greater return (15.0 percent) than would be warranted by its risk and is therefore undervalued.

Process of Arbitrage

Portfolio U thus presents a profit opportunity, which we can convert into a riskless arbitrage. For example, to construct a portfolio with the same risk as portfolio U, an investor could apportion half his investment to portfolio A and the other half to portfolio D. Since the risk of the resulting combination is simply a weighted average of the risks of the individual components ($1/2 \times .80 + 1/2 \times 1.20$), the risk of the combination would be 1.00. Correspondingly, the return of the combination would be a weighted average of the returns of the components ($1/2 \times 10.6$ percent $+ 1/2 \times 13.4$ percent),

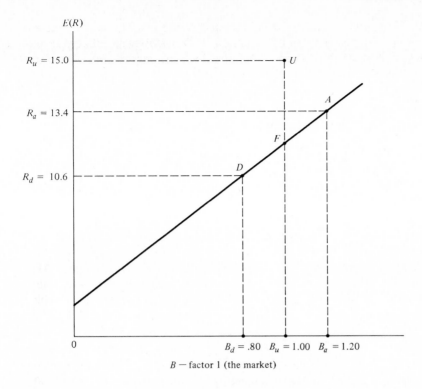

Figure 3-8 Arbitrage pricing model: single factor — the market.

or 12 percent for the combination. This return would be in line with the portfolio's riskiness as illustrated in Figure 3-8, but less than the 15 percent offered by portfolio U.

The data in Table 3-4 illustrate how we can convert the return differential between two portfolios of equal risk into a riskless arbitrage. For example, an investor could sell $1000 of portfolio F short, obtain the proceeds, and invest the $1000 long in portfolio U. Note that this transaction involves no net cash outlay by the investor as shown by the zero net investment in the arbitrage portfolio. Correspondingly, there would be no risk assumed as the two portfolios have identical risk and the process of buying and short selling equal amounts nets to a zero risk position — that is, an arbitrage portfolio beta of zero; however, there would be a positive return to the investor of $30.

Table 3-4 Undertaking a riskless arbitrage

	Investment	Return	Risk (B)
Portfolio U	+ $1000	+ $150	1.0
Portfolio F	− 1000	− 120	− 1.0
Arbitrage portfolio	0	$ 30	0

Since an investor can obtain a return with no investment and no risk, the investor (or investors) will continue to engage in this arbitrage. This activity of selling portfolio F (and hence portfolios A and D) short would drive down the price of portfolios A and D, while the activity of buying portfolio U would drive up its price. Again using our simple return equation, we can see that the return on portfolios A and D will increase as the price declines (the denominator decreases), and that the return on portfolio U will decrease as the price increases (the denominator increases):

$$E(R) = \frac{P_1 - P_0 + \text{dividend}}{P_0}$$

This activity will continue until the return on portfolio U equals that of portfolio F. All three portfolios—A, D, and U—will then lie on the line, thus illustrating how the arbitrage process keeps the risk-return relationship linear. Note that this process of arbitrage might just as well be considered in the context of the SML as the process preventing securities from diverging from that line. As before, however, we would expect that the presence of imperfections like transactions costs, taxes, and imperfect information means that securities plot only within a band around the line rather than on it.

CONCLUSION

Thus far, we've described two models of general equilibrium in the market: CAPM and APT. Each invokes different assumptions and employs a different method of analysis, but interestingly each arrives at a similar conclusion about the sort of risk-return relationship that should characterize the market. Examining both models provides us with a better understanding of the process of equilibrium and reinforces the idea of the existence of a risk-return relationship in the marketplace.

While it may be debatable whether the CAPM or the APT is the underlying theory for an equilibrium relationship in the market, it seems clear that there is strong theoretical reason for some sort of risk-return trade-off in the marketplace that resembles the SML. Furthermore, extensive empirical evidence, flawed though it may be in certain respects, appears to verify that such a relationship characterizes the capital markets studied. At the same time, we should note that there is only a general tendency toward equilibrium, as we might expect from the fact that such real-world market imperfections as transactions costs, taxes, and differential information will prevent the attainment of a complete equilibrium.

The fact that security prices show a tendency toward equilibrium, and that we can describe this equilibrium in terms of an SML, has great implications for practical portfolio management. First, it provides us with a benchmark for the evaluation of the relative attractiveness of securities. Correspondingly, the explicit risk measure that evolves from this model is useful with respect to individual security evaluation as well as overall portfolio analysis. Finally, these models demonstrate the importance of the general market in determining the returns of securities and especially portfolios of securities, thereby emphasizing the need to monitor the level of valuation of the general market. Chapter 5 describes how these insights can facilitate the management of a portfolio.

PROBLEMS

1 Refer to Table 3-2. Compute the returns to the three investors assuming that the market return is 5 percent and then 2 percent.

2 Assuming that the market price of risk is one-third, that the risk-free rate is 9 percent, and that the standard deviation of market return is 21 percent, determine the expected return on the market.

3 Assume that the risk-free rate is 9 percent and the expected return of the market is 15 percent. Graph the security market line (SML), and indicate where securities that are aggressive and those that are defensive would plot.

4 Security J has a beta of .70, while security K has a beta of 1.30. Calculate the expected return for these securities, using SML data from the previous problem.

5 Refer to the data in Table 3-4. Assume that there is another portfolio, 0, that has a beta of .9 and is offering a return of 10 percent. Illustrate the process of arbitrage that equilibrates the return of this portfolio.

6 Portfolio K pays a dividend of $2, sells at a current price of $50, and is expected to sell at $52 at the end of the year. It has a beta of 1.10. Refer to the data in Table 3-4 and determine the price at which the portfolio should sell to be in equilibrium with portfolios A and D.

SELECTED REFERENCES

Black, Fischer: "Capital Market Equilibrium with Restricted Borrowing," *Journal of Business,* July 1972, pp. 444–455.

Black, Fischer, Michael C. Jensen, and Myron Scholers: "The Capital Asset Pricing Model: Some Empirical Tests," in Michael C. Jensen (ed.), *Studies in the Theory of Capital Markets,* Praeger, New York, 1972.

Fama, Eugene F.: "Risk, Return and Equilibrium: Some Clarifying Comments," *Journal of Finance,* March 1968, pp. 29–40.

Fama, E. F. and J. D. MacBeth: "Risk, Return, and Equilibrium: Empirical Tests," *Journal of Political Economy,* May–June 1973, pp. 607–636.

Fouse, W., W. Jahnke, and B. Rosenberg: "Is Beta Phlogiston?" *Financial Analysts Journal,* January–February 1974, pp. 70–80.

Francis, Jack, C.: *Investments: Analysis and Management,* 3d ed., McGraw-Hill, New York, 1980.

Fuller, Russell, Jr.: "Capital Asset Pricing Theories—Evolution and New Frontiers," Monograph no. 12, Financial Analysts Research Foundation, Charlottesville, Va., 1981.

Gehr, Adam: "Test of the Arbitrage Pricing Model," Research Report no. 88, Institute for Quantitative Research in Finance, 1979.

Jensen, M. C.: "Risk, the Pricing of Capital Assets and the Evaluation of Investment Portfolios," *Journal of Business,* April 1969, pp. 167–247.

————: "Capital Markets: Theory and Evidence," *Bell Journal of Economics and Management Science,* Autumn 1972a, pp. 357–398.

Lorie, James H., and Mary T. Hamilton: *The Stock Market: Theories and Evidence.* Richard D. Irwin, Homewood, Ill., 1974.

Markowitz, Harry M.: "Portfolio Selection," *Journal of Finance*, March 1952, pp. 77–91.

————: *Portfolio Selection: Efficient Diversification of Investments,* John Wiley & Sons, New York, 1959.

Modigliani, Franco, and Gerald Pogue: "An Introduction to Risk and Return," *Financial Analysts Journal,* March–April 1974, pp. 68–86.

Roll, R.: "A Critique of the Asset Pricing Theory's Tests," *Journal of Financial Economics,* March 1977, pp. 129–176.

Ross, S.: "Return, Risk and Arbitrage," in I. Friend and J. Bicksler (eds.), *Risk and Return in Finance,* Ballinger, Cambridge, 1976.

———: "The Arbitrage Theory of Capital Asset Pricing," *Journal of Economic Theory,* December 1976.

Sharpe, William F.: "Capital Asset Prices: A Theory of Market Equilibrium under Conditions of Risk," *Journal of Finance,* September 1964, pp. 425–442.

———: *Portfolio Theory and Capital Markets,* McGraw-Hill, New York, 1970.

———: *Investments,* Prentice-Hall, Englewood Cliffs, N. J., 1978.

Sharpe, W. F. and G. M. Cooper: "Risk-Return Classes of New York Stock Exchange Common Stocks, 1931–1967," *Financial Analysts Journal,* March–April 1972, pp. 46–54.

Thompson, D. J.: "Sources of Systematic Risk, in Common Stocks," *Journal of Business,* April 1976, pp. 173–188.

Tobin, James: "Liquidity Preference as Behavior towards Risk," *Review of Economic Studies,* February 1958, pp. 65–85.

Treynor, Jack L.: "Toward a Theory of Market Value of Risky Assets," unpublished manuscript, 1961.

Vasicek, O. A., and J. A. McQuown: "The Efficient Market Model," *Financial Analysts Journal,* September–October 1972.

FOUR

THEORY OF VALUATION

INTRODUCTION

The previous two chapters have dealt primarily with risk. This chapter and the next will primarily deal with return, which is, as we have seen, the reward expected for bearing the risk. Both chapters will focus in particular on models for developing returns — that is, valuation models — because they provide the most direct way of generating explicit return forecasts. Also, these techniques have been subjected to the most extensive theoretical analysis, discussion of which is interesting in its own right. Finally, these models are being applied more and more extensively by investors as a means of both generating returns and imposing greater discipline in the investment management process.

This chapter deals with the basic theory underlying valuation models. It begins by discussing such concepts as time value of money and discounting, as they are basic to an understanding of valuation theory. We then move on to describe the most general form of a valuation model. With regard to specific tailoring of the model, we first describe bond valuation and then treat the more complex subject of stock valuation. In the process we link this discussion with that in Chapter 1 by describing how the four fundamental sources of risk (interest rate, purchasing power, business, and financial) fit into the valuation model framework.

Chapter 5 will discuss how these models can and have found application in solving practical problems of bond and stock valuation. Subsequent chapters will discuss other approaches to developing explicit return forecasts for individual securities as well as broader aggregates — that is, homogeneous stock groups or total market aggregates. Describing this process is essential because formal valuation models are not universally applicable in generating return forecasts and, as we will see, need to be supplemented by other approaches in order to work most effectively where applicable.

CONCEPTS OF DISCOUNTING

Before discussing models of valuation for stocks and bonds, it will be helpful to cover several basic concepts that in fact provide the general framework for security valuation models. These concepts are (1) compound growth or interest, (2) future value, (3) present value, and (4) internal rate of return. They're based on the principles of time value of money and, as we'll see in the process of discussion, each concept is related to the other.

In particular, the concept of compound interest can be used to determine the future value of principal. The existence of positive interest means that funds to be received in the future have a lower value at present than at the future date. Knowing the rate used to compound interest, one can determine a present value. Knowing the future value of principal as well as the present value, one can determine the interest rate or internal rate of return of the investment. This final concept relates most directly to valuation models, and covering it should be a good prelude to discussing valuation models.

Compound Interest and Future Value

Compound interest or growth can be viewed as the second simplest kind of growth. The simplest way for numbers to increase is by the addition of a constant value to the preceding value, say, 1.00, 1.10, 1.20, 1.30 and so on. Compound growth is only slightly more complex since the increase is a constant percentage of the preceding value instead of a constant absolute amount. An example is the increase of $1 deposited in a 10 percent per year savings account, producing $1.00, $1.10, $1.21, $1.33, and so on. Obviously, if more than $1 is invested, the series is simply multiplied by the initial amount invested to find the total value after any given number of periods.

Future value is the value at some point in the future of a quantity subject to compound growth. An example would be the value ten years from now of $1000 invested at 10 percent compound interest. One might also be interested in the values at the end of each of the years over the ten-year period or other periods for that matter. To find these values, the investor could allow P_0 to represent the starting principal, i the rate of interest earned, and t the period over which the interest compounded, and use the following formulation to find the future values P_t:

$$P_t = P_0(1 + i)^t \qquad (1)$$

Applying this formula to the above example, we find that $1000 (1.10)^5$ equals $1611. Actually, once the type of problem has been recognized, it is possible simply to use financial tables to look up the solution. Table A-1 at the end of the book shows the amount of $1 at compound interest over different periods. This table can be used to find the future value of $1000 simply by looking up the compound factor of 1.611 and multiplying by $1000 to obtain the $1611 value. Future values of other investment amounts over different periods can be similarly obtained.

Financial tables are also available to find the future value of investment streams known as *annuities*. These are payment patterns that provide a constant amount each year over a fixed number of years. As an example, presume that the previous flow had been $1000 each year from year 1 through year 5. The future value of this flow can be determined by referring to Table A-2 at the end of the book, which shows the value of an annuity of $1 per period. Note that the compound factor for interest of 10 percent over a five-year period is 6.105, which multiplied by $1000 gives a future value of $6105. Future values for other annuities could similarly be determined from Table A-2.

Finally, it is sometimes useful to know how long it will take an amount to double in value. Table 4-1 shows selected interest rates. A rough rule of thumb for doubling time is to divide the interest rate into 70. We get 70 years at 1 percent, 35 years at 2 percent, 17.5 years at 4 percent, and so on. Also, we can see that it will take 20 years to double at a growth rate of 3.8 percent, 10 years at 7.3 percent, and 5 years at 14.9 percent. From Table 4-1 it is apparent that the approximation is fairly close at low interest rates, but not so accurate at rates above 10 percent.

Present Value

As has been noted, the existence of positive interest rates means that funds to be received in the future have a lower value at present than at the future date. Knowing the rate used to compound interest, one can determine a present value for a payment to be received in the future. Future and present values can thus be made equivalent (or linked) by means of the compound interest rate. Figure 4-1 is a graph displaying the link between future value and present value. From the time lines it can be seen that future values can be converted into present values and vice versa. The explicit link, or equating factor, is the interest rate i, as illustrated by the following formula:

$$\text{Present value} = \frac{\text{future value}}{(1 + i)^t} \tag{2}$$

Note that this formula is in essence the inverse of the general compound interest formula. It can be used to determine the present value of a future payment if we know the interest rate i and the period t at which the payment will be received. Assuming we were to receive a payment of $1000 in the fifth year of an investment period and the current interest rate was 10 percent, the present value of the payment would be

$$\text{Present value} = \frac{\$1000}{(1.10)^5} = \frac{\$1000}{1.611} = \$621$$

Again, this problem and others could be solved most easily by reference to a table of present-value factors. Table A-3 at the end of the book shows the present-value factor at a 10 percent interest rate in the fifth year to be .621. Multiplying this by the $1000 future value gives the same present value as was determined more tediously by means of the formula.

Present-value tables are also available for determining the present value of a stream of annuity payments. Assuming an investment flow of $1000 per year for the next five years and an interest rate of 10 percent, the present value can be determined by reference to Table A-4 at the back of the book. This table shows a present-value factor of 3.791 when the interest rate is 10 percent and the investment horizon is five years.

Table 4-1 Time needed to double an amount

Interest rate, %	Years to double
1	69.7
2	35.0
4	17.7
6	11.9
8	9.0
10	7.3
15	5.0
20	3.8

Multiplying this factor by the $1000 payment stream shows a present value of $3791 for this annuity. Figure 4-2, like the previous figure, is a time line showing the link between the future and present values of an annuity.

Investors should be aware that the increasing availability of electronic calculators can circumvent the need to refer to tables like A-1 to A-4 to solve future-value and present-value problems. Those tables were derived simply by calculation from the basic

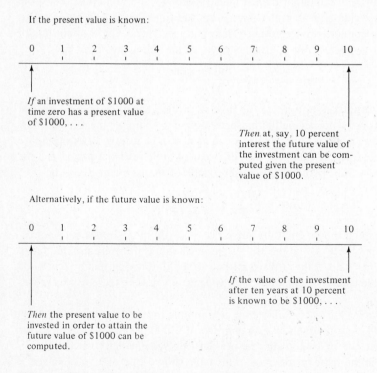

If the present value is known:

If an investment of $1000 at time zero has a present value of $1000, . . .

Then at, say, 10 percent interest the future value of the investment can be computed given the present value of $1000.

Alternatively, if the future value is known:

If the value of the investment after ten years at 10 percent is known to be $1000, . . .

Then the present value to be invested in order to attain the future value of $1000 can be computed.

Figure 4-1 Time lines linking present and future value.

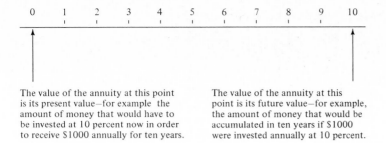

The value of the annuity at this point is its present value—for example the amount of money that would have to be invested at 10 percent now in order to receive $1000 annually for ten years.

The value of the annuity at this point is its future value—for example, the amount of money that would be accumulated in ten years if $1000 were invested annually at 10 percent.

Figure 4-2 Time line linkage between future and present value of an annuity. The periodic payment of, say, $1000 is made each year.

present-value and future-value formulas and reproduced as shown. Appendix A at the end of this chapter reviews the basic formulas for finding future and present values for both lump sums and annuities. The appendix shows how these formulas can easily be applied to a calculator so that investors can readily solve present-value or future-value problems.

Internal Rate of Return

As noted before, the internal rate of return (IRR) is related to the present-value concept. The problem that each is solving is framed similarly; the essential difference is the unknown value that is being derived. When calculating a present value, we know the interest (discount) rate and the future value of the payment flows, and we are interested in finding out how much the flows are worth. On the other hand, when deriving an IRR we know the current prices (present value) and the future value of the cash flows, and we are interested in finding a discount rate that equates the future value with the present value. This procedure is shown in the following formula:

$$\text{Present price} = \frac{\text{future value}}{1 + i} + \frac{\text{future value}}{(1 + i)^2} + \frac{\text{future value}}{(1 + i)^3} \qquad (3)$$

In this case we want to solve for the interest rate i that equates the present value of the cash inflows with the present price, or value, of the outlay. Solving this requires the following iterative ("trial and error") procedure. Given the future values (cash flows) and present prices, choose an interest rate at random and calculate the security's present value. If the difference between present value and current price is positive, choose a higher discount rate and repeat the procedure; if the present value is negative, choose a lower discount rate and repeat the procedure. That discount rate which makes the present value equal to the current price is the IRR, and the procedure is completed.

Table 4-2 gives an example of such a calculation for one hypothetical security that has a current price of $1000 and a cash flow of $300 per year over each of the next five years. Using a 12-percent discount factor, the net present value is positive ($81.50), and therefore a higher rate of 18 percent is chosen. Since this discount rate results in a

Table 4-2 Determining the internal rate of return (IRR)

Year	Cash flow (future value)	Present value 12% discount	18% discount	15% discount
1	300	267.9	254.1	261.0
2	300	239.1	215.4	226.8
3	300	213.6	182.7	197.4
4	300	190.8	154.8	171.6
5	300	170.1	131.1	149.1
Total	1500	1081.5	938.1	1005.9
Net present value		81.5	−61.9	5.9

negative present value ($61.90), a discount rate lower than 18 percent but higher than 12 percent is required. A 15 percent rate reduces the project's present value to approximately zero, so that by definition the project's IRR is 15 percent (the actual IRR is 15.24 percent). To solve more complex problems, a computer and a mathematical program using this iterative technique would be essential.

Figure 4-3 graphs the net present value (present value less cash outlay) as a

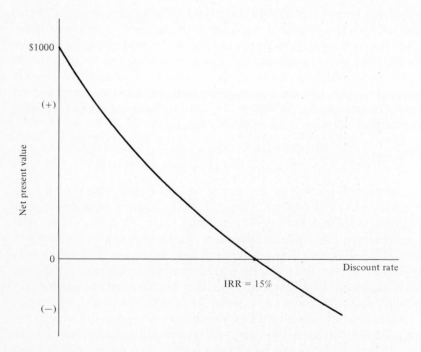

Figure 4-3 Net present value as a function of the discount rate.

function of the discount rate and further illustrates the link between the IRR and present-value concepts, as well as the method of deriving an IRR for an investment. Note that the IRR is located at the intercept with the horizontal axis — that is, at point IRR — since this is the rate of discount which reduces the net present value to zero. One can verify from this graph that for all discount rates less than the IRR the net present value is positive; conversely, for all discount rates greater than the IRR the net present value is negative.

While we generally need a computer or hand calculator with finance routines to solve most IRR problems, there is a particularly simple and interesting case that is of relevance in illustrating the general valuation problem. It is the case of a *perpetuity*, where a fixed cash inflow is expected at equal intervals forever. An example is the British consol, a bond with no maturity date, which carries the obligation of the British government to pay a fixed coupon perpetually.

Calculation of the IRR for a perpetuity can be illustrated by referring back to the previous example of a $1000 outlay with an annual cash inflow of $300. In this instance, however, we'll assume that the flow continues forever rather than for only five years. To begin with, we know that the return should be greater than 15 percent, since that was the return on the flow when it continued for only five years; in fact, the IRR would be 30 percent.

Table 4-3 illustrates the general formula for a perpetuity. Note that the IRR can be derived by merely dividing the annual inflow by the initial outlay. We now turn to the derivation of a similarly simple model of stock valuation as well as other aspects of security valuation.

Table 4-3 General formula for a perpetuity

We can show the general formulation for calculating a perpetuity by first writing out the cash outlay P and the inflow pattern CF for the hypothetical security in the form of an IRR problem and call it Equation A:

$$1000 = \frac{300}{(1 + k)} + \frac{300}{(1 + k)^2} + \frac{300}{(1 + k)^3} + \cdots + \frac{300}{(1 + k)^t} \tag{A}$$

When we multiply both sides of Equation A by $(1 + k)$, we obtain Equation B:

$$1000(1 + k) = 300 + \frac{300}{(1 + k)} + \frac{300}{(1 + k)^2} + \cdots + \frac{300}{(1 + k)^{t-1}} \tag{B}$$

Subtracting Equation A from Equation B, we obtain Equation C:

$$1000(1 + k) - 1000 = 300 - \frac{300}{(1 + k)^t} \tag{C}$$

As investment horizon becomes longer or as t approaches infinity, $300/(1 + k)^t$ approaches zero because the denominator becomes ever larger. As a result, we end up with:

$$1000k = 300 \tag{D}$$

$$k = \frac{CF}{P} = \frac{300}{1000} = 30\%$$

VALUATION MODELS

The preceding discussion of the concepts of time value of money and discounting has provided a fundamental background for the valuation of bonds and stocks, which we'll describe in the remaining sections of this chapter. Given this background, we can thus regard a security as simply a series of dividend or interest payments to be received over a period of time. At the most general level, then, the value of any security can be established as the present value of a future stream of cash flows as described by the following formula:

$$P = \sum_{t=1}^{T} \frac{CF_t}{(1 + k)^t} \tag{4}$$

In this formula, P represents the price or present value of the security, while CF is the cash flow or future value of cash flows and T is the time horizon over which the cash flows are expected to be received. The k term in the denominator is the discount rate (or compound interest rate factor); it is useful to think of this term as being composed of a risk-free return and a risk premium that is in turn composed of several factors: interest rate risk, purchasing power risk, business risk, and financial risk.

These factors are the same ones that we described in Chapter 1 as being fundamental sources of risk, and they have the same meaning in this context. Similarly, the degree of sensitivity of the security to any or all of those factors will determine the size of the discount rate or expected return for that security. The more sensitive the security is to those factors, the higher the discount rate will be, while the less sensitive the security is to them, the lower the discount rate. As noted before, we would expect stocks to be the most sensitive to all risk factors and thus carry the highest discount rate, while bonds would be less sensitive and carry lower discount rates.

Further relating back to Chapter 1, to the extent that expectations are in line with realizations, we anticipate that the realized return on securities will be representative of the discount rate demanded by investors over the time period of interest. To the extent that the return realized over the time periods analyzed in Chapter 1 were in line with anticipations, these realized returns may be more or less representative of the discount rates that are required by investors. Recall that stocks earned higher returns than bonds over the longer period, implying that the discount rate on stocks was higher than the discount rate on bonds, as can be expected from an analysis of the components of risk.

VALUATING A PERPETUITY

It's useful to begin describing how Equation 4 can be used to value different types of securities by discussing the special case of valuation of a perpetuity. Recall that a perpetuity pays out a fixed amount over an indefinitely long period; recall also that by using the techniques described in the section on internal rate of return we reduced a model of the same form as Equation 4 to the simplified form shown in the bottom of Table 4-3. In order to recast that expression into the form of a valuation model, we would simply rearrange the equation to solve for a price P rather than the rate of return k as shown in the table:

$$P = \frac{CF}{k} \tag{5}$$

This expression says that the price P or present value of the perpetuity is simply the fixed cash flow CF, either coupon or dividend, capitalized by the discount rate k that represents the required return on the security. This equation has particular relevance to the valuation of such special bonds as the British consol and to the broader class of preferred stocks that are generally committed to pay out a fixed dividend amount over an indefinitely long period. For example, for a preferred stock that paid a dividend (cash flow) of $6 and had a required return or alternatively a discount rate k of .12, we could use Equation 5 to calculate a value of $50:

$$P = \frac{\$6.00}{.12} = \$50$$

While perpetuities such as preferred stocks are a limited class of securities, evaluation of this security type is nevertheless instructive for the broader classes of bonds and common stocks. Bonds are similar to perpetuities in that they pay out a fixed amount of cash flow per period, but they differ in that they generally have a finite life. On the other hand, common stocks have an infinite life, like perpetuities, but they differ in that cash flows are not fixed. As a matter of interest, the expression for valuing a common stock is similar in form to that of Equation 5, with the difference being a modification to take account of the fact that cash flows to the common stock are expected to grow over time.

BOND VALUATION

We covered the valuation of a perpetuity first because of the insights it provides into valuing common stocks and bonds. We now cover bond valuation because bonds are easier to evaluate than stocks, mainly because the benefits which the bondholder expects to receive from holding a bond to maturity are specified. Analyzing this should in turn provide useful insights into the problem of stock valuation.

The cash flow from bonds consists of the coupon payments C, which are fixed, and the principal F, which is also set by contract. The period over which the coupons are to be paid and the maturity date t for the principal are also established by terms of the bond indenture. One can use the following valuation model to solve for the price P_b or the discount rate k, which is generally referred to as the yield to maturity:[1]

$$P_b = \frac{C}{1 + k} + \frac{C}{(1 + k)^2} + \cdots + \frac{C}{(1 + k)^t} + \frac{F}{(1 + k)^t} \tag{6}$$

[1] Bond interest is ordinarily paid semiannually, and a more general formulation would indicate semiannual compounding. However, for ease of exposition, we'll assume only annual payments and hence ignore the effect of semiannual compounding.

Since we generally know the price of the bond and are interested in determining the yield to maturity, bond valuation becomes a problem of solving for an internal rate of return (IRR). We could use the same trial and error methods described previously. Alternatively, bond yield tables are available, just as there are present-value tables for solving those problems. Table 4-4 shows a page from a bond yield book to illustrate the format of these tables. Moreover, hand calculators geared with the appropriate financial routines are convenient and provide quick solutions to problems.[2]

When the current price of the bond is $1000, it is selling at par (1000), and calculating its yield to maturity is simply a matter of dividing the coupon by the par value. For example, if the coupon were $100, the yield to maturity would be 100 divided by 1000, or 10 percent. If the current price were below $1000, it would be selling at a discount and the calculated yield to maturity for the bond would be greater than 10 percent in the case of a $100-coupon bond.[3] For example, if the term to maturity were three years and the current price were $952, the yield to maturity using Equation 5 would be 12 percent.

$$P_b = \frac{\$100}{1.12} + \frac{\$100}{(1.12)^2} + \frac{\$1100}{(1.12)^3}$$

$$= \$89 \ + \$80 \quad + \$783 = \$952$$

Conversely, if the current price were over $1000, then it would be at a premium and the calculated yield to maturity would be less than 10 percent in the case of a $100-coupon bond. For example, if the term to maturity were again three years and the current price were $1052, the yield to maturity using Equation 5 would be 8 percent.

$$P_b = \frac{\$100}{1.08} + \frac{\$100}{(1.08)^2} + \frac{\$1100}{(1.08)^3}$$

$$= \$93 \ + \$86 \quad + \$873 = \$1052$$

We can further use the bond valuation model (Equation 6) to demonstrate two elementary but important features of bonds as an investment medium. First, their prices vary inversely with changes in interest rates: if market interest rates k go up, prices P_b decline. Second, the amount of price variation necessary to adjust to a given change in interest rates is a function of the number of years to maturity. In the case of long-maturity bonds, a change in the discount rate k is cumulatively applied to the entire series of coupon payments C, and the payment on principal at maturity is discounted at the new rate for the entire number of years yet to run on the obligation. Short-maturity bonds, however, show only modest changes in price in response to a change in interest rates because the new discount rate k is applied to only a few coupon payments and similarly applies to principal for only a short period of time. Long-term bonds are more variable with respect to interest rate changes than short-term bonds.

Table 4-5 illustrates this for two hypothetical bonds differing only in term to maturity: one is a three-year bond, and the other is a six-year bond. Note that when the

---

[2] For example, the Texas Instruments MBA, as well as their more sophisticated programmable calculators, offers this capability. Hewlett-Packard is another manufacturer that markets this type of calculator.

[3] When price differs from par, the effective yield on a bond has two components: (1) the annual coupon rate and (2) the appropriate annual amount of the total discount added to (or premium subtracted from) the coupon rate.

Table 4-4 Bond yield table

7% **YEARS** and MONTHS

Yield	10-6	11-0	11-6	12-0	12-6	13-0	13-6	14-0
4.00	125.52	126.49	127.44	128.37	129.29	130.18	131.06	131.92
4.20	123.58	124.46	125.33	126.18	127.01	127.83	128.63	129.41
4.40	121.68	122.48	123.27	124.04	124.79	125.53	126.26	126.96
4.60	119.81	120.54	121.25	121.94	122.62	123.29	123.94	124.57
4.80	117.98	118.63	119.27	119.89	120.50	121.09	121.67	122.24
5.00	116.18	116.77	117.33	117.88	118.42	118.95	119.46	119.96
5.20	114.42	114.94	115.43	115.92	116.39	116.86	117.31	117.74
5.40	112.70	113.14	113.57	114.00	114.41	114.81	115.20	115.58
5.60	111.00	111.38	111.75	112.11	112.47	112.81	113.14	113.46
5.80	109.34	109.66	109.97	110.27	110.57	110.85	111.13	111.40
6.00	107.71	107.97	108.22	108.47	108.71	108.94	109.16	109.38
6.10	106.90	107.14	107.36	107.58	107.79	108.00	108.20	108.39
6.20	106.11	106.31	106.51	106.70	106.89	107.07	107.24	107.41
6.30	105.32	105.50	105.67	105.83	105.99	106.15	106.30	106.45
6.40	104.54	104.69	104.83	104.97	105.11	105.24	105.37	105.49
6.50	103.76	103.89	104.01	104.12	104.23	104.34	104.45	104.55
6.60	103.00	103.09	103.19	103.28	103.37	103.46	103.54	103.62
6.70	102.24	102.31	102.38	102.45	102.51	102.58	102.64	102.70
6.80	101.48	101.53	101.58	101.62	101.67	101.71	101.75	101.79
6.90	100.74	100.76	100.78	100.81	100.83	100.85	100.87	100.89
7.00	100.00	100.00	100.00	100.00	100.00	100.00	100.00	100.00
7.10	99.27	99.25	99.22	99.20	99.18	99.16	99.14	99.12
7.20	98.54	98.50	98.45	98.41	98.37	98.33	98.29	98.25
7.30	97.83	97.76	97.69	97.63	97.57	97.51	97.45	97.40
7.40	97.12	97.03	96.94	96.85	96.77	96.70	96.62	96.55
7.50	96.41	96.30	96.19	96.09	95.99	95.89	95.80	95.71
7.60	95.71	95.58	95.45	95.33	95.21	95.10	94.99	94.88
7.70	95.02	94.87	94.72	94.58	94.44	94.31	94.19	94.07
7.80	94.34	94.16	94.00	93.84	93.68	93.54	93.39	93.26
7.90	93.66	93.47	93.28	93.10	92.93	92.77	92.61	92.46
8.00	92.99	92.77	92.57	92.38	92.19	92.01	91.84	91.67
8.10	92.32	92.09	91.87	91.66	91.45	91.26	91.07	90.89
8.20	91.66	91.41	91.17	90.94	90.73	90.51	90.31	90.12
8.30	91.01	90.74	90.48	90.24	90.00	89.78	89.56	89.35
8.40	90.36	90.07	89.80	89.54	89.29	89.05	88.82	88.60
8.50	89.72	89.42	89.13	88.85	88.59	88.33	88.09	87.86
8.60	89.08	88.76	88.46	88.17	87.89	87.62	87.36	87.12
8.70	88.45	88.12	87.80	87.49	87.20	86.92	86.65	86.39
8.80	87.83	87.48	87.14	86.82	86.52	86.22	85.94	85.67
8.90	87.21	86.84	86.49	86.16	85.84	85.53	85.24	84.96
9.00	86.60	86.22	85.85	85.50	85.17	84.85	84.55	84.26
9.10	85.99	85.59	85.22	84.86	84.51	84.18	83.86	83.56
9.20	85.39	84.98	84.59	84.21	83.86	83.51	83.19	82.88
9.30	84.79	84.37	83.96	83.58	83.21	82.86	82.52	82.20
9.40	84.20	83.76	83.35	82.95	82.57	82.20	81.86	81.52
9.50	83.61	83.16	82.73	82.32	81.93	81.56	81.20	80.86
9.60	83.04	82.57	82.13	81.71	81.30	80.92	80.55	80.20
9.70	82.46	81.98	81.53	81.10	80.68	80.29	79.91	79.56
9.80	81.89	81.40	80.94	80.49	80.07	79.67	79.28	78.91
9.90	81.33	80.83	80.35	79.89	79.46	79.05	78.65	78.28
10.00	80.77	80.26	79.77	79.30	78.86	78.44	78.04	77.65
10.20	79.67	79.13	78.62	78.14	77.67	77.23	76.82	76.42
10.40	78.58	78.03	77.50	76.99	76.51	76.06	75.63	75.21
10.60	77.52	76.94	76.39	75.87	75.38	74.91	74.46	74.04
10.80	76.48	75.88	75.31	74.77	74.26	73.78	73.32	72.88
11.00	75.45	74.83	74.25	73.70	73.17	72.68	72.20	71.76
11.20	74.44	73.81	73.21	72.64	72.10	71.59	71.11	70.66
11.40	73.45	72.80	72.19	71.61	71.06	70.54	70.04	69.58
11.60	72.48	71.82	71.19	70.59	70.03	69.50	69.00	68.52
11.80	71.53	70.85	70.21	69.60	69.03	68.49	67.98	67.49
12.00	70.59	69.90	69.24	68.62	68.04	67.49	66.97	66.48

Source: Expanded Bond Values Tables, Desk Edition, Financial Publishing
Company, Boston, 1970, p. 734.

rate of interest (yield to maturity) is 10 percent, both bonds sell at $1000. However, when the rate of interest moves to 11 percent, the price of the long-term bond declines by 4.7 percent to $953, while the shorter-term bond declines by 2.6 percent to $974. The longer-term bond is in fact more sensitive to interest rate movements than the shorter-term bond.

Figure 4-4 illustrates this relative interest rate sensitivity more dramatically. The figure shows a perpetuity with a $100 coupon (with values calculated by inserting differing interest rates into Equation 5) and a three-year bond with a $100 coupon (calculated as illustrated in Table 2-5). Note that the perpetuity shows a much greater variation in value than the short-term bond as interest rates vary over a range of 7 percent to 13 percent. Long-term bonds are characteristically more sensitive to interest rate changes than short-term bonds — or, alternatively, long-term bonds generally have greater exposure to the interest rate risk.

DURATION

We noted in Chapter 1 that all securities are exposed to the interest rate risk and that longer-term securities are more vulnerable to this risk than short-term securities. Table 4-5 and Figure 4-4 show this and indicate that maturity of a security provides a gauge of the sensitivity to interest rate risk. Maturity is, however, an imprecise gauge of a security's exposure to the interest rate risk.

To begin with, a maturity measure ignores interim cash flows to the bond and focuses only on the final payment at maturity. Coupon payments (interim cash flows) are important in this regard, and it's well known that bonds with higher coupons are less sensitive to interest rates than those with lower coupons. This is because the investor receiving the higher coupon is in effect recouping his investment sooner by means of the faster payback of cash flows than the investor in a bond with a lower coupon.

Table 4-5 Maturity and interest rate sensitivity

	Bond A	Bond B
Term to maturity	3 years	6 years
Current price	$1000	$1000
Coupon	$100	$100
Yield to maturity	10%	10%
Present value at 11% interest rate		
Year 1	$ 90	$ 90
Year 2	81	81
Year 3	803	73
Year 4		66
Year 5		59
Year 6		584
Total	$974	$953
Change in price, %	−2.6	−4.7

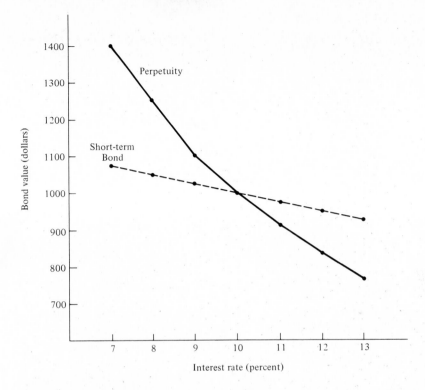

Figure 4-4 Values of long-term and short-term bonds — 10 percent coupon rates, at differing market interest rates.

Table 4-6 illustrates this deficiency for three hypothetical securities, all with the same three-year maturity. Each currently sells at $1000 and has a yield to maturity of 10 percent; however, the patterns of cash flow differ substantially. Security A pays the entire cash flow at the end of the period; it's a discount bond. Security B pays out its cash flow evenly over the three-year period, somewhat like a mortgage. Security C is the same $100-coupon bond from the previous example and illustrates the pattern of cash flow associated with a coupon bond.

The table shows the effect on the prices of the three instruments of an increase in interest rate from 10 percent to 11 percent. Note that security A, the discount bond, declines the most — by 2.8 percent — as its cash flow is deferred the longest. On the other hand, security B, which pays out an even flow of cash, shows the least decline in price as it provides the earliest payback of investment. Security C, the coupon bond, as might be expected, shows an intermediate price decline of 2.6 percent.

Despite the same maturity, the three securities show different sensitivities to interest rate changes. Maturity in this instance would have provided little insight into the relative vulnerability of the three securities to the interest rate risk. Duration is, however, a measure that allows one to evaluate the relative exposure to the interest rate risk of securities with differing patterns of cash flow, because it specifically takes into account both interim and final cash flow payments to the security.

Table 4-6 Interest rate sensitivity

	Security A	Security B	Security C
Current price	$1000	$1000	$1000
Cash flow			
Year 1	0	400	100
Year 2	0	400	100
Year 3	1331	400	1100
Yield to maturity, %	10	10	10
	Present value at 11% interest rate		
Year 1	$ 0	$ 360	$ 90
Year 2	0	325	81
Year 3	972	292	803
Total	$ 972	$ 977	$ 974
Change in price, %	−2.8	−2.3	−2.6

Figure 4-5 illustrates the basic notion of the duration measure, using the hypothetical security with a level cash flow over the three years. Note that this hypothetical security would have an average life of two years, as shown in the top panel of the figure. A more refined measure of the life of the cash flow would, however, take account of the present value of the flows. In this case the objective would be to calculate the average time point by weighting each payment by the present value of the payment rather than simply the flow of raw dollar amounts. This measure of the time to each payment weighted by the present value of that payment is termed *duration d;* it is illustrated in the bottom panel of the figure. Note that because earlier payments have a higher present value than later payments the duration will be less than the average life.

Computation of the duration of a bond is similar to computation of a bond price. The formula for computing duration d is

$$d = \left[1\frac{C_1}{(1 + k)} + 2\frac{C_2}{(1 + k)^2} + 3\frac{C_3}{(1 + k)^3} + t\frac{(C_n + F)}{(1 + k)^t}\right]\Big/P \qquad (7)$$

Notice that the equation consists of setting out a series, 1 through t, representing the time from the present to each receipt of cash by the bondholder, and then weighting each number. The weights are the present values of the cash receipts, coupon C and redemption F. Finally, the sum of these weighted time intervals is divided by the sum of the weights, which is simply the price P obtained by using Equation 6.[4]

[4] We can see this by showing the formula for duration in a more general format:

$$D = \frac{\sum_{t=1}^{T} \dfrac{C(t)}{(1 + k)^t}}{\sum_{t=1}^{T} \dfrac{C_t}{(1 + k)^t}}$$

Note that the denominator is merely the price of the bond as determined by the present-value formulation (Equation 6). The numerator is also a present-value concept of price, except that all the cash flows are weighted according to the length of time to receipt.

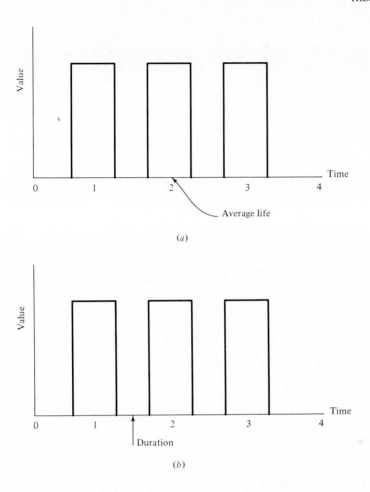

Figure 4-5 *(a)* Average life of cash flow; *(b)* duration of cash flow.

Table 4-7 uses Equation 7 to calculate the durations of our three hypothetical securities. Note that discount bond *A* has a duration of three years, which is the same as its maturity. Discount bonds have a duration equal to their maturity as the entire cash flow is received at the end of the holding period. On the other hand, securities that make interim payments have durations that are shorter than their maturity. Therefore, coupon bond *C* has a duration of 2.7 years, which is, of course, less than its three-year maturity. Bond *B* with its level cash flow has an even shorter duration, 1.9 years, because it pays even more before maturity.

DURATION AND INTEREST RATE SENSITIVITY

The most obvious superiority of duration over maturity as a measure of how long investors must wait for their money shows up in measuring sensitivity of bond price to changes in yield. It is generally true that for two bonds with different maturities a 1 percent change in yield will produce a larger price change in the bond with the longer maturity. But this is not true if the bonds have different coupons, as we've just seen, and in any case there is no neat relationship between maturity and price sensitivity. Duration, instead, gives a precise measure:

$$\text{Percent change in price} = \frac{-\text{duration} \times \text{change in yield}}{1 + \text{yield}} \tag{8}$$

To illustrate, we can use coupon bond C from Table 4-7. Recall that we calculated a duration of 2.7 years for the coupon bond, and we can again assume an increase in interest rates from 10 percent to 11 percent. Using these inputs for the bond, we derive an expected price change

Table 4-7 Calculating the duration of a bond

$$d = \left[1\left(\frac{C_1}{K_1}\right) + 2\left(\frac{C_2}{K_2}\right) + 3\left(\frac{C_3}{K_3}\right) \right] \Big/ P$$

Bond A (discount)

$$d = \left[1\left(\frac{0}{1.10}\right) + 2\left(\frac{0}{1.21}\right) + 3\left(\frac{1331}{1.331}\right) \right] \Big/ 1000$$

$$= [1(0) + 2(0) + 3(1000)]/1000$$

$$= \frac{3000}{1000} = 3 \text{ years}$$

Bond B ("mortgage")

$$d = \left[1\left(\frac{400}{1.10}\right) + 2\left(\frac{400}{1.21}\right) + 3\left(\frac{400}{1.33}\right) \right] \Big/ 1000$$

$$= [1(364) + 2(331) + 3(301)]/1000$$

$$= \frac{1929}{1000} = 1.9 \text{ years}$$

Bond C (coupon)

$$d = \left[1\left(\frac{100}{1.10}\right) + 2\left(\frac{100}{1.21}\right) + 3\left(\frac{1100}{1.33}\right) \right] \Big/ 1000$$

$$= [1(90) + 2(81) + 3(827)]/1000$$

$$= \frac{2733}{1000} = 2.7 \text{ years}$$

$$\frac{\Delta P}{P} = -d\left(\frac{\Delta k}{1 + k}\right) = -2.7\left(\frac{.01}{1.10}\right) = -2.5 \text{ percent}$$

This compares with the actual price decline of 2.6 percent calculated in Table 4-6. The difference arises from the fact that the duration-derived measure works best when gauging relatively small changes in interest rate and loses precision as the change in interest rate becomes larger. The assumed change of 1 percent — 100 basis points — would be a relatively large change over a short period. Alternatively, we might deduce that the analysis works best when evaluating prospective changes in interest rate and price over shorter intervals, say, over a one- to six-week forecasting period.[5]

Table 4-8 shows duration values for bonds of varying maturities with coupons at three different interest rates: 12, 14, and 16 percent. Note that bonds of longer maturity generally have greater duration than bonds of shorter maturity.[6] For example, at the 14 percent interest rate level, a twenty-year bond paying a 10 percent coupon has a duration of 6.98, while the ten-year bond has a duration of 5.68 and the five-year bond a duration of 3.71. At the same time, note that duration is lower at higher levels of interest rates than at lower levels. For example, the twenty-year bond with a duration of 6.98 at the 14 percent interest rate level has a duration of 7.74 at the 12 percent interest rate level but a duration of 6.30 at the 16 percent level.

It will be instructive to conclude this section by relating this analysis of duration back to our earlier discussion of the components of risk for securities in Chapter 1. There we noted that securities with a greater interest rate risk should carry a higher premium or discount rate in a valuation framework than securities with less exposure to the interest rate risk. The analysis in this section has indicated that securities with longer durations are more sensitive to interest rate changes than securities with shorter durations. We would thus expect longer-duration securities to carry greater discount rates (all other risk factors being equal) than shorter-duration securities to compensate for this greater risk.[7]

[5] As the formula for calculating duration shows, duration itself changes when yield changes. A rise in yield shortens duration. So duration is a precise measure of price sensitivity to yield change only for very small yield changes. A large yield change will change the duration and the sensitivity. The sensitivity of duration to yield changes is an interesting measure, the usefulness of which is largely unknown.

[6] Duration increases at a diminishing rate as maturity increases owing to the effect of discounting back to present value, which becomes more pronounced at higher discount rates. In some instances the duration of very long-term bonds is actually less than that of shorter term bonds, again owing to the effect of discounting back to present value.

[7] We should note that duration has limitations as a risk measure. First, duration relates change in price, not change in rate of return, to yield change. For some purposes this may not matter much. Second, duration relates price change to change in the yield of a particular bond, not to changes in interest rates generally. The price of a bond with a ten-year duration and a yield of 8 percent, will move 0.9 percent if the yield corresponding to a twenty-year duration, changes by 1 basis point; and the price of a bond with a five-year duration and a yield of 7 percent will change by 0.45 percent if the yield changes by 1 basis point. But one cannot conclude that the risk exposure to interest rate changes is twice as great for the ten-year bond, unless the two yields can be expected to change by the same amount. In general, long rates fluctuate less than short rates, and the ten-year-duration bond has less than twice the risk exposure to interest rate changes as the five-year-duration bond. How much less involves a subjective estimate of the relative magnitude of probable interest rate changes across the yield curve.

Table 4-8 Duration, coupon rate, and yield to maturity

Years to maturity	Coupon			
	6%	8%	10%	12%
		Yield = 12%		
1	.93	.92	.92	.92
5	4.05	3.91	3.78	3.68
10	6.61	6.23	5.95	5.73
15	7.96	7.46	7.13	6.88
20	8.53	8.05	7.74	7.52
		Yield = 14%		
1	.92	.92	.91	.91
5	3.98	3.83	3.71	3.60
10	6.33	5.95	5.68	5.46
15	7.37	6.91	6.59	6.37
20	7.65	7.24	6.98	6.80
		Yield = 16%		
1	.91	.91	.90	.90
5	3.91	3.76	3.63	3.53
10	6.05	5.68	5.41	5.20
15	6.80	6.38	6.09	5.89
20	6.86	6.51	6.30	6.15

Source: John Rountree, "Duration, an Easily Calculated Risk Measure," Kidder, Peabody & Co., Inc., New York, Mar. 24, 1980.

STOCK VALUATION MODELS

Stock valuation is more difficult than bond valuation. Whereas in the case of bonds both the cash flow stream (interest) and time horizon (maturity) are well specified, these factors need more careful consideration in the case of stocks. To introduce the subject of stock valuation, then, it will be appropriate to consider what constitutes return for a stock, first for a one-year horizon and then for an infinite horizon. The purpose of this is to show that the fundamental determinant of value for a stock is the same for investors with a short or a long horizon. To begin with, recall that the formula for holding-period returns to determine stock returns for an investor with less than an infinite investment horizon is

$$k = \frac{D + P_1 - P_0}{P_0}$$

In words this says that return k is dividends paid D plus any change in price $P_1 - P_0$ over the period, in this case assumed to be one year, divided by the initial price P_0. Restating this formula in terms of the familiar present-value format, we obtain

$$P_0 = \frac{D}{1 + k} + \frac{P_1}{1 + k}$$

This says that the current price is a function of dividends to be paid at the end of the year plus the price of the stock at year-end discounted back at the rate k. In the case of an investor with a longer horizon, we can restate the formula more generally as follows:

$$P_0 = \sum_{t=1}^{T} \frac{D_t}{(1 + k)^t} + \frac{P_T}{(1 + k)^T}$$

As the investor's horizon gets longer — as T approaches infinity — the second term becomes insignificant. It tends to go to zero, so that we are left with expected return consisting entirely of the dividend flow. Expected return is then determined by solving the following equation for k.

$$P_0 = \sum_{t=1}^{T} \frac{D_t}{(1 + k)^t}$$

This formula demonstrates that for an investor with an infinite horizon or, for practical purposes, anyone with a sufficiently long-time perspective, the fundamental determinant of stock value is the dividend flow. Less directly we can also deduce that the flow of dividends is the fundamental determinant even for an investor with a relatively short horizon who buys with the intention of selling. The reason is that the price received when the investor sells the stock will be determined by what other investors perceive as the expected flow of dividends from it.

It should be noted that this same analysis applies whether the stock is currently paying dividends or not. In the case of a non-dividend-paying stock, as typified by very high-growth stocks, the stockholder with a less than infinite horizon expects to obtain his sole return by selling the stock at a higher than current price. Again, this selling price is a function of the projected dividends to be paid out at some time in the future. Thus, ultimately, it is the dividend that determines the value of a corporation for an investor with a short- or long-term perspective. We'll illustrate this analysis again in a more rigorous format in Chapter 5.

DIVIDEND CAPITALIZATION MODEL

The preceding section indicated that the relevant cash flows of interest are dividends for stocks and coupon payments for bonds. It was also indicated that the relevant time horizon for stocks is perpetual, whereas for bonds it is finite and set by terms of the bond indenture. Despite these differences we can still state the basic stock valuation model in the same general IRR form used for bond evaluation (see Equation 3). Using P_s as stock price, D as dividend, k as the discount rate for stocks, and t as the time period over which the dividends are received, we can express the stock model as

$$P_s = \frac{D_1}{1 + k} + \frac{D_2}{(1 + k)^2} + \frac{D_3}{(1 + k)^3} + \cdots + \frac{D_t}{(1 + k)^t} = \sum_{t=1}^{T} \frac{D_t}{(1 + k)^t} \qquad (9)$$

This model is commonly known as the generalized version of the dividend capitalization model. In this form, however, it is unsuitable for practical application, as one would have to develop estimates of the individual cash flows, or dividends

$(D_1, D_2,$ etc.) over a very long period — in theory, to infinity. Since this is obviously impossible, there is need to develop modifications — simplifications, if you will — of this model in order to implement it for practical purposes of stock valuation.

We'll discuss two simplifications of the model that are, in fact, suitable for practical application and sufficiently flexible to accommodate the various types of common stock available. In this regard, two types are needed in order to accommodate the two major categories of common-stock dividend growth: (1) normal or generally average growth, and (2) supernormal or generally above-average growth. In this chapter we'll cover the first modification of the model for normal or generally average dividend growth, along with the assumptions involved, and then, in the next chapter, discuss the modification for supernormal growth companies and the reasons it is needed. Chapter 5 will also illustrate how investors can develop suitable inputs for these models and develop data for use in portfolio construction.

As noted, the most basic simplification of the dividend capitalization model applies to the case of normal growth. Developed by several authors, it is now probably most closely associated with Gordon. In developing the model a couple of key assumptions are made. The first is that dividends grow at a constant rate g over an infinite time horizon, and the second is that the discount rate k is greater than the growth rate g. When we assume that dividends grow at a constant rate over time, we can eliminate the necessity of considering the dividends year by year over time. In this case we apply a growth rate to an initial dividend, and the dividend rate at a particular year becomes the initial dividend compounded out, just as in our discussion of compound interest, to a future value at that date. We can then convert the generalized form of the dividend capitalization model to the following form:

$$P_s = \frac{D_0(1 + g)}{(1 + k)} + \frac{D_0(1 + g)^2}{(1 + k)^2} + \frac{D_0(1 + g)^3}{(1 + k)^3} + \cdots + \frac{D_0(1 + g)^t}{(1 + k)^t} \qquad (10)$$

We can then use applicable techniques for converting into a simpler form cash flow streams that continue at a constant rate over an infinite time — that is, perpetual annuities or perpetuities. The application of these techniques is described in greater detail in Appendix B to this chapter. Meanwhile, applying these techniques to Equation 10 and making the assumption $k > g$ reduces the model to the desired simpler form shown below:[8]

$$P = \frac{D}{k - g} \qquad (11)$$

This simplified form of the dividend capitalization model is the version that is applicable to the problem of valuating companies that are growing at normal or average rates. In words the model says that the value of a stock is equal to its year-ahead forecasted dividend per share D capitalized by the difference between the company's discount rate k and its growth rate g. For example, if a company was expected to pay

[8] This assumption is necessary, for if g is greater than k, then all values become infinite, and if g is almost equal to k, then all values become too large to be meaningful.

$2 in dividends and was growing at a rate of 5 percent, and if the appropriate discount rate for that company was 9 percent, then the price of the stock would be

$$P = \frac{2.00}{(.09 - .05)} = \$50$$

Stock Value and Differing Model Inputs

It's useful to redefine some of the terms of the dividend capitalization model both for help in understanding the factors that create differences in values (prices) and for greater ease of practical implementation. To begin with, we can define E as earnings and b as the retention rate for earnings, so that $1 - b$ becomes the payout rate. We can then regard dividends as the payout rate $1 - b$ times the earnings level E. Correspondingly, when we define r as the rate of return on retained earnings, then we can multiply this by the retention rate b to obtain a growth rate.[9] Inserting these new definitions into the model, we have

$$P = \frac{(1 - b)E}{k - br}$$

In turn, we can convert this model into a price earnings (P/E) ratio model simply by moving the earnings variable to the left-hand side of the equation (dividing both sides by E):

$$P/E = \frac{(1 - b)}{k - br} \qquad (12)$$

[9] We can analytically show that $g = rb$, as follows. First, we assume that the firm will maintain a stable dividend policy (keep its retention rate constant) and earn a stable return on new equity investment I over time. Since growth in earnings arises from the return on new investments, we can represent earnings at a given time as

$$E_t = E_{t-1} + rI_t$$

Since the firm's retention rate is constant, then

$$E_t = E_{t-1} + rbE_{t-1} = E_{t-1}(1 + rb)$$

Growth in earnings is the percentage change in earnings, or

$$g = \frac{E_t - E_{t-1}}{E_{t-1}} = \frac{E_{t-1}(1 + rb) - E_{t-1}}{E_{t-1}} = rb$$

Since a constant proportion of earnings is assumed to be paid out each year, the growth in earnings equals the growth in dividends, or

$$g_E = g_D = rb$$

In estimating the return on retained earnings one can assume that the return on investment will be similar to the returns on total investment. Value Line regularly publishes the historical return on net worth as well as one-, two-, and five-year forecasts of this return. Using this data and the estimated retention rate, one can develop a projected growth rate. We'll illustrate this more fully in Chapter 5.

In words this model says that the P/E ratio is equal to the dividend payout rate $1 - b$ divided by the difference between the discount rate k and growth rate g as represented by the retention rate b times the return on retained earnings r. We can use this model to analyze the effects of changes in the fundamental input on the P/E ratio. We can best illustrate this for a hypothetical security that pays a $2 dividend out of $4 in earnings per share (target payout rate of 50 percent), shows a 14 percent rate of return on investment, and has a growth rate of 7 percent and a discount rate of 12 percent. The P/E ratio with these inputs would be 10, as shown below:

$$P/E = \frac{(1 - b)}{k - br} = \frac{.50}{.12 - (.5)(.14)} = 10$$

Table 4-9 on page 104 shows the effect on the P/E ratio of varying the discount rate and rate of return on retained earnings of the company, holding the payout rate constant. The left-hand column of the table shows the range of discount rates considered, while the top row of figures under rate of profitability shows the effect of varying the rate of return on retained earnings and hence the growth rate of the company. Each of the numbers in the body of the table shows the P/E ratio at that rate of return on retained earnings and that discount rate.

Note that the P/E ratio varies directly with the return on retained earnings of the company. For example, at the 12 percent discount rate, the P/E ratio is 8.3 when the return is 12 percent, 10 when the return is 14 percent, and 12.5 when it is 16 percent. All other things being equal, highly profitable companies sell at higher P/E ratios than companies with lower profits. On the other hand, the P/E ratio of a company varies inversely with its discount rate. For example, at the 14 percent profitability level, the P/E is 25 when the discount rate is 9 percent, 12.5 when it is 11 percent, and 8.3 when it is 13 percent. Companies with high discount rates should sell at lower P/E ratios than those with lower discount rates.

Price Earnings Ratio and the Discount Rate

As a final note, we might indicate that there are two instances where the P/E ratio would be an appropriate indicator of the discount rate for a stock. One obvious case is where the company pays out all its earnings as dividends, so that the earnings variable becomes identical to a dividend variable and the P/E ratio is the same as a price dividend ratio. In terms of our formulation, the retention rate b would be zero, and the P/E ratio is then equal to the reciprocal of the discount rate.

$$P/E = \frac{(1 - b)}{k - br} = \frac{(1 - 0)}{k - (0)r} = \frac{1}{k} \tag{12}$$

The second instance is where the company has opportunity only to reinvest earnings at the discount rate. This is indicative of the absence of growth opportunities and is the classic finance case known as *expansion,* where the growth rate is expected to be only average. In terms of our formulation, where the return on reinvested earnings is equal to the discount rate ($r = k$), the P/E ratio is then equal to the reciprocal of the discount rate.

$$P/E = \frac{(1 - b)}{k - br} = \frac{(1 - b)}{k(1 - b)} = \frac{1}{k} \tag{13}$$

Referring again to Table 4-9, we can see that when the stock has no growth opportunities, as indicated by a return rate r and discount rate k both equal to 12 percent, the P/E in the bottom-left-hand portion of the Table is 8.3 The inverse of the P/E in this case is also 12 percent and is therefore an appropriate estimate of the actual discount rate. In the presence of growth, which generally characterizes most stocks, the E/P ratio would, however, be an underestimate of the discount rate for stocks. For example, at a P/E ratio of 10 the simple inverse estimate of the discount rate would be 10 percent. Note in the table that the E/P ratio of 10 percent would underestimate the discount rate for a stock with a profitability rate of 14 percent by two percentage points. The true discount rate should be 12 percent, as shown in the left-hand column of the table. In these cases, generally for most stocks, there is thus need to use a model that considers growth, such as the dividend discount model.

DISCOUNT RATE: INTEREST RATE RISK

It will be useful at this point to analyze those factors that should have an impact on the level of the discount rate for stocks: (1) interest rate risk, (2) purchasing power risk, (3) business risk, and (4) financial risk. We can in fact analyze interest rate risk within the duration framework just as we used duration to evaluate the exposure of bonds to this risk. In the case of stocks, dividend payments are presumed to continue over an indefinite period — that is, infinity — so that developing duration for stocks comes within the general category of developing duration for a perpetuity. For perpetuities such as preferred stocks, where dividend payments are fixed, or British consols (bonds), where interest payments continue indefinitely, the formula for calculating duration is[10]

$$d = \frac{1}{k} \tag{14}$$

As before, k represents the required return on the security, and the resulting expression is simply the inverse of the required return. Since we are dealing with perpetuities, like preferreds and consols, the required return k can be determined by merely observing the current yield of the security. For example, a preferred stock paying a $12 dividend and selling at $100 would have a current yield of 12 percent. Presuming that this is representative of the required return on the security, and using Equation 14, we can calculate the duration of the preferred stock as follows:

$$d = \frac{1}{k} = \frac{1}{.12} = 8.3 \text{ years}$$

---

[10] This expression for duration assumes continuous compounding, and for purposes of illustrating duration for perpetuities like preferred stocks and common stocks we'll consider that the assumption of continuous compounding is appropriate. When discrete compounding is assumed, the expression for the duration of a perpetuity like a preferred stock is:

$$d = \frac{1 + k}{k}$$

This expression is only slightly more complex than the one in the text but would tend to obscure the analytical exposition.

Table 4-9 P/E ratio as a function of the return on retained earnings and the discount rate

Discount rate k	Rate of profitability r				
	12	13	14	15	16
9	16.7	20.0	25.0	33.3	50.0
10	12.5	14.3	16.7	20.0	25.0
11	10.0	11.1	12.5	14.3	16.7
12	8.3	9.1	10.0	11.1	12.5

The equation for calculating the duration of a common stock is similar, except for the need to consider the fact that common-stock dividends are expected to grow over the longer term. Again using g to represent the growth rate of the dividend, we can amend the previous equation to account for the expected growth in dividends. The equation for calculating the duration of common stock is then

$$d = \frac{1}{k - g} \tag{15}$$

Note that the denominator of the expression has the same form as that of the dividend capitalization model (see Equation 11). Rearranging the dividend capitalization model, we see that

$$D/P = \text{dividend yield} = k - g$$

In words, this says that the dividend yield D/P of the stock is equal to the difference between the required return k and the growth rate g. Substituting for $k - g$, we see that duration for the stock is simply the inverse of the dividend yield:

$$\text{Duration} = \frac{1}{\text{dividend yield}} \tag{16}$$

This, in turn, indicates that stocks with low dividend yields have long durations and are relatively more sensitive to discount rate changes. High-growth stocks are generally characterized by relatively low dividend yields and would be more subject to this risk than low-growth stocks. We would expect high-growth stocks to carry a higher discount rate to compensate for this risk than lower-growth stocks.

We can best illustrate this discount rate sensitivity or duration effect by means of the data in Table 4-10. This table shows two stocks, each paying $1 in dividends, with a discount rate of 10 percent, but one having a growth rate of 7 percent and the other a growth rate of 4 percent. Stock A has a duration of 33.3 years, while stock B has a duration of 16.7 years. When the discount rate increases to 11 percent, the high-growth stock shows a 25-percent change in price compared to a 14 percent change in price for the low-growth stock. Correspondingly, a decrease in the discount rate to 9 percent leads to a 50 percent change in price for the high-growth stock and a 20 percent price change for the low-growth stock. The longer-duration stock (33 years) thus shows greater variability with respect to discount rate changes than the short-duration stock (17 years) as indicated by the preceding analysis.

Since the measure of duration for stocks is similar to the measure of duration for bonds, we can thus compare the duration of stocks and bonds to evaluate the relative riskiness of the two broad security types to interest rate changes. As proxy input data we can use the returns generated by stocks and the returns generated by bonds over the fifty-three-year period 1926–1978 (the same data as shown in Chapter 1). We can then use Equation 6 to calculate bond duration and Equation 14 to calculate stock duration.

Table 4-11 shows the input data and calculated durations for stocks and bonds. Note that over the fifty-three-year period the bonds, based on an index of returns of 5 percent for an average maturity of twenty years, had a duration of twelve years, whereas the stocks showed an average dividend return of 4 percent and a growth rate of 5 percent, indicating a duration of twenty-five years. At year-end 1979, stocks were yielding 5 percent and showed a duration of twenty years, while a high-grade twenty-year government bond yielding 10 percent showed a duration of eight years. Because of their perpetual life and positive growth character, stocks typically show a duration considerably in excess of bonds, which have fixed maturity periods and, of course, no growth characteristics. Stocks should be considerably more responsive to changes in real interest rates than bonds and correspondingly carry a higher premium in the discount rate than bonds to compensate for this component of risk.

Table 4-10 Sensitivity to discount rate changes

	Stock A	Stock B
Dividend D	$ 1.00	$ 1.00
Growth rate g	7%	4%
Discount rate k	10%	10%
Price $= \dfrac{D}{k-g}$	$33.3	$16.7
Duration $= \dfrac{1}{k-g}$	$\dfrac{1}{(.10-.07)} = 33.3$	$\dfrac{1}{(.10-.04)} = 16.7$
Discount rate k	11%	11%
Price $= \dfrac{D}{k-g}$	$25	$14.3
Price change	25%	14%
Discount rate k	9%	9%
Price $= \dfrac{D}{k-g}$	$50	$20
Price change	50%	20%

Table 4-11 Relative duration — stocks versus bonds

	1926–1978	12/31/79
Bonds		
Average coupon	$5	$10
Maturity	20 years	20 years
Average interest rate	5%	10%
Duration	12 years	8 years
Stocks		
Average dividend	$4	$5
Growth rate	5%	8%
Average discount rate	9%	13%
Duration	25 years	20 years

PURCHASING POWER RISK

It is, however, not so clear how responsive stocks should be to changes in nominal interest rates. Nominal rates include both a real interest rate component R_r and an inflation premium component I. Nominal rates should adjust up or down as the rate of inflation changes. Nominal rates should increase as the inflation component rises when inflation is high; conversely, nominal rates should decline as the inflation component declines when inflation is low.

Since bond coupons are fixed, we would expect bonds to be fully subject to this component of risk. In particular, as the discount rate rises, the price of the bond with a fixed coupon must adjust fully by declining to compensate for the increase in the interest rate. With stocks, however, there is an opportunity to offset inflation through an increase in dividends. We can best illustrate this by referring back to the basic stock valuation equation (7) and in this case augmenting it with an increased dividend growth rate, $1 + I$, to compensate for inflation. Thus

$$P = \frac{D(1 + I)}{k(1 + I) - g(1 + I)} \tag{17}$$

Note that all three variables (dividends, growth, and discount rate) have been augmented with the inflation factor $1 + I$. When inflation increases, we would expect the discount rate to be higher by $k(1 + I)$ to reflect the higher rate. If the corporate growth rate and dividend increased directly in line with the inflation increase, or by $g(1 + I)$ and $D(1 + I)$, the company would be expected to offset inflation entirely, and there should be no effect on price. In this case we can factor out the $1 + I$ terms as shown below:

$$P = \frac{(1 + I)D}{(1 + I)(k - g)} = \frac{D}{(k - g)}$$

If, however, the corporation cannot increase its rate of growth in line with inflation, or if there is only a partial adjustment, there should be a negative effect on stocks. This happens because the discount rate will increase more than the growth rate and dividend level, thus resulting in the application of a net higher discount rate. In the extreme situation where the corporation is completely unable to increase growth in the face of inflation, the dividend becomes almost like a fixed coupon payment. In this case the stock acts more or less like a bond in bearing the full brunt of an increase in the discount rate.

Table 4-12 illustrates the dividend growth adjustment under three different scenarios: (1) a full dividend growth adjustment to inflation; (2) a partial adjustment — in this case only a 50 percent adjustment to an increase in inflation; and (3) a zero, or bondlike, adjustment. Note that when inflation increases by 2 percent, there is essentially no effect on stock prices if growth increases in tandem with inflation; however, stock prices depreciate by 35 percent if there is no adjustment and by 21 percent if there is only a partial adjustment for inflation.

How stocks adjust to inflation — that is, which of the three scenarios seems to fit stocks best — is essentially an empirical question. Studies seem to indicate that stocks adjust rather fully to inflation over longer periods of time; however, over shorter periods the indications are not so clear. Recent experience indicates that stocks have not adjusted fully, suffering severely during the 1973–1977 period, when in terms of the dividend capitalization model the change in g lagged the change in k. This lag may be due to tax laws, stickiness in prices, or a multitude of other factors that are under investigation. Research over the coming years is likely to provide better perspective on the issue.

BUSINESS AND FINANCIAL RISK

Within the equity market there are varying degrees of exposure to business and financial risk. Companies that are small, hold secondary positions within their industry, have heavy fixed costs and extensive operating leverage, show substantial sensitivity to the business cycle, and that demonstrate significant variability in earnings would be expected to have a lot of business risk. Companies in this category that finance heavily with debt would have further significant exposure to financial risk. We would expect

Table 4-12 Inflation and stock prices

Stock	Zero inflation	5% inflation		
		100% adjustment	50% adjustment	Zero adjustment
Dividend	1.00	1.02	1.01	1.00
Growth rate	.05	.0710	.0605	.05
Discount rate	.09	.1118	.1118	.1118
Stock price	$25.00	$25.00	$19.69	$16.18
Price change, %	—	− 0	− 21	− 35

such companies to carry the highest discount rates to compensate investors for relatively extensive exposure to these risks.

On the other hand, companies that are large, are leading factors in their industry, have relatively low sensitivity to the business cycle, and show a stable pattern of earnings would be expected to have a lesser degree of business risk. Companies in this category that also have clean balance sheets—that is, financed entirely with equity—would, of course, show no exposure to financial risk. Because of the relatively limited business risk and the absence of financial risk, we would expect the discount rates of these "highest quality" companies to be significantly lower than those of the previous category of companies.

CONCLUSION

This chapter has dealt with the underlying theory of valuation models. We've seen that these models provide a way of explicitly developing returns for both stocks and bonds. Furthermore, we've seen that these models allow us to develop a greater understanding of how fundamental sources such as interest rate, inflation, and business and financial risk impact the risk-return characteristics of bonds and stocks. Developing explicit returns and understanding the risk-return characteristics of securities are, of course, critically important as inputs for generating portfolios of securities that are optimal in terms of risk and return.

APPENDIX A USING A CALCULATOR TO FIND FUTURE AND PRESENT VALUES OF LUMP SUMS AND ANNUITIES

The financial tables are calculated from four basic formulas that can be used directly when tables are not available. Like the tables, the formulas are specified in terms of a $1 initial amount.

FUTURE VALUE OF LUMP SUM

The formula for the compound value of an initial value of $1 is given by

$$FV = (1 + i)^n \qquad (A\text{-}1)$$

where i = the interest rate per period (in decimal form) and n = the number of time periods.

This equation can easily be solved by using a hand calculator that has the exponential function x^y, where x and y correspond to $1 + i$ and n, respectively. For example, a 10 percent interest rate over ten years results in the following compound-value calculation:

$$FV = (1 + i)^n = (1.1)^{10} = 2.594$$

PRESENT VALUE OF LUMP SUM

The formula for the present value of a $1 future value is

$$PV = \frac{1}{(1 + i)^n} \qquad \text{(A-2)}$$

This value is simply the reciprocal of the compound value illustrated above (A-1). Where $i = .10$ and $n = 10$, the present value of a $1 future value is

$$PV = \frac{1}{(1 + i)^n} = \frac{1}{(1.10)^{10}} = \frac{1}{2.594} = .3855$$

FUTURE VALUE OF AN ANNUITY

The formula for the future value of an annuity of $1 per year for n years is

$$FVA = \frac{(1 + i)^n - 1}{i} \qquad \text{(A-3)}$$

The calculation is a simple variation of those shown above where 1 is subtracted from the compounded-value term $(1 + i)^n$ and the difference is divided by the interest rate. The example given below is for $i = .10$ and $n = 10$.

$$FVA = \frac{(1 + i)^n - 1}{i} = \frac{(1.10)^{10} - 1}{.10} = \frac{2.594 - 1}{.10} = \frac{1.594}{.10} = 15.94$$

PRESENT VALUE OF AN ANNUITY

The formula for the present value of an annuity may be expressed as

$$PVA = \frac{(1 + i)^n - 1}{i(1 + i)^n} \qquad \text{(A-4)}$$

The only complex terms involve $(1 + i)^n$ and are easily calculated using the x^y function. Continuing with the example given above, the present value of the annuity is given by

$$PVA = \frac{(1 + i)^n - 1}{i(1 + i)^n} = \frac{(1.10)^{10} - 1}{.10(1.10)^{10}} = \frac{2.594 - 1}{.10 \times 2.594} = \frac{1.594}{.2594} = 6.145$$

Note that this result is equal to the present value of the compounded annuities value:

$$PVA = \frac{FVA}{(1 + i)^n} = \frac{15.94}{(1.10)^{10}} = \frac{15.94}{2.594} = 6.145$$

APPENDIX B SIMPLIFYING THE DIVIDEND CAPITALIZATION MODEL

In simplifying the dividend capitalization model two critical assumptions are made. The first is that dividends will grow at a constant rate g over a long period of time — in theory, to infinity. This allows us to restate the basic dividend capitalization model as

$$P = \frac{D(1 + g)}{1 + k} + \frac{D(1 + g)^2}{(1 + k)^2} + \frac{D(1 + g)^3}{(1 + k)^3} + \cdots + \frac{D(1 + g)^T}{(1 + k)^T} \tag{B-1}$$

Converting this then becomes similar to the process used to illustrate the return on an annuity. First, multiplying by $1 + k/1 + g$ we obtain

$$\frac{P(1 + k)}{1 + g} = D + \frac{D(1 + g)}{1 + k} + \frac{D(1 + g)^2}{(1 + k)^2} + \cdots + \frac{D(1 + g)^{T-1}}{(1 + k)^{T-1}} \tag{B-2}$$

When we subtract Equation B-1 from Equation B-2, we eliminate the middle terms, to obtain

$$\frac{P(1 + k)}{1 + g} - P = D - \frac{D(1 + g)^T}{(1 + k)^T} \tag{B-3}$$

Simplifying, we then obtain

$$P(k - g) = D\left[1 - \frac{(1 + g)^T}{(1 + k)^T}\right] \tag{B-4}$$

At this point we make the second critical assumption, which is that the expected return is greater than the expected growth rate of the dividend — that is, $k > g$. Making this assumption allows us to eliminate the complex term on the right-hand side in the brackets. For example, if $g = 1$ and $k = 2$, this term would be $(\frac{2}{3})^T$, and as T approaches infinity, the term would approach zero. When this term disappears and $D = D_0(1 + g)$ is defined as the year-end dividend, this expression simplifies to Equation 10 in the body of the chapter:

$$P = \frac{D}{k - g} \tag{B-5}$$

In reviewing, the analysis is based on two key assumptions. The first, constant growth of the dividend, allows us to simplify the stream of dividend payments. The second, $k > g$, allows us to reduce the expression to its final simplified form. The second assumption is also critical so that the equation does not give nonsense results. If k equals g, the equation blows up and yields an infinite price; if k is less than g, a negative price results. When either of these two conditions is present, there is need for modification of the model, which will be treated in Chapter 5.

PROBLEMS

1 Assume there is a bond paying an $80 coupon with a term to maturity of three years. Calculate the yield to maturity when the bond sells at (a) par, (b) $800, and (c) $1100.

2 Assume there are two bonds paying a $100 coupon, but one has a term to maturity of four years and the other a term to maturity of seven years. Determine the price of the bonds when the yield to maturity is 8 percent. Then determine the price of the two bonds when the yield is 12 percent, and calculate the percentage change in price from the prior yield.

3 Determine the duration for the following securities:

- (a) a bond due to pay $1200 (interest and principal) at the end of four years and selling at $900;
- (b) a bond paying a $100 coupon, selling at $800, and having a maturity value of $1000 in four years;
- (c) a "mortgage" type of security making level payments of $500 per annum over a life of four years;
- (d) a preferred stock selling at $560 and paying a dividend of $4 per share; and
- (e) a common stock selling at $50, paying a $4 dividend that grows at the rate of 4 percent, and having a required return of 11 percent.

4 Determine the expected price change for each of the above securities associated with a .10 percent change in the required return (discount rate) of each.

5 A common stock pays out 40 percent of its earnings, which are expected to be $3 at year-end. The return on retained earnings is 15 percent, and the required return on the stock is 14 percent. Determine the P/E ratio.

6 The return on retained earnings for the stock is now expected to be 18 percent rather than 15 percent, but the required return is also expected to increase to 16 percent. Determine the P/E ratio for the stock assuming the earnings and payout ratio remain unchanged.

7 A common stock is earning $2 and pays out $0.80 in dividends. The required return on the stock is 16 percent, and the projected growth rate in dividends is 9 percent. Inflation increases from 9 percent to 11 percent. Determine the change in stock price assuming (a) no ability to adjust for the increased inflation and (b) a 75-percent adjustment to the change in inflation.

SELECTED REFERENCES

Bauman, W. Scott: "Investment Returns and Present Values," *Financial Analysts Journal,* November–December 1969, pp. 107–118.

Brigham, Eugene F., and James L. Pappas: "Duration of Growth, Changes in Growth Rates, and Corporate Share Prices," *Financial Analysts Journal,* May–June 1966, pp. 157–162.

——— and Myron J. Gordon: "Leverage, Dividend Policy, and the Cost of Capital," *Journal of Finance,* March 1968, pp. 85–104.

Fewings, David: "The Impact of Corporate Growth on the Risk of Common Stocks," *Journal of Finance,* May 1975, pp. 525–531.

Gordon, Myron: *The Investment, Financing, and Valuation of the Corporation,* Irwin, Homewood, Ill., 1962.

Graham, B., D. Dodd, and S. Cottle: *Security Analysis,* 4th ed., McGraw-Hill, New York, 1962.

Haugen, R. A., and D. W. Wichern: "The Elasticity of Financial Assets," *Journal of Finance,* September 1974, pp. 1229–1240.

Holt, Charles C.: "The Influence of Growth Duration on Share Price," *Journal of Finance,* September 1961, pp. 465–475.

Hopewell, M. H., and G. G. Kaufman: "Bond Price Volatility and Term to Maturity: A Generalized Respecification," *American Economic Review,* September 1973, pp. 749–753.

Lerner, Eugene M., and Willard T. Carleton: *A Theory of Financial Analysis,* Harcourt Brace Jovanovich, New York, 1966.

Malkiel, Burton G.: "Equity Yields, Growth, and the Structure of Share Prices," *American Economic Review,* December 1963, pp. 467–494.

———— and John G. Cragg: "Expectations and the Structure of Share Price," *American Economic Review,* September 1970, pp. 601–617.

Mao, James C. T.: "The Valuation of Growth Stocks: The Investment Opportunity Approach," *Journal of Finance,* March 1966, pp. 107–118.

Miller, M. H. J., and F. Modigliani: "Dividend Policy, Growth, and the Valuation of Shares," *Journal of Business,* October 1961, pp. 411–433.

Modigliani, F., and M. H. Miller: "The Cost of Capital, Corporation Finance and the Theory of Investment; Corporate Income Taxes, and the Cost of Capital: A Correction," *American Economic Review,* June 1958, pp. 433–443.

Nichols, D. A.: "A Note on Inflation and Common Stock Values," *Journal of Finance,* September 1968, pp. 655–657.

Reilly, F.: "Companies and Common Stocks as Inflation Hedges," *N. Y. U. Bulletin,* 1975–2.

Solomon, Ezra: *The Theory of Financial Management,* Columbia University Press, New York, 1963.

FIVE

APPLYING VALUATION MODEL METHODS

INTRODUCTION

The previous chapter discussed the underlying theory of valuation models. This chapter describes how these models can be and have been applied in solving practical problems of evaluation. To begin with, we'll see that the valuation model needs to be specialized for the particular kind of company being analyzed, since companies differ significantly in operating characteristics. Some companies have highly stable earnings patterns, while others have erratic or cyclical patterns of earnings. Similarly, some companies are expected to show a strong pattern of growth in earnings, while most others will grow more or less in line with the broad average. These differing operating patterns in turn require modification of the basic dividend capitalization model in order to properly accommodate the differences. We here discuss what these modifications are and how they apply to the different kinds of companies.

We'll also see that no matter what variation of the model is used, there is a critical need to ensure that inputs to these models are developed as carefully as possible. Poorly developed or inappropriate inputs will degrade the performance of even the most elegantly constructed model. Developing appropriate inputs is the responsibility of the fundamental analyst, and the greater the skill and effort of the analyst in developing the inputs, the better the performance of the model will be. As a result, we'll illustrate this process by describing a framework that analysts would typically use to develop inputs for a valuation model. We'll also describe examples of how the framework can be used.

The final part of the chapter describes a framework for simultaneously considering the risk and return of common stocks. It is, in fact, the empirical counterpart of the security market line (SML) described in a theoretical context in Chapter 3. We'll first show how the market line is constructed in practice. In the process it should become clear that this framework provides an explicit link between valuation theory and models of the risk-return relationship (like the SML and APT) that grow out of portfolio and capital-market theory. Once we've described how the line is constructed, we'll illustrate the three major uses of the market line: (1) assessing the relative valuation level of the market, (2) assessing the risk-return trade-off in the equity market, and (3) identifying relatively undervalued and overvalued individual securities.

DIVIDEND CAPITALIZATION MODEL: SIMPLIFIED FORM

To this point we have analyzed the dividend capitalization model as a way of determining a price or value for a stock. Generally, however, the variable of most interest to investors is the discount rate k for the stock. This is because the price of the stock can readily be found, while variables, such as the current dividend and the growth rate, can be estimated, albeit with varying degrees of ease. We can use the simplified form of the dividend capitalization model for this purpose by rearranging it into a suitable form for estimating the discount rate k, as shown below:

$$k = \frac{D}{P} + g \tag{1}$$

This equation says that the discount rate k for a stock is a function of two variables: the dividend yield, which is the year-ahead dividend D divided by the stock price P, and the growth rate of the dividend g. Estimating the dividend and growth rate of the dividend can in turn be facilitated by first redefining these variables. Defining E as earnings and $1 - b$ as a payout rate, dividends can be thought of as a function of a payout rate and an earnings level $D = (1 - b)E$. Further defining b as a retention rate and r as a return on equity, or a measure of profitability, we can think of the growth rate of the dividend as a function of the retention rate and return on equity $g = br$. Using these alternative definitions, the equation for determining the discount rate becomes

$$k = \frac{(1 - b)E}{P} + br \tag{2}$$

Note that, in this form, generating inputs thus becomes a task of developing estimates for the following variables: the level of earnings E; the retention rate b or, alternatively, the payout rate $1 - b$; and the basic level of profitability r. The retention or payout rate is a policy variable established by the management of the company. It can be assessed by gauging the behavior of the corporation from past payouts of earnings or more directly from the stated policy of the corporation; for example, the management may have a policy of paying out 50 percent of earnings over a longer period of time. Estimating the level of earnings E and the productivity of retained earnings r is, however, a function of the fundamental analyst.

A particularly useful framework that a fundamental analyst can use is assessment of the earnings level and the return on reinvested earnings of the corporation, as shown in Table 5-1. The top row of the figure shows that the level of earnings per share of the company is a function of five variables: (1) profit margin, (2) capital turnover, (3) a financial leverage factor, (4) a tax rate effect, and (5) level of book value. The exact definition of these variables is shown at the bottom of the table. Note that when the first

Table 5-1 Fundamental factors in corporate profitability

$\text{EPS} = M \times T \times L \times U \times B$

Return $r = \text{EPS}/B = M \times T \times L \times U$

where M = the ratio of net operating income to sales
       T = the turnover ratio, defined as the ratio of sales to total tangible assets
       L = the extent to which the return on equity has been raised by the use of leverage, i.e., using debt
           together with equity
       U = the after-tax rate $U = (1 - t)$, where t is the tax rate
       B = the book value per share

---

four variables are multiplied together, we obtain the rate of return which is the earnings per share divided by the book value per share as shown in the second row of the figure. We should note from this relationship that the rate of return of the company will be high when the capital turnover is high, profit margins are high, the tax rate is low, and leverage is high and positive. Conversely, the rate of return of the company will be low when the capital turnover is low, profit margins are low, the tax rate is high, and leverage is low. The earnings level will also vary directly with the rate of return on equity and will be correspondingly higher or lower as the book value of the company increases or decreases.

Book value increases as earnings are retained and will be higher or lower depending on the retention rate b. The retention rate interacts with the rate of return on retained earnings to produce growth $g = br$. The growth in book value and hence in earnings and dividends will be higher as the rate of retention and return on retained earnings increases. Conversely, it will be lower as the rate of retention and return on retained earnings decreases. While there are other sources of growth, it is especially helpful to think of growth in terms of retention and rate of return on retained earnings, since over the long term this is the only sustainable source of growth for the firm. In fact, some have referred to it as *sustainable growth,* as other potential sources of growth are by their nature limited in the extent to which they can change and hence do not represent sustained, or recurring, sources of growth.[1]

The contribution of earnings retention and investment return to growth can be specifically illustrated by comparing two hypothetical corporations, as shown in Table 5-2. Company A has a return on investment of 18 percent and retains two-thirds of its earnings (one-third payout), while company B has a return on investment of 12 percent and retains one-third of its earnings (two-thirds payout). The table shows that company A's earnings will grow by \$0.216, or 12 percent, over the next year, while company B's earnings will grow by \$0.048, or 6 percent, over the next year. These are, of course, the same percentage changes that are implied by the sustainable growth calculation br for both companies. High return and retention leads to high growth as expected, while low return and retention leads to low growth also as expected.

[1] Growth of equity per share has two principal sources: (1) the sale of new stock at a price higher than the existing book value per share; and (2) the plowing back of earnings into the business — that is, paying out only a portion of net income in cash dividends to common stockholders and retaining and reinvesting the balance. Of these two sources, the second is far and away the most important for most companies.

Table 5-2 Retention, rate of return, and growth

	Company *A*	Company *B*
Book value per share *B*	10.00	10.00
Rate of return on equity *r*	18%	12%
Earnings per share *B* × *r*	1.80	1.20
Retention rate *b*	⅔	⅓
Retained earnings *b* × EPS	1.20	0.40
Earnings on retained earnings *r* × *RE*	0.216	0.048
New level of earnings	2.016	1.248
Growth rate of earnings	(2.016/1.80) − 1 = 12%	(1.248/1.20) − 1 = 4%
Sustainable growth *br*	12%	4%

ESTIMATING THE DISCOUNT RATE

We can most easily illustrate the use of the dividend capitalization model in developing a discount rate by estimating the discount rate, or expected return, of the market as a whole. To begin with, the model should be applicable to the total market since the market is simply an aggregation of individual stocks, and if it applies to the individual components, it should apply to the total. Furthermore, when dealing with an aggregate rather than an individual stock, errors in measuring inputs tend to cancel out; that is, overestimates tend to be offset by underestimates. There is, in effect, an automatic smoothing or normalizing of the data that makes it more suitable for direct use in the simplified version of the dividend capitalization model.

Table 5-3 shows some relevant valuation data for a fairly representative index of the U. S. equity market: the Standard & Poor's Composite Index of 500 Stocks. This table shows, for the five-year period 1975–1979, data on earnings, payout ratios, return on investment, and retention rate times the return on investment. Note that the payout ratio averaged about 40 percent but showed a slight downward trend over the period, while the return on investment increased from 12.1 to 16.1 percent, averaging 14.1 percent for the period.

The 1979 retention rate and return on investment imply a sustainable growth of 10 percent. At year-end 1979 the value of the S&P 500 was 108 and the dividend rate was 5.65, giving a yield of 5.2 percent. Combining this with a sustainable growth of 10 percent indicates a discount rate, or expected return, of 15.2 percent for the S&P 500. Of course, this is an average and will differ across companies owing to differences in risk, as we'll see later in the chapter.

Table 5-3 also compares this current "expected" return of 15.2 percent with that earned by stocks over the fifty-three-year period 1926–1978. While the absolute return is now higher than that realized over the 1926–1978 period, it is not necessarily so when inflation is taken into account. In particular, the 8.9 percent return was earned over a period when the rate of inflation averaged only 2.5 percent, providing a real return of 6.4 percent (8.9 percent less 2.5 percent) for stocks. In the five-year period 1975–1979 inflation averaged 8 percent, and some have estimated that the underlying rate of

Table 5-3 The S&P 500 — expected return

Year	Earnings E	Payout ratio $1 - b$	Return on investment r	Dividends D	Retention rate b	Growth rate br
1975	7.96	46%	12.1%	3.68	.54	6.5%
1976	9.91	41	13.9	4.05	.59	8.2
1977	10.89	43	14.0	4.67	.57	8.0
1978	12.33	41	14.6	5.07	.59	8.6
1979	14.86	38	16.1	5.65	.62	10.0

$$\text{Expected return } E(R) = \frac{(1 - b)E}{P} + br$$

$$= 5.2\% + 10.0\% = 15.2\%$$

Inflation rate	9.0%
Expected real return	6.2
Realized return 1926–1978	8.9
Inflation	2.5
Realized real return	6.4

Source: Standard and Poor's Security Price Index Record, Standard and Poor's Corporation, New York, N. Y.

inflation is 9 percent. This figure would imply a real return on stocks of 6.2 percent (expected return of 15.2 percent less underlying inflation of 9 percent).

Despite the fact that the current expected nominal return on stocks is substantially different from the past average, the current "expected" real return on stocks is fairly close to that earned over the longer term. This apparent relative stability in real return might in turn be helpful in developing a forecast of future return on stocks. In particular, one might build a return forecast by estimating the inflation rate and adding it to the real return.

Besides application to the overall market, the simplified form of the model is also appropriate for use with certain types of companies that we might characterize as being of a stable, more mature variety. For such companies the earnings patterns as well as retention rates and returns on investment are fairly stable over time. This is because their investment opportunities, which are a prime consideration in setting the retention rate, are fairly constrained and their basic profitability is pretty constant over time.

As a result, developing the inputs and applying them to the model is a fairly straightforward task for rather mature, stable companies. For example, we might use the simplified form of the dividend capitalization model to estimate the expected return for Kellogg. At year-end 1979 Kellogg was selling at $19 and paying a dividend of $1.32, to provide a yield of 6.9 percent. The company's sustainable growth rate was 9.5 percent. Combining these two inputs would indicate an expected return of 16.4 percent for the company.

While the formula is useful in cases like Kellogg, it must be modified substantially to deal with companies that have a highly cyclical operating pattern, like General Motors (GM), or companies that are expected to show exceptionally high rates of earnings growth, like Wang Labs. The problem with cyclical companies is one of casting the inputs in a suitable form for use in the model. The problem with high-growth companies is that the simplified form of the model is not suitable for use. An alternative form is needed, which we'll describe in a later section of this chapter. Meanwhile, it will be useful to describe the problems that must be overcome in analyzing cyclical companies.

CYCLICAL COMPANIES

The basic problem in using the valuation model for cyclical companies is to normalize the earnings of the company, which means "to adjust the earnings of the company to what they would be at the midpoint of an economic cycle."[2] The purpose here is to abstract the earning power of the company from abnormal economic influences such as recession or boom. This concept emanates from Graham and Dodd, who describe it extensively in their textbook *Security Analysis.*

We can most easily describe this concept by referring to Figure 5-1, which shows the idealized earnings trend of a hypothetical cyclical company. The vertical axis is a scale indicating the earnings level, while the horizontal axis is a time line starting at year zero. Note that the earnings line fluctuates up and down regularly, depicting the cyclical earnings pattern of the company. Note also that while the line fluctuates it shows an upward trend over time, indicating a basic growth rate for the company's

[2] Graham B., D. Dodd, and S. Cottle, *Security Analysis,* 4th ed., McGraw-Hill, New York, 1962.

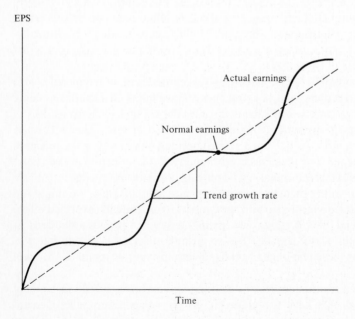

Figure 5-1 Cyclical growth pattern.

earnings. The objective of the normalization procedure is, in effect, to smooth out the fluctuating pattern of earnings in order to determine what the earnings are at a normal level, such as that designated "normal earnings" by point n on the graph. The objective is also to discern the trend or sustainable rate of earnings growth as depicted by the slope of the dashed line fitted to the fluctuating earnings line. Once we've done this, we have earnings and growth-rate data suitable for input to the valuation model.

The method of normalizing earnings can best be illustrated by again referring to the analytical framework shown in Table 5-1, where the earnings per share of a company were expressed as a function of five variables: (1) profit margin, (2) capital turnover, (3) a financial leverage factor, (4) tax rate effect, and (5) level of book value. We can discern from this framework that earnings can change owing to changes in any of the variables. However, changes in the first four variables — margin, turnover, leverage, and tax effect — cannot be relied upon to sustain growth over a long period of time. Specifically, changes in margin will occur, but upward moves will be limited by competition in the market. Similarly, changes in turnover are almost inevitable, but plant capacity or the state of technology will limit the volume of sales relative to capital. Likewise, the degree of leverage available to a company is limited, either by the willingness of creditors or by the prudence of management. Tax cuts are, of course, a very limited source of growth.

In any one period, changes in these four variables may be critical in determining the level of earnings. Over time, however, they all have a tendency to fluctuate about some normal value, which will depend on the nature of the industry, the level of the economy, or management discretion, especially with regard to taxes and debt. As has been noted, for a stable company, such as Kellogg, the fluctuations will be negligible and the need to analyze them limited. On the other hand, for a highly cyclical company, such as GM, changes in these variables can be quite sizable, and there is a corresponding need to analyze them in depth. For the more cyclically oriented companies we need to determine the normal levels for margins, turnover, leverage, and taxes, and then multiply them together to obtain a normalized rate of return. Given a normalized rate of return r and a normal retention rate b, we can compute a sustainable growth rate g for normalized earnings per share (EPS) as $g = br$.

APPLICATION OF TECHNIQUE

Perhaps it will be helpful to use GM's operating record over the 1973–1974 period as a prime example of this kind of analysis. First, the 1973–1974 period was one of severe recession, which actually stretched into 1975. During such a period auto sales are especially adversely affected, resulting in a highly negative effect on turnover and profitability variables. Specifically, fewer sales and a fairly constant capital investment cause a decline in the turnover ratio. Also, fewer sales adversely affect unit costs, leading in turn to a shrinkage in profit margins. The decline in profitability from these two sources is further compounded by a certain amount of debt in capital structure, so that there is a reversal in leverage. In 1974, earnings were below normal owing to these factors. Actual reported earnings were $3.27 as compared with 1971–1973 earnings of between $7 and $8.

Table 5-4 shows the normalized 1974 GM earnings. The first row gives the actual 1974 earnings along with actual values of the five variables: margin M, turnover T, leverage L, taxes U, and book value B. The middle part of the table shows the values of the variables for the prior three years, 1971–1973, along with an average of the variables over the three years. Averaging the three years of data serves to smooth out cyclical influences and hence develop normal values for the variables.

We should note, however, that there are alternative and superior ways of developing normal values for the basic profitability variables. To begin with, one might well wish to evaluate the relationships over several business cycles rather than only one; that is, perhaps a twelve-year period would provide more representative figures. Alternatively, it might be preferable to focus on specific years when the economy and presumably the company were operating at a "normal" level and use these values as typical or representative. In either case historical values should only be used as an initial guideline, and the typical, or "normal," values of the past should be adjusted where there may have been a fundamental change. For example, the significant change in the relative price of gasoline and the increasing competition from auto imports may well have changed the fundamental profitability of the auto industry. Professional fundamental analysts would incorporate those kinds of changes into their evaluation of the prospective profitability of the company.

Meanwhile, using the three-year average to illustrate the normalization process, the final row in Table 5-4 shows that by multiplying the four "normal" values for the variables together, we obtain a "normal" return of approximately 18 percent.[3] Using this return and the same book value of $42.8 indicates that earnings of GM would have been $7.75 if 1974 had been a "normal" year. GM has a policy, or at least a tradition, of paying out approximately two-thirds of its earnings; hence it has a retention rate b of one-third. Since GM's normalized return on investment r is about 18 per-

[3] Note that in this example we have merely been applying historical relationships and not adjusting for future changes in company fundamentals. In particular, the shift to smaller cars is bound to have some effect on the basic profitability of the industry. Some professional analysts believe that this means that GM's profitability has shifted downward to something like 15 percent from the historical 18 percent. One should amend the analysis to account for these changes. Also, the analysis in this section should be considered merely illustrative.

Table 5-4 Normalizing earnings — General Motors

	M	$\times$ T	$\times$ L	$\times$ U	$=$	r	$\times$ B	$=$ EPS
1974 actual values	5.8	1.54	1.50	.57		7.7%	$42.8	$3.27
Historical values								
1971	13.4	1.54	1.70	.52				
1972	14.0	1.66	1.50	.51				
1973	12.9	1.75	1.60	.53				
Three-year average	13.4	1.63	1.60	.52				
1974 normal values	13.4	1.63	1.60	.52	$=$	18.1%	$42.8	$7.75

cent, then sustainable growth g is on the order of 6 percent—that is, $g = br$, $1/3(18 \text{ percent}) = 6$ percent.

Once these growth and earnings factors have been assessed, we can then apply them directly to the simplified formulation of the dividend capitalization model illustrated in Table 5-5. Inserting the $7.75 computed as normal earnings and the normal dividend payout of two-thirds gives a dividend of $5.15. Relating this to $30, the price at which GM stock was selling as of the end of 1974, indicates a yield of 17.2 percent, which only represents a potential, not actual, yield. With a sustainable growth of 6 percent this formulation would then provide an expected return of 23.2 percent.

We should note, however, that this return should only be considered approximate, as applying it in this fashion assumes that the company immediately reaches the computed normalized earnings level. It might ordinarily take a cyclical company like GM two or even three years to come out of the trough of an economic cycle and reach its normal earnings level. The assumption of a premature return to normal gives the estimated return an upward bias. Use of a more elaborate formulation, such as the one illustrated in Appendix A to this chapter, would eliminate the bias and show that the "true" return should be 22 percent rather than the previous estimate of 23.2 percent. For purposes of exposition the simplified model, as we've shown, is useful, but for purposes of practical application use of the more elaborate formulation would be warranted.[4]

GROWTH STOCKS AND THE TWO-STAGE GROWTH MODEL

The most obvious case in which one cannot use the simplified valuation formula to estimate the discount rate for stocks is that of a rapidly growing company. Such companies are unable to conform to the main assumptions used in deriving the simplified form of the dividend capitalization model. Recall that in developing this model we made two critical assumptions: (1) that the growth rate was constant over an

[4] We thus obtain an estimate that is approximately equal to the estimate obtained from the more elaborate formulation. This estimate is somewhat higher because it assumes an earlier flow of higher dividends than other formulations. The bias here is, however, less severe than if one used only a current dividend rate and a sustainable growth in line with the basic profitability of the company—that is, 6 percent. In this case the estimate would have been only 16 percent for expected return. Whether this would have been more appropriate cannot be determined definitively. We do know, however, that GM doubled in price during 1975, outperforming most stocks and giving some credence to the higher estimated return.

Table 5-5 Discount rate — General Motors

$$\text{Expected return } E(R) = \frac{(1 - b)E}{P} + br$$

$$= \frac{(\tfrac{2}{3})7.75}{30} + \frac{1}{3}(18\%)$$

$$= 17.2\% + 6.0\% = 23.2\%$$

infinitely long period and (2) that the discount rate k was greater than the growth rate g. Constant growth was needed to simplify the dividend progression over time, while the second assumption was necessary to avoid an infinite or negative stock price.

High-growth companies are unlikely to fulfill either of these assumptions. In particular, these companies can be characterized as ones that are growing at quite rapid rates relative to general economic growth. To provide a benchmark, these companies would be classified as growing at rates of 15–30 percent, compared with the growth rate of 9–10 percent that was shown to be representative of the current S&P 500 and might be used as a benchmark for the growth rate of the "nongrowth" stocks. Companies growing at these quite rapid rates of 15–30 percent are unlikely to conform to the assumption of a discount rate that is greater than the growth rate.

At the same time we cannot assume that this rapid growth will remain constant, but should anticipate a transition to a more normal pace (in line with general economic growth) at some stage. No company could normally be expected to maintain an abnormally high pace of growth, as the mere compounding effect of its growth would at some stage result in its becoming such a large proportion of the economy (if not the total economy itself) as to foreclose further prospects of growth. For example, IBM, a premier growth company, showed an earnings growth rate of 18 percent from 1945 to 1980. If the company continued this relative pace of growth and total corporate profits grew at the historical rate, IBM profits would represent something like 60–70 percent of total corporate profits in fifteen years. Though possible, continuation of this sort of growth seems highly unlikely.

One convenient way of capturing a pattern of growth proceeding at a quite rapid pace in the initial stages and then declining to a rate more in line with the general corporate average is the two-stage growth model. It is the most direct elaboration of the simplified form of the dividend capitalization model. Other multistage elaborations are more complex and allow greater flexibility in the practical application of valuation techniques; however, since they are based on the framework of the two-stage growth model, analyzing this model is instructive with regard to more complex elaborations. In addition, the two-stage growth model can be used in developing appropriate valuations for growth stocks, as we'll illustrate in this and the following section. For those interested in the multistage growth model, the development and application of this model is described in Appendix A to this chapter.

Figure 5-2 illustrates the general pattern of growth assumed by the two-stage growth model to accommodate the expected slowdown in corporate growth. Essentially the model presupposes that dividends grow at rate g, which represents the rate associated with supernormal growth, for N periods. It then assumes that the company grows at a rate g_s, which is in line with that of the general corporate average, sometimes referred to as a standard share rate from $N + 1$ to infinity.

As a matter of interest, it would appear that a 10 percent rate of growth is a representative estimate of the current rate of growth of a standard stock. It is in line with the sustainable growth estimate derived in Table 5-3 for the S&P 500, which might be a useful proxy for a standard share. It's also approximately equal to the rate of growth in dividends for the recent 1975–1980 period, when the rate of dividend growth increased to compensate for higher levels of inflation. Table 5-6 shows the rate of dividend growth in the S&P 500 over various periods from 1950 to 1980.

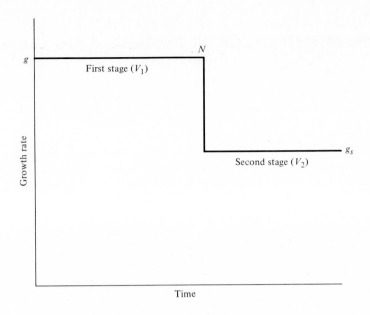

Figure 5-2 Two-stage growth model pattern.

The price of the stock thus becomes a function of two dividend flows: (1) the flow from period 1 to N, which we'll call V_1, and (2) the flow from period $N + 1$ to infinity, referred to as V_2. The total value, or price P, of the stock is then a sum of the two flows:

$$P = V_1 + V_2 \tag{3}$$

The two streams can be evaluated by using the techniques for appraising dividend flows which we covered in Chapter 4. The V_1 component, in particular, can be evaluated by using the most generalized version of the dividend capitalization model. Using D to represent the beginning dividend, g the growth rate during the period of abnormal

Table 5-6 Rate of growth (%) in dividends of the S&P 500

			To			
From	1955	1960	1965	1970	1975	1980
1950	2.2	2.8	4.2	3.9	3.7	4.9
1955		3.4	5.2	4.4	4.1	5.4
1960			6.9	4.6	4.3	5.9
1965				2.9	3.0	5.6
1970					3.2	7.0
1975						10.8

Source: Standard & Poor's Security Price Index Record, Standard and Poor's Corporation, New York, N. Y.

growth, N the period of abnormal growth, and k the discount rate, which is constant over the period, the value for the first stage of growth becomes

$$V_1 = \frac{D(1 + g)}{1 + k} + \frac{D(1 + g)^2}{(1 + k)^2} + \frac{D(1 + g)^3}{(1 + k)^3} + \cdots + \frac{D(1 + g)^N}{(1 + k)^N} = \sum_{i=1}^{N} \frac{D(1 + g)^i}{(1 + k)^i}$$

To estimate the value of the flow from year $N + 1$ to infinity, we can use the same procedure for simplifying a sum of dividends as was used in Chapter 4 to derive the simplified form of the dividend capitalization model. We should note, however, that the initial dividend for applying the procedure is at period N rather than period 1 and has a future value $D(1 + g)^N$ that is discounted back at $(1 + k)^N$ to give it a present value. We again make the standard assumption of constant growth at the rate g_s, which is reasonable since we've assumed that growth was only in line with the corporate average at that time and that the discount rate was the same in the second stage as in the first stage of the valuation process. We then end up with the following expression for the second-stage value:

$$V_2 = D\frac{(1 + g)^N (1 + g_s)}{(1 + k)^N (k - g_s)}$$

The following equation shows the model for valuing growth stocks as a combination of two components: (1) V_1 representing the period of above-average growth, and (2) V_2 representing the period in which the stock has begun to grow at a rate equivalent to that of the average stock.

$$P = \qquad V_1 \quad + \qquad V_2$$
$$= \sum_{i=1}^{N} \frac{D(1 + g)^i}{(1 + k)^i} + D\frac{(1 + g)^N}{(1 + k)^N}\left(\frac{1 + g_s}{k - g_s}\right) \tag{4}$$

Finally, we should note that this formulation is also useful in illustrating that the price of a stock in the future is a function of the projected flow of dividends into the future. In particular, note that the V_2 component of the expression can be considered the discounted price at the rate k of the share at the end of period N; this, in turn, is a function of the flow of dividends expected beyond that time. As a result, an investor with a shorter horizon selling stock at time N realizes return as a combined flow of dividends over the holding period and a value P_N at the end of the holding period N.

$$P = \sum_{i=1}^{N} \frac{D(1 + g)^i}{(1 + k)^i} + \frac{P_N}{(1 + k)^N} \tag{5}$$

Note that we are discounting the price P_N that the investor receives at the end of the holding period N (future value) at the rate $1 + k$ to derive its present worth to the stockholder. This thereby demonstrates that the dividend capitalization model is equivalent as a perpetual flow of dividends or as a flow of dividends and a terminal price, which, in turn, is based on a perpetual flow of dividends. The model is thus helpful for illustrating in a more rigorous fashion the discussion in Chapter 4 of how dividends give value to a stock for an investor with either a short- or long-term horizon.[5]

VALUATING A GROWTH STOCK

We might use the following as an example of the use of the two-stage model for valuating a growth stock. Assume that the growth rate for a hypothetical company in its period of above-average growth is 20 percent per annum and, for purposes of illustration, that the rate lasts for five years. Beyond the fifth year we then make the (heroic) assumption that the rate of growth immediately declines to 10 percent, so that from the sixth year onward the company grows at that rate. The rate of 10 percent is again the same as that derived earlier for the S&P 500 and is presumed to be in line with the growth rate of an average or standard stock. Analysts typically assume that this is the appropriate terminal (final) rate to use in the application of the two-stage or multistage model.

Figure 5-3 is similar to Figure 5-2 except that it illustrates the growth pattern with data pertinent to the hypothetical company of this example. The graph shows the standard two-stage growth formulation, and the input data for this example is inserted into the formulation below. When the discount rate for the stock is assumed to be 15 percent, the price of the hypothetical stock is $33. We can see here that the first stage of growth—the V_1 component—provides a value of $5.70, or 17.3 percent of the total, while the second stage of growth—the V_2 component—provides a value of $27.30, or 82.7 percent of the total. Note that the future value, or price, of the stock in its transition to normal growth would be $55, but when discounted back to present value it becomes $27.30 as noted above.

While solving for a price, or present value, provides a useful illustration of how the formulation works, ordinarily one would know the price of the stock from generally available market quotes and be interested in determining the discount rate. Knowing the price, one then solves for the discount rate by using the trial-and-error method described in Chapter 4 or by resorting to standard computer routines. As shown in Figure 5-3, when the price is $33, the discount rate is 15 percent, while at a price of $41.61 the discount rate is lower, 14 percent, and at a price of $27.75, it is higher, 16 percent, as shown in the formulation below the table.[6] This illustrates that the discount rate moves inversely to the price, just as in the simplified formulation.

Table 5-7 shows the effect that variations in the rate of growth and duration of growth inputs at a fixed discount rate of 15 percent have on the value of the stock. Note that when the rate of growth in a five-year growth period increases, for example, from 20 percent to 30 percent, the price increases to $48, while a decrease in the rate to

---

[5] In this analysis we're assuming that the discount rate k for the stream of dividends in both stages is constant. However, one might well make the case that the risk of the dividend streams differ in the two periods; that is, the risk associated with high dividend growth in period 1 might be considered greater than in period 2. As a result, use of a different discount rate for the two periods would be warranted. We only mention this as a possible refinement, but we will not pursue it further.

[6] We should note that because of rounding, many of these values will not work out precisely if one uses a hand calculator.

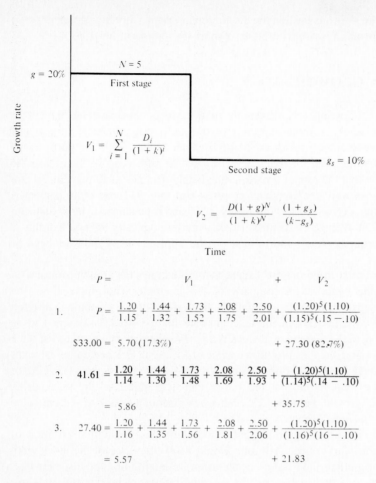

$$P = \qquad V_1 \qquad + \qquad V_2$$

1. $$P = \frac{1.20}{1.15} + \frac{1.44}{1.32} + \frac{1.73}{1.52} + \frac{2.08}{1.75} + \frac{2.50}{2.01} + \frac{(1.20)^5(1.10)}{(1.15)^5(.15 - .10)}$$

$$\$33.00 = 5.70 \ (17.3\%) \qquad\qquad + 27.30 \ (82.7\%)$$

2. $$41.61 = \frac{1.20}{1.14} + \frac{1.44}{1.30} + \frac{1.73}{1.48} + \frac{2.08}{1.69} + \frac{2.50}{1.93} + \frac{(1.20)^5(1.10)}{(1.14)^5(.14 - .10)}$$

$$= 5.86 \qquad\qquad\qquad + 35.75$$

3. $$27.40 = \frac{1.20}{1.16} + \frac{1.44}{1.35} + \frac{1.73}{1.56} + \frac{2.08}{1.81} + \frac{2.50}{2.06} + \frac{(1.20)^5(1.10)}{(1.16)^5(16 - .10)}$$

$$= 5.57 \qquad\qquad\qquad + 21.83$$

Figure 5-3 Two-stage growth model.

10 percent reduces the price to $22. As a matter of interest, note in the latter case that the first- and second-stage growth rates are identical; that is, g becomes a constant, so that valuation can be carried out with the simplified form of the dividend capitalization model. When the length of superior growth (20 percent) increases, for example, from five to seven years, the price increases to $38, and when it is reduced from five to three years, the price declines to $28. Higher and longer growth thus leads to higher prices, while lower and shorter growth leads to lower prices.

As a final note, when estimating dividends and growth rates for the two-stage growth models, we can usefully employ the same sort of analytical techniques described earlier with regard to the simplified version of the dividend capitalization model. The major additional requirement for developing inputs to this model is to assess the duration of the superior rate of growth; that is, there is need to estimate the length of the first stage of superior growth. One framework for helping to assess this

Table 5-7 Two-stage growth model — effect of rate and duration of growth in first stage on stock price

Rate of growth, %	Duration of growth (years)						
	3	5	7	10	12	15	20
10	$22	$22	$ 22	$ 22	$ 22	$ 22	$ 22
15	25	27	29	32	34	37	42
20	28	33	38	46	53	63	84
25	32	40	49	67	81	108	170
30	36	48	64	96	125	184	347
40	44	68	104	192	287	522	1405

transition from rapid to more normal growth is the industrial life cycle, as depicted in Figure 5-4.

The industrial life cycle is a representation of an industry's life as it goes through three distinct stages of growth. The initial pioneering stage, the investment maturity stage, and the stability stage are characterized by varying growth patterns in sales and earnings as the industry is born, matures, and stabilizes over time in the competitive economic environment. The investor might use this to determine the period of superior

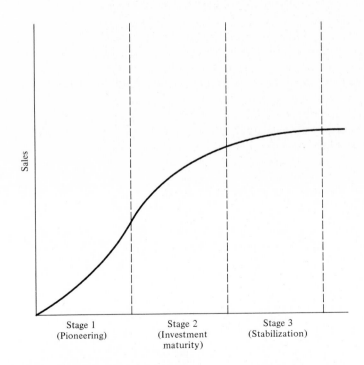

Stage 1
(Pioneering)

Stage 2
(Investment maturity)

Stage 3
(Stabilization)

Figure 5-4 The industrial life cycle.

growth by ascertaining where the company of interest stands with respect to this cycle. For example, a company still in the pioneering stage of development would be expected to have a longer duration of superior growth than one that has entered the expansion phase of development.

While the life cycle theory provides this framework, we should note that it is not without deficiencies. First, the theory is a highly idealized and more or less subjective view of how industries grow and mature. Second, there is no guarantee that a specific industry will systematically pass through the three stages described by the theory. Finally, there is nothing inherent in the theory that provides a way of identifying in advance when an industry will pass from one stage to another.

THE MARKET LINE TECHNIQUE

We'll conclude this chapter by discussing the empirical counterpart to the security market line (SML). It is a technique that provides not only a way of simultaneously considering risk and return but also an explicit link between the theory of valuation and valuation models and the more formal models of the relationship between risk and return (like the SML and APT) growing out of portfolio theory and capital-market theory. It is thus appropriate that we cover this approach here as a way of connecting the material on valuation in this chapter and Chapter 4 with the prior discussion of risk in Chapters 2 and 3.

A growing number of organizations are beginning to implement the market line approach, as it is perhaps the simplest and most direct way of explicitly considering risk and return for equities. The originator of the approach, Wells Fargo Bank, is also representative of the way the approach has been implemented more widely, and therefore its application can most easily be illustrated by referring to the Wells Fargo experience. We'll first describe how the line is constructed and then discuss its three main uses as a means of (1) evaluating the overall attractiveness of the market, (2) assessing the relationship between risk and return in the equity market, and (3) evaluating the relative attractiveness of individual stocks.

In using the market line approach the organization would need to develop return estimates and risk measures for each of the individual stocks in its universe. Wells Fargo monitors a universe of about 340 companies, so there would be need to develop 340 pairs of risk-return estimates. We can most easily illustrate the nature of these estimates by focusing on fifteen companies that are representative of the other 325 companies being monitored. Table 5-8 shows risk and return estimates for each of these fifteen companies as of the end of 1976, along with ticker symbols that will be useful for identifying the securities when they are graphed.

To begin with, the return estimates are generated according to the same dividend-discount model approach that we have been describing in this chapter and the previous one. Wells Fargo, however, uses a three-stage variant of the model, which is described in Appendix A to this chapter, rather than the more simplified forms previously discussed. With respect to inputs, Wells Fargo requires analysts covering the various companies in the universe to develop explicit dividend forecasts. Given these dividend

Table 5-8 Selected stocks — Wells Fargo market line

Expected return-risk sector, 1976

		Expected return	Risk sector
Above-average-expected return stocks			
Raychem	(RYC)	16.7	5
Great Lakes Chemical	(GLC)	15.3	4
Emery Air Freight	(EMY)	14.6	3
ACF Industries	(ACF)	14.4	2
Gulf Oil	(GO)	14.2	1
Average-expected return stocks			
Data General	(DATA)	13.8	5
SEDCO	(SED)	13.7	4
ARA	(ARA)	13.5	3
Bethlehem Steel	(BS)	12.9	2
Texas Utilities	(TXU)	12.1	1
Below-average-expected return stocks			
First Charter	(FCF)	12.3	5
Walt Disney	(DIS)	12.1	4
Xerox	(XRX)	11.7	3
Getty Oil	(GET)	11.7	2
Ralston Purina	(RAL)	11.3	1

estimates and using the three-stage model, returns are generated like those shown for the fifteen companies in the table. Note that the estimated return ranged from a low of 11.3 percent for Ralston Purina to a high of 16.7 percent for Raychem.

As noted before, there is also need to develop a risk estimate for each of the companies in the universe. This risk estimate might simply be a beta using, for example, monthly returns over the last five years and calculated in the way that was illustrated in Chapter 2. Alternatively, one could use statistical techniques, such as those suggested by Blume, to adjust for the tendency of betas of securities to gravitate toward a mean of 1 over time. Finally, one could also use such data as income and balance sheet ratios to adjust for changes in the fundamental riskiness of the company. Wells Fargo calculates betas using historical data but adjusts the betas to reflect any changes in the underlying position of the company.

For ease of comparison Wells Fargo groups companies into five sectors according to riskiness: the 10 percent most risky in the fifth sector, the 20 percent next most risky in the fourth, the next 20 percent in the third, the next 20 percent in the second, and the 30 percent least risky in the first. The first sector has the highest percentage of companies because the larger and presumably more significant companies are in this lowest risk category, while the fifth sector contains the smallest percentage because the smaller and less significant companies are in the highest risk category. The table shows

three companies and their return estimates for each of the five sectors. Raychem, Data
General, and First Charter are in the highest risk sector, while Gulf Oil, Texas Utilities,
and Ralston Purina are in the lowest.

Given risk and return estimates like those in Table 5-8 for each of the companies
in the universe, we could then plot them on a risk-return diagram, as illustrated in
Figure 5-5. The vertical axis refers to return, the horizontal axis to risk, and the
numbers from one to five just above the axis and in the body of the chart represent
midpoints of the risk sectors. The numbers at the bottom of the lines extending down
from the horizontal axis are beta values that bracket the risk sectors. Note that in this
case the chart shows the risk-return plots of the fifteen stocks shown in Table 5-8. For
example, plotting Raychem would be a matter of moving up the vertical axis to
16.7 percent and then across the horizontal axis to the midpoint of risk sector five.
Raychem is a high-risk stock offering a high return, as indicated by its plot on the
diagram. The other fourteen stocks are similarly plotted on the diagram.

If we did this for all 340 stocks in the Wells Fargo universe, we would have a great
number of plots that we could fit a line to. We would, in fact, use statistical
techniques — namely, *regression techniques* — to fit the line to these plots. The line on
the chart in Figure 5-5 has been fitted by regression techniques to the plots for the 340

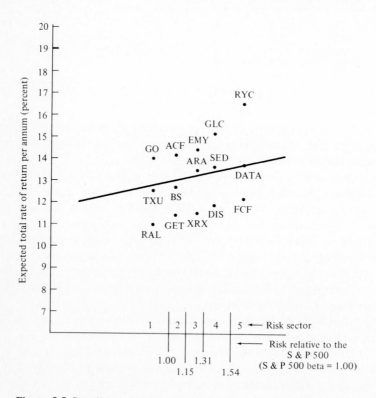

Figure 5-5 Security market line, December 1976. (*Source: Wells Fargo Bank Trust Department,
San Francisco, Calif.*)

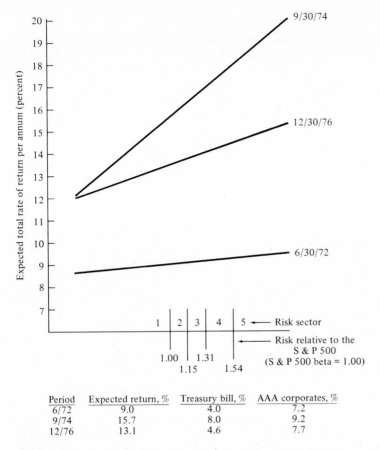

Period	Expected return, %	Treasury bill, %	AAA corporates, %
6/72	9.0	4.0	7.2
9/74	15.7	8.0	9.2
12/76	13.1	4.6	7.7

Figure 5-6 Security market line—historical high and low, 1972–1976. *(Source: Wells Fargo Bank Trust Department, San Francisco, Calif.)*

companies. It is the market line as of the end of 1976 based on the estimates of analysts. Wells Fargo updates the line monthly to incorporate any changes in inputs as well as to reflect the impact of changes in stock prices on the position of the line.

MARKET LINE USES

As noted before, the market line has several uses. We can best illustrate its dual use in monitoring the attractiveness of the overall market and assessing the risk-return trade-off in the equity market by referring to Figure 5-6. It is a risk-return diagram showing the position of the Wells Fargo market line at three different dates—June 1972, September 1974, and December 1976—based on inputs for generating expected returns and expected risks at those dates. The 1972 line reflects the peak of a bull market, the 1974 line reflects the bottom of a bear market, and the 1976 line represents an intermediate market level. The level of the line reflects the general attractiveness or unattractiveness of stocks based on expected returns; the slope of the line reflects the risk-return relationship in the market, allowing the investor to assess the relative attractiveness of high- versus low-risk stocks.[7]

The bottom left-hand portion of Figure 5-6 shows the expected returns of the stocks at each of the three dates. These can be read on the chart by running a vertical line from the beta level of 1 to intersect with the market line and then reading off the vertical (return) axis. For example, running a line up from a beta of 1 we would first encounter the 1972 market line. Reading over to the vertical axis we would see that the return at that date was 9 percent. Continuing to extend the line upward we would next meet the 1976 line, and again reading over to the vertical axis we would see that the return at that date was 13.1 percent. Further extending the line we would encounter the 1974 line, and reading from the vertical axis we would find that the return at that date was 15.7 percent.

Figure 5-6 also shows the returns of treasury bills and AAA corporate bonds at each of these three dates. This allows us to compare equity returns with returns on risk-free security and a high-quality fixed-income instrument, so that we can derive an expected risk premium as well as a premium over the return on corporate bonds. For example, in 1976 the expected premium over treasury bills was 8.5 percent, simply the difference between the expected return of 13.1 percent on stocks and the return of 4.6 percent on treasury bills. We can then compare this with the premium provided by stocks over longer periods of time to help us assess the relative attractiveness of stocks. For this purpose we can refer to the data from the Ibbotsen-Sinquefeld study in Chapter 1, which indicated that stocks earned approximately a 7 percent premium over treasury bills and a 5 percent premium over long-term corporates over the fifty-three-year period 1926–1978.

Note that stocks were offering a return of 9 percent at the June 1972 high level compared with the 15.7 percent offered in the market trough of September 1974. While the 1972 return was in line with the 9 percent earned on average over the 1926–1978 period, the premium over treasury bills of 5 percent was below the longer-term average of 7 percent. Furthermore, the real return on stocks, which tends to equate with the risk premium over time, was below the longer-term average — 5 percent in 1972 compared with the longer-term average of 7 percent. On the other hand, in the 1974 market low the expected risk premium on stocks was 7.7 percent, or higher than the longer-term average. Also, inflationary forces were peaking at that time, so that the real return on stocks was expected to expand over the subsequent period.

Also observe that the market line in 1972 was rather flat. There was little premium for assuming greater risk in the equity market: low-beta stocks were offering virtually the same return as high-beta stocks. This contrasts with the situation in 1974 when higher-beta stocks were offering significantly greater returns than lower-beta stocks. This, of course, was evidenced by the steep upward slope of the market line at that time. This information can be highly useful both in making better asset allocation decisions

---

[7] Wells Fargo draws the market line to extend only over the range of risk-return estimates for securities in the universe of interest. Since no security in the universe had betas of zero or even close to zero, the line does not extend to the vertical axis. As a result, Wells Fargo shows no intercept, but one could easily extend the line to gauge the location of the intercept.

and in structuring the equity portion of the portfolio advantageously. For example, a market line in the position shown for 1972 in Figure 5-6 might indicate the efficacy of shifting from equities to fixed-income securities and perhaps restructuring the equity portion of the portfolio toward lower-beta stocks. Conversely, a market line positioned similarly to the 1974 line might indicate the advantage of shifting more heavily toward equities and perhaps restructuring the equity portion of the portfolio toward higher-beta stocks. We'll discuss the use of the market line for these purposes in greater detail when we cover asset allocation and market timing strategies in Chapter 7.

Meanwhile, we should note that stocks in general, and especially high-risk stocks, proved to be unattractive in June 1972. This is evidenced in Figure 5-6 by the upward movement of the market line as prices dropped and the upward rotation of the line until September 1974 as prices of high-risk stocks dropped even faster than the average. Conversely, stocks in general, and especially high-risk stocks, proved to be quite attractive in September 1974. We can again see this in the downward movement of the line as well as the downward rotation of the line to its position at the end of 1976. This occurred as stock prices rose in general and high-risk stocks rose even faster than the average.

EVALUATION OF INDIVIDUAL SECURITIES

As noted before, the market line is used to assess the relative attractiveness of individual stocks.[8] Recall from Chapter 3 that in the SML context, high-risk stocks are expected to offer high returns by virtue of their risk level, while low risk stocks are expected to offer low returns, again by virtue of their risk level. The question is whether the stock — low-risk or high-risk — is offering returns more or less than proportional to their risk. Figure 5-7, which reproduces Figure 3-4 in Chapter 3, illustrates the framework for this analysis. In particular, it shows that hypothetical stocks X, Y, and Z are overvalued, stocks A, B, and C are undervalued, and stocks M, N, and O are appropriately valued in the market line context.

We can now illustrate this analysis with some actual data by referring back to Table 5-8, showing the fifteen stocks used to demonstrate the construction of the market line. Note that these fifteen stocks were grouped into three broad classes in terms of expected return: (1) above average, (2) average, and (3) below average. Also, each of the five stocks in each group represents one of the risk classes. The group at the top of the table shows above-average returns for their risk class and are therefore

---

[8] We should note here that the market line we are using as a benchmark for security selection is fitted to the individual risk-return plots by means of a regression equation, similar to the way that researchers have fitted ex post data in testing the SML relationship (see Chapter 3). The fitted relationship here differs from that used by researchers to test the SML relationship in that the risk-return plots are forecast (ex ante) values for these variables rather than historically derived. Use of ex ante variables is, of course, more in keeping with the SML, which, as we've noted, is an ex ante rather than an ex post relationship. Presumably, one might well use this data to develop superior tests of the relationship than have been possible in the past; however, developers of this technique have not emphasized this use and have used it, rather, primarily as a means of improving portfolio management.

plotted above the forecasted market line.[9] The group at the bottom of the table shows below-average returns and are thus plotted below the market line. Finally, the group in the middle of the table shows about average returns for their risk class and are plotted on the market line.

Ideally one would prefer to construct a portfolio of stocks from those that plot above the market line. To ensure maximum return at a given risk level, we used the simplified portfolio optimization techniques as developed by Elton and Gruber and illustrated in the appendix to Chapter 8.[10] Use of these techniques provides us with the weightings for the five stocks of above-average attraction shown in Table 5-9.

Note that the portfolio has a weighted average (expected) return of 14.6 percent, along with a portfolio beta of 1.08, and would therefore plot above the market line illustrated in Figure 5-8. This portfolio would be offering a 1.4 percentage points greater return than a portfolio plotted on the market line — in other words a portfolio constructed of stocks of only average attraction. In the language of the capital-asset pricing model (CAPM) the portfolio would have a positive expected alpha.

Realizing this hoped-for positive excess return would depend, in practice, on whether there was actual mispricing in the marketplace or whether the existence of securities plotting off the market line merely represented (1) misestimated returns for individual securities and/or (2) a mistaken risk measure. The reader may have deduced from the discussion on estimating inputs to the valuation model and the attendant difficulties that there are bound to be errors emanating from this source. Moreover, our earlier discussion also indicated that beta is an incomplete measure of risk, so that it, too, is often a cause of error. Despite these potential errors we can still develop some perspective on the degree of mispricing as well as the opportunity for developing above-average performance by measuring the actual performance of this kind of strat-

[9]The line we are using here is fitted to the ex ante risk-return values for individual stocks. This is a good property when using the line for stock selection, as the least-squares regression technique generally results in a distribution where half the points (individual stocks) will be above the line and the other half below the line. As a result, one obtains a measure, or benchmark, of the relative attractiveness of stocks that does not depend on the movements of the market; that is, presumably those above the line will outperform those below the line regardless of the direction of the market.

An alternative way to use the line would be to assess the risk-free rate, determine the expected return on the overall market, and then connect the two points to form the forecast market line. The line constructed in this way would not, however, ensure that an equal number of stocks would plot above and below the line. In fact, it's likely that an unequal number will plot either above or below, so that the relative positioning of the stocks would depend on the forecast of the risk-free return and the market return.

As a result, determining the relative attractiveness of stocks would depend not only on the quality of the inputs in estimating the risk and return of individual stocks but also on the accuracy of the forecast of the risk-free rate and the market return. For those who possess some capability in forecasting these returns, the use of the market line in the latter way may well be preferable. However, for those who do not wish to forecast market returns, either for lack of predictive accuracy or for avoidance of extra risk, the approach that we've outlined in the body of this chapter seems more appropriate. In fact, we'll see in Chapter 6 that this process works quite well within the context of an investment process that is primarily oriented toward achieving superior overall performance by focusing exclusively on stock selection.

[10]Recall that this method of generating an optimum portfolio relies on the assumption that the single-index model is an appropriate description of the return-generating process for stocks. We've seen, however, that this model is an oversimplification, and a multi-index model that more adequately describes the return-generating process is needed to solve the portfolio selection problem most satisfactorily. For ease of exposition, however, we've used the single-index model.

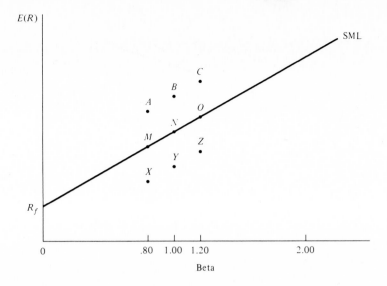

Figure 5-7 The market line and security valuation.

egy over time. We'll discuss ways of measuring this as well as the results of the evaluation in the next chapter.

CONCLUSION

This chapter has discussed the practical problems of using valuation models to develop explicit returns for common stocks. We've emphasized the importance of developing inputs of the highest quality for the valuation model and illustrated a framework of analysis for developing such inputs. We concluded by showing how the outputs of such

Table 5-9 Above-average return portfolio
Risk objective of 1.08

Stock	Weight	Beta	Expected return, %
Raychem	.08	1.65	16.7
Great Lakes Chemical	.09	1.40	15.3
Emery Air Freight	.17	1.25	14.6
ACF Industries	.26	1.05	14.4
Gulf Oil	.40	.85	14.2
Above-average return portfolio	1.00	1.08	14.6
Market line portfolio	—	1.08	13.2
Return differential	—	—	1.4

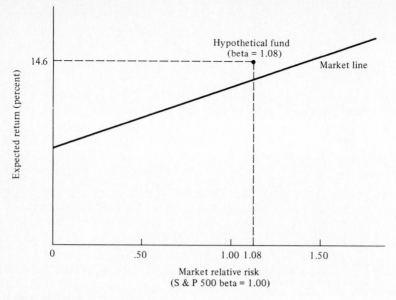

Figure 5-8 Risk-return diagram.

a valuation model could be cast in a risk-return framework that has use with regard to both overall market valuation and individual stock selection. We'll see in the next chapter that this method has been used as a component of an actual on-line stock selection process that has, in fact, been shown to have facility in distinguishing between attractive and unattractive stocks.

APPENDIX A THE THREE-STAGE DIVIDEND CAPITALIZATION MODEL

Molodovsky, May, and Chottiner (see references) developed the three-stage dividend capitalization model. The two-stage and three-stage dividend capitalization models differ essentially in the way that they allow for a shift in above-normal growth to growth in line with the corporate average. The two-stage model assumes an abrupt one step down in the growth rate, while the three-stage model, because of the provision of a middle stage, allows for a gradual tapering in the growth rate. This middle stage offers a generally more realistic way of portraying the real-world pattern of growth and decline than the two-stage model. At the same time, it allows the flexibility of modeling the two-stage pattern where needed by allowing the middle stage of growth to be zero. For these reasons the three-stage model has been the most popular for practical application.

Figure 5-A1 illustrates the general pattern of growth portrayed by the three-stage model. It shows a hypothetical company that is growing at a rate of 20 percent in the initial period N_g, assumed to last five years, after which the growth rate begins to decline. The model assumes that this growth rate declines linearly over a ten-year period N_d to a 10 percent terminal growth rate. This linear decline means that the growth rate is simply reduced by 1 percent per annum, so that the company would grow at a rate of 20 percent in the fifth year, 19 percent in the sixth year, 18 percent in the seventh, and so on, until the growth rate finally declines to 10 percent rate in the fifteenth year. The 10 percent terminal growth rate is assumed to be in line with the general corporate average and, again, is a current estimate for the S&P 500 from Table 5-3.

The bottom part of the Figure 5-A1 shows the general formulation for the three-stage model, and Figure 5-A2 provides a more elaborate illustration of the model. For ease of exposition the formula assumes that the initial dividend rate D_0 is $1. To determine the price of a stock where the dividend differs from $1, simply multiply the actual dividend by the derived price (or, in this sense, dividend multiplier). Note that the first and third components of the three-stage model are essentially identical to the two-stage model. In particular, the first stage merely represents compounding of the

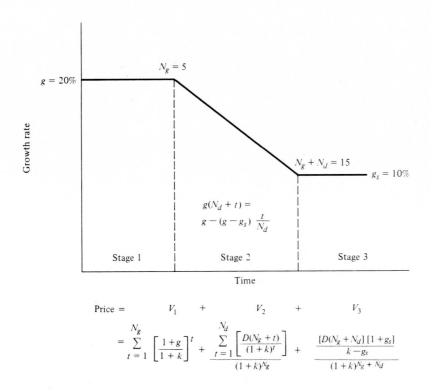

Figure 5-A1 Three-stage growth model.

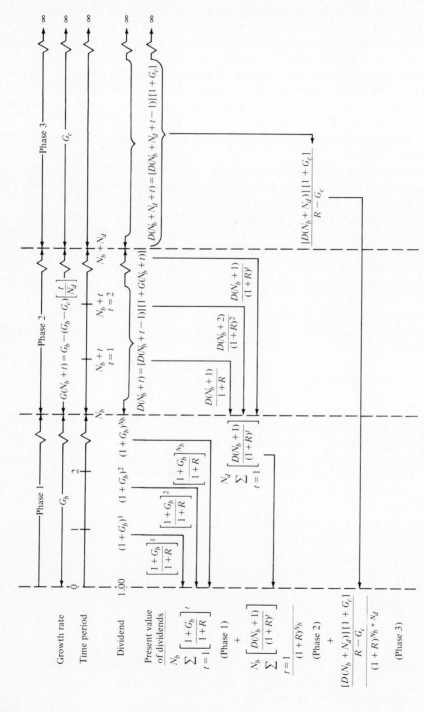

Figure 5-A2 Graphic derivation of the three-stage dividend discount model. *(Source: Russ Fuller, "Programming the Three-Phase Dividend Discount Model," Journal of Portfolio Management, Summer 1979.)*

dividend at the supernormal rate and discounting to obtain a value for the supernormal growth phase. The third stage represents the value of the stock when it settles into a growth rate in line with the standard phase. Here the dividend at the end of both the superior and declining growth stages is capitalized and discounted back to present value over both stages.

The three-stage model differs from the two-stage model in requiring a middle segment V_2 to represent the phase when the superior growth rate is declining to that of an average (or standard) stock. The formulation indicates that we take the dividend at the end of the first phase of growth and apply a diminishing growth rate to it over the period of decline. The formulation in the body of the Figure 5-A2 shows how to calculate the appropriate growth rate to use for each period of the declining growth phase. For example, in the fifth year of the declining growth phase, the rate of growth would be

$$g - (g - g_s)\frac{t}{N_d} = 20 - (20 - 10)5/10 = 15 \text{ percent}$$

These dividends are in turn discounted back to derive a present value of the stock for the second phase of growth.

While the formulation to represent this model is more elaborate than that for the two-stage model, the burden of estimation is not significantly greater. In particular, the method would normally require for the first stage explicit estimates of the company's dividend for each of the first five years of the planning period or, alternatively, merely an estimate of the supernormal rate of growth in this initial phase. The second stage would call for an estimate of the rate of growth of the company at the beginning of the period as well as the number of years over which that rate is expected to decline to grow in line with the general corporate average. The third-stage input would be an estimate of the rate of growth of the standard share or, alternatively, the growth rate of the general corporate average.

These kinds of inputs can reasonably be expected either because they are in keeping with the normal tasks of analysts or can be developed by making some standard assumptions. For example, developing explicit dividend estimates for the first stage is a task that can be reasonably expected of an analyst, just as five-year projected income and balance sheet data are the sorts of information that the analyst should be providing as a matter of course. The major difficulty would only be recasting the information in a suitable form for the model. In addition, estimates of the way that above-average rates of growth will taper to be in line with the economy can be facilitated by using some rather simple rules of thumb. Finally, the third-stage model input becomes a matter of providing an estimate based on general economic analysis of the likely rate of general corporate growth.

To illustrate how the formulation can be used to derive an expected return, Table 5-A1 shows the calculation for the hypothetical stock illustrated in Figure 5-A1. Note that at a price of $33 we would derive, by the same process of trial and error illustrated with the two-stage model, an expected return (discount rate) of 16.5 percent, compared with an expected return of 15 percent when we used the two-stage model to

Table 5-A1   Calculating the discount rate for the three-stage model

$$V_1 = \frac{1.20}{1.165} + \frac{1.44}{(1.165)^2} + \frac{1.73}{(1.165)^3} + \frac{2.07}{(1.165)^4} + \frac{2.49}{(1.165)^5} = 5.46$$

$$V_2 = \frac{2.96}{(1.165)^6} + \frac{3.49}{(1.165)^7} + \frac{4.09}{(1.165)^8} + \frac{4.74}{(1.165)^9} + \frac{5.45}{(1.165)^{10}} + \frac{6.22}{(1.165)^{11}} + \frac{7.03}{(1.165)^{12}}$$

$$+ \frac{7.87}{(1.165)^{13}} + \frac{8.73}{(1.165)^{14}} + \frac{9.61}{(1.165)^{15}} = 11.29$$

$$V_3 = \left[\frac{10.57}{(.165 - .10)}\right]\left[\frac{1}{(1.165)^{15}}\right] = 16.24$$

$$\text{Price} = V_1 + V_2 + V_3$$
$$= 5.46 + 11.29 + 16.24 = \$33$$

determine the value for this hypothetical stock. The assumption of a middle stage —
declining growth phase — adds 1.5 percent to the return of the stock.

Using the formulation in Table A-1 is tedious, however, as it entails generating the
dividend flow and, most importantly, determining the appropriate discount rate by trial
and error. Fortunately, there are computer programs, such as the one illustrated in
Figures 5-A3 and 5-A4, which greatly ease the task of calculating discount rates. Figure 5-A3 illustrates the use of the program, while Figure 5-A4 gives the program code.
This program is written in FORTRAN and should be generally usable on most computers, including personal computers; conversion to BASIC would be necessary for use
on most hand calculators.

To estimate the appropriate discount rate, one only needs to generate the required
inputs shown in Figure 5-A3. Given these inputs, the program would then quickly solve
for the same discount rate, 16.54 percent, obtained by the tedious method. Note that
the figure shows the present values of the dividend stream for each of the three stages
to assist in evaluating the impact of changes in input variables. In addition, the program
has the capability of solving for a price if the discount rate is known. This option is
designated *dividend multiplier*.

Figure 5-A3 Program code: three-stage dividend discount model.

```
SOLVE FOR DIVIDEND MULT.        (DIVM)
      OR  DISCOUNT RATE         (RATE)
      OR  END                   (END )
RATE
ENTER ALL DATA AS XXX.XX ON ONE LINE IN ORDER:
PHASE 1 GROWTH RATE
PHASE 1 GROWTH PERIOD
PHASE 2 GROWTH PERIOD
PHASE 3 GROWTH RATE
LATEST DIVIDEND
DIVIDEND MULT.
(EXAMPLE: 20.00   5.00 10.00 10.00   1.00 33.00)

20.00   5.00 10.00 10.00   1.00 33.00
                          ASSUMPTIONS & RESULTS
          3 PHASE DIVIDEND DISCOUNT MODEL SOLVED FOR DISCOUNT RATE

PHASE 1 GROWTH PERIOD          5      DIVIDEND MULTIPLIER:
PHASE 1 GROWTH RATE        20.00      PHASE 1 VALUE              5.46
PHASE 2 GROWTH PERIOD         10      PHASE 2 VALUE             11.29
PHASE 3 GROWTH RATE        10.00      PHASE 3 VALUE             16.24
DIVIDEND                    1.00      TOTAL                     33.00
PRICE                      33.00
DISCOUNT RATE              16.54


                          TIME PATH
          3 PHASE DIVIDEND DISCOUNT MODEL SOLVED FOR DISCOUNT RATE

          TIME        GROWTH RATE           DIVIDEND
          ----        -----------           --------
PH.1        1            20.00                1.20
            2            20.00                1.44
            3            20.00                1.73
            4            20.00                2.07
            5            20.00                2.49


          ----        -----------           --------
PH.2        6            19.00                2.96
            7            18.00                3.49
            8            17.00                4.09
            9            16.00                4.74
           10            15.00                5.45
           11            14.00                6.22
           12            13.00                7.03
           13            12.00                7.87
           14            11.00                8.73
           15            10.00                9.61


          ----        -----------           --------
PH.3       16            10.00               10.57

MORE ? (OR END)
END
```

Figure 5-A4 Program code: three-stage dividend discount model.

```
C                                                                    00010001
C         MAIN ROUTINE FOR COMPUTING THE THREE PHASE DIVIDEND DISCOUNT MODEL00020001
C                                                                    00030001
          REAL DIVS(99),GRS(99),PHASE(3),                            00040001
        X    M1/'MORE'/,E1/'END '/,M2/'M   '/,E2/'E   '/             00050001
C                                                                    00060001
   10     CALL   INPUT (GB,NB,ND,GC,R,DIVM,DO,IT)                    00070001
          GRS(1)           = GB                                      00080001
          IF (NB + ND + 1.GT.99) GO TO 998                          00090007
          GRS(NB + ND + 1) = GC                                      00100001
          IF (IT.EQ.1) CALL PHASER(NB,ND,R,DIVM,DO,PO,PHASE,DIVS,GRS) 00110001
          IF (IT.EQ.2) CALL FINDR (NB,ND,R,DIVM,DO,PO,PHASE,DIVS,GRS) 00120001
          IF (IT.EQ.3) GO TO 999                                    00130001
          CALL   OUTPUT(NB,ND,R,DIVM,DO,PO,PHASE,DIVS,GRS,IT)       00140001
C                                                                    00150001
   20     WRITE(6,1001) M1,E1                                       00160001
          READ(5,1002) ANS                                          00170001
          IF (ANS.EQ.M1.OR.ANS.EQ.M2)  GO TO 10                     00180001
          IF (ANS.NE.E1.AND.ANS.NE.E2) GO TO 20                     00190001
          GO TO 999                                                 00200008
C                                                                    00210001
 1001 FORMAT(1X,A4,' ? (OR ',A3,')')                                00220001
 1002 FORMAT(A4)                                                    00230001
 1003 FORMAT(' PH.1 GROWTH OF',I4,' + PH.2 GROWTH OF',I4,' IS TOO BIG.')00240007
C                                                                    00250001
  998     WRITE(6,1003) NB,ND                                       00260007
          GO TO 10                                                  00270007
  999     RETURN                                                    00280001
          END                                                       00290001
```

```
          SUBROUTINE FINDR (NB,ND,R,DIVM,DO,PO,PHASE,DIVS,GRS)      00680001
C                                                                    00690001
C         SOLVING FOR THE DISCOUNT RATE                             00700001
C                                                                    00710001
          INTEGER T                                                 00720001
          REAL PHASE(1),DIVS(1),GRS(1)                              00730001
C                                                                    00740001
C INITIALIZE                                                         00750001
C                                                                    00760001
          TOLER = .000001                                           00770001
          IF (DIVM.LT.0) JSIGN =  1                                 00780001
          IF (DIVM.GT.0) JSIGN = -1                                 00790001
          TDIVM = DIVM + .01*JSIGN*(-1)                             00800001
          DIF   = TDIVM-DIVM                                        00810001
          RADD  = .1                                                00820001
C                                                                    00830001
C FIND R TO TOLERANCE LEVEL                                          00840001
C                                                                    00850001
    5     R = R + RADD*JSIGN                                        00860001
          OLDT  = TDIVM                                             00870001
          CALL          PHASER(NB,ND,R,TDIVM,DO,PO,PHASE,DIVS,GRS)  00880001
          OLDDIF = DIF                                              00890001
          DIF    = TDIVM-DIVM                                       00900001
          IF (ABS(OLDDIF-DIF).LE.TOLER) GO TO 80                    00910001
```

Figure 5A-4 (*Continued*)

```
C                                                                    00920001
C TEST FOR DIRECTION CHANGE                                          00930001
C                                                                    00940001
          SWITCH = 0                                                 00950001
      IF((OLDT.GT.DIVM.AND.JSIGN.LT.0).OR.(OLDT.LT.DIVM.AND.JSIGN.GT.0))00960001
     X    SWITCH = 1                                                 00970001
      IF (OLDT)   50,60,60                                           00980001
 50   IF (SWITCH)  5,70,5                                            00990001
 60   IF (SWITCH) 70,5,70                                            01000001
 70   JSIGN = JSIGN * (-1)                                           01010001
      RADD = RADD/10                                                 01020001
      GO TO 5                                                        01030001
 80   DIVM = TDIVM                                                   01040001
C             '                                                      01050001
 999  RETURN                                                         01060001
      END                                                            01070001
```

```
      SUBROUTINE PHASER(NB,ND,R,DIVM,DO,PO,PHASE,DIVS,GRS)            00300001
C                                                                    00310001
C     SOLVING FOR THE DIVIDEND MULTIPLIER                            00320001
C                                                                    00330001
      INTEGER T                                                      00340001
      REAL PHASE(1),DIVS(1),GRS(1)                                   00350001
C             '                                                      00360001
      NBPLND = NB+ND                                                 00370001
      NBPND1 = NBPLND + 1                                            00380001
C PHASE1                  .                                          00390001
      DIVS(1) = 1*(1+GRS(1))                                         00400001
      PHASE(1) = ((1+GRS(1))/(1+R))**1                               00410001
      IF (NB.LE.1) GO TO 15                                          00420001
      DO 10 T = 2,NB                                                 00430001
      GRS(T) = GRS(1)                                                00440001
      DIVS(T) = DIVS(T-1)*(1+GRS(T))                                 00450001
      PHASE(1) = PHASE(1) +((1+GRS(1))/(1+R))**T                     00460001
 10   CONTINUE                                                       00470001
C PHASE2                                                             00480001
 15   PHASE(2) = 0.0                                                 00490001
      IF (ND.LE.0) GO TO 30                                          00500001
      DO 20 T = 1,ND                                                 00510001
      NBT = NB + T                                                   00520001
      GRS(NBT) = GRS(1)-(GRS(1)-GRS(NBPND1))*(FLOAT(T)/FLOAT(ND))    00530001
      DIVS(NBT) = (DIVS(NBT-1))*(1+GRS(NBT))                         00540001
      PHASE(2) = PHASE(2) + DIVS(NBT)/((1+R)**T)                     00550001
 20   CONTINUE                                                       00560001
      PHASE(2) = PHASE(2) / (1+R)**NB                                00570001
C PHASE3                                                             00580001
 30   PHASE(3) = ((DIVS(NBPLND)*(1+GRS(NBPND1))) / (R-GRS(NBPND1)))  00590001
     X           / ((1+R)**NBPLND)                                   00600001
      DIVS(NBPND1)=  DIVS(NBPLND)*(1+GRS(NBPND1))                    00610001
C DIVIDEND MULTIPLIER                                                00620001
      DIVM = PHASE(1) + PHASE(2) + PHASE(3)                          00630001
      PO = DO*DIVM                                                   00640001
C             '                                                      00650001
 999  RETURN                                                         00660001
      END                                                            00670001
```

Figure 5A-4 *(Continued)*

```
      SUBROUTINE INPUT(GB,NB,ND,GC,R,DIVM,DO,IT)                        01080004
C                                                                       01090001
C     OBTAIN NECESSARY INPUTS                                           01100001
C                                                                       01110001
      REAL ARRAY(10),                                                   01120012
     XTANS(3)/'DIVM','RATE','END '/,     TANS2(3)/'D   ','R   ','E '/,   01130012
     X ALD(4)/'LATE','ST D','IVID','END '/,A1(3)/' 16.','5   ','1.00'/,  01140012
     X ADR(4)/'DISC','OUNT',' RAT','E   '/,                             01150012
     X ADM(4)/'DIVI','DEND',' MUL','T.  '/,A2(3)/' 1.','00 3','3.00'/    01160012
C                                                                       01170001
 10   WRITE(6,1001) ADM,TANS(1),ADR,TANS(2),TANS(3),TANS(3)             01180013
      READ(5,1002)  ANS                                                 01190001
      IT = 0                                                            01200001
      DO 20 I = 1,3                                                     01210001
      IF (ANS.EQ.TANS(I).OR.ANS.EQ.TANS2(I)) IT = I                     01220012
 20   CONTINUE                                                          01230001
      IF (IT.LE.0) GO TO 10                                             01240001
      IF (IT.EQ.3) GO TO 999                                           01250001
C                                                                       01260001
      IF (IT.EQ.1) WRITE(6,1003) ADR,ALD,A1                            01270012
      IF (IT.EQ.2) WRITE(6,1003) ALD,ADM,A2                            01280012
      READ(5,1004) GB,ANB,AND,GC,A,B                                    01290006
      GB = GB/100.                                                      01300006
      NB = ANB                                                          01310006
      ND = AND                                                          01320006
      IF (NB.LT.1) GO TO 998                                           01330001
      GC = GC/100.                                                      01340001
      IF (IT.EQ.1) R   = A/100.                                         01350001
      IF (IT.EQ.1) DO  = B                                              01360001
      IF (IT.EQ.2) DO  = A                                              01370001
      IF (IT.EQ.2) DIVM = B                                            01380001
      GO TO 999                                                         01390004
C                                                                       01400001
 1001 FORMAT(' SOLVE FOR ',4A4,T35,' (',A4,')',                         01410003
     X       /'        OR  ',4A4,T35,' (',A4,')',                       01420002
     X       /'        OR  ', A4,T35,' (',A4,')')                       01430001
 1002 FORMAT(A4)                                                        01440001
 1003 FORMAT(' ENTER ALL DATA AS XXX.XX ON ONE LINE IN ORDER:',         01450011
     X /' PHASE 1 GROWTH RATE',/' PHASE 1 GROWTH PERIOD',               01460001
     X /' PHASE 2 GROWTH PERIOD',/' PHASE 3 GROWTH RATE',2(/1X,4A4),    01470009
     X /' (EXAMPLE: 20.00  5.00 10.00 10.00',3A4,')')                   01480012
 1004 FORMAT(6F6.3)                                                     01490011
 1005 FORMAT(' ERROR: ',A4)                                             01500001
C                                                                       01510001
 998  WRITE(6,1005) ANS                                                 01520001
      GO TO 10                                                          01530001
 999  RETURN                                                            01540001
      END                                                               01550001
```

```
      SUBROUTINE OUTPUT (NB,ND,R,DIVM,DO,PO,PHASE,DIVS,GRS,IT)          01560001
C                                                                       01570001
C     PRODUCE ONE OF TWO OUTPUTS                                        01580001
C                                                                       01590001
      REAL PHASE(1),DIVS(1),GRS(1),PS(3)/'PH.1','PH.2','PH.3'/,         01600001
     X                    AC1(5)/'DIVI','DEND',' MUL','TIPL','IER '/,    01610001
     X                    AC2(5)/'DISC','OUNT',' RAT','E   ',' '/        01620001
```

Figure 5A-4 *(Continued)*

```
                                                                   01630001
C      I                                                           01640001
       NB1       = NB + 1                                          01650001
       NBPLND    = NB + ND                                         01660001
       J         = NB + ND + 1                                     01670001
       DO 10 I = 1,J                                               01680001
   10  GRS(I)    = GRS(I) * 100                                    01690001
C                                                                  01700001
       R2= R  * 100                                                01710001
       IF (IT.EQ.1) WRITE(6,1001)                                  01720001
    X  AC1,NB,GRS(1),PHASE(1),ND,PHASE(2),GRS(J),PHASE(3),DO,DIVM,PO,R201730001
       IF (IT.EQ.2) WRITE(6,1001)                                  01740001
    X  AC2,NB,GRS(1),PHASE(1),ND,PHASE(2),GRS(J),PHASE(3),DO,DIVM,PO,R201750001
       IF (IT.EQ.1) WRITE(6,1002) AC1                              01770001
       IF (IT.EQ.2) WRITE(6,1002) AC2                              01780001
       WRITE(6,1003)                                               01790001
       WRITE(6,1004) PS(1),((I,GRS(I),DIVS(I)),I=1,NB)             01800001
       WRITE(6,1003)                                               01810001
       IF (ND.GT.0) WRITE(6,1004) PS(2),((I,GRS(I),DIVS(I)),I=NB1,NBPLND)01820010
       WRITE(6,1003)                                               01830001
       WRITE(6,1004) PS(3),  J,GRS(J),DIVS(J)                      01840001
C                                                                  01850001
 1001  FORMAT(T32,'ASSUMPTIONS & RESULTS  ',                       01860001
    X  /T10,'3 PHASE DIVIDEND DISCOUNT MODEL SOLVED FOR ',5A4,     01870001
    X//' PHASE 1 GROWTH PERIOD',T25,I10,T40,'DIVIDEND MULTIPLIER:',01880001
    X /' PHASE 1 GROWTH RATE',T25,F10.2,T40,'PHASE 1 VALUE',T65,F10.2,01890001
    X /' PHASE 2 GROWTH PERIOD',T25,I10,T40,'PHASE 2 VALUE',T65,F10.2,01900001
    X /' PHASE 3 GROWTH RATE',T25,F10.2,T40,'PHASE 3 VALUE',T65,F10.2,01910001
    X /' DIVIDEND',          T25,F10.2,T40,'TOTAL',T65,F10.2,      01920001
    X /' PRICE',             T25,F10.2,                            01930001
    X /' DISCOUNT RATE',     T25,F10.2)                            01940001
 1002  FORMAT(T32,'TIME PATH',                                     01950001
    X      /T10,'3 PHASE DIVIDEND DISCOUNT MODEL SOLVED FOR ',5A4, 01960001
    X      //T10,'TIME',T20,'GROWTH RATE',T40,'DIVIDEND')          01970001
 1003  FORMAT(T10,'----',T20,'-----------',T40,'--------')         01980001
 1004  FORMAT(1X,A4,T10,I4,T20,F11.2,T40,F8.2,                     01990001
    X      100(/T10,I4,T20,F11.2,T40,F8.2))                        02000001
C      '                                                           02010001
  999  RETURN                                                      02020001
       END                                                         02030001
```

PROBLEMS

1 Assume that because of increased competition and energy price changes GM's normal profit margin is now 11 percent. Calculate GM's normalized rate of return for 1974, as well as its normal earnings and projected sustainable rate of growth.

2 Calculate the sustainable growth for a company that has a policy of paying out 40 percent of its earnings and has shown the following financial characteristics over the past three years.

Year	M	I	L	V
1978	8%	1.9	1.30	.55
1979	12	2.6	1.60	.45
1980	10	2.1	1.30	.50

3 Determine the discount rate for a company paying a $1 dividend that is expected to grow at a rate of 30 percent per annum for the next five years and then grow at a rate of 10 percent beyond that period. Assume a 16 percent discount rate (required return) for the stock.

4 Determine the discount rate for the company in the previous problem using the previously determined price, but assume that the period of superior growth is (a) three years and (b) seven years.

5 Assume that a stock is expected to grow at a rate of 25 percent over the next five years and then decline over the next three years (years 6 through 8) to a growth rate of 10 percent. Determine the price of the stock that is currently paying a $1 dividend and has a 17 percent discount rate.

6 Determine the discount rate for the stock in the previous problem, but where the company is now expected to grow at a rate of 30 percent for five years and then decline to a growth rate in line with the economy (10 percent) over the next five years (years 6 through 10). Use the previously determined price.

7 Determine the optimum portfolio weights for the companies in Table 5-7 using the Elton and Gruber method, as shown in Appendix A to Chapter 8, but assume that Raychem has an expected return of 18.5 percent, Great Lakes Chemical a return of 17 percent, and Gulf Oil a return of 13.7 percent.

SELECTED REFERENCES

Babcock, G.: "The Concept of Sustainable Growth," *Financial Analysts Journal,* May–June 1970, pp. 108–114.

Babcock, G.: "The Roots of Risk and Return," *Financial Analysts Journal,* January–February 1980, pp. 56–63.

Baylis, R., and S. Bhirud: "Growth Stock Analysis," *Financial Analysts Journal,* July–August 1973, pp. 63–71.

Beaver, W., P. Ketler, and M. Scholes: "The Association Between Market Determined and Accounting Determined Risk Measures," *Accounting Review,* October 1970, pp. 654–682.

Bernstein, Peter L.: "Growth Companies vs Growth Stocks," *Harvard Business Review,* September–October 1956, pp. 88–95.

Blume, Marshall: "Betas and their Regression Tendencies," *Journal of Finance,* June 1975, pp. 785–795.

Cohen, J., E. Zinbarg, and A. Zeikel: *Investment Analysis and Portfolio Management,* Richard D. Irwin, Homewood, Ill., 1973.

Durand, David: "Growth Stocks and the Petersburg Paradox," *Journal of Finance,* September 1956, pp. 305–315.

Farrell, J.: "Modern Portfolio Theory and the Common Stock Investment Process," Heubner Foundation Lecture Series in Life Insurance Investment, 1976.

Fouse, W.: "Risk, Liquidity and Common Stock Prices," *Financial Analysts Journal,* May–June 1976, pp. 35–45, and January–February 1977, pp. 40–45.

Fuller, Russ: "Programming the Three-Phase Dividend Discount Model," *Journal of Portfolio Management,* Summer 1979, pp. 28–32.

Gordon, Myron: *The Investment, Financing, and Valuation of the Corporation.* Richard D. Irwin, Homewood, Ill., 1962.

Graham, B., D. Dodd, and S. Cottle: *Security Analysis,* 4th ed., McGraw-Hill, New York, 1962.

Hamada, Robert: "The Effect of the Firm's Capital Structure on the Systematic Risk of Common Stocks," *Journal of Finance,* May 1971, pp. 435–452.

Holt, Charles C.: "The Influence of Growth Duration on Share Price," *Journal of Finance,* September 1961, pp. 465–475.

Jahnke, William: "The Growth Stock Mania," *Financial Analysts Journal,* May–June 1973, pp. 65–69.

———: "What's Behind Stock Prices?," *Financial Analysts Journal,* September–October 1975, pp. 69–76.

Malkiel, Burton G.: "Equity Yields, Growth, and the Structure of Share Prices," *American Economic Review,* December 1963, pp. 467–494.

Molodovsky, Nicholas, C. May, and S. Chottiner: "Common Stock Valuation: Theory and Tables," *Financial Analysts Journal,* March–April 1965, pp. 104–123.

Porter, Michael: "Industry Structure and Competitive Strategy: Keys to Profitability," *Financial Analysts Journal,* July–August 1980, pp. 30–41.

Price, Lee: "Choosing Between Growth and Yield," *Financial Analysts Journal,* July–August 1979, pp. 57–67.

Rosenberg, B., and W. McKibben: "The Prediction of Systematic and Specific Risk in Common Stocks," *Journal of Financial and Quantitative Analysis,* March 1973, pp. 317–333.

Thompson, Donald: "Sources of Systematic Risk in Common Stocks," *Journal of Business,* April 1978, pp. 173–188.

Wendt, Paul E.: "Current Growth Stock Valuation Methods," *Financial Analysts Journal,* March–April, 1965, pp. 91–103.

PART

TWO

MANAGING THE
EQUITY PORTFOLIO

DISCIPLINED STOCK SELECTION

INTRODUCTION

So far we have provided basic background and analytical concepts with respect to capital-market behavior, portfolio analysis, capital-market theory, and valuation models. The next five chapters will build on these concepts, introduce some new ones, and illustrate how these can be applied to practical portfolio management. The first three chapters are primarily concerned with analyzing the domestic equity investment process, with Chapter 6 focusing on stock selection, Chapter 7 on asset allocation and market timing, and Chapter 8 on opportunities associated with major groups. Chapter 9 introduces and discusses foreign equity investment, building on techniques already described with regard to domestic equity investing but allowing a broadening of the investment horizon. Chapter 10 discusses bond analysis and management.

As noted, this is the first in a series of three chapters on the equity investment process and is primarily concerned with stock selection. It begins by describing active and passive strategies of investing. This discussion, in turn, provides some perspective, for this chapter as well as the next two chapters, regarding approaches to equity management in the domestic market. We then go on to discuss a framework for comparing a disciplined stock selection strategy with other types of strategies, as well as a method of establishing specific objectives for that strategy. We'll then move on to ways of designing the investment process and implementing the strategy. We'll conclude with discussion of the results of tests as well as the active implementation of the disciplined stock selection strategy.

ACTIVE-PASSIVE STRATEGIES

Figure 6-1 provides a framework for thinking about investment strategies and is based on analysis from Chapter 2. Note that the diagram is concerned with both risk and

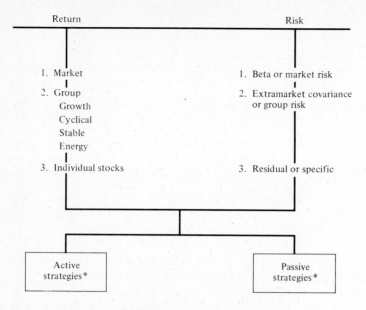

*Active and passive strategies are investment vehicles with specific risk and return characteristics and are designed to fulfill the differing needs of investors. (The text provides specific examples of types of investment strategies.)

Figure 6-1 Breakdown of types of investment judgments.

return. It indicates that the returns accruing to an individual stock derive from three sources: (1) overall market effect, (2) affiliation to the industry or broad market sector,[1] and (3) unique characteristics of the individual security. Correspondingly, there are risks associated with each of these components, identified respectively as (1) market risk, (2) group risk or extramarket covariance,[2] and (3) specific or residual risk. In endeavoring to achieve investment objectives, organizations can pursue an active or a passive strategy with respect to each or a combination of these risk-return components.

Organizations that pursue an active strategy with respect to the market component are known as *market timers*. In particular, an organization pursuing such a strategy with a forecast of a rising market would raise the beta of its portfolio either by shifting from cash to stocks or by raising the beta of the equities in the portfolio, or by a combination of both techniques. Conversely, a forecast of a declining market would indicate that the organization should decrease the beta of its portfolio either by shifting to cash from

[1] Benjamin King, "Market and Industry Factors in Stock Price Behavior," *Journal of Business,* January 1966, pp. 139–191, showed that an industry effect explained approximately 10 percent of the realized returns of stocks over the 1926–1960 period. James L. Farrell, Jr., "Analyzing Covariation of Returns to Determine Homogeneous Stock Groupings," *Journal of Business,* April 1974, pp. 181–207, showed that a broader than industry effect explained an additional 15 percent of the realized returns of stocks over the 1961–1969 period.

[2] Barr Rosenberg, "Extra-Market Components of Covariance in Security Returns," *Journal of Financial and Quantitative Analysis,* March 1974, pp. 263–274.

equities or by decreasing the beta of the equities in the portfolio, or by a combination of both techniques. Correspondingly, organizations that wish to maintain a passive stance with respect to market timing should at all times maintain the beta of their portfolios in line with the target for achieving longer-term portfolio objectives.

An active strategy with respect to industries or broad market sectors has been termed a policy of *group rotation*.[3] Pursuit of such a strategy would entail under-weighting or overweighting the group or industry with respect to its weight in the market index according to whether the outlook for the group has been assessed as favorable or unfavorable. For example, an organization that assessed the outlook for growth stocks as unfavorable and cyclicals as favorable in 1972 would have under-weighted the growth component and overweighted the cyclical component of the market. Again, an organization that decided it had no capability to forecast in this respect and desired to pursue a passive strategy with regard to this risk-return compo-nent would set portfolio weights in the broad market sectors and major industries in line with their weightings in the market index.

An active strategy with respect to individual stocks (stock selection) is used extensively by investment organizations. Stocks that are identified as most attractive would be overweighted relative to their weighting in the market index, while those considered unattractive would not be held or underweighted relative to their position in the index. Organizations typically hold many individual stocks to hedge against the fact that their knowledge of the outlook for individual stocks is at best imperfect. In portfolio analysis this is known as *diversification*. When an organization considers it has no ability to assess the outlook for individual stocks, it would logically hold many stocks and weight them in accordance with their weighting in an index. The most efficient way to attain this objective is to create an index fund, which is the ultimate in totally passive strategies.

A STOCK SELECTION STRATEGY

Given this kind of framework for thinking about individual components of the return-generating process for stocks, we can begin to describe more specifically the kinds of investment strategies that an organization might offer based on combinations of active and passive strategies associated with each component. In this regard we have chosen to analyze three types of strategies that would seem to be general enough to provide perspective on a multitude of variations. These strategies include: (1) remaining totally passive with respect to all three return components — stock, group, and market; (2) remaining passive with respect to market and group components and active with respect to stock selection; and (3) deciding to be active with respect to all three components.

Figure 6-2 illustrates the risk-return characteristics of the three types of strategies. These are labeled (1) totally passive or index fund, (2) disciplined stock selection, and (3) totally active. The horizontal line is a performance benchmark for return relative to

[3] James L. Farrell, Jr., "Homogeneous Stock Groupings: Implications for Portfolio Management," *Financial Analysts Journal,* May–June 1975, pp. 50–62.

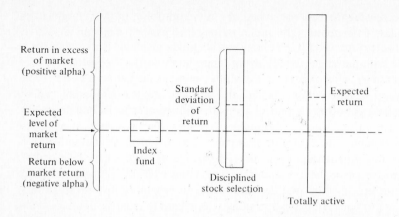

Figure 6-2 Risk-return characteristics of investment strategies. Note: The dashed line across the bar represents the expected return to the strategy, while the height of the bar represents the risk of the strategy as measured by the standard deviation.

the market: anything above the market-return line is an above-average return; anything under the market-return line is a below-average return. The dashed line represents the expected return relative to the market associated with each strategy. The height of the bar represents the expected return range or risk associated with that strategy.

Note that the index fund strategy is located at the lower end of the risk-return spectrum as it remains totally passive with respect to return opportunities. An index fund is expected not only to offer no incremental return relative to the index but also to show relatively little divergence from that neutral performance. At the other extreme, the totally active strategy undertakes to take advantage of all three return opportunities: market timing, group rotation, and individual stock selection.[4] If an organization had predictive capability with respect to all three return opportunities, it would earn a return above that of the market or index fund. At the same time it would experience a greater expected return range or risk associated with that return. No one's predictions are always right.

[4]When an organization undertakes an active strategy using both market timing and group rotation, it is likely that the market risk of the portfolio will at times diverge from a beta of 1, a risk in line with the market. An organization that engages in an actual policy of "timing" the market will at times have betas that differ from that of the market. For example, an organization acting on a forecast of a falling market should have a beta of less than 1, while a forecast of a rising market would imply a beta greater than 1. The diagram in Figure 6-2 assumes that over a market cycle the positive beta divergences will be offset by negative beta divergences. As a result, this diagram presumes that over time the organization's market risk will average out to that of the market — that is, have a beta of 1 as measured against a broadly representative market index.

For those organizations deliberately pursuing a long-run policy of keeping the market risk of their portfolio above or below the market level — that is, a beta above or below 1 — this diagram would be inadequate, as it assumes that the realized return is at the same level as the market risk. When risk differs from the market, the returns earned in excess or below the market may or may not be representative of above- or below-average performance. These returns would have to be adjusted for the experienced risk level of the fund to determine whether the performance had in fact been inferior or superior. Chapter 12 discusses techniques for making this adjustment.

The intermediate case actively capitalizes on stock selection capability. It is passive or neutral with respect to market and group influence. With predictive capability in stock selection an organization would expect to earn an above-average return — not as much as the totally active strategy but greater than the index fund. At the same time the organization would expect to experience return variability greater than an index fund but less than the totally active strategy. The potential for error is not so great as with the totally active strategy because it is not exposed to the risks of the other two return opportunities. We'll focus on the elements needed to execute the disciplined stock selection strategy in the rest of this chapter, and then discuss still other elements needed to carry out the totally active strategy in Chapters 7 and 8.

DESIGNING THE INVESTMENT PROCESS

To successfully execute the disciplined stock selection strategy, several critical elements must be present in the investment process. First, there is need to ensure that the organization has predictive capability with respect to individual stocks; that is, it must be able to distinguish between relatively attractive and unattractive individual stocks. This, in turn, implies the need for some method of measuring or assessing predictive capability. There is also need for a systematic portfolio construction procedure, to ensure that predictions for individual stocks are appropriately built into the portfolio. Finally, operating the system over time means that there will be portfolio rebalancing as well as transactions costs associated with that activity. This calls for explicit consideration of the magnitude of transactions costs, and methods of controlling those costs must be developed to avoid a degrading of performance over time.

Figure 6-3 illustrates the necessary elements of the investment process and shows how these fit together to produce the desired strategy. The top of the diagram shows risk on one side and return on the other, similar to the first diagram in this chapter, but this figure is specifically oriented to the stock selection strategy. The middle part of the diagram shows how risk and return can be considered simultaneously to develop an optimum portfolio. The lower part of the diagram illustrates how the process is implemented, while the dashed line extending from the bottom of the diagram indicates that investing over time is a matter of repeating the process.

Note that the return side in Figure 6-3 shows multiple sources — in this case, four — for identifying relatively attractive and unattractive stocks. Use of multiple sources is superior to reliance on a single method of stock selection when individual sources have predictive content and are complementary and not redundant. The block labeled "composite forecast" indicates the need to put these individual forecasts together in an optimum fashion in order to maximize their predictive value. The risk side of the diagram indicates the need for explicit consideration of five major components of risk: general market, growth, cyclical, stable, and energy. We can do this most effectively by means of a multi-index model described in Chapter 2.

Given composite return estimates and the multi-index risk model, we can use optimization techniques like those described in Chapter 2 to obtain a portfolio with the

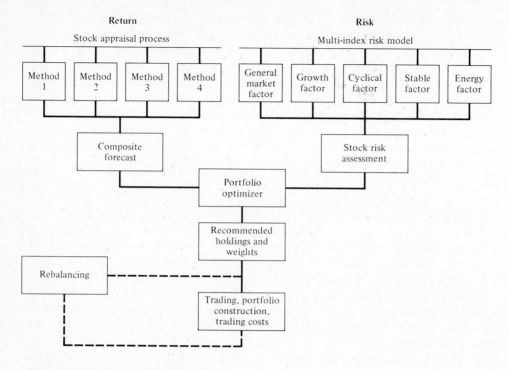

Figure 6-3 The equity investment process.

highest return at a minimal risk. Once the optimum portfolio has been generated, it is then a matter of purchasing the securities in the amounts indicated by the optimization model. Trading in securities, however, means incurring transactions costs, and it is important to consider and properly control these to avoid unduly dissipating a performance advantage. This is especially significant when there is need to recycle through the process illustrated in Figure 6-3 and rebalance the portfolio over time.

MEASURING PREDICTIVE ABILITY

As noted before, pursuit of an active strategy of stock selection presumes some ability to identify relatively attractive and unattractive stocks, as well as the need for some method of measuring this stock selection ability. While there are alternative techniques for measuring predictive ability, perhaps the best for analyzing stock selection capability is the information coefficient (IC) method. Some of the particular advantages of this method are (1) facility of identifying whether there is a consistent ability to select stocks; (2) ease of distinguishing between stock selection capability and the capability of identifying general market and major group moves; and (3) provision of the framework for optimally combining several different sources of stock selection.

Table 6-1 Predicted ranking versus realized ranking — paper industry

Company	Predicted ranking	Realized return, (12 months)	Ex post ranking
International Paper (IP)	1	25	1
Hammermill Paper (HML)	2	20	2
Mead Corp. (MEA)	3	18	3
Westvaco Corp. (W)	4	17	4
Union Camp (UCC)	5	14	5
St. Regis (SRT)	6	11	6
Fort Howard Paper (FHP)	7	8	7
Kimberly-Clark (KMB)	8	4	8
Consolidated Papers (CPER)	9	1	9
Crown Zellerbach (Z)	10	− 5	10

The method essentially involves correlating outcomes with predictions. The first step in the procedure is to rank the stocks in the universe of interest from relatively most attractive to relatively least attractive.[5] The performance in a succeeding period is then observed, and the stocks in this same universe are ranked from relatively best performing to relatively worst performing.

Table 6-1 illustrates this process more specifically with hypothetical data for ten companies in the paper industry. The first column shows the analyst's forecast of the relative performance of the stocks in the industry over the prior twelve-month period. For example, the table shows that International Paper was forecast to show the best performance (rank of 1) and Crown Zellerbach the worst (rank of 10) over the one-year period. The second column shows the actual performances in terms of companies' rates of return over the twelve-month forecast period along with the ranking of the companies by their ex post performances. International Paper was the best performer (+25 percent) and Crown Zellerbach the worst (−5 percent), with the others lining up exactly in concert with their predicted ranking. We can use the following model to measure the relationship between the forecast ranking FR and the actual ranking AR.

$$AR = a + IC(FR) + e \qquad (1)$$

This equation says that the actual ranking depends on a constant term *a,* the forecast ranking FR, the slope IC of the line relating FR to AR, and an error term *e* with

[5] When ranking securities in a universe, one is automatically making a judgment of the performance on a relative basis; that is, the performance of a security should be considered relatively better or worse than the average of the universe or the average as represented by, say, a broad market index. We're illustrating a more refined method, where the ranking is within industries, such as the paper industry, or within broad market groupings, such as growth, cyclical, stable, and energy groups. Ranking within groupings allows one to make the assessment against more comparable securities and thereby control for the differing riskiness of securities. In the former case the resulting ranking might be construed as representing nonmarket returns — that is, returns in excess of or below the market return. To the extent that the latter procedure of grouping controls for the riskiness of securities, the returns might be considered as risk-adjusted excess returns, or alphas.

a zero mean and standard deviation. Since the distribution of the two rankings, FR and AR, have identical means and standard deviations, the constant term *a,* the slope IC, and standard deviation of error *e* can be given unambiguous interpretations. Appendix A to this chapter provides further perspective on the meaning of the terms in Equation 1.

In this case the information coefficient (IC) would be 1, the constant term zero, and the standard deviation of error zero. As might have been deduced from inspection of data, this would indicate perfect forecasting ability. At the other extreme, a complete lack of forecasting ability implies an IC (slope) of zero, a constant term *a* equal to the average of the ARs, and a standard deviation of error *e* equal to the standard deviation of the ARs. All sets of ICs between zero and 1, constant terms between AR and zero, and standard errors between the average standard deviation of the ranks and zero imply a level of forecasting ability that is less than perfect but better than random.

Figure 6-4 shows three scatter diagrams plotting actual outcomes against predictions as well as the measured ICs (information coefficients), to further illustrate different degrees of predictive capability.[6] The first diagram, or part (*a*), illustrates a correlation coefficient of +1, which would indicate an ability to anticipate the ex post ranking of stocks perfectly, as was represented by the hypothetical data in Table 6-1. This, of course, would be highly unlikely in a stock market that is highly competitive and efficient, as most participants would acknowledge. Part (*b*) illustrates the correlation coefficient of zero, which indicates no ability to rank the subsequent per-

[6] Information coefficients, ICs, are correlation coefficients. When calculating an IC with raw data, the IC is the same as a raw correlation coefficient, while the IC is a rank correlation coefficient when calculating the correlation using ranked data. In theory, the raw correlation coefficient is the slightly better measure; generally, however, there will be little difference between the resulting correlation coefficients, whether the calculation is based on raw or ranked data; that is, the rank correlation coefficient and raw correlation coefficient will be virtually identical. Furthermore, rank correlation coefficients are easier to calculate and equal the beta coefficient when regressing ranks against ranks, as illustrated in Appendix A to this chapter.

More importantly, with regard to practical application, the rank correlation coefficient is the preferred measure, because of the necessity of working with ranked rather than raw data when measuring the predictive capability of an investment process. For a fundamental analyst providing a subjective evaluation of a stock, it is perhaps the only way to obtain some sort of an explicit statement of the relative attractiveness of a security. Even in the case of valuation model data, where the raw predictions are in the form of explicit return predictions, the use of rankings is generally preferable. This process smooths the data by pulling in extremely high or low return forecasts that are more than likely merely reflective of major forecasting errors.

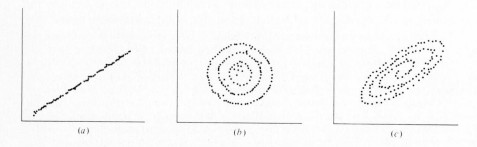

(*a*)　　　　　　　(*b*)　　　　　　　(*c*)

Figure 6-4 Information coefficients: (*a*) IC = 1.00; (*b*) IC = 0; (*c*) IC = .15.

formance of stocks, which would be consistent with a stock market that is perfectly efficient. Part (c) represents the intermediate situation of an imperfect degree of forecasting ability as indicated by the .15 information coefficient.

The .15 information coefficient appears to represent a standard of good performance with regard to stock selection. Several empirical studies that have measured stock selection capability from several different sources (fundamental analyst, valuation models, etc.) document that the capability of individuals is in line with this standard.[7] Among these are the Wells Fargo market line approach (which was described in the previous chapter), the Value Line timeliness ratings on stocks, insider trading patterns, and several institutions and brokerage analytical research departments. While the figure is relatively small — a lot closer to zero than to +1 — it can be quite useful in generating above-average performance, as we'll demonstrate in a later section. This is so, however, only if that level of predictive ability is used within the context of a well-defined investment process, such as the kind being described in this chapter.

COMPOSITE FORECASTING

As noted, predictive capability is available from several different sources, but it is at best only modest. It is also an empirical fact that no single source provides a constant level of predictive capability over each and every period of time; the capability fluctuates — sometimes showing above-average results, other times below-average results. Fortunately, there is a method known as *composite forecasting* that has the potential of stabilizing predictive capability (reducing the fluctuations) and at the same time increasing the power of the predictions. Using multiple sources to stabilize and increase the predictive power of stock selection is analogous to the use of diversification

---

[7] There are several methods of individual-stock selection that have been subjected to the sort of rigorous analysis that indicates their predictive power. One of the first methods to be analyzed extensively was patterns of insider trading. Research studies, beginning in the early 1960s and more recently updated, have universally indicated that insiders have predictive capability to a statistically meaningful degree. The Value Line stock valuation method has also been subjected to analysis, first by Shelton and then by Black. These researchers demonstrated that the model has facility in identifying mispriced securities and hence potential in earning superior returns. Finally, Wells Fargo has evaluated the success of the dividend-discount valuation model as cast in the framework of the SML in discriminating attractive from unattractive stocks. This analysis suggests that the method has potential for allowing an organization to earn superior risk-adjusted returns.

Ambachtsheer has also applied the IC method to evaluation of the success of several approaches to selecting individual stocks. He has evaluated the predictive capability of valuation models in this context, with particular emphasis on the Value Line and "market" line methods of stock selection. His studies were consistent with earlier analyses, indicating that both approaches had statistically significant ICs over a reasonably large universe of stocks. His firm, Canavest House, has also evaluated the judgmental capability of analysts from a number of different organizations over a period of years. This monitoring showed that analysts as a group had a modest but statistically significant ability to identify the relative attractiveness of stocks.

While these studies indicated that some methods of stock selection had predictive content, the degree to which this capability existed could not be regarded as extensive. With regard to studies using the IC method, the measured ICs ranged from about .05 to as high as .20 when analyzed over reasonable amounts of data. In terms of Figure 6-2, the capability was more on the order of that represented by part (c) — if not less — rather than that represented by part (a).

as a means of reducing the variability of a portfolio from the variability attendant on investing in only a single security.

This method involves putting together separate individual sources to form a multiple source or composite prediction. It works only when two conditions are present. First, the individual sources must have predictive content — that is, a positive IC; sources without predictive content cannot be used in combination to enhance the forecast. Second, the individual sources should provide some different perspective on stocks — should not provide information already being provided by another source. In fact, the process works best when the individual sources provide completely independent readings — that is, when they show zero cross-correlation.

Table 6-2 uses four different sources of stock selection as an example of how the process of composite forecasting operates. Note that each source has predictive capability as evidenced by a measured IC of .10; also, each has equal predictive capability. We're also assuming that each of the sources gives a different perspective on stocks and, for purposes of illustration, that they are independent: the correlation across the sources is zero. As a matter of practical interest, experience has shown that sources like those based on valuation models, both long-term and short-term in orientation, as well as the perspective provided by fundamental analysts have characteristics that broadly fit these specifications.

Appendix B to this chapter demonstrates that for sources with predictive capability that provide independent readings (uncorrelated with one another), the optimum way of combining them is to weight each source according to its predictive power. Since each of the sources in our example has equal predictive power (IC = .10), the optimum way of combining them is to weight them equally in forming the composite forecast. Using all four sources in tandem would result in a composite IC of .20, or double the predictive power of .10 when relying on only one source. The formulation at the bottom of Table 6-2 shows that the individual ICs combine in proportion to the square of their values with the resulting composite IC, the square root of the combined total.[8]

[8] The development of linear composite prediction is generally ascribed to J. M. Bates and C. W. J. Granger, "The Combination of Forecasts," *Operations Research Quarterly*, 20, 1969, pp. 451–468. Robert Falconer and Charles M. Sivesind, "Dealing with Conflicting Forecast: The Eclectic Advantage," *Business Economics*, September 1977, pp. 5–11, illustrate the use of composite forecasting with respect to economic data analysis. Keith Ambachtsheer and James L. Farrell, Jr., apply the approach to stock market analysis in "Can Active Management Add Value?" *Financial Analysts Journal*, November–December 1979, pp. 39–47.

Table 6-2 Stock selection source

Stock selection source	Predictive content (IC)
1	.10
2	.10
3	.10
4	.10
Composite IC = $[(.10)^2 + (.10)^2 + (.10)^2 + (.10^2)]^{1/2} = [.04]^{1/2} = .20$	

When sources of predictive capability are correlated (not perfectly independent), the formula is not so simple, but the principle is generally the same. There is need in this case to adjust the composite IC for any dependence, or correlation, across the differing sources of information. The composite IC will be lower as the degree of positive correlation across sources increases, so that if there were positive correlation across the four sources in the example, the resulting IC would be less than .20. If the sources in this example were perfectly correlated (or totally redundant), then the composite IC would be .10, or the same as when only a single source was used. Combining in this instance would not be beneficial.

Ambachtsheer and Farrell demonstrated that this composite forecasting approach could be implemented in practice by evaluating two different sources of stock predictions.[9] The first source evaluated was the Wells Fargo market line approach to stock selection, which we described in Chapter 5. It is primarily based on a dividend discount valuation model, and to characterize their approach and generalize it, Ambachtsheer and Farrell referred to it as long-term fundamental (LTF). The second source was the Value Line timeliness ratings of stocks, an approach based on relative P/E ratios and earnings momentum. To characterize it and contrast it with the LTF approach, the authors referred to it as short-term fundamental (STF).

The top two rows of Table 6-3 show the ICs of the two sources measured at six-month intervals from September 1973 to September 1976. Note that the LTF method shows a positive IC in each interval and averages out to close to .15, which is a standard level of good performance. The STF method generally shows positive ICs and averages out to a lower but still positive IC. The evaluation indicates that the models do in fact have predictive capacity, which is, of course, a necessary condition if these models are to have use in developing above-average performance. In addition, statistical tests indicate that the two models provide generally independent readings on stocks, another necessary condition for usefulness as part of a composite forecasting process.

The third row of Table 6-3 shows the results of combining the LTF and STF methods for use in developing forecasts of individual stock performance. Note that the combined IC averages out to .15 for the full period, thereby providing a higher IC than either individual method. Furthermore, the combined IC appears to fluctuate less than

[9]Keith Ambachtsheer and James L. Farrell, Jr., "Can Active Management Add Value?" *Financial Analysts Journal,* November–December 1979, pp. 39–47.

Table 6-3 Six-month ICs for the long-term and short-term fundamental methods (LTF and STF)

Source	9/73–3/74	3/74–9/74	9/74–3/75	3/75–9/75	9/75–3/76	3/76–9/76	Mean (IC)
LTF	.12	.16	.01	.13	.08	.31	.135
STF	.17	.04	−.09	.16	.11	.01	.067
Combined	.17	.18	.00	.16	.10	.30	.152

Source: Keith Ambachtsheer and James L. Farrell, Jr., "Can Active Management Add Value?" *Financial Analysts Journal,* November–December 1979, pp. 39–47.

the individual methods over the test period. In sum the results were in line with expectations in terms of increasing predictive ability as well as seeming to add stability to the capability of the two sources over time.

GENERATING RETURN FORECASTS

Once an organization has assessed that it has predictive capability (a positive IC), it then becomes a problem of structuring the analytical process in such a way as to systematically generate return forecasts for each stock in the universe. In doing this the organization first needs to obtain over- or undervaluation judgments on individual stocks from its security analysis process, whether these result from estimates by individual analysts, a more formal valuation model, or perhaps even other methods of appraisal. It is then necessary to express these judgments more explicitly as return forecasts, or more properly as returns apart from those attributable to market and group effects. The final step is to adjust the return forecasts for the degree of predictive capability possessed by the organization — that is, adjust the forecasts for the imperfect predictive accuracy of even the best investment organizations.

With respect to the first step in the process — generating judgments of value — the organization needs to ensure that these are unbiased and on the same scale. As an extreme example, the organization will want to avoid biases that would result in recommendations of either purchase or sale for all individual stocks. It will instead desire to have purchase recommendations in balance with sale recommendations. Also, the organization will be interested in being able to compare qualitative judgments such as buy, hold, and sell evaluations from a security analyst with rate of return estimates generated from valuation models. Placing evaluations on the same scale allows comparison across many disparate sources.

To eliminate scale and bias problems, the organization might use a rating scheme, with the ratings serving as proxies for the judged degree of relative over- or undervaluation. The rating scheme could, for example, simply consist of five valuation categories, with 1 the most attractive and 5 the least attractive, and could be applied directly to the selection universe using a simple allocation rule such as the one illustrated in Figure 6-5. The bottom part of the figure applies this rule to the stock-ranking data from Table 6-1. Note that setting up a fixed number of valuation categories eliminates the scale problem, while using the simple allocation rule of Figure 6-5 eliminates biases from the judgment process.

Generating a Return Distribution

From knowledge of the cross-sectional distribution of annual stock returns, the rating distribution can then be transformed into a return distribution. For example, analysis has shown that in recent years, the standard deviation of residual returns (nonmarket and nongroup related) has been on the order of 18 percent with an average value or expectation of zero. Assuming normally distributed returns, this means that two-thirds of all stocks in a typical year will earn returns of between ±18 percent. Alternatively,

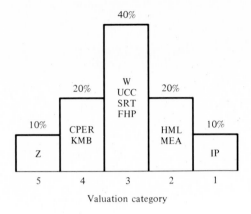

Figure 6-5 Allocation rule.

this means that one-sixth of the stocks will earn returns exceeding 18 percent, while one-sixth of the stock universe will show losses exceeding 18 percent.

We can superimpose the 5-point rating scheme on this kind of distribution by first converting the rating points into units of standard deviation from the mean. For this rating distribution the upper part of Figure 6-6 indicates a standard deviation of 1.1 rating points. Using this standard deviation means that a rating of 5, which is 2 rating points from the mean, is also 1.8 (2 ÷ 1.1) standard deviations from the mean. Similarly, a rating of 4 or 2, which is 1 rating point from the mean is also .9 (1 ÷ 1.1) standard deviations from the mean. Naturally, a rating of 3 would be zero deviations away from the mean.

When we multiply this converted rating by the standard deviation of the return distribution, we obtain the returns illustrated in the middle portion of Figure 6-6. Note that a rating of 1 converts to a return of 32 percent return (1.8 standard deviation times 18 percent standard deviation of return), while a rating of 5 converts to a loss of 32 percent (−1.8 standard deviation times 18 percent standard deviation of return). Similarly, a rating of 2 becomes a 16 percent return (.9 times 18 percent), while a rating of 4 converts to a loss of 16 percent (−.9 times 18 percent). A rating of 3, or an average ranking, converts to a zero return as would be expected for this neutral rating. In a sense this converted return distribution presents the opportunity for explaining these gains and losses, and an organization with perfect forecasting ability (an IC of +1) would be confronted with the total potential of this distribution.

Adjusting for Predictive Capability

As noted before, however, empirical research indicates that predictive capability with respect to individual stocks is far less than perfect, with ICs on the order of .15 representing quite satisfactory levels of performance in a highly competitive environment. Thus there is need to adjust the empirical return distribution for less than perfect

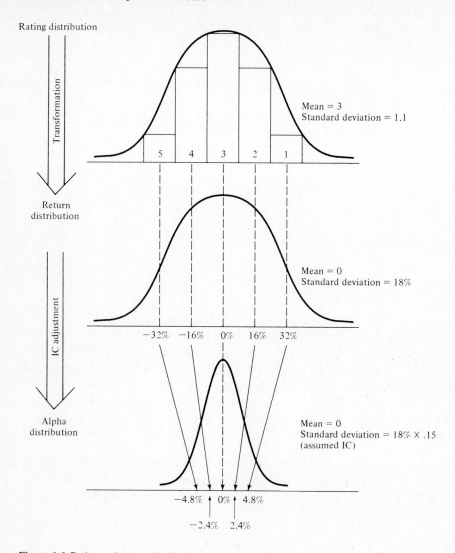

Rating distribution

Transformation

Mean = 3
Standard deviation = 1.1

| 5 | 4 | 3 | 2 | 1 |

Return
distribution

IC adjustment

Mean = 0
Standard deviation = 18%

−32%   −16%   0%   16%   32%

Alpha
distribution

Mean = 0
Standard deviation = 18% × .15
(assumed IC)

−4.8%   0%   4.8%

−2.4%   2.4%

Figure 6-6 Rating and return distributions.

predictive capability. An organization can adjust the return distribution for its level of predictive capability by means of the following formula:

$$R = IC(FR) + e \qquad (2)$$

This formula says that the return on the stock R comprises two components: (1) the forecast $IC(FR)$; and (2) the error e in the forecast. The error term has an expected value of zero, $E(e) = 0$, and a variance $e = (1 - IC^2) \, \text{Var}(R)$. To illustrate the role of the error term in the forecast, assume that the standard deviation of stock return is 18 percent, or has a variance of 324, and that the organization has an IC of .20. Given the forecast, the stock-return variance R becomes $(1 - IC^2) \text{Var}(R) = (1 - .20^2)(324) = 311$.

When the IC has a value of 1, the error term becomes zero; there is perfect forecasting ability, and the actual return is completely explained by the forecast return. On the other hand, when the IC is zero, there is no forecasting ability; the forecast return explains nothing, and the resulting return and error are equivalent. The organization has no opportunity to explain any part of the distribution of returns.

Assuming some level of predictive capability — for example, the .15 level, which represents the standard of performance — the formula allows us to see the effect of the IC adjustment for partial predictive capability. Recall for example, that a stock rated 1, or most highly rated, would have a return equivalent of 32 percent using the historical return distribution. Adjusting the IC to reflect an imperfect degree of forecasting capability would, however, considerably reduce the return that the investor should expect. Using the previous equation and taking its expected value, so that the error term disappears $E(e) = 0$, we obtain an expected return for the stock, as shown:

$$E(R) = IC(FR) \tag{3}$$
$$= .15(+32\%)$$
$$= 4.8\%$$

Adjusting to the levels of predictive capability that are likely to be encountered in actual practice reduces the return distribution considerably, as reflected in the bottom part of Figure 6-6. The IC adjustment, in effect, shrinks the whole distribution to one with a standard deviation of 2.7 percent from the original one with a standard deviation of 18 percent. The highest rated stocks, the 1s, now have expected returns of 4.8 percent and the stocks rated 2 have returns of 2.4 percent, while the lowest rated stocks, the 5s, have expected losses of 4.8 percent and the stocks rated 4 are expected to lose 2.4 percent. Organizations with greater or lesser ICs would be faced with wider or narrower return distributions. An organization with no forecasting capability, or an IC of zero, would be faced with no opportunity range around a mean of zero.

As a further note, the resulting distribution of adjusted returns as shown at the bottom of Figure 6-6 might be considered as an alpha distribution. These alphas would have the same meaning as the alphas discussed in Chapter 2; that is, they represent returns expected apart from market and group effects and again represent a potential bonus return or penalty, as the case may be. In this case, we generate the alphas in an indirect way, whereas in the case of the market line method, as described in Chapter 5, the alphas represented by the distance above and below the line were generated directly. The approach just described is more flexible, however, in that expectations about stocks from disparate sources can be converted into alphas that are comparable across the sources.

TRANSACTION COSTS

Finally, the organization needs to know the transactions costs and to compare them with the return opportunities facing the organization. Transactions costs include both commissions and the price impact of the transaction — the rise in price when buying or the decline when selling. Wagner and Cuneo evaluated those costs for institutional investors and showed that the round-trip transactions costs (commissions and market impact) were on the order of 3 percent.[10] This study was, however, prior to the removal of fixed commission rates, which has resulted in lower average commission rates, at least for institutional investors. Currently commission rates average approximately 0.4 percent of the cost of a transaction compared with perhaps 1 percent prior to the demise of fixed commission rates. Presuming that the price impact of transactions averages another 0.4 to 0.6 percent, the cost of a one-way transaction would be about 1 percent, or 2 percent for a round-trip transaction.

Transactions costs represent a kind of hurdle rate that a return opportunity must surpass in order to justify trading. For example, if round-trip transactions costs are 2 percent, a purchase opportunity and a sale opportunity must show a more than 2 percent spread to justify action. The lower the transactions costs, the lower the hurdle rate can be, and the higher the transactions costs the higher the hurdle rate.

An organization with a high IC — that is, high predictive capability — would be justified in developing more trades than an organization with a low IC. This is because the organization with the higher IC would have a greater margin of return for overcoming transactions costs than an organization with a low IC; that is, the organization with greater predictive capability would have a greater adjusted return distribution, as illustrated in Figure 6-6, than the low-IC organization. Consequently, high ICs at a given transactions cost imply high turnover, while low ICs imply low turnover, as there is less margin to overcome the cost of transacting. Correspondingly, high transactions costs at a given IC imply that low turnover is optimum, while low transactions costs at a given IC imply higher turnover is justified.

APPLIED COMPOSITE FORECASTING

It's useful at this point to illustrate how the investment-counseling firm with which the author is associated uses the process just described to assess the relative attractiveness of 800 stocks in a stock selection universe. This universe includes only companies with market capitalization in excess of $100 million, so it is most representative of large institutional-grade stocks. It includes all 500 companies in the S&P market index. The other 300 companies provide exposure to industries such as the specialty chemical industry which are not components of the S&P 500 index and which allow for a more complete selection.

In monitoring the stock selection universe, we gather information about these 800 companies from four different sources. We continue to rely on the same two broad valuation categories — long-term fundamental and short-term fundamental, as in the original study. The specific models within the categories differ in particular but not in spirit. We've supplemented these with two other stock evaluation categories that are

[10]Wayne Wagner and Larry Cuneo: "Reducing the Cost of Stock Trading," *Financial Analysts Journal*, November–December 1975, pp. 35–44.

Table 6-4 Stock universe monitor

	Long-term fund	Short-term fund	Trading fund	Analyst judgment	Alpha
			Forest Products		
Evans Products	2	3	1	4	2.7
Weyerhaeuser	4	3	2	3	1.0
Boise Cascade	3	4	1	3	0.6
Champion International	2	4	3	3	0.0
Louisiana-Pacific	2	4	3	3	−0.2
Pacific Lumber	3	3	3	3	−0.8
Willamette Industries	2	5	3	3	−1.7
Georgia-Pacific	3	4	3	4	−3.4
Potlatch	3	4	4	3	−4.8
			Paper		
Westvaco	2	4	1	2	4.9
Kimberly-Clark	3	3	1	3	4.8
Great Northern Nekoosa	3	3	3	2	2.4
James River	3	3	3	3	0.6
Union Camp	3	3	3	3	0.0
St. Regis Paper	2	4	3	3	0.0
Mead	1	4	5	3	−0.7
Crown Zellerbach	3	4	3	3	−0.8
Hammermill Paper	3	3	4	3	−0.8
Fort Howard Paper	5	1	3	4	−1.9
Consolidated Papers	3	3	3	4	−1.9
International Paper	3	3	4	3	−2.3
Domtar, Inc.	3	5	3	3	−3.1
			Paper Containers		
Federal Paper Board	3	2	3	3	1.6
Maryland Cup	4	3	3	3	−1.0
Bemis	3	3	4	3	−2.0
Diamond International	5	3	5	4	−7.7

Source: James L. Farrell, Jr., "A Disciplined Stock Selection Strategy," *Interfaces,* October 1982.

termed (1) trading fundamentals and (2) analyst judgment. The general category of trading fundamentals includes such information as that provided by share repurchase programs or insider trading patterns, while the analyst judgment category monitors the buy-hold-sell recommendations of security analysts. Since each of the four sources has demonstrated predictive content and since statistical measures indicate that the four sources are mutually independent, the sources are well suited for the composite forecasting process described previously in this chapter.

Table 6-4 is from a regularly generated report that provides for each of the 800 companies in the universe information with respect to each of the four broad evaluation categories as well as a composite ranking. The companies are classified according to standard S&P 500 industries, which are, in turn, further grouped into one of the four homogeneous stock groupings: growth, cyclical, stable, or energy. In this instance, the report shows companies in three industries (forest products, paper, and paper containers) that are in turn classified into the cyclical sector. Companies are ranked within industries according to their alpha value.

The first four columns show the ratings of the companies within each of the four evaluation categories according to the same five-way ranking scheme described previously. Note, for example, that Westvaco ranks quite high — 1 — with respect to trading fundamentals and moderately high — 2 — with respect to both long-term fundamentals and analyst judgmental categories but is rated relatively unattractive — 4 — according to short-term fundamentals. The final column of the table shows the combined rating of the stock converted into a projected excess return, or alpha, using the composite IC and the technique of converting ratings that we've been discussing. As a general rule, stocks with alphas in excess of 3.0 are considered highly attractive, while stocks with alphas below -3.0 are considered highly unattractive.

With regard to the stocks shown in the table, we would consider Westvaco and Kimberly-Clark to be highly attractive, because their alphas are positive and large. If we were constructing a portfolio anew or did not currently hold these stocks, we should consider them for inclusion. On the other hand, Georgia-Pacific, Potlatch, Domtar, and Diamond International have quite negative alphas, and we would consider them to be unattractive. We should avoid these, or if we held these in a portfolio we should consider replacing them with stocks showing large positive alphas, such as the ones listed above. In considering such a switch, however, one should compare the potential pickup in added return to the cost of the transaction.

In building a portfolio, our first step is to identify the most attractively priced stocks, which generally turn out to be the 120 stocks with the highest positive alphas. Once identified, they are analyzed in order to ensure that the basic inputs to the evaluation are valid. We also assess whether there might be an impending change in the basic evaluation inputs that has not been captured in the processing. Finally, we attempt to incorporate into our analysis factors that cannot be structured into a formal evaluation framework. This further analysis usually reduces the list of potential investment candidates. From this reduced list, we then construct the portfolio according to the guidelines and procedures outlined in the following sections of this chapter.

PORTFOLIO CONSTRUCTION

Once the organization has made return forecasts and adjusted them for the level of predictive capability, it is then a matter of ensuring that these predictions are properly embodied in the portfolio. This in turn means that the organization needs to develop a well-defined set of portfolio construction guidelines and that the portfolio construction process is carried out in a controlled and disciplined fashion. This is especially important because predictive capability, where it exists, is modest at best and can easily be lost or dissipated at other stages in the investment process.

Table 6-5 shows the broad guidelines that the organization should follow in constructing the portfolio. These three guidelines are consistent with the objective of the strategy, which is to rely on stock selection alone in attempting to attain above-average performance, without capitalizing on the opportunities associated with the market and group components of return. The guidelines also conform to the framework of thinking about risk and return that we described in the opening section of this chapter.

Since the objective is to rely exclusively on stock selection, there is need to control the risk associated with the market and group components of return. In order to control the risk associated with market timing, the organization should keep the portfolio as fully invested in equities as possible. Alternatively, it should keep the cash position at a minimum; a maximum of 2 percent would seem to be a workable rule. Correspondingly, the organization should keep the beta of the equity portion of the portfolio at 1 or within a range of, say, .95 to 1.05 in order to maintain the market risk of the equity portion in line with the market as measured by an index like the S&P 500.

To control the risk associated with major groups, it is necessary to ensure that the portfolio is well-diversified. In particular, there is need to ensure that the portfolio is not overweighted with respect to a particular group or, alternatively, that it is not tilted too heavily in the direction of one of the major nonmarket factors. Conversely, it is necessary to ensure that the portfolio is not underweighted with respect to the major groups or, alternatively, unduly tilted away from one of the major factors. For example, if energy stocks represented 20 percent of the weighting in the overall market, it would be important to construct the portfolio so that this factor had the same representation — neither significantly more nor less.

The third major requirement, or guideline, for the portfolio-construction process is to ensure that the portfolio includes a sufficient number of stocks — say, between sixty and ninety stocks. Holding a sufficient number of stocks helps diversification by reducing specific risk in the fashion analyzed in Chapter 2. Holding a sufficient number of stocks is, however, also consistent with the fact that our predictive ability is going to be modest at best. We expect our judgments — bets, if you will — to work out on average, not with respect to each and every one: our ICs are not +1. The greater the number of stocks, the more likely that the averages will work in our favor.

PORTFOLIO OPTIMIZATION

Once the guidelines have been established, there are two main procedures for implementing the portfolio-construction strategy. One is to use more traditional types of

Table 6-5 Portfolio construction objective

1. Portfolio market risk should be in line with that of the S&P 500.
2. Portfolio should be highly diversified with respect to group/industry risk.
3. Portfolio should have many individual stock judgments with high predictive content working at the same time.

constraints, like industry guidelines, minimum numbers of stocks to include in a portfolio, or maximum size of individual holdings. This approach can work effectively when the objectives are explicitly defined and the process has been specifically delineated, as it has in this instance. Furthermore, it has the merits of being simple and least costly to operate.

The other approach is to use optimization procedures like those identified and discussed in Chapter 2. These approaches are more costly, though not prohibitively so, and more complex. Furthermore, it is essential that the procedure used is based on an appropriate model of the risk-return generating process. In this regard we recommend use of the multi-index, or multifactor, approach that was discussed in earlier chapters. It takes into account those major effects impacting stocks — general market, growth, cyclical, stable, and energy — and at the same time provides most of the economy of operation and ease of interpretation of the simplest model of the return-generating process — the single-index model.

Given return estimates and using the multi-index risk model, the optimization procedure works in the following way.[11] It seeks out those stocks having the most favorable returns. At the same time it balances these return opportunities against the riskiness of the stocks. The intent here is to hedge against market and group risks, as well as to reduce specific risk as much as is consistent with the objective of obtaining a high return. The result should be a mix of stocks that best fulfills the objective of the portfolio — that is, to obtain a high return at a minimal risk.

Table 6-6 shows an actual portfolio constructed at the end of 1979 using optimization techniques and built to conform to the sort of guidelines that we've been discussing in this chapter. The table shows the names of the companies as well as their weights in the portfolio.[12] Note that the weights sum to 100 percent, which indicates that the portfolio is fully invested in equities, so that the cash position of the portfolio is zero, as is shown at the bottom of the table. This is, of course, consistent with the practical portfolio guideline calling for no more than 2 percent cash in the portfolio.

Note also that the second column of the table shows the beta values of the individual stocks as a measure of their exposure to general market risk. We can obtain a beta value for the overall portfolio by simply using the individual beta value and the weight of the company in the portfolio to calculate a weighted average beta for the portfolio, as was illustrated in Chapter 2. Commonly referred to as a cross-sectional beta, it provides a way of estimating the exposure of the overall portfolio to general market risk at a given point in time. Note that the weighted average, or cross-sectional,

[11] Those interested in a more elaborate description of how an optimization technique works should refer to Appendix A in Chapter 8. Using the simplified portfolio techniques of Elton and Gruber, this illustrates the generation of an optimal portfolio. While the single-index model, rather than the multi-index model, was used in that process, the example should nevertheless be illustrative of the way that an optimization technique selects securities for inclusion in a portfolio and determines the optimum weightings for these securities.

[12] In generating the portfolio, several weighting constraints were established. One was that no individual security would represent more than 3 percent of the portfolio weighting, with the exception of AT&T, Exxon, and IBM, which represent more than 3 percent weightings in the S&P 500. An additional constraint was that the weightings of the portfolio in the growth, cyclical, stable, and energy groupings would be in line with the S&P 500 weighting. Given these constraints, the objective was to obtain a maximum return while minimizing residual risk (standard error) at a beta level of 1.

beta of the portfolio was 1.03, in line with a practical guideline calling for a .95–1.05 beta range for the portfolio. On balance the portfolio was well-controlled with respect to market risk.

With regard to group risk, one way of measuring exposure is to simply compare the weighting of the portfolio in these major sectors with the weighting of that sector in the overall market to determine whether there is underweighting or over-weighting with respect to the market. The bottom part of the Table 6-6 shows the weighting of the portfolio in each of the four major sectors as well as the weighting of the sectors in the S&P 500, which we're using as a generally acceptable proxy for the market. Note that the portfolio is well-diversified, or hedged, with respect to group risk; the weights of the portfolio are virtually the same as the weighting in the overall market. The portfolio optimization procedure, of course, ensures the control of this kind of risk most efficiently.

Two other related diagnostics that provide perspective on the overall level of diversification of the portfolio are the coefficient of determination R^2 and the standard error of the portfolio. (Appendix A provides perspective on the meaning of these two portfolio diagnostics.) Both measure how closely the portfolio will move in tandem with the market. A high R^2 and a low standard error indicate that the portfolio will move closely in tandem with the market, while a low R^2 and a high standard error indicate that the portfolio will tend to move out of phase with the overall market. As a benchmark, the typical actively managed institutional portfolio will have an R^2 of between .90 and .93 and a standard error on the order of 7 percent.

Note that the portfolio in Table 6-6 has an R^2 of .98 and a standard error of 2 percent, which are well within the guidelines established for diversification of a portfolio that is designed for the stock selection strategy. At the same time the portfolio is more highly diversified than the typical actively managed portfolio because of the conscious decision to control market and major group risk closely, as well as the intent to hold a reasonably large number of securities in the portfolio. Note that the portfolio contains sixty-nine stocks, which is again within the guidelines. This means that specific risk is controlled, while the opportunity for the weighted average projected alpha of 3.5 percent (shown as portfolio alpha in the table) to be realized is maximized.

MANAGING THE PROCESS OVER TIME

The final problem is that of managing the process over time. The dashed line leading from the bottom part of Figure 6-3 indicates that this involves repeating the procedures that we've been describing in this chapter. In particular, it means continuing to generate return forecasts for individual stocks and combining them with the appropriate weights to develop an updated list of stock-return estimates. Presumably these estimates will change both because of continual reassessment of the future prospects for companies by the stock selection sources and owing to changes of prices in the marketplace. This means that optimization with these revised estimates will lead to different recom-

Table 6-6 Stock selection portfolio, 12/31/79

Security	% of portfolio market value	Beta
Aetna Life & Casualty Co.	1.50	1.43
Alcan Aluminum Ltd.	1.00	1.05
Amax, Inc.	0.50	1.13
Amerada Hess Corp.	2.00	1.32
American Home Products	1.00	0.70
AT&T	5.00	0.67
Anheuser-Busch, Inc.	1.00	1.07
Atlantic Richfield	2.00	0.87
Bethlehem Steel	1.00	1.48
Burroughs Corp.	1.50	1.06
Cameron Iron Works	1.00	1.28
Campbell Soup Co.	1.00	0.74
Carnation Co.	1.00	0.98
CBS, Inc.	0.50	1.19
Chase Manhattan Corp.	1.50	1.23
Coca-Cola Co.	1.00	0.78
Conoco, Inc.	2.00	0.86
Digital Equipment Corp.	1.50	1.45
Dow Chemical Co.	1.00	1.08
Emerson Electric	1.00	0.98
Exxon Corp.	5.00	0.83
Federated Department Store	1.00	1.30
Florida Power & Light	1.50	1.05
Foster Wheeler Corp.	1.50	1.36
Gannett, Inc.	1.50	0.95
General Electric	2.00	0.98
General Motors	2.50	1.04
Georgia-Pacific	1.50	1.08
Gulf Oil Corp.	3.00	0.82
INA Corp.	1.00	1.51
Ingersoll Rand	1.00	1.13
IBM	3.50	0.87
Johnson & Johnson	1.00	0.77
Koppers, Inc.	1.00	1.31
Kroger Co.	1.00	0.98
Lone Star Industries	1.00	1.20
R. H. Macy & Co., Inc.	1.50	1.44
Maytag Co.	1.00	0.96
McDonald's Corp.	2.00	1.32
Medtronic, Inc.	0.50	1.47
Melville Corp.	1.50	1.20
Merck & Co., Inc.	1.00	0.84
Midland Ross Corp.	1.00	1.32
Minnesota Mining & Manufacturing	2.00	0.96
Monsanto Co.	1.00	1.18
Motorola, Inc.	0.50	1.32
NCNB Corp.	1.50	1.23

Table 6-6 (*Continued*)

Security	% of portfolio market value	Beta
Newmont Mining	1.00	1.16
Northern Natural Gas Co.	1.50	0.96
Owens Illinois	1.00	1.08
Perkin Elmer Corp.	0.50	1.47
Philip Morris, Inc.	2.00	0.73
Phillips Petroleum	2.00	0.92
Revlon, Inc.	1.00	1.07
R. J. Reynolds Industries	1.00	0.50
Rockwell International Corp.	2.00	0.94
Schering Plough Corp.	1.00	1.02
Schlumberger Ltd.	3.00	0.85
Seaboard Coast Line	0.70	1.37
Southern California Edison	1.50	0.84
Southern Railway	0.80	1.00
St. Regis Paper Co.	1.50	1.12
Standard Oil (Ohio)	2.00	1.05
Texaco, Inc.	3.00	0.85
Texas Instruments	0.50	1.31
Thomas & Betts Corp.	0.50	1.10
Union Carbide Corp.	1.00	1.01
United States Fidelity & Guaranty Co.	1.00	1.43
Wang Labs, Inc.	1.00	1.64
Total portfolio	100.00	1.03
Cash	0.0	$R^2 = .98$
Portfolio alpha=3.5%		Standard error 2.2%

Sector	% of portfolio	% of S&P 500
Growth	31	32
Cyclical	23	23
Stable	25	25
Energy	21	20
Total	100	100

mended portfolio holdings, which in turn means rebalancing — portfolio turnover — with the attendant trading and transactions costs.[13]

[13] Setting the optimum rebalancing cycle is an important but difficult task. Too frequent rebalancing and turnover can lead to foregone profits on securities and excessive transaction costs, while an overlong rebalancing cycle can lead to dissipation of gains on formerly profitable holdings. The ideal of course would be to set the rebalancing cycle so that securities are sold as they are peaking in terms of relative performance and replaced with more highly ranked securities. The optimum period is likely to depend on the types of stock selection method used and the phase of the market cycle. Analysis of the time trend and peaking behavior of the ICs of a source or sources of stock selection may be helpful but hardly conclusive in this important though highly difficult area.

In this regard the organization should be especially alert to monitoring the return-estimating process. This is a matter of continuing to monitor the ICs of the separate sources to ensure that they are continuing to provide useful information. We know that sources will show fluctuating patterns with regard to predictive capability, and the analyst should bear this in mind before eliminating a source that may temporarily show a deterioration in performance. The analyst should ascertain whether there has been a long-term fundamental deterioration in predictive capability. Coincidental with the monitoring of the individual sources, there should be an analysis of how well the combining process is working by measuring whether the sources are continuing to provide complementary information, or independent readings. A trend toward redundancy or too high an intercorrelation would call for elimination of the source.

The second major factor to monitor over time is transactions costs, since predictive capability and transactions costs are interrelated. In particular, an organization with predictive capability should act on those predictions in order to take advantage of performance opportunities. This in turn will result in trading and the attendant transactions costs. The greater the predictive ability, the more the organization should be inclined to trade and, of course, be subject to transactions costs. Failure to account for transactions costs can result in a dissipation of performance and in the extreme could lead to subpar performance.

Here the process would be to make sure that the level of transactions costs is properly established and monitored over time to ensure that the estimated cost level remains appropriate. For example, if transactions costs prove to be higher than originally estimated, then a lower level of turnover would be appropriate at a given level of predictability. Conversely, if transactions costs prove to be less, then there would be a greater latitude for acting on predictions. It would also be useful to investigate over time how transactions costs have varied across different types of stocks. Perhaps there is merit to establishing different trading costs for different classes of securities — for example, using a higher cost for smaller, less liquid stocks than for large, actively traded stocks. Finally, it might be useful to investigate trading strategies that would help minimize those costs.

PERFORMANCE OF STRATEGY OVER TIME

It is useful to conclude this chapter by describing the performance results of a test of the strategy that is described in the same Ambachtsheer and Farrell article "Can Active Management Add Value?" discussed in an earlier section.[14] In testing the strategy the authors developed three variations, differing only with respect to the source of return estimates. One variant used only the Value Line, or short-term fundamental (STF), stock selection method as a sole source of return inputs, while another variant used the Well Fargo, or long-term fundamental (LTF), method as the sole source of return inputs. The third variant used the stock selections

---

[14] Keith Ambachtsheer and James L. Farrell, Jr., "Can Active Management Add Value?" *Financial Analysts Journal,* November–December 1979, pp. 39–47.

Table 6-7 Stock selection performance, 9/30/73–9/30/76

Stock selection strategy	Average annual return, %
Combined stock selection	10.0
LTF	9.0
STF	5.5
S&P 500	3.3

Source: Keith Ambachtsheer and James L. Farrell, Jr., "Can Active Management Add Value?" *Financial Analysts Journal,* November–December 1979, pp. 39–47.

generated by combining the two individual sources, STF and LTF, within the composite forecasting framework. The authors compared the performance of the three strategy variants over a three-year period with the S&P 500.

Table 6-7 shows the performance results. Note that all three variants of the strategy outperformed the S&P 500. In addition, the performance advantage of each was directly in line with the predictive content of the information source. The STF method, with the lowest IC of .07, showed the least differential of 2.2 percent, while the combined source, with the highest IC of .15, showed the greatest differential of 6.7 percent. Test results showed that "low-quality" predictive information about stocks could be translated into above-average performance, with the magnitude of the IC indicating the degree of the performance advantage.

Subsequent to this study, the disciplined stock selection approach underwent further testing and simulation until in 1979 it was applied to management of equity funds. It is now being used by the investment-counseling firm with which the author is associated to manage over $250 million in equity assets. The current application, while similar to the earlier phase of design and testing, differs in three respects. First, the stock selection process relies on four rather than two independent sources of predictions. As noted above, each of these sources has predictive content and the composite forecasting method has worked as before. Second, the universe of stocks from which selections are made is broader; it includes 800 of the largest stocks as opposed to a 200-stock universe used for purposes of the test. Finally, the portfolios being managed are somewhat larger in terms of individual issues (80 versus 60), and the risk control somewhat tighter than for the test.

Table 6-8 shows the performance of the strategy over the period of simulation and implementation. The period of simulation spans the first five years, while the actual implementation is reflected in the performance results for the three years beginning in 1979. Note that the strategy outperformed the S&P 500 by approximately 2 percent or better in each of the years from 1974 to 1981. The data in the lower part of the table indicate that the performance margin was delivered during both bull and bear markets. The strategy not only provided a longer-term favorable result but also delivered this with consistency, that is, low risk.

Table 6-8 Disciplined stock selection investment performance

Year	Disciplined stock selection	S&P 500	Disciplined stock selection advantage
1974*	−20.2%	−26.4%	+6.2%
1975	+45.3	+37.3	+8.0
1976	+33.7	+24.0	+9.7
1977	−2.7	−7.2	+4.5
1978	+13.6	+6.6	+7.0
1979[†]	+21.4	+18.5	+2.9
1980	+34.2	+32.5	+1.7
1981	−2.8	−5.1	+2.3
Average up market year			
	+29.6	+23.8	+5.8
Average down market year			
	−8.6	−12.9	+4.3

*Period of design, testing, and simulation.
[†]Results from application to management of equity funds.
Source: James L. Farrell, Jr., "A Disciplined Stock Selection Strategy," *Interfaces,* October 1982, pp. 3–12.

CONCLUSION

This chapter began by describing the main opportunities available to managers of domestic equities: stock selection, group rotation, and asset allocation-market timing. We then emphasized the importance of the need to analyze the investment process so as to emphasize those areas of strength in the organization through active strategies and to downplay those areas of weakness by using passive investment strategies. We thus introduced the notion of active-passive investment strategies. We then described the components and organizational structure necessary to implement an active strategy of stock selection. This structure has, in fact, been successfully implemented and used to derive above-average returns consistently over time. This not only verifies the efficacy of the systematic approach advocated in this book but also provides evidence counter to the most extreme version of the efficient-market hypothesis.

APPENDIX A DEFINING THE FORECASTING REGRESSION EQUATION

In the simple linear regression model between a dependent variable Y and an independent variable X,

$$Y = a + bX + e$$

the following relationships hold:

$$b = \frac{\text{Cov}(X, Y)}{\text{Var}(X)} = \frac{\rho_{xy}(S_x S_y)}{S_x \cdot S_x} = \frac{\rho_{xy} S_y}{S_x} \tag{1}$$

$$a = \overline{Y} - b\overline{x} \tag{2}$$

It should be apparent that if the two variables are in no way related, meaning they are uncorrelated, $\rho_{xy} = 0$, then $b = 0$. If $b = 0$, $a = Y$. If the two variables are perfectly related, $\rho_{xy} = 1$, and also have the same mean and standard deviation (one can be sure that they would when using ranked data), then $b = 1$. If $b = 1$, then $a =$ zero.

To provide perspective on the meaning of the error term, note that the total variability of the dependent variable Y can be partitioned into two parts: (1) that explained by the independent variable X; and (2) the unexplained part, or error. Substituting the regression equation for Var(Y), we obtain:

$$\text{Var}(Y) = \text{Var}(a + bX + e)$$

Since Var(a) = 0, and the Var(bx) = b^2 Var(X), this equation becomes

$$\text{Var}(Y) = b^2 \text{Var}(X) + \text{Var}(e)$$
$$= \text{explained variance} + \text{variance of the error}$$

When we take the square root of the Var(e), we obtain the standard deviation, a measure commonly referred to as the standard error. It provides a measure of the dispersion of individual plots around a regression line, as illustrated graphically in Figure A-1. A small standard error would reflect a narrow scatter of plots around the line, indicating a well-defined relationship. In contrast, a large standard error would reflect a wide scatter of plots around the line, indicating a loosely defined relationship.

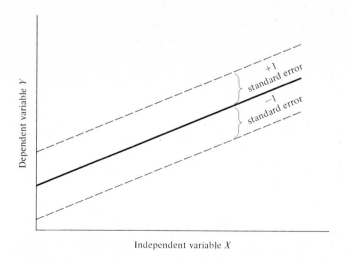

Figure 6-A1 Standard error of the regression.

The standard error is, in turn, related to the coefficient of determination R^2, which is a measure of the portion of the variance explained by the underlying relationship. It is calculated as follows:

$$\frac{\text{Explained variance}}{\text{Total variance}} = \frac{b^2 \, \text{Var}(X)}{\text{Var}(Y)} = R^2$$

At the same time the standard error, or variance of the error, measures the portion that is unexplained and is calculated as follows:

$$\frac{\text{Unexplained variance}}{\text{Total variance}} = \frac{\text{Var}(e)}{\text{Var}(Y)} = 1 - R^2$$

APPENDIX B COMBINING FORECASTS

This appendix illustrates the procedure for the special case of combining forecasts from two different methods, where each has a positive IC and the two sources are independent (cross-correlation is zero). In this regard it might be easier to demonstrate the process of combining forecasts by working with forecast errors, or the unexplained portion of realized return. This is in contrast to the discussion in the body of the study, which focuses on the correlation coefficient, or the explained portion of returns. Error reduction is, however, equivalent to maximizing the correlation by combining.

To begin with, we can designate the two forecasting methods as F_1 and F_2, and denote the variance of errors associated with each as $\text{Var}(F_1)$ and $\text{Var}(F_2)$ and the correlation between the errors of the two methods as ρ_{12}. Note that the method with the smaller error would be one with the higher IC. In addition, the objective in combining forecasts is to minimize forecast errors, which as noted would be equivalent to maximizing correlation. We can further let k represent the weight of the first method and $1 - k$ the weight of the second, where the weights sum to 1, thereby ensuring that the combined forecast is unbiased. The variance of errors in the combined forecast, $\text{Var}(C)$, can then be written as

$$\text{Var}(C) = k^2 \, \text{Var}(F_1) + (1 - k)^2 \, \text{Var}(F_2) + 2\rho_{12}k(\text{Var}(F_1))^{1/2}(1 - k) \, (\text{Var}(F_2))^{1/2}$$

Note that the extent of error reduction depends on the correlation between methods, ρ_{12}, as can best be illustrated by analyzing two extreme cases mentioned in the body of the study: zero correlation and perfectly positive correlation between methods. We first assume that the forecasting methods have the same predictive power, or that $\text{Var}(F_1) = \text{Var}(F_2)$. We also assume that both forecasts carry the same weight in the combining formula, or that $k = 1/2$. Substituting in the original formulation produces the following expression, where $\text{Var}(F)$ is a general representation of the error from both methods:

$$\text{Var}(C) = 1/2 \, \text{Var}(F) + 2\rho_{12}(1/4) \, \text{Var}(F)$$

When the methods are independent, the variance of the combined forecast is one-half that of an individual forecast because the zero correlation, $\rho_{12} = 0$, eliminates the covariance term in the expression. On the other hand, when the correlation is perfectly positive, $\rho_{12} = +1$, the variance of the combined forecast is the same as that of an individual forecast, because the covariance term becomes equivalent to the error of an individual forecast.

As noted before, we can also illustrate that weighting of forecasting methods in proportion to their forecasting power is optimum. We can specifically illustrate this by first differentiating the original expression in this appendix with respect to k, then equating to zero. This provides the following expression where the combined error is minimum (combined IC is greatest):

$$k = \frac{\text{Var}(F_2) - \rho_{12}\,\text{Var}(F_1)^{1/2}\,\text{Var}(F_2)^{1/2}}{\text{Var}(F_1) + \text{Var}(F_2) - 2\rho_{12}\,\text{Var}(F_1)^{1/2}\,\text{Var}(F_2)^{1/2}}$$

Where $\rho_{12} = 0$, this reduces to:

$$k = \frac{\text{Var}(F_2)}{\text{Var}(F_1) + \text{Var}(F_2)}$$

Note that where each method has equal forecasting power the errors would be equal and the numerator would be one-half the denominator. This would indicate that equally powerful methods should be weighted equally to obtain the optimal reduction in forecasting error.

PROBLEMS

1 Describe the various active strategies that are available for obtaining above-average return, and indicate the passive alternative to these active strategies.

2 An organization needs to assign ratings to stocks from three different industries: 5, 15, and 20 stocks, respectively. Determine how many stocks will be in each of the five rating categories for each of the three industries, using the rule illustrated in Figure 6-5.

3 What are the benefits of composite forecasting, and under what conditions is it appropriate to use this method?

4 An organization evaluates three independent sources of information and assesses each as having an IC of .15. It decides to use a composite forecasting method. Determine the combined IC for the organization using the three sources.

5 Refer to Figure 6-6 and assume that the standard deviation of the stock-return distribution is 26 percent and that the organization's IC is now .10. Determine the adjusted return distribution for that organization.

6 Discuss the importance of considering transactions costs when rebalancing the portfolio.

7 Outline the basic elements needed to execute an active strategy of stock selection.

SELECTED REFERENCES

Ambachtsheer, Keith P.: "Portfolio Theory and Security Analysis," *Financial Analysts Journal,* November–December 1971, pp. 53–57.

——: "Profit Potential in an 'Almost Efficient' Market," *Journal of Portfolio Management,* Fall 1974, pp. 84–87.

——: "Where Are the Customers' Alphas?" *Journal of Portfolio Management,* Fall 1977, pp. 52–56.

——and James L. Farrell, Jr.: "Can Active Management Add Value?" *Financial Analysts Journal,* November–December 1979, pp. 39–47.

Bates, J. J., and C. W. J. Granger: "The Combination of Forecasts," *Operations Research Quarterly,* 1969, pp. 451–468.

Bidwell, Clinton: "A Test of Market Efficiency: SUE/PE," *Journal of Portfolio Management,* Summer 1979, pp. 53–58.

Black, Fischer: "Yes, Virginia, There Is Hope: Tests of the Value Line Ranking System," *Financial Analysts Journal,* September–October 1973, pp. 10–14.

Elton, Edwin J., Martin Gruber, and Manfred Padberg: "Optimal Portfolios from Simple Ranking Devices," *Journal of Portfolio Management,* Spring 1978, pp. 15–18.

Falconer, Robert, and Charles M. Sivesind: "Dealing with Conflicting Forecasts: The Eclectic Advantage," *Business Economics,* September 1977, pp. 5–11.

Farrell, James L., Jr.: "The Multi-Index Model and Practical Portfolio Analysis," Occasional Paper no. 4., Financial Analysts Research Foundation, 1976.

——: "A Disciplined Stock Selection Strategy," *Interfaces,* October 1982, pp. 3–12

Fouse, William: "Risk and Liquidity: The Keys to Stock Price Behavior," *Financial Analysts Journal,* May–June 1976, pp. 35–45.

Hodges, Stewart, and Richard Brealey: "Portfolio Selection in a Dynamic and Uncertain World," *Financial Analysts Journal,* March–April 1973, pp. 50–65.

Lorie, James, and Victor Niederhoffer: "Predictive and Statistical Properties of Insider Trading," *Journal of Law and Economics,* April 1968, pp. 35–53.

Newbold, P., and C. W. J. Granger: "Experience with Forecasting Univariate Time Series and the Combination Forecasts," *Journal of the Royal Statistical Society,* 1974, pp. 131–146.

Shelton, John P.: "The Value Line Contest: A Test of the Predictability of Stock Price Changes," *Journal of Business,* July 1967, pp. 251–269.

Treynor, Jack, and Fischer Black: "How to Use Security Analysis to Improve Portfolio Selection," *Journal of Business,* January 1973, pp. 66–86.

Treynor, Jack: "Long-Term Investing," *Financial Analysts Journal,* May–June 1976, pp. 56–59.

Wagner, Wayne, and Larry Cuneo: "Reducing the Cost of Stock Trading," *Financial Analysts Journal,* November–December 1975, pp. 35–44.

SEVEN

ASSET ALLOCATION/MARKET TIMING

INTRODUCTION

This chapter deals with both asset allocation and market timing. Asset allocation can be considered strategic decision making. With a time horizon of at least three to five years, it is longer term than market timing, which can be considered a tactical approach to capitalizing on return opportunities that are perceived to be available in the more immediate term.

The purpose of the asset allocation process is to put assets together in a portfolio in such a way as to maximize return at a level of risk consistent with the investor's objective. This process involves four key elements. First, the investor needs to determine the assets that are eligible for the portfolio. Second, it is necessary to determine expected return for these eligible assets over a holding period or planning horizon. Third, once returns have been estimated and risk assessed, the techniques of optimization described in Chapter 2 should be used to find portfolio mixes providing the highest return for each level of risk. The final step is to choose the portfolio (from the efficient frontier) that provides the maximum return at a tolerable risk level. Since we've described the kinds of assets that are available in the investment universe in Chapter 1, we'll discuss the other three elements in this chapter, with special emphasis on determining the expected return for assets of interest to the portfolio manager.

After treating asset allocation, we'll discuss market timing. Since a decision to actively engage in market timing first involves assessing whether the organization has predictive capability, we'll describe techniques for making this measurement. Correspondingly, we'll discuss a framework for determining to what extent the organization should reallocate its asset mix based on a shorter-term market forecast. We'll then briefly deal with some methods that forecasters use in assessing the relative attractiveness of the market. The chapter will conclude with a discussion of the risks and degree of success that organizations have had in this endeavor.

181

ASSET ALLOCATION

As has been noted, once the universe has been defined, it is necessary to develop risk and return estimates for the assets of interest. There are essentially two methods of estimating the risk-return relationship among securities. The first is to assume that the future will be like the past and to extrapolate this past experience into the future. At the other extreme is the scenario approach, which involves establishing appropriate economic scenarios and then assessing the returns and risks associated with these scenarios. Generally, forecasts using this approach have a three- to five-year planning horizon. Forecasting by extrapolating the past into the future implicitly presumes an infinite planning or forecasting horizon. We'll begin by describing this approach and then cover the more complex scenario approach to forecasting risk-return relationships.

USING THE PAST TO FORECAST THE FUTURE

Since we'll first describe forecasting by the analysis of past data, we've reproduced the returns and risks associated with asset classes in Table 7-1. Note that we're considering only three asset classes: common stocks, long-term bonds, and short-term treasury bills. This will simplify the analysis and improve the illustration. The returns and risks associated with the assets were developed over the 1926–1978 period. The returns are realized returns and include income and capital gains, while the risks are the standard deviation of return and correlation among the asset classes.

Note that stocks showed the highest return and treasury bills the lowest return, with bonds showing intermediate return. The risk of the assets as measured by the standard deviation of return was in line with the realized return where stock returns were the most variable and treasury bills the least variable. Finally, stocks showed negative correlation over the period with treasury bills and slightly positive correlation with bonds, while treasury bills showed virtually no correlation with bonds.

In forecasting, investors will ordinarily assume that the standard deviations and correlations among assets realized over the past will persist in the future. They will, however, adjust projected returns for current levels of inflation, as theory and empirical research indicate investors are primarily concerned with real rather than nominal returns. Projections then assume that the real return earned in the future will be the same

Table 7-1 Risk and return characteristics of major asset classes, 1926–1978

Asset class	Return, %	Standard deviation, %	Correlation		
			Stocks	Bonds	Treasury bills
Stocks	8.9	22.5	1.0		
Bonds	4.0	5.6	0.1	1.0	
Treasury bills	2.5	2.2	−0.2	0.0	1.0

Source: Roger Ibbotson and Rex Sinquefeld, "Stocks, Bonds, Bills, and Inflation: Historical Returns (1926–1978)," Financial Analysts Research Foundation, Charlottesville, Va., 1979.

as that earned in the past. Nominal returns projected into the future will differ from past returns by the differences in the assumed future level of inflation and the rates realized in the past.

Table 7-2 shows the inflation rate for the 1926–1978 period, the realized real return for the three asset classes, and projected nominal returns incorporating current levels of inflation. Over the 1926–1978 period inflation was 2.5 percent, so that the real return on stocks was 6.4 percent, on bonds 1.5 percent, and on treasury bills close to zero. According to current estimates, inflation was to proceed at a rate of 9 percent, or 6.5 percentage points more than in the past. Adding the current inflation rate to the real returns of the past period provides projected nominal returns, higher than in the past, of 15.4 percent for stocks, 10.5 percent for bonds, and 9 percent for treasury bills.

Subdividing Historical Data

We can develop further insights into projecting past data into the future by subdividing the past fifty years into five natural periods. The first, 1929–1933, was a period of extreme deflation without recovery in the economy. The second, 1934–1938, was also a period of deflation, but with prospects of recovery in the economy. The third period, 1939–1945, was an extreme case of a controlled economy with both prices and interest rates set by regulatory agencies. The fourth, 1946–1965, was an extended period of stable prosperity. In the final period, 1966–1978, inflation began to accelerate and real growth slowed.

Table 7-3 shows the performance of stocks, bonds, and treasury bills over these five periods. The five historical capital market environments with their frequency of occurrence are shown across the top of the table. The frequency of occurrence was determined simply as the percentage of the total fifty-year period encompassed by a particular market environment; for example, the market was in an environment of deflation with no hope of recovery for the five-year period 1929–1933, or 10 percent for the 1929–1978 period. The return realized by the asset classes and the inflation rates over each of the five periods are also shown. Finally, the table shows the real return (nominal return less inflation rate) for each of the asset classes, the inflation premium (CPI rate of change), and the equity risk premium (stock return less treasury bill return) over each of the five periods.

Note that stocks did poorly during the initial period of deflation with no recovery and during the recent period of inflation. On the other hand, stocks did quite well during

Table 7-2 Nominal returns, inflation, real returns, and projected returns for major asset classes, %

Asset class	Nominal return (1926–1978)	Inflation rate (1926–1978)	Real return (1926–1978)	Expected inflation (1979)	Projected return
Stocks	8.9	2.5	6.4	9.0	15.4
Bonds	4.0	2.5	1.5	9.0	10.5
Treasury bills	2.5	2.5	0.0	9.0	9.0

the period of deflation with recovery as well as during the 1946–1965 period, when real economic growth was favorable and inflation moderate. Stocks performed moderately well during the period of controls. Real economic growth and low inflation appear to be favorable environments for stocks, while high inflation and low or declining real growth are unfavorable for stocks.

Bonds performed well during the two deflationary periods and showed relatively poor performance during the three periods subsequent to 1938. In a sense, bonds provide a hedge against slow economic growth and deflation but suffer in a relative sense in other periods. Treasury bills, on the other hand, appear to provide some hedge against inflation, as indicated by their performance in line with the rate of inflation in the most recent period, 1966–1978. During other periods treasury bills are less attractive relative to both stocks and bonds.

Adjusting Historical Data

In addition to accommodating current inflation rates, we could also adjust the return series for unusual events that might be distorting the data for certain periods. For example, during the 1940s and early 1950s the Federal Reserve pegged interest rates at artificially low levels. This, of course, not only depressed bond and treasury bill returns for that period but also lowered the longer-term average return for these assets. This, in turn, would distort the differential relationship between the return earned on stocks

Table 7-3 Historical capital-markets experience, 1929–1978, %

Capital-market environments	Deflation		Controls	Good times	Inflation
	Without recovery	With recovery			
Years	(1929–1933)	(1934–1938)	(1939–1945)	(1946–1965)	(1966–1978)
Frequency of occurrence	0.10	0.10	0.14	0.40	0.26
Average annual returns					
Stocks	−6.7	15.3	11.5	15.0	5.6
Bonds	6.2	7.8	3.5	2.3	4.6
Treasury bills	1.9	0.2	0.2	1.9	5.7
CPI	−5.0	1.3	3.9	2.9	6.0
Wages	−4.6	7.7	7.3	4.9	6.4
Average annual return components					
Real rate	6.9	− 1.2	− 3.7	− 1.0	−0.3
Inflation premium	−5.0	1.3	3.9	2.9	6.0
Equity risk premium	−8.6	15.1	11.3	13.1	−0.1

Source: Roger Ibbotson and Rex Sinquefeld, "Stocks, Bonds, Bills, and Inflation: Historical Returns (1926–1978)," Financial Analysts Research Foundation, Charlottesville, Va., 1979.

as well as on other fixed-income instruments. Excluding this period would result in a difference or realized risk premium for stocks of 5 percent rather than the 6.4 percent derived by using the full fifty-year period. Presumably this amended calculation would be more representative and hence more useful for projection into the future.

Another more fundamental adjustment for further adapting history to the future might be to adjust the historical frequencies of occurrence to reflect today's best judgment as to what kind of economic environments the future will bring. For example, we might foresee little likelihood of a controlled type of environment in the future and greater probability of a high-inflation environment. We would therefore lower the odds on the controlled environment and increase those on the inflationary, and then re-calculate the return series. Again, these recalculations would presumably be more representative of future experience.

SCENARIO FORECASTING

The other major approach to developing returns and assessing risk for securities is the scenario approach. The scenario approach differs from the historical approach with respect to both the analytical difficulty in developing the forecast and the appropriate time horizon for the forecast. To begin with, the scenario approach requires greater analytical effort and forecasting skill than the approach of extrapolating history into the future. The trade-off is, of course, the greater flexibility in dealing with changing environments and hence deriving more effective forecasts of future returns.

While forecasting with the historical approach implies an infinite forecasting hori-zon, the scenario approach requires a more explicit statement of the forecast period. Generally, forecasters will choose an intermediate-term forecasting horizon of, say, three to five years. This time horizon forces planners to look beyond seasonal and cyclical events and focus on sociopolitico-economic trends and their implications for stock prices and interest rates. At the same time, this planning horizon is not so remote as to be beyond the capability of developing some objective and useful forecasts of value.

In addition, this time horizon provides the appropriate perspective for shorter-term portfolio decision making. Once longer-term benchmark yields and price levels for security classes have been established, tactical portfolio decisions flow naturally from the interaction of (1) short-term fluctuations around these benchmark yields and price levels and (2) a predetermined long-term investment plan. It is in this latter respect that we can differentiate market timing, which is a shorter-term tactical approach, from asset allocation, which is a longer-term strategic approach to determining and changing the composition of the portfolio. We'll discuss market timing and its integration with the asset allocation process later in this chapter.

Figure 7-1 illustrates the necessary steps to implement the forecast. The diagram shows that the first step is to identify the possible range of economic environments that could exist. There are five scenarios listed, and the task here is to describe the real growth-inflation paths that could occur in each. The next step is to develop for each scenario the implications for interest rates, stock prices, and holding-period returns for each asset class. The third step is to determine the probability associated with the occurrences of each scenario.

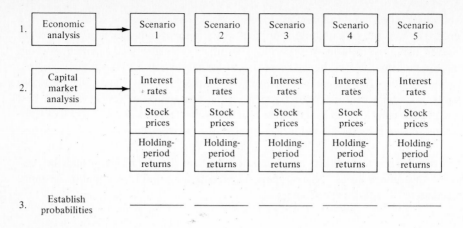

Figure 7-1 Scenario forecasting process.

Determining Scenarios

The number of economic scenarios will vary over time as economic conditions change. It will also vary across different forecasters, as some deal with as few as three and some with as many as a dozen or even more. We'll deal with five, as this number is large enough to be descriptive of the current economic environment but small enough to be analytically tractable. In addition, we noted previously that the economic environment of the past fifty years could be classified into five different episodes. We'll find it useful to compare some of the current scenarios to these past economic environments.

Figure 7-2 shows the five scenarios developed by a well-known forecasting organization, Canavest House, to describe the 1979–1983 economic environment. These five scenarios are designated (1) deflation with no recovery, DEF(NR); (2) deflation with recovery, DEF(WR); (3) good environment, OK; (4) inflation with collapse, BB; and (5) stagflation, SF. The figure shows the rate as well as the pattern of GNP growth associated with each scenario. It also shows the rate and pattern of inflation as measured by the CPI associated with the scenario. Finally, it indicates the probability of occurrence of each of the scenarios. Appendix A to this chapter describes the rationale for these scenarios, while Appendix B discusses the setting of the probability for the scenarios.

Note that the two deflationary environments correspond to those that occurred in the 1929–1933 and 1934–1939 periods. Bonds would be expected to do well during such times, while stocks would show mixed performance, doing well when recovery is in prospect and poorly when no recovery is foreseen. The OK environment might be construed as similar to the "good times" environment of the 1946–1966 period. Stocks would be expected to perform quite well during such a period, while bonds and treasury bills would be expected to show relatively inferior performance. The boom-bust and stagflation scenarios might in combination be compared with the inflationary environment of the 1966–1978 period. Treasury bills would be expected to perform well during this sort of period, while stocks and bonds would be expected to perform less favorably.

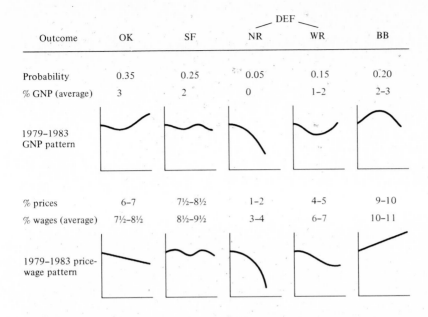

| Outcome | OK | SF | DEF | | BB |
			NR	WR	
Probability	0.35	0.25	0.05	0.15	0.20
% GNP (average)	3	2	0	1–2	2–3
1979–1983 GNP pattern					
% prices	6–7	7½–8½	1–2	4–5	9–10
% wages (average)	7½–8½	8½–9½	3–4	6–7	10–11
1979–1983 price-wage pattern					

Figure 7-2 Economic scenarios (1979–1983). (*Source: "A Special Report on Investment Policies and Objectives,"* Canavest House, Ltd., Toronto, June 1979.)

Capital-Market Implications

Figure 7-3 shows holding-period returns associated with each scenario for each of the asset classes: stocks, bonds, and treasury bills. Note that treasury bill returns are generally high when bond returns are low and vice versa. Bonds are expected to provide a hedge against deflation, while treasury bills are expected to provide a hedge against inflation. It is thus not surprising that these two assets exhibit contrary return behavior, as they are hedging against contrary economic phenomena—upward and downward changes in the prices of goods and services.

Note also that stocks show the greatest absolute and relative return in the OK or most favorable economic scenario. They provide a means of participating to the greatest extent in the favorable fortunes of the economy, whereas treasury bills and bond prospects are by nature quite limited. Stocks provide dramatically different returns depending on the sort of deflationary environment in prospect. According to one scenario, stocks act as a sort of hedge against deflation and would be highly correlated with bonds, but in the other diverge quite sharply from bond performance. Stocks, like treasury bills, perform moderately well in the stagflation environment, but show considerably poorer performance in the BB (boom-bust) environment. On balance, stocks tend to act independently of bonds and treasury bills.

Table 7-4 compares for each asset class the expected return developed by the scenario approach and the return derived from historical data. The scenario-based expected return was developed by weighting the return associated with each scenario by the probability of occurrence of the scenario. It is, in other words, simply a weighted

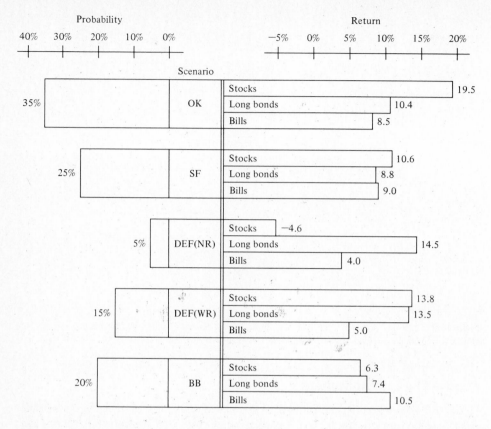

Figure 7-3 Four-year holding period return (1979–1983). (*Source: "A Special Report on Investment Policies and Objectives," Canavest House, Ltd., Toronto, June 1979.*)

average return. The historically derived return was derived by adjusting the return realized over the past fifty years for current rates of inflation, as described in the previous sections.

The table also compares the standard deviations and correlation coefficients derived by each of the forecasting methods. The risk measures for the historical methods are simple extrapolations of the realized risk over the past fifty years. The standard deviations and correlation coefficients for the scenario approach are derived by using the usual standard deviation and correlation coefficient formulas along with the probabilities associated with each of the scenarios.

While the return and risk measures generated by the two methods are fairly similar, they differ in some significant respects. First, note there is a narrower spread between the scenario-derived expected return for stocks and bonds than between that developed historically. This partially reflects the fact that bond returns were artificially depressed during the 1940–1953 period, thereby causing an unnaturally large spread between realized bond and stock returns for both the short and longer historical periods. Also, the scenario-based forecast does not place as high a probability on very favorable

Table 7-4 Risk and return — scenario versus historical forecast

	Expected returns	
	Forecast, %	Historical, %
Stocks	12.6	15.4
Long-term bonds	10.1	10.5
Treasury bills	8.3	9.0

	Standard deviation	
	Forecast, %	Historical, %
Stocks	18.0	22.5
Long-term bonds	5.5	5.6
Treasury bills	1.5	2.2

	Correlations					
	Forecast			Historical		
	S	LB	TB	S	LB	TB
Stocks	1.0	—	—	1.0	—	—
Long-term bonds	0.1	1.0	—	0.1	1.0	—
Treasury bills	0.0	−0.9	1.0	−0.2	0.0	1.0

environments as the historical return incorporates. The most favorable environment for stocks — the OK scenario — is projected to occur with a probability of .35, whereas historically the environment occurred with a frequency of .40.

   With regard to risk measures the historically derived standard deviation is higher for stocks than the scenario-based derivation. This is because the scenario-based projection places less weight on the most unfavorable scenario — deflation with no recovery — than occurred historically: .05 versus .10. Also, the correlation between bonds and treasury bills is highly negative (−.9) whereas historically there was zero correlation. This is because treasury bills are projected to track inflation more closely than in the past, whereas bonds are a more explicit hedge against deflation. Stocks are also expected to show less negative correlation with treasury bills primarily because they are projected to suffer less in an inflationary environment than they did previously.

DETERMINING THE OPTIMUM MIX

The next step in the asset allocation process is to develop mixes of assets that provide optimum risk-return combinations. We can use the portfolio optimization techniques described in Chapter 2 to develop these optimum portfolios.[1] Recall that one needs

---

[1]Since there are only a limited number of asset classes and variance and covariance inputs can be readily derived, it is usual to directly use the full covariance Markowitz formulation to generate portfolio mixes for an asset allocation.

returns, standard deviations, and covariances for the asset under consideration as inputs to these optimization models. For purposes of illustration we'll use the risk and return statistics developed as a part of the scenario approach as inputs.

Table 7-5 shows five optimum portfolios representing selected risk levels along the efficient frontier.[2] It shows the expected return associated with each portfolio and the risk of the portfolio as measured by the standard deviation. In addition, the table shows the composition of the portfolio—the percentage weighting of each asset class in the portfolio. Finally, it shows the probability of the return on the portfolio not exceeding a certain minimum level. This represents a sort of hurdle rate, or threshold, that an investor would presumably be especially concerned about exceeding; for purposes of illustration we're setting the hurdle rate at 5 percent.

Note that the proportion of stock held in optimum portfolios is directly related to their risk. As risk-return increases, the optimum equity portion increases; the reverse is true with treasury bills, as large holdings are associated with lower-risk portfolios. Bonds have higher weights in medium-risk portfolios than in either high- or low-risk mixes. The highest-risk portfolio has a .74 probability of exceeding the 5 percent hurdle rate, while the lowest-risk portfolio has a .89 probability of exceeding the hurdle rate.

The final step in the asset allocation process is to choose the portfolio that meets the requirements of the investor. Those with a high tolerance for risk would choose the

[2] Peter Deitz of Frank Russell Company conducted a study to determine the minimum and maximum percentages of a portfolio that should be represented by stocks and bonds. He obtained historical return data for these asset classes over the 1900–1975 period, formed portfolios with varying mixes of stocks and bonds, and computed the return and risk associated with the portfolio using the historical return data. Dietz calculated this for all combinations of stocks and bonds, varying the time periods to obtain risk and return characteristics for a whole range of portfolios over many differing historical return episodes.

The study showed that portfolios should have a minimum of 35 percent or a maximum of 60 percent in bonds and a minimum of 40 percent and a maximum of 65 percent in stocks to obtain the best reward per unit of risk. Portfolios with bond or stock allocations outside those boundaries had a significantly less favorable reward-risk ratio than those within those bounds. Portfolios that were structured within those bounds had reward-risk ratios that were fairly similar. The study is interesting in cautioning against extreme divergences in asset mix for a portfolio.

Table 7-5 Optimum portfolios, %

	Portfolio				
	A	B	C	D	E
Expected return	12.1	11.9	11.6	11.3	10.8
Standard deviation	10.9	9.7	8.2	6.7	4.8
Asset mix					
Stocks	85	75	63	50	35
Bonds	5	15	25	25	10
Treasury bills	10	10	12	25	55
Total	100	100	100	100	100
Probability of not exceeding 5% return	26	24	21	17	11

higher-risk portfolio. Presumably these investors are willing to tolerate a higher probability of not achieving a certain minimum return in order to earn a higher return. On the other hand, those with a lower tolerance for risk would choose the lower-risk portfolio. They are presumably more interested in achieving a certain minimum return, as illustrated by their 5 percent level in Table 7-5.

MARKET TIMING

As noted before, the expected return, standard deviation, and covariance inputs to the asset allocation process are of a longer-term nature, which can be defined here as a period of more than three years; however, these longer-term asset class expectations embody short-term risk-return parameters. In particular, the short-term return — say, the one-year return — will likely diverge above or below the average to be realized over the longer period. In the absence of special information, it is best, however, to proceed as if the year-by-year results will be identical to the longer-term average. For example, if the expected return on stocks is 13 percent over a four-year forecasting period, one would assume that the return realized each year would be 13 percent.

On the other hand, one can take the position that he has special knowledge about the return from an asset class that differs from the average expected over the longer period. The investor can vary the asset mix from the position established on the basis of longer-term projections to take advantage of the short-term forecast. For example, if the expected return on stocks that an organization is using for long-term planning purposes is 13 percent, but it forecasts a declining market for the coming twelve months, it could use this judgment to reduce its exposure to stocks below a level consistent with its long-term view.

This process of forecasting shorter-term return movements and varying the asset mix accordingly is popularly known as *market timing*. It is an activist management style, analogous to company or industry group selectivity. It is consciously taking an incremental risk in order to achieve incremental return. Engaging in this activity, however, presumes some sort of predictive capability with respect to market moves. The following section describes how to assess predictive ability and provides a framework for assessing the appropriate amount of risk-taking to obtain the incremental return.

ASSESSING PREDICTIVE ABILITY

A requisite for engaging in market timing is some level of predictive ability. The information coefficient (IC) method described in Chapter 6 provides a way of measuring this capability just as it does with respect to measuring stock selection capability. Before describing the application to market timing we should be aware that actual measurement of predictive accuracy in calling market moves is not easy. Whereas predictive accuracy tests on individual company judgments typically yield as many judgments per measurement period as the size of the stock selection universe, only one market judgment can be made per measurement period. In order to develop as large a sample for market judgments as for individual stocks, many measurement periods must pass. The statistics pertinent to evaluating market timing capability are, in short, much less readily available than for stock selection.

Figure 7-4 shows that measuring market timing capability is a three-step procedure. The first step is to compile an expression of the degree to which the market is over- or undervalued. We can again use the 5-point rating scheme, where rating 1 represents an extremely undervalued market, which would occur 10 percent of the time; 2 represents a moderately undervalued market, which occurs 20 percent of the time; 3 represents a neutral market, occurring 40 percent of the time; 4 represents a moderately overvalued market, occurring 20 percent of the time; and 5 represents an extremely overvalued market, which occurs 10 percent of the time.

Once these return categories are set, they must be converted into explicit return forecasts. As part of this process, we need to express rating categories in terms of standard deviations from the mean of the rating distribution. For the rating distribution used here, the standard deviation is 1.1 rating points. In this case, a rating of 5 or 1, which is 2 rating points away from the mean, is also 1.8 ($2 \div 1.1$) standard deviations away from the mean. Similarly, a rating of 4 or 2, which is 1 rating point away from the mean, is also .9 ($1 \div 1.1$) standard deviations away from the mean. Naturally, a rating of 3 would be zero deviations away from the mean.

Given the ratings distribution and using a forecast standard deviation of 18 percent for the market, the explicit return forecasts become those illustrated in step 2 of Figure 7-4. This shows that we convert a rating of 1, which is 1.8 standard deviations above the mean, into a 32 percent outperformance (1.8×18), while we convert a rating of 5, which is 1.8 below the mean, into a 32 percent underperformance. Similarly, we convert a rating of 2, which is .9 standard deviations from the mean, into a 16 percent outperformance ($.9 \times 18$), and a rating of 4, which is .9 below the mean, into a 16 percent underperformance. Naturally, a rating of 3, which is right at the mean of the distribution, converts into a performance that is in line with the longer-term expectation for the market—13 percent in this case. In this regard note that we're indicating underperformance or outperformance relative to the average expected return for the market over the longer term. This means that a projected rating of 5 converts into an expected return of -19 percent, or 13 percent less the forecast shortfall of 32 percent.

The third step involves adjusting the raw return adjustments for the assessed degree of accuracy in making the return forecast. Some predictive accuracy in turn implies some ability to create a correlation IC between forecast return deviations $F(D)$ and actual return deviations D. This is expressed in the following formula:

$$D = ICF(D) + \text{error} \qquad (1)$$

The formula tells us that the return deviation comprises two components: (1) that part explained by the forecast $ICF(D)$ and (2) the error in the forecast, or the remainder. When the ability to predict is perfect, $IC = 1.0$, the error in the forecast is zero and the actual deviation becomes equal to the forecast deviation—$D = F(D)$. On the other hand, when there is no predictive ability, $IC = 0$, the forecast explains no part of the deviation and actual deviation is then equal to the error term—$D = e$.

These are, of course, extremes, and as we've noted before, where predictive ability

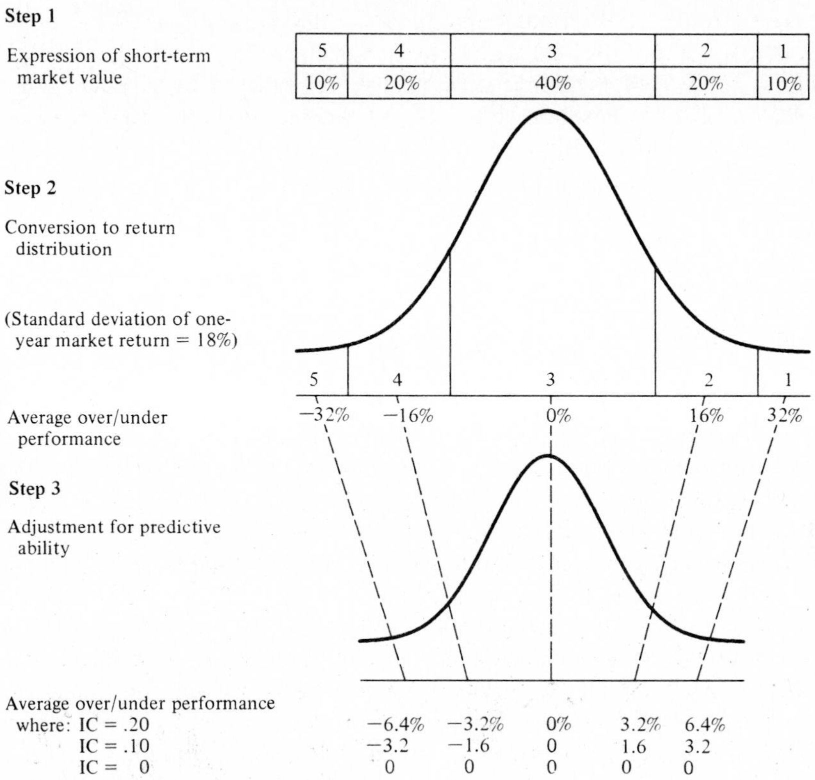

Step 1

Expression of short-term
  market value

5	4	3	2	1
10%	20%	40%	20%	10%

Step 2

Conversion to return
  distribution

(Standard deviation of one-
  year market return = 18%)

5	4	3	2	1
−32%	−16%	0%	16%	32%

Average over/under
  performance

Step 3

Adjustment for predictive
  ability

Average over/under performance
where: IC = .20
       IC = .10
       IC = 0

	−6.4%	−3.2%	0%	3.2%	6.4%
	−3.2	−1.6	0	1.6	3.2
	0	0	0	0	0

Figure 7-4 Evaluating market timing capabilities.

does exist, it's likely to be on the order of .10 to .20. To illustrate the case of some predictive ability, we'll assume that the organization has made an assessment that the market is moderately overvalued—a rating of 4 on our five-way rating scale. This, in turn, converts to an expected return deviation of −16 percent. Presuming that the organization has predictive capability on the order of .10, the expected deviation $E(D)$ becomes[3]

$$E(D) = \mathrm{IC}F(D) = .10(-.16) = -1.6$$

[3] To further illustrate, we can indicate that the market return R_M will be a function of its long-term expected return (13 percent) and a deviation D around that return:

$$R_M = 13 + D$$

The deviation D has an expected value $E(D)$ of zero and a variance $\mathrm{Var}(D) = 18^2 = 324$. As noted in the body of the chapter, the deviation can be explained as follows:

$$D = \mathrm{IC}F(D) + error$$

The error has an expected value $E(e)$ of zero and a variance $\mathrm{Var}(e) = (1 - \mathrm{IC}^2)\,\mathrm{Var}(D)$. The market variance, given the forecast, then becomes $(1 - \mathrm{IC}^2)\,\mathrm{Var}(D) = (1 - .10^2)(324) = 321$.

The diagram further illustrates this adjustment for three levels of predictive capability: .20, .10, and zero. When one adjusts for less than perfect predictive capability, the return forecast divergences become much smaller than indicated by the raw returns. For example, a rating of 5, which converts to a -32 percent return, becomes a forecast of -6.4 percent when adjusted for .20 predictive capability and -3.2 percent when adjusted for .10 predictive capability. Note that zero predictive capability means that low return divergences adjust to a zero forecast return divergence, automatically implying no activity with regard to market timing.

MANAGING MARKET SENSITIVITIES

Presuming some predictive ability and given a market forecast, the organization needs to adjust the portfolio accordingly to take advantage of the forecast. For example, forecast of a rising market would suggest reducing cash or increasing the portfolio beta, or a combination of the two. Conversely, forecast of an overvalued market and presumably an impending market decline would suggest increasing cash or decreasing the beta of the portfolio, or again a combination of the two. How much adjustment to the portfolio is warranted to take advantage of this extra return opportunity requires, however, a more formal analytical framework, which we can illustrate as follows.

To begin with, we can assume that an investor engaging in market timing would desire to maintain the same trade-off between risk and return as when maintaining the asset mix constant over time — that is, not engaging in market timing. We can express this quantitatively as the desire to maintain a constant ratio of expected return in excess of the risk-free rate to the standard deviation of return. Also known as the Sharpe ratio, it can be expressed as

$$\text{Sharpe ratio} = \frac{\text{expected return} - \text{risk-free rate}}{\text{standard deviation of return squared}} \tag{2}$$

To illustrate, we can again use our long-term expected return of 13 percent and forecast standard deviation of 18 percent for the market along with an assumed risk-free rate of 6 percent. We'll assume that the organization not only bases its longer-term forecast on this data but also uses it as a forecast for the forthcoming year — that is, the assumed data remains the same year by year. We'll call the ratio of return to risk derived from this data the "no special information" ratio and use it as a benchmark. Using the assumed data, the ratio becomes[4]

$$\frac{\text{Long-term expected return} - \text{risk-free rate}}{\text{Standard deviation of return squared}} = \frac{13 - 6}{18^2} = .0216$$

To illustrate market timing we can refer again to the organization that views the market as moderately overvalued. Recall from the prior section that with a predictive accuracy of .10 its raw 16 percent deviation forecast $F(D)$ should be adjusted to $.10(-16)$ for an expected deviation $E(D)$ of -1.6 percent. Given this, the portfolio manager should

---

[4] This calculation assumes that the stock portfolio has a market sensitivity (beta) of 1 and carries no specific risk.

adjust his beta in such a way as to maintain the "no special information" ratio of excess expected return to variance, which in the example is .0216. Assuming the one-year forecast does not significantly affect the standard deviation, the appropriate new beta level can be approximated by the ratio of the forecast one-year expected return to the "no special information" long-term excess expected return:[5]

$$\text{Beta} = \frac{E(RM) - R_f - E(D)}{E(R_m) - R_f} = \frac{13 - 6 - 1.6}{13 - 6} = .77 \qquad (3)$$

The formula thus calls for a reduction of the beta for the portfolio from the prior assumed level of 1.00 to .77. The formula represents a formal rationale for why an organization that considers the market extremely overvalued is unlikely (and unjustified in doing so) to go to a 100 percent cash position — reducing the beta to zero. The rather modest adjustment in the beta derives in turn from the fact that the return deviation was adjusted for imperfect forecasting ability. It also reflects an intention to incur no overall added risk in pursuit of greater return — that is, maintain the "no special information" ratio of excess expected return to variance.

CYCLICAL BEHAVIOR OF THE MARKET

Table 7-6 shows the performance of the S&P 500 in rising and falling market periods — bull and bear markets, if you will. The table shows the duration of the rising or falling markets and the percentage change in the index over those time spans. Note that since World War II there have been ten market declines, which in recent periods have been more severe and prolonged. Correspondingly, the rising, or bull, markets were more prolonged in the earlier period. Keep in mind that when these broad market movements occur, virtually all stocks are affected at least to a certain degree. In particular, in a long bull market, virtually all stocks experience some appreciation, while in a long bear market virtually all stocks experience some decline.

The changing behavior of the market has relevance to the ease of implementing a strategy of market timing. For example, it would have been quite difficult to operate with market timing strategies during the 1950s and early 1960s. This was a period of unusually favorable market experience, where returns were high on average and market declines were relatively short-lived, averaging only nine months in length, with the longest being fifteen months. Investors attempting to forecast the market and recommending selling would have had to have been quite nimble to successfully time a sale and repurchase in the space of nine months. This problem would have been especially severe for large investors, where substantial time is needed to establish positions. On the other hand, the market declines of eighteen months in 1969–1970 and twenty-one months in 1973–1974 were more severe and protracted

---

[5] This is so because the required condition is

$$B_p = \frac{E(R_M) - R_F + E(D)}{\text{Variance of portfolio}} = \frac{E(R_M) - R_F}{\text{Var}(D)} = \frac{13 - 6}{324} = .0216$$

If $\text{Var}(P) = B_p^2 \text{Var}(D)$, the equality condition is met by allowing B_p to take on a value equal to the ratio of the forecast risk premium over the "no special information" risk premium.

Table 7-6 Major bear and bull markets, 1929–1976, and performance of the S&P 500

Dates	Duration, months	Change, %
Sept. 1929–June 1932	33	− 84.8
June 1932–Feb. 1934	20	137.3
Feb. 1934–Mar. 1935	13	− 25.7
Mar. 1935–Feb. 1937	23	115.3
Feb. 1937–Apr. 1938	14	− 45.3
Apr. 1938–Oct. 1939	18	30.4
Oct. 1939–Apr. 1942	30	− 39.2
Apr. 1942–May 1946	49	138.5
May 1946–June 1949	37	− 25.3
June 1949–Jan. 1953	43	87.4
Jan. 1953–Sept. 1953	8	− 11.1
Sept. 1953–July 1956	34	109.6
July 1956–Dec. 1957	17	− 17.3
Dec. 1957–July 1959	19	48.1
July 1959–Oct. 1960	15	− 10.1
Oct. 1960–Dec. 1961	14	33.5
Dec. 1961–Oct. 1962	10	− 21.7
Oct. 1962–Jan. 1966	39	66.1
Jan. 1966–Oct. 1966	9	− 17.3
Oct. 1966–Dec. 1968	26	38.1
Dec. 1968–May 1970	17	− 28.6
May 1970–Dec. 1972	18	55.2
Dec. 1972–Sept. 1974	21	− 46.6
Sept. 1974–Dec. 1976	27	53.8

than in the previous period. Funds attempting to protect against a market decline would have had greater opportunity to successfully time a sale and repurchase over a period of eighteen to twenty-one months than in the nine-month interval of the earlier period.

The impact of differing market environments on the opportunity to use market forecasts profitably is illustrated by the data in Table 7-7. It shows hypothetical fund performance over two peak-to-peak market cycles. The first cycle includes a relatively short bear market (nine months) and should be representative of market forecasting results within the longer-term (1953–1968) favorable equity environment. The second cycle includes the eighteen-month bear market of 1969–1970 and should be representative of potential results in the more difficult equity markets of the 1970s.

First assume that a fund can position up to 25 percent of its assets in cash and the remainder is invested in equities represented by the S&P 500. Further assume that the fund can act on a forecast of market peaks and troughs (1) with a lead of two quarters, (2) with a lead of one quarter, (3) precisely at the peak or trough, (4) with a lag of one quarter, and (5) with a lag of two quarters. Table 7-7 shows the percentage added to the fund performance under each of the five lead-lag positioning assumptions for the two peak-to-peak market cycle periods.

Table 7-7 Hypothetical fund performance in two peak-to-peak market cycles, %

	1/1/66–12/31/68		1/1/69–12/31/72	
	Return	Added return	Return	Added return
S&P 500 performance (buy and hold)	23.9	—	29.5	—
Fund performance (cash-equity transfer)				
Two-quarter lead	24.2	0.3	34.7	5.2
One-quarter lead	26.7	2.8	36.0	6.5
Precise positioning	30.4	6.5	44.2	14.7
One-quarter lag	27.7	3.8	38.4	8.9
Two-quarter lag	22.6	−1.3	34.0	4.5

Note that the full-cycle return of the S&P 500 was approximately the same in both periods, with the latter period showing a somewhat greater return. A shift from a fully invested position in equities to 25 percent cash at the peak and a redeployment of cash to equities at the market trough would, however, have been relatively more beneficial in the latter cycle than in the earlier one. Cash management would have provided an incremental return of 14.7 percent versus 6.5 percent for the one-quarter lead. In addition, in the latter cycle cash management activities would have provided higher returns than in the earlier cycle under all lead-lag assumptions. Finally, there would have been positive benefits to cash management under all lead-lag assumptions in the latter cycle, whereas in the earlier cycle the two-quarter lag would have had a negative impact.

FORECASTING THE MARKET

There are any number of techniques for forecasting the market. The particular method or variety of methods depends on the preference of the forecaster. The success in using the technique or techniques depends in turn on the skill of the forecaster in interpreting the data. There are three major categories of techniques: (1) valuation-based methods, (2) business cycle and monetary indicators, and (3) technical indicators. We'll comment on each of these categories and illustrate some specific methods in the rest of this chapter.

Valuation Indicators

One of the more useful kinds of indicators of market value derives from the market line described in Chapter 5. Recall that the market line provides an indication of the overall level of stock prices as well as of the risk-return trade-off in the market. One can simply compare current market returns with those in other periods to develop some perspective on the current level. It is more useful, however, to compare the current absolute returns with the return on alternative investments, such as bonds and treasury bills, to develop some perspective on relative attractiveness. In addition, one may also want to compare the return with current inflation rates to assess what sort of real return is being offered by stocks and how it has varied in the past.

Figure 7-7 in Chapter 5 shows the actual Wells Fargo market line at various dates during the period 1972–1977. The line for June 1972 reflects the peak of the 1971–1972 bull market, while that for September 1974 reflects the bottom of the 1973–1974 bear market; the other line represents the market situation for a more normal period. The expected returns offered by stocks on each of the three dates represented by the lines are also presented in the figure. Expected returns on treasury bills and long-term bonds as well as the current inflation rates are presented for comparison.

It is noteworthy that stocks were offering 9 percent returns in the June 1972 market peak compared with 15.7 percent in the market trough of September 1974. Relating these absolute returns to the returns on treasury bills shows a spread, or risk premium, of 5 percent in 1972 and a risk premium of 7.7 percent in 1974. Since treasury bill rates and inflation rates were fairly similar, the real returns for stocks as of the two dates were virtually the same as the risk premiums as of the same dates. The real returns and risk premiums in June 1972 were below and in September 1974 above the 6.4 percent realized for both over the 1926–1978 period. As a matter of interest, inflation was in the process of accelerating in 1972, whereas in 1974 it was in the process of decelerating, albeit from a higher level than in 1972.

It is useful also to point out that the scenario framework itself can provide some immediate perspective in evaluating the current attractiveness of the market. Recall that the scenario approach entails determining scenarios, developing the capital-market implications of the scenarios, and assigning the probabilities of occurrence of the scenarios. Given this data, we can determine the expected return on assets under consideration; in our example we determined the expected return of stocks, bonds, and treasury bills over a four-year holding period.

One can, however, reverse this process by first assessing the expected return for the asset, given current price levels and consensus-input estimates, and then determining what the market seems to be assigning as probabilities to the different scenarios. For example, at year-end 1979, as we indicated previously, the S&P 500 was providing a yield of 5.4 percent. The growth rate implied by current return on equity and retention rate was generally in the 10 percent range, and adding these together (yield plus growth) provided an implied return of 15.4 percent compared with the 13 percent return developed from the scenario forecast.

Table 7-8 shows the five economic scenarios described earlier, the return for stocks associated with each scenario, and the probabilities of occurrence that lead to a scenario-related expected return of 13 percent for stocks. The final column shows a set of probabilities that may represent the weighting of scenarios implied by the return of 15 percent indicated by the alternative method of forecasting. Note that these implied probabilities give greater weight to more favorable scenarios and less weight to less favorable scenarios. If this implied weighting were to seem particularly unreasonable, then the course of action might be to reduce the stock weights in the portfolio from its longer-term target to take advantage of an apparent overvaluation.

Table 7-8 Stock return and probability of scenario, %

Scenario	Scenario-related return	Original probability of scenario	Consensus probability of scenario
OK	19.5	0.35	0.45
SF	10.6	0.25	0.35
DEF(NR)	4.6	0.05	0.0
DEF(WR)	13.8	0.15	0.20
BB	6.3	0.20	0.0
Expected return		12.6	15.4

Economic and Technical Indicators

Use of business cycle and monetary indicators to forecast the market is based on the fact that there should be some relationship between economic activity and stock returns. This relationship derives from the fact that dividends and the pricing of dividends are the fundamental source of value for the market. The dividend-paying ability of corporations and the discount rate for dividends should, in turn, be a function of general economic conditions.

Table 7-9 illustrates the relationship of stock returns to real GNP, inflation (CPI), and profits over both the 1953–1968 and 1969–1974 periods. Note that stocks showed an average annual return of 14 percent in the earlier period but an average loss of 3 percent in the latter period. The change in the return behavior of stocks might be attributed to a change in the general economic environment between the two periods. In particular, inflation increased and interest rates rose substantially, increasing the discount rate for dividends. Correspondingly, corporate profitability did not keep pace, leading to a below average rate of dividend growth.

Economic indicators are used to anticipate changes on a shorter-term basis. Some types of economic indicators used in this regard are (1) the rate of change of corporate profits, (2) growth in the real money supply, and (3) the GNP gap. We should note, however, that relating economic data to stock prices on a short-term basis is much more problematical than assessing longer-term relationships. This is because of the leads and lags in the relationships and the fact that these can vary over time.

While use of economic indicators has theoretical support, technical indicators are mainly based on empirically derived relationships. One indicator that seems to have been successful in the past is a simple relation of recent returns to past returns on the market. When returns have been high in recent times, the market is likely to regress to a lower level, while the converse is true when returns have been low in the recent period. The framework of a four-year period seems to work best, and it may be related to the business cycle, which has averaged about four years over time. There are, of course, myriad other technical indicators, but discussing them would be beyond the scope of this book.

Table 7-9 Stock returns and economic variables, %

	Compound annual trend	
	1954–1968	1969–1974
S&P 500 (total return)	14.0	−3.4
GNP (real)	3.9	3.2
Inflation (CPI)	1.7	5.6
Dividends	5.7	3.4
Interest rates		
Treasury bills	3.1	6.1
AAA corporates	4.3	7.6

RISKS IN MARKET TIMING

Market timing is a controversial subject. Many contend that it is impossible to be successful in the effort, while others contend that it is too risky to undertake in the first place.[6] At the same time there are only a very limited number of studies available that provide any perspective on the question; those few which deal with the subject come up with conflicting results.

Two studies by Treynor[7] and Jensen[8] evaluated the market timing activities of mutual funds in the 1950s and early 1960s, when market timing would presumably have been more difficult. Their studies indicated little evidence of a facility of funds, on average, to profit from forecasts of the market. At the same time the studies indicated no extraordinary losses, on average, from the attempt to forecast, implying little realized risk from the endeavor.

In a study of market timing Farrell evaluated the performance of funds over that earlier period as well as over the 1969–1975 period, when market timing would presumably have been easier.[9] His results were consistent with those of the previous two studies for the earlier period. The results also indicated that funds, on average, showed little return or realized loss from the endeavor in the latter period; however, in that period he found several funds that demonstrated some above-average capability to add to performance by market timing.

[6]In a study "Likely Gains from Market Timing" (*Financial Analysts Journal*, March–April 1975, pp. 60–69), William Sharpe estimated the degree of predictive capability necessary to be successful in market timing. He assumed a particular market timing strategy on the part of a hypothetical market timer, incorporated transactions costs, and simulated the strategy over the 1929–1972 period. His results showed that the timer had to be correct in his forecast 75 percent of the time to do well with a buy-and-hold strategy over the same period. The study is interesting both for its analytical method and its indication of the difficulty of achieving success through market timing strategies.

[7]Jack L. Treynor and Kay Mazuy, "Can Mutual Funds Outguess the Market?" *Harvard Business Review*, July–August 1966, pp. 131–236.

[8]Michael C. Jensen, "The Performance of Mutual Funds in the Period 1945–1964," *Journal of Finance*, May 1968, pp. 389–416.

[9]James L. Farrell, Jr., "Is Market Timing Likely to Improve Performance?" paper presented at the Spring 1976 seminar of the Institute for Quantitative Research in Finance, Scottsdale, Ariz.

CONCLUSION

This chapter has indicated that the portfolio analysis model described in Chapter 2 provides the explicit framework for determining an asset allocation that best meets the longer-term goals of the investor. We have also explained the scenario approach to developing risk and return inputs for asset classes. This approach places the heaviest burden of estimation on the user, but it has the greatest potential of providing the most useful input for the analysis. It's an analytical technique that can be applied to many other areas of forecasting.

We then discussed market timing, which has a shorter-term orientation with the objective of improving the portfolio return by opportunistically shifting the weighting of the assets from their longer-term allocation. Here we described an analytical framework that explicitly considers our assessed degree of forecasting ability and thereby establishes the proper amount to "bet" on this activity. We further described those analytical tools which might be useful in assessing the relative attractiveness of the overall market. The review in the final part of the chapter indicates that the limited number of studies on market timing are rather inconclusive as to the likely success of this investment activity.

APPENDIX A POSSIBLE 1979–1983 ENVIRONMENTS[10]

1. *The OK environment.* A moderate recession takes place in late 1979 and early 1980. Real output is back on an upward track by late 1980. Inflation decelerates over the period to a 5–6 percent rate by 1983. In short, gradualism works.
2. *The SF environment.* The trend toward inflation immunization and acceptance continues. Real output moves up and down in fits and starts. Inflation remains in the current 8–9 percent range as the various constituencies attempt to maintain their share of an apparently constant economic pie.
3. *The DEF(NR) environment.* A combination of policy errors, a consumer strike, a credit crisis, and new supply shocks set off a cumulative downward spiral in an economy already moving into a recession. The inflation process is broken, but at a very high cost in terms of unemployment and bankruptcies. No recovery is in progress at the end of the horizon.
4. *The DEF(WR) environment.* Events at first unfold as per the DEF(NR) environment, but concerted efforts on the part of the major economic constituencies within the United States and abroad restore confidence. A recovery is in progress in the early 1980s accompanied by a 3–4 percent inflation rate.
5. *The BB (boom-bust) environment.* The widely anticipated late 1979–early 1980 recession does not occur. Instead, the focal point of attention becomes protection against an accelerating inflation rate. Purchasing of real goods and credit expansion

[10]Keith Ambachtsheer, *A Special Report on U.S. Stock Prices and Interest Rates,* Canavest House, Ltd., Toronto, June 1979.

continues until emergency measures are taken, which might include, for example, credit allocation and price and wage controls. The early 1980s now see a confusing combination of collapsing "auction market" prices (from levels much higher than today) and a bureaucratic takeover of "institutional market" pricing, with the latter prices moving up at double digit rates prior to the emergency measures.

APPENDIX B PROBABILITIES OF SCENARIOS[11]

1. *The OK environment.* For this environment to unfold, a "common good" concensus has to evolve. This evolution could be aided by a transfer of resources out of the public sector into capital formation. It also implies a reasonable alignment of economic expectations and possibilities. While these developments are far from certain, they are certainly possible. Assigned probability: .35
2. *The SF environment.* The incomes-share battle in this environment is fought with the expectation that high inflation rates will be a permanent fixture. All constituencies learn to live with it as best as they can. Indexation becomes a widespread phenomenon. Changes of course in monetary and fiscal policies prevent both inflationary and deflationary spirals. Assigned probability: .25
3. *The DEF(NR) environment.* Even *Crash of 1979* author Erdman admits this scenario is not likely. Yet, it seems imprudent to totally ignore this possibility in an interdependent world with a highly levered credit structure and a serious oil-supply problem. Assigned probability: .05
4. *The DEF(WR) environment.* This is the preferred outcome of the "it will hurt but it's worth it" school. The inflation cycle can be broken, but only with the drawing of sufficient economic blood. While a consciously produced deep recession does not seem likely, the previously cited uncertainties surrounding the consumer and monetary policy (past, present, and future) make it a possibility. Assigned probability: .15
5. *The BB (boom-bust) environment.* If the acceleration of food, energy, and commodity prices continues, industrial prices and wages are almost certain to follow. This would set the stage for full-scale double-digit inflation, which in a presidential election year like 1980 would give the electorate a choice between Democratic controls and a Republican credit crunch. Either outcome would be very unpleasant socioeconomically speaking. Assigned probability: .20

PROBLEMS

1 Discuss how market history may be useful in setting probabilities for differing market scenarios.

2 Outline and discuss the major steps in asset allocation.

[11]Keith Ambachtsheer, *A Special Report on U.S. Stock Prices and Interest Rates,* Canavest House, Ltd., Toronto, June 1979.

3 Compare and contrast the historical and scenario approaches to developing input data for asset allocation.

4 Calculate the standard deviation of the rating distribution shown in Figure 7-4. Then calculate the standard deviation assuming that the probability of falling into each of the five rating categories is equal — that is, 20 percent for each.

5 Assume that the standard deviation of the market is 22 percent and the organization has a predictive capability on the order of .15 (IC = .15). Determine the adjusted return distribution for that organization using the format in Figure 7-4.

6 Assume that the organization in the previous problem determines that the market is moderately undervalued — rates it 2. Determine the appropriate portfolio beta.

7 Describe how the scenario approach can be used as a benchmark for comparing current consensus expectations for market return.

SELECTED REFERENCES

Ambachtsheer, Keith: "On the Risks and Reward of Market Timing," paper presented at the Spring 1976 seminar of the Institute for Quantitative Research in Finance, Scottsdale, Ariz.

Cagan, P.: "Common Stock Values and Inflation — The History Record of Many Countries," National Bureau Supplement, National Bureau of Economic Research, New York, 1974.

Dietz, Peter: "Setting Objectives and Allocating Assets: The Pension Manager's Dilemma," paper presented at the Spring 1976 seminar of the Institute for Quantitative Research in Finance, Scottsdale, Ariz.

Edesess, Michael, and George A. Hambrecht: "Scenario Forecasting: Necessity, Not Choice," *Journal of Portfolio Management,* Spring 1980, pp. 10–15.

Fama, E. F., and G. W. Schwert: "Asset Returns and Inflation," *Journal of Financial Economics,* November 1977, pp. 115–146.

Fanning, James: "A Four-Indicator System for Forecasting the Market," *Financial Analysts Journal,* September–October 1971, pp. 49–56.

Farrell, James L., Jr.: "Is Market Timing Likely to Improve Performance?" paper presented at the Spring 1976 seminar of the Institute for Quantitative Research in Finance, Scottsdale, Ariz.

Fong, Gifford: "An Asset Allocation Framework," *Journal of Portfolio Management,* Winter 1980, pp. 58–66.

Grant, Dwight: "Market Timing and Portfolio Management," *Journal of Finance,* September 1979, pp. 1119–1131.

Gray, William: "Developing a Long-Term Outlook for the U. S. Economy and Stock Market," *Financial Analysts Journal,* July–August 1979, pp. 29–39.

Ibbotson, Roger, and Rex Sinquefeld: "Stocks, Bonds, Bills, and Inflation: Historical Returns (1926–1978)," Financial Analysts Research Foundation, Charlottesville, Va., 1979.

Jensen, Michael C.: "The Performance of Mutual Funds in the Period 1945–1964," *Journal of Finance,* May 1968, pp. 389–416.

Keran, Michael W.: "Expectations, Money, and the Stock Market," *Federal Reserve Bank of St. Louis Review,* January 1971, pp. 18–26.

Leuthold, Steven: "Interest Rates, Inflation and Deflation," *Financial Analysts Journal,* January–February 1981, pp. 28–41.

Lintner, J.: "Inflation and Common Stock Prices in a Cyclical Context," National Bureau of Economic Research, 1973 Annual Report, pp. 23–36.

Modigliani, Franco, and Richard Cohn: "Inflation and the Stock Market," *Financial Analysts Journal,* March–April 1979, pp. 24–44.

Moore, Geoffrey H.: "Stock Prices and the Business Cycle," *Journal of Portfolio Management,* Spring 1975, pp. 7–13.

Moskowitz, Arnold, and George A. Harben: "Keep Profits: The True Discount Factor," *Journal of Portfolio Management,* Summer 1978, pp. 5–15.

Nelson, C. R.: "Inflation and Rates of Return on Common Stocks," *Journal of Finance,* May 1976, pp. 24–44.

Rozeff, Michael: "The Money Supply and the Stock Market," *Financial Analysts Journal,* September–October 1975.

Sharpe, William: "Likely Gains from Market Timing," *Financial Analysts Journal,* March–April 1975, pp. 60–69.

Sharpe, William F.: *Investments,* Prentice-Hall, Englewood Cliffs, N. J., 1978.

Smith, Rodger, and Thomas Richard: "Asset Mix and Investment Strategy," *Financial Analysts Journal,* March–April 1976, pp. 67–71.

Terborgh, George: "Inflation and Profits," *Financial Analysts Journal,* May–June 1974, pp. 19–22.

Treynor, Jack L., and Kay Mazuy: "Can Mutual Funds Outguess the Market?" *Harvard Business Review,* July–August 1966, pp. 131–236.

Wallich, Henry: "Investment Income during Inflation," *Financial Analysts Journal,* March–April 1978, pp. 34–37.

EIGHT

HOMOGENEOUS STOCK GROUPINGS

INTRODUCTION

This chapter is concerned with homogeneous stock groupings and is the last of a series of three dealing with the domestic equity investment process. It begins by discussing the results of a statistical test for relevant stock groupings and the characteristics of the stock groupings that emerged from the analysis. It then examines the uses of stock groupings: first within the context of a passive portfolio strategy, and then within the context of an active management strategy.

TEST FOR STOCK GROUPINGS

We'll begin by reviewing the results of a statistical test for relevant stock groupings published by Farrell.[1] This analysis was oriented toward determining whether the price action of stocks conformed to the classes of growth, cyclical, stable, and energy (oil) stocks.[2] Table 8-1 defines these classes of stocks and gives some examples of the types of companies represented in these classes.

To test whether stocks actually group accordingly, Farrell first selected a sample of 100 stocks and then developed monthly returns for each of the stocks over the 1961–1969 period. It was not possible, however, to work directly with the unadjusted returns as virtually all stocks are correlated with a general market effect. It was therefore necessary to remove this effect and see if there was added co-movement among stocks that conformed to the classification into growth, cyclical, stable, and energy stocks. (Those who are interested in the technicalities of making this adjustment should read the published material.)

---

[1] James L. Farrell, Jr., "Analyzing Covariation of Return to Determine Homogeneous Stock Groupings," *Journal of Business,* April 1974, pp. 181–207.

[2] In Farrell's original study the fourth group was identified as oil; however, subsequent analysis indicates that the group is more broadly identified as representing an energy effect.

Table 8-1 Definitions and examples of growth, cyclical, stable, and energy stocks

---

Growth stocks

Earnings of these companies are expected to show a faster rate of secular expansion than the average company.
Examples:
  Electronics companies, such as Hewlett-Packard, Perkin Elmer, AMP, and Texas Instruments
  Office equipment companies, such as Digital Equipment and Wang Labs
  Drug and hospital supply companies, such as Baxter Labs, Becton Dickinson, and Merck

---

Cyclical stocks

These companies have an above-average exposure to the economic cycle. Earnings would be expected to be down more than the average in a recession and up more than the average during the expansion phase of the business cycle.
Examples:
  Metals companies, such as Phelps-Dodge, Asarco, Alcoa, and Bethlehem Steel
  Machinery companies, such as Caterpillar, Ingersoll Rand, Cincinnati Milacron, and Deere
  Building-related companies, such as Johns-Manville and Weyerhauser
  General industrial companies, such as Goodyear, International Paper, Square D, Continental Group, and Eaton

---

Stable stocks

These companies have a below-average exposure to the economic cycle. Earnings would be expected to be down less than the average in a recession and up less than average during the expansion phase of the business cycle. Earnings of these companies are the most adversely impacted by inflation but fare relatively the best in periods of decelerating inflation, or disinflation.
Examples:
  Utilities, such as American Electric Power
  Food and beverage companies, such as General Foods, Coca-Cola, and Kellogg
  Retailers, such as Sears and Federated Department Stores
  Banking, insurance, and finance companies, such as Chase Manhattan, Transamerica, and Household Finance
  General consumer merchandising companies, such as Gillette, Reynolds, and Procter and Gamble

---

Energy stocks

Energy companies supply energy to both producers and consumers. The earnings of these companies are affected by the economic cycle but, most importantly, by trends in the relative price of energy.
Examples:
  Coal companies, such as Pittston and Westmoreland Coal
  Crude-oil producers, such as Pennzoil, General American Oil, and Superior Oil
  Domestic oil companies, such as Shell Oil, Atlantic Richfield, and Union Oil
  International oil companies, such as Exxon, Texaco, and Standard Oil of California

---

Once returns had been adjusted, a coefficient of correlation between each stock in the sample and every other stock was calculated. Since there were 100 stocks in the sample and each was being correlated with every other, this resulted in $100 \times 100 = 10,000$ correlation coefficients. If stocks group according to growth, cyclical, stable, and energy characteristics, one would expect them to be positively and highly correlated within groupings and generally uncorrelated across groups. More specifically, one would expect growth stocks to be highly correlated with other growth stocks but not to be correlated with cyclical, stable, or energy stocks; cyclical stocks to be highly correlated with other cyclical stocks but uncorrelated with growth, stable, or energy stocks; stable stocks to be highly correlated with other stable stocks but uncorrelated with growth, cyclical, or energy stocks; and energy stocks to be highly correlated with other energy stocks but uncorrelated with growth, cyclical, or stable stocks.

This expected pattern of correlation is illustrated by the matrix of correlation coefficients in Figure 8-1. The correlation coefficients within each of the classes of growth, cyclical, stable, and energy stocks are arranged along the diagonal of the matrix. These within-group correlation coefficients should show high and positive values; they are identified by the letter H and a plus sign. The correlation coefficients off the diagonal represent the correlation of stocks between groups (growth with cyclical, cyclical with stable, etc.). These correlation coefficients, which one expects to be low, are identified by the letter L.

Cluster Analysis

To analyze whether the actual correlation matrix in fact showed this expected pattern, Farrell used cluster analysis. This technique systematically examines the matrix of correlation coefficients and separates stocks into groups or clusters within which stocks are highly correlated and between which stocks are poorly correlated. The stepwise

	Growth	Cyclical	Stable	Energy
Growth	Growth stocks H+	L	L	L
Cyclical	L	Cyclical stocks H+	L	L
Stable	L	L	Stable stocks H+	L
Energy	L	L	L	Energy stocks H+

Figure 8-1 Matrix of correlation coefficients — growth, cyclical, stable, and energy stocks.

nature of this method permits use of a simple, rapid computer program that involves (1) searching the correlation matrix for the highest positive correlation coefficient, (2) combining these stocks to reduce the matrix by one, and (3) recomputing the correlation matrix to include the correlation between the combined stock or cluster and the remaining stocks or clusters.

This process can be illustrated with a specific example. Presume that of all possible stock pairs two electronic stocks, Hewlett-Packard and Perkin Elmer, were the most highly correlated. The routine would combine these stocks to form a cluster of two stocks, simultaneously reducing the number to be clustered from 100 to 99. It would then search the correlation matrix for the next highest pair of correlation coefficients. Again, for purposes of illustration, assume that AMP, another electronics company, and the Hewlett-Packard/Perkin Elmer cluster were the most highly correlated. AMP and the Hewlett-Packard/Perkin Elmer cluster would then be combined to form a larger three-stock cluster, again simultaneously reducing the number to be clustered by one, from 99 to 98. This iterative routine continues until all positive correlation coefficients are exhausted or until (on the ninety-ninth pass) all 100 stocks form a single cluster.

At each scanning the stocks are classified into one less groups than on the previous pass, thus yielding, for example, $100 - 50 = 50$ groups on the fiftieth pass. If the hypothesis that the 100 stocks in the sample could be categorized was correct, then by the ninety-sixth pass the four remaining groups should correspond to those hypothesized. Furthermore, all positive correlation coefficients should be exhausted by the ninety-sixth pass, thus terminating the procedure. This, in turn, would indicate not only that the sample data can be explained by four independent groupings, but also that there is a low degree of correlation across stock groupings.

Figure 8-2 provides four diagrams of the results of the cluster routine, showing the stage where pairs or groups of stocks joined and the value of the correlation coefficient at that stage. The number of stocks in each cluster is growth 31, cyclical 36, stable 25, and energy (oil) 8. Stocks classified a priori as growth, cyclical, stable, or energy (oil) actually clustered within their allocated groups. All group clusters appeared to contain highly intercorrelated stocks, as final stocks, or groups of stocks clustering into individual groups, did at relatively high levels of positive correlation: .19 for growth, .15 for stable, .18 for cyclical, and .27 for energy (oil). The final four groups were not positively correlated, as evidenced by the fact that the routine terminated on the ninety-sixth pass, as the positive correlation of .15 was the lowest positive correlation on the prior (ninety-fifth) pass.

Index Procedure

To determine the degree of positive correlation within each of the four groupings of growth, cyclical, stable, and energy stocks, as well as the extent to which the stocks were uncorrelated with other groupings, Farrell then employed an index procedure. This involved first developing a rate of return (adjusted for general market effects) for each of the four stock groupings. Stocks that clustered into the four groups were formed directly into four monthly indexes composed of growth, cyclical, stable, and energy

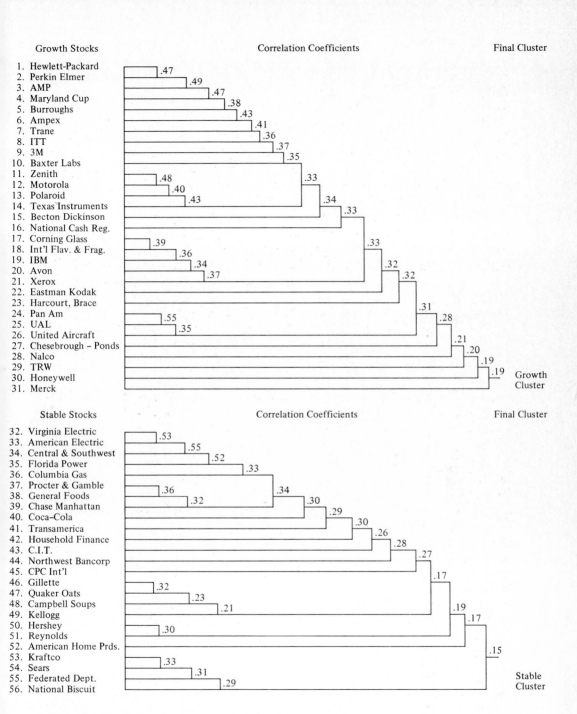

Figure 8-2 Cluster diagram. *(Source: James L. Farrell, Jr., "Analyzing Covariation of Return to Determine Homogeneous Stock Groupings," Journal of Business, April 1974, pp. 184–208.)*

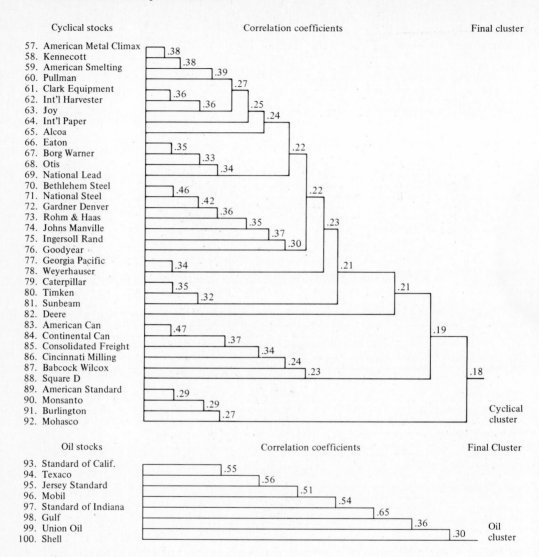

Figure 8-2 *(Continued)*

stocks. The adjusted return of each stock in the index was then averaged month by month to provide a series of monthly returns over the 1961–1969 period.

Between the adjusted returns of each stock in the sample of 100 stocks and each of the four indexes, 400 different correlation coefficients were calculated. If the four groupings of growth, cyclical, stable, and energy (oil) stocks represent homogeneous groups, one would expect the correlation coefficient of a stock with its corresponding index to be positive and significantly far from zero. In addition, one would expect its correlation with the other three indexes to be limited. This pattern is, of course, implied by the previously described expectation for the matrix of correlation coefficients of the grouped stocks (see Figure 8-1).

Figure 8-3 shows the average value of the correlation coefficients for growth, cyclical, stable, and energy stocks in the sample with the corresponding index as well as with the other three indexes for the 1961–1969 period (this 4×4 matrix thus summarizes the 4×100 correlation matrix of stocks and indexes). Note that the average values of the correlation coefficients of stocks with the corresponding index are all positive and highly significant. Inspection of the complete correlation matrix of stocks and indexes also indicates that most of the stocks in the group average are positively correlated with the respective index at a statistically significant level. At the same time, note that the average value of the correlation coefficients of stocks with other indexes shows a low degree of correlation. These results indicate that the four return-determined stock groupings are homogeneous, as the return behavior of stock within each group is highly correlated, while the return behavior between groups is independent.

Test for Stability of Relationship

In order to test for the stability of the relationships established in the study, the analysis was updated to a later period (1970–1977) and a larger sample of stocks was used.[3] There were 354 stocks in this sample, including virtually all 100 stocks analyzed in the earlier study. These stocks were mainly of large institutional quality, with 260 of them representing approximately 90 percent of the market weighting of the S&P 500, compared with 50 percent for the original 100 stocks. The companies in the sample were also spread over 90 of the S&P 500's 108 industry groupings, thereby providing great diversity as well as encompassing the major market portion of the index.

Monthly returns were calculated for each stock for the 1970–1977 period. These returns were adjusted for general market effects by running a regression of the monthly returns against the returns of the S&P 500. Correlation coefficients based on these adjusted returns were calculated between each stock and every other stock in the sample in order to generate a correlation matrix for the more recent 1970–1977 period.

In order to assess the group behavior exhibited by the stocks over this period, a cluster procedure similar to the one in Farrell's original study was again employed. This analysis showed that four clusters were adequate to explain the correlation matrices for both the 1961–1969 and 1970–1977 periods. For both periods these clusters were identified as containing growth, cyclical, and stable stocks, with the fourth cluster being more appropriately identified as an energy group rather than a more narrowly defined oil group. The cluster results were by and large in line with those from Farrell's original study, indicating the stability of return-determined homogeneous groups over time.[4]

---

[3] The update is described in James L. Farrell, Jr., George Pinches, and James Scott, "Growth Stock Fundamentals: Implications for Portfolio Management," unpublished paper, 1981.

[4] While the cluster analysis indicated that the same four stock groupings were appropriate for explaining the data, we should note that there were instances where individual stocks switched group affiliation; that is, there was migration of individual stocks across the groupings. This was especially true with respect to the growth grouping, where stocks fell into one of the nongrowth groupings in the latter period of analysis. This, of course, should be expected from the fact that the fundamental distinguishing feature of a growth stock is investor expectation of superior growth in earnings and that this superior growth is finite, that is, limited in duration. Once the company has exhausted its opportunities to generate superior growth, we would then expect its price action to conform to that of a nongrowth stock.

	Growth index	Cyclical index	Stable index	Energy index
Growth average	.40	−.07	−.08	−.13
Stable average	−.08	.34	.05	−.03
Cyclical average	−.11	.01	.39	.00
Energy average	−.23	−.08	.04	.48

Figure 8-3 Matrix of residual correlation coefficients — averages of stocks and four stock indexes (1961–1969). *(Source: James L. Farrell, Jr., "Analyzing Covariation of Return to Determine Homogeneous Stock Groupings," Journal of Business, April 1974, pp. 184–208.)*

Application of the index procedures provided Figure 8-4, which is similar to Figure 8-3, except that the data is for the 1970–1977 period. It also shows an average value of the correlation coefficients for the four groups of stocks with the corresponding index as well as with the other three indexes. Note again that the average values of the correlation coefficients with the corresponding index were all positive and highly significant, while the average values of the correlation coefficients with other indexes show low correlation. The results for the 1970–1977 period are generally in line with those from the 1961–1969 period, thus indicating stability or consistency in the appearance of the four return-determined homogeneous groupings over time.

HOMOGENEOUS GROUPINGS

Now that we've covered the statistical test for stock groupings, it will be useful at this point to emphasize the main findings of the test. It shows that large well-known stocks of the type analyzed — S&P 500 type stocks, if you will — can be grouped into categories of growth, cyclical, stable, and energy stocks. Furthermore, these groups are homogeneous in the sense that stocks within each group show a strong co-movement and at the same time tend to act independently of other stock groupings.

When we say that stocks within a group show strong co-movement, it means that stocks tend to do well or poorly as a group. When Texas Instruments or some other growth stock does poorly, it's likely that other growth stocks, like Hewlett-Packard

	Growth index	Cyclical index	Stable index	Energy index
Growth average	.36	−.10	−.09	−.14
Cyclical average	−.04	.38	.04	−.06
Stable average	−.10	.13	.37	−.07
Energy average	−.26	−.11	−.10	.54

Figure 8-4 Matrix of residual correlation coefficients — averages of stocks and four stock indexes (1970–1977). *(Source: James L. Farrell, Jr., George Pinches, and James Scott, "Homogeneous Stock Groupings: Fundamental Determinants," unpublished paper, 1981.)*

or Baxter Labs, will do poorly. Also, for example, when a cyclical stock, such as Bethlehem Steel, does well it's likely that others, such as Alcoa or International Paper, will also perform well. This carries over to the case of stable companies, so that when, for example, American Electric Power does poorly, it's likely that General Foods or Household Finance will do poorly. As a final example, when some energy stocks, such as Exxon or Shell, do well, it's likely that the rest of the group will perform well.

As noted, the groups also tend to perform independently or differently from one another. When growth stocks are doing poorly, cyclicals may be doing well while energy and stable stocks are turning in neutral performances; or stable stocks could be doing well while cyclicals are doing poorly and the others are performing in a neutral fashion. In other words, the groups tend to move out of phase with one another, as seen in Figure 8-5. This chart shows the relative performance of indexes for groups of growth, cyclical, stable, and energy stocks. The 50 percent line indicates neutral market performance; any stocks above that line are performing above average and any below that line are performing below average.

In a sense these groups can be thought of as representing four different equity markets within the overall domestic equity market. There is in effect (1) a growth-stock market, (2) a cyclical-stock market, (3) a stable-stock market, and (4) an energy-stock market. In turn, the existence of these differing markets of homogeneous stock groupings has implications for the general area of portfolio management. We intend to focus primarily in this chapter on their application to active and passive portfolio management strategies.

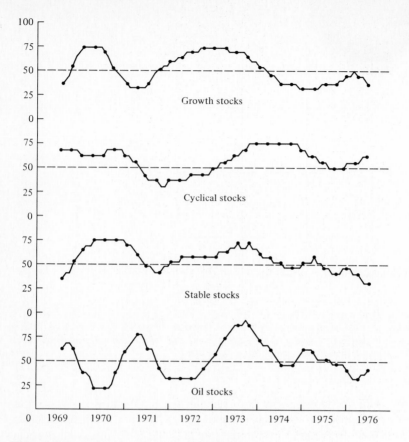

Figure 8-5 Independently varying stock group returns.

PORTFOLIO CONSTRUCTION/PASSIVE STRATEGY

Homogeneous stock groupings have implications in developing a passive strategy, to which we alluded in Chapter 6. It's useful at this stage to reinforce that earlier analysis and more completely illustrate its importance. In particular, it's important when constructing a portfolio to compare the fund weighting in the four groupings (growth, cyclical, stable, and energy) with a market average, such as the S&P 500. This is to determine whether the fund is concentrated in a particular area or well-diversified relative to the average. A fund proportioned in line with the average ensures against overexposure to poor performance by a particular grouping. If the fund is to outperform the average, it must be heavily concentrated in a grouping with a favorable outlook. (Needless to say, it risks underperformance if the favorable outlook does not materialize.)

The data in Table 8-2 provide a more specific illustration of the use of homogeneous groupings for purposes of portfolio construction. This table shows the weighting

Table 8-2 Portfolio construction — S&P 500 and mutual funds, %

	S&P 500	Affiliated Fund	T. Rowe Price
Stock sector			
Growth	39.8	10.5	80.2
Cyclical	24.0	57.5	8.7
Stable	20.0	18.0	4.1
Energy (oil)	16.2	14.0	7.0
Total	100.0	100.0	100.0
Portfolio beta	1.00	1.09	1.11
Fund performance (12/31/72–7/31/74)	−29	−16	−42

Source: James L. Farrell, Jr., "Homogeneous Stock Groupings: Implications for Portfolio Management," *Financial Analysts Journal,* May–June 1975.

of the four groupings of growth, cyclical, stable, and energy (oil) stocks in the S&P 500. In addition, it shows the portfolio structure of two large mutual funds — Affiliated Fund and T. Rowe Price Growth — classified by the four homogeneous groups. Finally, it shows the portfolio betas calculated from monthly data over the 1968–1972 period, as well as the total return performance of the two funds and the S&P 500 between December 31, 1972, and July 31, 1974.

Affiliated Fund was heavily weighted (approximately twice as heavily) relative to the S&P 500 in the cyclical group, while T. Rowe Price Growth was heavily weighted (approximately twice as heavily) relative to the S&P 500 in the growth group. Both funds had approximately the same beta: 1.11 for T. Rowe Price and 1.09 for Affiliated. The performance of the two funds and the S&P 500 was, however, substantially different over the December 31, 1972 to July 31, 1974 period. The S&P 500 declined 29 percent, Affiliated was down 16 percent, and T. Rowe Price was down 42 percent.

With both funds having betas in excess of 1, they would have been expected to decline by more than the S&P 500 in the bear market of December 31, 1972 to July 31, 1974. Affiliated Fund was down significantly less than the market because cyclical stocks performed especially well over this period (being down only 10 percent). T. Rowe Price underperformed the market and did even worse than expected on a beta-adjusted basis because growth stocks performed especially badly over this period (declining by 42 percent). The data illustrate the merits of both diversifying to avoid the wrong group (growth stocks) at the wrong time and concentrating in the right group (cyclicals) at the right time.

GROUP ROTATION/ACTIVE STRATEGY

Many managed portfolios or funds have a policy of concentrating investments in a particular category of stocks. For example, T. Rowe Price, as noted previously, has a long-standing policy of investing in growth stocks. It does not shift the weighting of the fund over time to different categories of stocks, such as from growth to cyclical. T. Rowe Price has been quite successful with this policy, rewarding long-term holders of the fund with above-average returns. The policy also helps fund holders establish a consistent risk exposure.[5]

An alternative to this philosophy of concentration is to pursue a policy of shifting fund weightings among the four groupings of growth, cyclical, stable, and energy stocks. If the outlook for a particular group is favorable, the strategy would be to give that group more weight in the portfolio than it enjoys in the S&P 500. On the other hand, if the group outlook is unfavorable, the strategy would be to give the group less weight. This policy, which can be termed *group rotation,* is the active counterpart to the passive strategy discussed in the previous section.

The potential rewards if one is correct in forecasting the direction of the groups can be quite substantial. To illustrate these potential rewards, we assumed (1) perfect foresight with respect to groups, (2) total investment in only one of the four groups at a particular time, and (3) no transactions costs. While these assumptions are obviously unrealistic with respect to real-world portfolio procedures, they are useful for illustrating the potential of group rotation as an investment strategy.

In a study of the returns from group rotation Farrell assumed that the fund shifted into growth stocks as of December 31, 1970, then into energy (oil) stocks as of June 30, 1971, and finally into cyclicals as of June 30, 1973.[6] Pursuing this strategy over the period from December 31, 1970 to June 30, 1974 would have provided a total return of 97 percent, as shown in Table 8-3. Over this same period the S&P 500 stock index provided a return of 4 percent, so that there was a net advantage to group rotation of 93 percent over the period.

An update of the strategy for the period from mid-1974 to the end of 1977 suggested the following shifts. First, the strategy would have been to shift into stable stocks as of June 30, 1974, and hold them until December 30, 1975, when it would have been profitable to shift back into cyclicals and hold them through 1976; the final shift would have been into energy stocks for the twelve months of 1977. The total gain from this strategy from June 30, 1974, to December 31, 1977, would have been 119 percent compared with 29 percent for the S&P 500, producing a net advantage of 90 percent to the group rotation investment strategy.

Table 8-3 shows the detailed breakdown of the group rotation strategy over the full period from December 31, 1970, to December 31, 1977. It shows the returns accruing to each of the favorably positioned groups within the subperiods as well as the return of the S&P 500 over that period. Note that the favorable group outperforms the S&P 500 by a substantial margin in each of the subperiods. The total return from the group rotation strategy over the full seven-year period would have been 324 percent in comparison to a return of 35 percent on the S&P 500, for a net gain of 298 percent over this time period.

[5] We should note that T. Rowe Price was one of the premier performers over the 1963–1971 period. It showed an average annual return of 12.6 percent over the period, or 2.7 percentage points better than the average annual return of 9.9 percent for the S&P 500.

[6] James L. Farrell, Jr., "Homogeneous Stock Groupings: Implications for Portfolio Management," *Financial Analysts Journal,* May–June 1975, pp. 50–62.

Table 8-3 Returns to investment strategies: group rotation versus buy and hold S&P 500, 1971–1977

Period	S&P 500	Growth stocks	Oil stocks	Cyclical stocks	Stable stocks	Net advantage to rotation
		Initial test (12/70–6/74)				
12//70–6//72	21.7%	48.5%				26.8%
6/72–6/73	0.2%		22.5%			22.3%
6/73–6/74	− 14.5%			8.5%		23.0%
Policy Buy-and-hold S&P 500	4.2%					
Rotate stock groups (12/70–6/74)	97.3%					93.1%
		Test update (6/74–12/77)				
6/74–12/75	12.4%				45.0%	32.6%
12/75–12/76	24.0%			41.1%		17.1%
12/76–12/77	− 7.2%		7.3%			15.5%
Policy Buy-and-hold S&P 500	29.3%					
Rotate stock groups (6/74–12/77)	119.5%					90.2%
		Full period results				
Buy-and-hold S&P 500 (12/70–12/77)	34.7%					
Rotate stock groups (12/70–12/77)	323.9%					289.2%

Source: James L. Farrell, Jr., "Homogeneous Stock Groupings: Implications for Portfolio Management," *Financial Analysts Journal,* May–June, 1975.

FUNDAMENTAL FACTORS: GROWTH STOCKS

The previous data and analysis indicates there is substantial opportunity for improving portfolio performance through identifying the appropriate group in an investment strategy of group rotation. To take advantage of these opportunities, one needs some predictive capability in assessing the relative attractiveness of the groupings, just as one needs predictive capability to engage successfully in stock selection or market timing. Developing an understanding of the fundamental factors that characterize or discriminate between stock groups should be an important step in gaining the ability to success-fully anticipate group moves.[7]

We have chosen to concentrate first on assessing the fundamental factor that distinguishes growth stocks from the other stock groupings—cyclical, stable, and energy. To facilitate this comparison, we'll consider the other three groupings an overall class of nongrowth stocks. We'll see in a later section that the three nongrowth groupings are affected by fundamental determinants of a different sort.

To begin with, growth stocks can be broadly characterized as those expected to grow at superior rates, while nongrowth stocks can be characterized as growing at rates in line with the economy. Since growth expectations are unobservable, one needs to resort to proxies to assess the sort of growth that an investor expects for a stock or group of stocks. We have chosen two measures that would best seem to approximate these growth expectations: (1) return on investment times retention rate or sustainable growth and (2) dividend yield.[8]

Sustainable growth is a fairly direct and objective measure of the growth prospects of a company, although it suffers from the usual deficiencies associated with accounting data. On the other hand, dividend yield is a market-determined variable that is not subject to accounting deficiencies. Furthermore, we should expect a negative trade-off between dividend yield and growth both through companies' earnings retention versus dividend payout and through the pricing of superior growth prospects by the market. The two variables should thus be complementary, albeit negatively related, for cap-turing investor expectations for future growth.

Using dividend yield and sustainable growth rate variables, the two stock groupings—growth and nongrowth—are distinguished as follows. First, we expect growth stocks to be characterized by high retention rates and high profitability rates (or some combination of the two), while we expect nongrowth stocks to be characterized by low retention rates and/or relatively lower profitability. Correspondingly, we expect companies sustaining high growth rates to pay relatively lower dividends as well as to show even lower dividend yields to the extent that superior growth prospects are built into the price of the stock. Conversely, we expect nongrowth companies to pay higher dividends and be characterized by even higher dividend yields to the extent that the price of the nongrowth stock does not reflect superior growth prospects.

SUSTAINABLE GROWTH-DIVIDEND YIELD CHARACTERISTICS

To illustrate that sustainable growth and dividend yield variables in fact distinguish these two groups of stocks, we can turn to the same sample of 354 stocks used to evaluate the price behavior of stocks. We calculated a measure of sustainable growth and a dividend yield for each of the stocks in the sample over the periods 1961–1969 and 1970–1977. These are the same periods used in the previous analyses and serve an additional function in assessing the stability of the relationships.

[7] Developing an understanding of the fundamental factors distinguishing stocks is also important for the following two reasons: (1) to ensure that the groupings or effect will persist over time; and (2) to ensure that individual stocks are classified into appropriate groupings.

[8] Recall that in Chapter 5 we described ways of estimating the sustainable growth rate for companies.

Figure 8-6 shows the sustainable growth-dividend yield relationship for growth and nongrowth stocks over the 1961–1969 period, while Figure 8-7 shows the same relationship for the 1970–1977 period. The vertical axis refers to the growth rate as measured by the sustainable growth rate (retention times return on equity), while the horizontal axis refers to the dividend yield. The stocks classified as growth stocks according to their price behavior in the market are plotted with circles, while stocks classified as nongrowth (cyclical, stable, or energy) are plotted with dots.

Note that in both figures most of the growth stocks plot together in the upper-left-hand portion of the quadrant, while the majority of the nongrowth stocks plot in the lower-right-hand portion of the quadrant. Growth stocks are thus characterized by high sustainable growth and low dividend yield, while nongrowth stocks are characterized by relatively low sustainable growth and relatively high yields. Furthermore, the figures illustrate that growth and dividend yield are negatively related as might be expected.

For further evaluation of the yield and growth distinctions between stock groups, Table 8-4 shows average values of the variables for the two groups, growth and nongrowth, over the 1961–1969 and 1970–1977 periods. Note that the average dividend yield and the average sustainable growth for the growth and nongrowth groups are substantially different for both periods of the test. In particular, the sustainable growth rate for the growth group is quite high in relation to the nongrowth group: 2.24 (12.10/5.41) times in the first subperiod and 1.93 (12.44/6.44) times in the second period. Correspondingly, the dividend yield variable for the growth stock group is quite low in relation to the nongrowth group: .45 (1.57/3.51) times in the first period and .34 (1.58/4.70) times in the second period.

As a final measure of the power of the fundamental variables to distinguish groupings, Appendix A to this chapter describes how a statistical technique known as *discriminant analysis* can be used to classify stocks according to sustainable growth and dividend yield characteristics into the appropriate groupings.

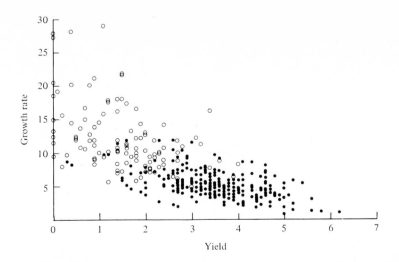

Figure 8-6 Growth-yield characteristics (circles = growth; dots = nongrowth), 1961–1969.

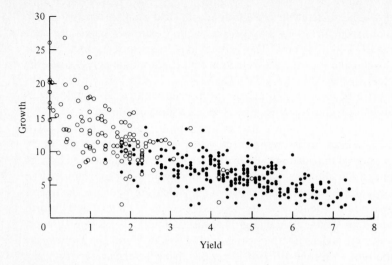

Figure 8-7 Growth-yield characteristics (circles = growth; dots = nongrowth), 1970–1977.

VALUATING GROWTH STOCKS

The previous section showed that growth stocks as a class are expected to grow at significantly more rapid rates than the average stock or the class designated as non-growth stocks. We've also seen that growth stocks provide significantly lower yields and sell at higher price-earnings (P/E) ratios than nongrowth stocks because of their prospects for superior growth. In effect, the investor in a growth stock incurs an immediate cost or suffers a penalty in the form of a higher price in order to obtain the benefit of a superior growth rate.

Table 8-4 Means and standard deviations for dividend yield and sustainable growth variables for growth and nongrowth stocks

		1961–1969			1970–1977	
	No.	Dividend yield	Sustainable growth	No.	Dividend yield	Sustainable growth
Growth	112	1.57	12.10	124	1.58	12.44
		(0.93)*	(4.87)		(1.06)	(4.18)
Nongrowth	229	3.51	5.41	230	4.70	6.44
		(0.99)	(2.10)		(1.34)	(2.30)
Total	341	2.87	7.61	354	3.61	8.54
		(1.33)	(4.54)		(1.95)	(4.22)

*Numbers in parentheses indicate standard deviation.

Source: James L. Farrell, Jr., George Pinches, and James Scott, "Growth Stock Fundamentals: Implications for Portfolio Management," unpublished paper, 1981.

It would be useful to assess the length of time that the superior rate of growth needs to persist in order to offset the initial penalty of a higher price. This would in a sense represent a sort of payback period when the investor would break even on his investment. The higher the initial price paid and the lower the growth rate for the stock, the longer the payback period. Conversely, the lower the initial price and the higher the growth rate for the stock, the shorter the payback period. Since investors should generally prefer growth stocks with shorter payback periods to those with longer payback periods, a measure of the relative attractiveness of a growth stock would be its assessed payback period.

Using the general framework of the two-stage dividend discount model, Holt developed a simple yet useful model for assessing from current market prices such a payback period.[9] The resulting model essentially allows one to determine the extent to which a growth stock's relatively higher P/E ratio is compensated by a relatively higher growth rate. Presuming that a market average such as the S&P 500 is representative of the P/E and growth rate characteristics of the average stock, we can represent the duration of growth model as follows:

$$\frac{\text{P/E growth stock}}{\text{P/E market average}} = \left[\frac{1 + \text{growth rate (growth stock)}}{1 + \text{growth rate (market average)}}\right]^{T} \qquad (1)$$

In words, this equation says that the ratio of the P/E ratios of the growth stock and the market average is equal to the ratio of their composite growth rates raised to the Tth power. For this purpose the composite growth rates include growth due to reinvested dividends, so that the growth rate is a sort of total return rate. The time period T might be considered the period when the higher growth rate of the growth stock "pays back," or offsets, the initial penalty of a higher P/E ratio. All other things being equal, the shorter this payback period, the more attractive the stock should be, while the longer the payback period, the less attractive the stock.

To illustrate the application of this valuation technique, we can use Wang Labs, a company in the office equipment industry, as representative of a high-growth stock, and the S&P 500 as representative of stocks growing at only average rates. In June 1981, Wang Labs was selling at a P/E ratio of 23 times, while the S&P 500 was selling at a P/E ratio of 9 times, so that Wang Labs had a relative P/E ratio of 2.56 times the

[9] Charles C. Holt, "The Influence of Growth Duration on Share Prices," *Journal of Finance,* September 1962, pp. 465–475, derived an expression for determining the period of superior growth within the framework of the two-stage dividend capitalization model. This implies that once the period of superior growth is completed, the growth stock assumes the characteristics of a nongrowth stock and is priced accordingly; that is, it assumes the same P/E as a nongrowth stock. In addition, Holt suggested that the dividend payout of the growth stock increased to that of a nongrowth stock when it completed the period of superior growth. Finally, he postulated that growth and nongrowth stocks were equivalent in terms of riskiness. This assumption implies that the returns to growth and nongrowth stocks should be equalized over time and facilitates the derivation of the years of superior growth estimates.

While this assumption facilitates the derivation of a simplified formulation, we should be aware that growth stocks are as a group likely to be riskier than average growth stocks. For one thing, growth stocks have greater exposure to the interest rate risk and as a consequence should generally provide a premium return over the average stock. This introduces a bias in favor of growth stocks into the analysis, but given the fact that the measure is mainly intended as a broad gauge indicator of valuation, the bias is not likely to be a serious impediment to practical application.

S&P 500. At the same time, Wang Labs was paying a negligible dividend that resulted in a yield of .4 percent, and expectations were for a growth rate of 30 percent into the future, which implied a total return growth rate of 30.4 percent, whereas the S&P 500 had a dividend yield of 5 percent and sustainable growth rate of 10 percent, which implied a total return of 15 percent. Assuming that these data are representative, we then input to the equation as follows:

$$\frac{23.0}{9.0} = \left[\frac{1 + .304}{1 + .150}\right]^T$$

$$2.56 = [1.13]^T$$

We can now solve for the expected period of superior growth T by using logarithms:

$$\ln[2.56] = T\ln[1.13]$$

$$T = \frac{.94000}{.12222} = 7.7 \text{ years}$$

These results indicate that the market is implicitly assuming that Wang Labs can continue to grow at this composite rate (30.4 percent) for 7.7 years, after which it is assumed that the company will grow at the same rate as the aggregate market, as represented by the S&P 500.[10] Given this calculated value, the investor could then interpret whether this seemed reasonable in view of the market conditions and the basic character of the company. Assessment that the implied duration of growth was too optimistic might well provide the basis for sale of the stock, while assessment that the implied duration was less than seemed appropriate might lead to purchase of the stock. For example, if the investor's view was that the period of superior growth would only persist for, say, five years, then he might consider the stock overvalued, while if the investor's analysis indicated that the period of growth would persist for, say, ten years, then the stock would be considered undervalued.

Similarly, we can apply this technique to valuing growth stocks as a class. This analysis is, in fact, particularly enlightening for illustrating the extreme valuation to which growth stocks as a class had risen at the end of 1972. At that time, growth stocks were selling at a P/E ratio of 32 times and the total return growth rate implied for the group was 13 percent, whereas the S&P 500 was selling at a P/E ratio of 14.0 times with an implied total return growth rate of 9.5 percent. Using the previously noted formulation, along with these inputs, we solve for an implied period of superior growth of over 25 years. To use an oft-cited Wall Street aphorism, growth stocks were discounting the hereafter. Growth stock performance subsequent to 1972 was decidedly inferior, underperforming the S&P 500, for example, by 40 percent over the 1973–1977 period.

---

[10] The Holt model assumes that the two-stage growth model is the appropriate one for modeling the growth progression of a growth stock. This model presumes an immediate transition and no gradual declination in the rate of superior growth of a growth stock. Immediate transition is a less realistic assumption and may create a slight bias in the estimate of the period of superior growth. Incorporating a different growth transition would, however, unnecessarily complicate the model and add little to the analysis, which is only intended as a broad-gauged indicator of valuation in the first place.

FUNDAMENTAL CHARACTERISTICS OF NONGROWTH GROUPINGS

When attempting to discriminate among nongrowth groupings of cyclical, stable, and energy stocks, it would be more useful to directly analyze the companies' sources of profit. One of the fundamental sources of profit is, of course, the price level of the companies' products and services. The general level of prices is set in a macroeconomic context and changes as inflationary forces are moderate or intensify. Companies, in turn, differ in their reaction to changes in prices. Those with greater flexibility in pricing their products and services fare better than others during inflationary periods, while other companies fare relatively better during periods of decelerating price changes or when the general level of prices remains stable.

Table 8-5 shows the major categories of industries included within the three groupings of cyclical, stable, and energy stocks. It should be helpful in illustrating the responses of different types of companies to changes in price levels. Note that the

Table 8-5 Industries classified by major sectors

Growth	Cyclical
Hospital management companies	Aluminum
Pollution control	Copper
Cosmetics	Miscellaneous metals
Drugs	Autos
Hospital supplies	Auto parts and trucks
Electronics	Building materials
Entertainment	Chemicals
Hotels and restaurants	Containers
Computers	Textiles
Oil service companies	Tires
Newspapers and broadcasters	Electrical equipment
Specialty chemicals	Machinery
Growth retailers	Forest products and paper
	Steel
	Railroads

Stable	Energy
Food processors	Coal
Beverage	Domestic oil
Tobacco	International oil
Household products	Crude-oil producers
Retailers	
Utilities	
Telephones	
Banks	
Insurance	
Finance	

energy sector consists of companies that provide the most basic input to the manufacture and consumption of goods and services. On the other hand, the stable sector consists of companies that provide goods and services at the final stage of demand: they primarily market to the consumer. The cyclical sector consists primarily of companies at an intermediate stage of processing: their customers are primarily other companies.

We would in turn expect the stable sector to be the most adversely impacted by accelerating inflation. Food, beverage, tobacco, and retailer companies would have difficulty in passing on increased prices to consumers because of the well-known phenomenon of consumer resistance to increased prices during such a period. At the same time, the costs of such companies usually keep pace with inflation, resulting in a squeeze on profit margins. Utilities, as regulated entities, encounter lags in adjusting rates or rate allowances that are not fully compensating and consequently suffer during periods of accelerating inflation. Banks, finance companies, and life insurance companies are significant net creditors and therefore suffer like other creditors during inflationary periods. Casualty insurance companies, as net creditors, are also exposed and suffer further impairment of underwriting margins when regulatory lags fail to adjust rates fully and promptly for inflationary effects. Conversely, we would expect stable companies to fare relatively well as inflation decelerates and during periods of price stability.

While stable companies would have difficulty passing on rising costs to final demanders — the consumers — cyclical companies as intermediate producers would have greater flexibility in this regard. In particular, we would expect cyclical companies to pass on costs to other companies with greater ease when demand for the product is high, capacity is limited, and inflationary pressures are widespread. We would, of course, expect that during periods of relatively slack demand and excess capacity it would be difficult for cyclical companies to raise prices, so that their profit margins and overall profitability would suffer accordingly.

Energy companies, which supply a primary factor of production, would seem to have the greatest flexibility in pricing their product and passing on costs to customers at either the producer or consumer level. A rising trend in energy prices seems to have the most favorable consequences for profitability and hence relative performance. Conversely, a declining trend in energy prices seems to be the most useful indication of declining profitability and hence relatively inferior performance by energy-related companies.

RELATIVE PERFORMANCE OF NONGROWTH GROUPINGS

An indicator of the relative swings in profitability between stable companies, or final-stage producers, and cyclical companies, or intermediate producers, is the relationship between producer or wholesale prices (WPI) and consumer prices (CPI). In this respect, we can broadly regard the CPI as representative of the prices that the final-goods producers (stables) receive, while the WPI is representative of those companies costs but also indicative of the prices that intermediate producers (cyclicals) receive. As a result, we would expect that the profit margins of final-goods companies would be relatively favorably impacted when the CPI is rising relative to the WPI, while the profitability of intermediate-goods companies would be relatively favorably impacted when the WPI is rising relative to the CPI.

Figure 8-8 plots the returns of the stable grouping, adjusted for general market effects against the WPI/CPI ratio, while Figure 8-9 plots the returns of cyclical companies also adjusted for general market effects against this same ratio. Note that the performance of the stable group moves counter (inversely) to the WPI/CPI ratio, indicating that this group performs well when the ratio is declining but poorly when it is rising, as might be expected from the likely impact on the relative profitability of these companies. Conversely, the performance of cyclical companies is positively related to the WPI/CPI ratio, indicating that this group performs well when the ratio is rising but poorly when it is declining. This again is what we would expect from the likely impact that changes in the ratio should have on the profitability of these companies.

Figure 8-10 shows an index of energy stock returns adjusted for general market effects and plotted against the rate of inflation measured as an average of the previous three years and the year-ahead change in an index of energy prices. Note that the energy

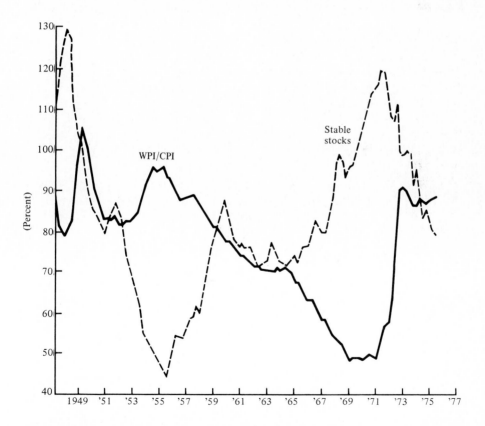

Figure 8-8 Stable stocks and the consumer price index.

stocks performed in line with the relative price index for energy, as would be expected. Energy companies performed especially well during the energy crises of 1970–1972 and 1977, when prices rose at a relatively rapid rate. These companies performed poorly when energy prices relatively declined.

In effect, what we have described here is a sort of stage of processing model for understanding the relative performances of the different nongrowth groupings. To a certain extent the favorable effect of changing prices for one group might adversely impact the performance of another group. For example, rising energy prices would favorably impact oil companies but unfavorably impact the cost structure of inter-mediate producers, such as chemical companies. We might further expect prices at these various stages of processing to accelerate or decelerate as the economy moves through the business cycle. For example, over the cycle the prices of primary products tend to lead those of intermediate products, which in turn lead the prices of final goods.

Given these differing group reactions to changes in the price level or its com-ponents, we as portfolio managers would react in the following way to expected changes in prices. A forecast of accelerating inflation would call for an underweighting of stable companies in the portfolio, while a forecast of decelerating inflation would

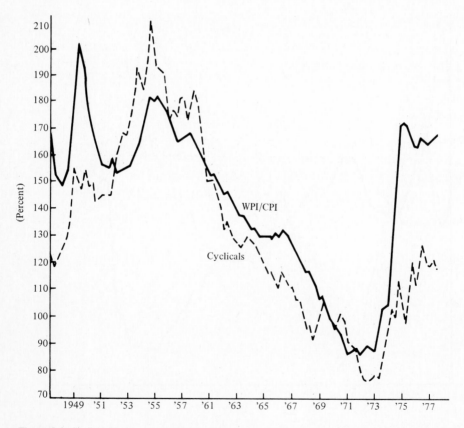

Figure 8-9 Cyclical stocks and the WPI to CPI ratio.

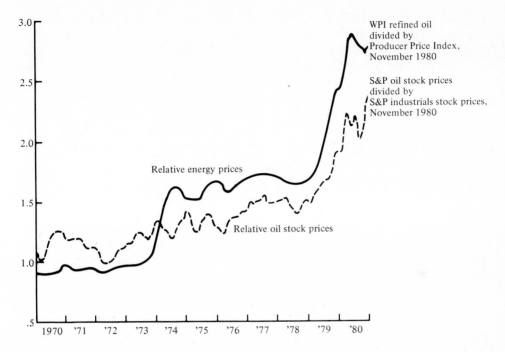

Figure 8-10 Energy stocks and the relative price of energy *(Source: C. J. Lawrence, Inc., New York, N.Y.)*

imply an overweighting of these companies. A forecast of increasing energy prices would indicate the relative attractiveness of energy companies and call for an over-weighting of this group, while a forecast decrease would call for the opposite reaction. Finally, a forecast of a rising WPI would call for an increased position in cyclicals, while a forecast decrease would imply an underweighted position.

ADJUSTING FORECASTS

Presuming some capability for predicting these group moves, either through the kind of analysis that we've just outlined or some other, the question then becomes one of determining to what extent the organization should act on these forecasts.[11] In particular, we need to determine to what extent a favorably positioned grouping — one with a positive return forecast — should be overweighted in the portfolio, and to what extent the group should be underweighted when an inferior performance is projected. The

[11] In estimating the return of the four groupings, one might well consider applying a scenario approach similar to the one described in Chapter 7. In generating scenarios one should be especially concerned with the implications for the rate of real economic growth as well as for the overall trend in inflation and the impact of relative prices, especially energy and wholesale prices. The returns to growth stocks will, of course, be especially affected by the trends in real growth, while the return to stable stocks will be affected by the overall rate of inflation, the return to cyclical stocks by the trend in wholesale prices, and the return to energy stocks by the trend in energy prices.

method of doing this essentially involves applying some of the principles discussed in earlier chapters along with more formal techniques of active-passive portfolio management.

This procedure can be outlined as follows. The first step is to generate forecasts of relative attractiveness for the four groups: growth, cyclical, stable, and energy stocks. The second step is to convert these into explicit forecasts of nonmarket return. The third step is to adjust these forecasts by means of the information coefficient (IC) method for the organization's presumed degree of forecasting capability. Once we've developed the return forecast, we need to consider the riskiness of each group to determine its optimum weighting in the portfolio.

The upper part of Figure 8-11 shows how we can use the same sort of rating technique described earlier with regard to stock selection and market timing for expressing the relative attractiveness of the groups. Note that we've assigned the following hypothetical ratings to the groups: energy stocks are rated 1, or most attractive; cyclical stocks are 2, or moderately attractive; growth stocks are 4, or moderately unattractive; and stable stocks are 5, or least attractive. Even though we only have four groups to

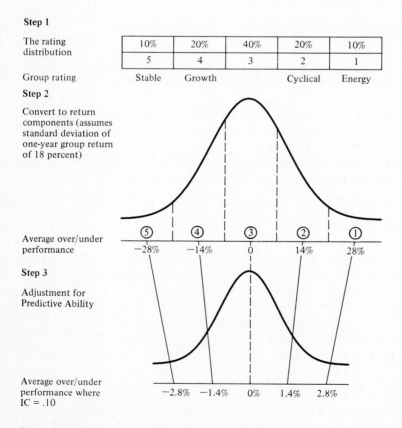

Step 1

The rating distribution

10%	20%	40%	20%	10%
5	4	3	2	1

Group rating Stable Growth   Cyclical Energy

Step 2

Convert to return components (assumes standard deviation of one-year group return of 18 percent)

Average over/under performance

⑤ ④ ③ ② ①
−28% −14% 0 14% 28%

Step 3

Adjustment for Predictive Ability

Average over/under performance where IC = .10

−2.8% −1.4% 0% 1.4% 2.8%

Figure 8-11 Forecasting group returns.

rate, the ratings still result in the desired average of 3, indicating an unbiased set of ratings. The standard deviation of the ratings is 1.3.[12]

Empirical research indicates that the cross-sectional distribution of group returns unrelated to general market effects (nonmarket returns) has averaged about 18 percent per annum. This means that for two-thirds of the time in any given year — assuming normally distributed returns — the nonmarket-related return of the group will be ±18 percent. Therefore, for one-sixth of the time the return will be higher than 18 percent, while for another one-sixth of the time it will be lower than 18 percent.

The middle section of Figure 8-11 shows the mapping of the rating distribution onto the empirical return distribution. Note that a rating of 1 converts to a return of 28 percent for the energy group, a rating of 2 to a 14 percent return for the cyclical group, a rating of 4 to a 14 percent loss for the stable group, and a rating of 5 to a 28 percent loss for the stable group. The center of the distribution is zero, indicating that the average, or expected, return is centered at zero. This would, in effect, be the kind of distribution or opportunity available to a forecaster with perfect predictive capability — an IC of +1.

We know, however, that it is necessary to adjust the distribution for the fact that predictive capability, where it exists, is likely to be imperfect at best. The bottom part of Figure 8-11 shows the adjustment that would be made for a hypothetical forecaster with an IC of .10. For this forecaster the expected return for the highest-rated group (energy stocks) becomes 2.8 percent, and for the cyclical group 1.4 percent, while the expected loss for the growth group becomes 1.4 percent and for the stable group 2.8 percent. The standard deviation of this distribution becomes 1.8 percent, compared with the original 18 percent, and represents the degree of shrinkage of the distribution owing to imperfect forecasts.

OPTIMUM WEIGHTING

In order to determine how extensively to overweight or underweight the groups in a portfolio, we need to consider the market and nonmarket risks of the groups as well as the return opportunities. For example, we would presumably want to overweight the energy group and underweight the stable group in the portfolio to take advantage of the return opportunity and avoid the potential loss. This would add nonmarket

---

[12] Recall from the previous two chapters that the first step in this process is to convert the rating of a grouping into standard deviations from the mean rating of 3. We do this by dividing the rating by the standard deviation of the rating distribution, which in this case is 1.3. For example, the cyclical group has a rating of 2, which is $1 \div 1.3 = .77$ standard deviations above the mean, while the growth group, which has a rating of 4, is .77 standard deviations below the mean. Correspondingly, the energy group, which is rated 1, is $2 \div 1.3 = 1.54$ standard deviations above the mean, while the stable group, which is rated 5, is 1.54 standard deviations below the mean.

Once the ratings have been converted into standard deviations, we then multiply these by the standard deviation of the return distribution, which in this case is 18 percent. For example, the energy group, which is 1.54 standard deviations above the mean, converts to a return of 28 percent (1.54×18), while the stable group, which is 1.54 standard deviations below the mean, converts to a return of −28 percent. Correspondingly, the cyclical group converts to a return of 14 percent ($.77 \times 18$), while the growth group, which is .77 below the mean, has a return of −14 percent.

risk to the portfolio and could move the portfolio beta to above or below 1, exposing the portfolio to market risk.

Figure 8-12 illustrates the importance of considering both risk and return in developing the optimum weightings of the groups in the portfolio. The solid curve shows the risk and return of various portfolios containing different combinations of the four groups: growth, cyclical, stable, and energy. Point M represents the market portfolio; it contains market proportions of the four groups. Points G and C are portfolios with group weights that diverge from the market portfolio and thus contain "bets" on the groups.

Note that point G provides a higher return and is at a higher risk level than point M. Portfolio G, however, provides a higher return per unit of risk than the market portfolio. The angle of the line extending from R_f, representing the risk-free rate, to point G is greater than the angle of the line extending from R_f to point M. Note also that the line is tangent to the curve at point G, indicating that it is at the maximum angle. Any portfolio to the right of point G would provide a less favorable return-risk ratio; the weightings of the groups in these portfolios would be less than optimum.

In fact, as one moves to the right along the line, the return-risk ratio becomes even less favorable than that provided by market M. For example, portfolio C, on the line to the right of G, provides a higher return than either G or M and yet has significantly higher risk, which results in a less favorable return-risk ratio than the market — that is,

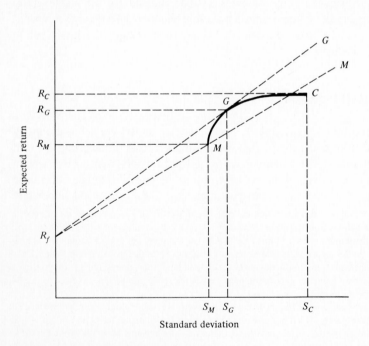

Figure 8-12 Optional group weights.

a line from R_f to point C would have a lesser slope than the line R_fM. This shows that overconcentration in the pursuit of high return leads to an excessive build-up of nonmarket risk.

In order to consider nonmarket risk explicitly and thereby develop an optimal portfolio, as illustrated by point G in Figure 8-12, we can again resort to the optimization techniques described in Chapter 2. Appendix B illustrates the way that weights are developed for the groups using the simplified portfolio optimization techniques of Elton and Gruber.[13] As noted before, the merits of these techniques are that they allow the analyst to see explicitly the risk-return trade-offs of assets under consideration and thereby better understand the reasons for the inclusion and weighting of groups in the optimal portfolio.

Since Appendix B describes the application of the optimization technique, we'll merely discuss the results of analysis as shown in Table 8-6. The table shows the weightings of the groups in the optimal portfolio as well as approximate weightings of the groupings in the market that allows a comparison of the divergence of portfolio weighting from the market. Note that optimum portfolio G has greater weighting in the energy and cyclical groups than the market, as might be expected given their relatively favorable rating. At the same time, the growth and stable groups have a zero weighting, which is, of course, less than their weighting in the general market. The portfolio is in effect long the energy and cyclical groups and short the growth and stable groups.

Table 8-6 also shows the weighted average return and risk as measured by the standard deviation of return for this optimum portfolio as well as the ratio of the excess return to standard deviation of the portfolio. This ratio is known as the Sharpe ratio, and in terms of Figure 8-12 it measures the slope of the line from the risk-free return to the risk-return plot of the portfolio. Table 8-6 also shows the same risk-return statistics for market portfolio M and for a concentrated portfolio invested entirely in the

[13] Edwin Elton, Martin Gruber, and Manfred Padberg: "Optimal Portfolios from Simple Ranking Devices," *Journal of Portfolio Management,* Spring 1978, pp. 15–19.

Table 8-6 Portfolio weighting and risk-return characteristics

Stock group	Market portfolio M (1)	Optimum portfolio G (2)	Divergence (2) − (1) = (3)	Concentrated portfolio C (4)	Divergence (4) − (1) = (5)
Cyclical	0.25	0.45	+ 0.20	1	+ 0.75
Energy	0.20	0.55	+ 0.35	0	− 0.20
Growth	0.30	0.0	− 0.30	0	− 0.30
Stable	0.25	0.0	− 0.25	0	− 0.25
Expected excess return	7%		9%		9.8%
Standard deviation of return	18%		21%		26%
Return/standard deviation	0.39		0.43		0.38

most attractive group in terms of return—cyclical stocks. This concentrated portfolio might be construed as representative of portfolio C in Figure 8-12.

Note that the risk-return ratio of .43 for the optimum portfolio exceeds ratio of .39 for the market portfolio. At the same time, the risk-return ratio of .38 for the concentrated portfolio is less than the ratios for both the optimum and market portfolio. These cases are depicted in Figure 8-12, where portfolio G shows a more favorable plotting than portfolio M, while portfolio C shows a less favorable positioning than either M or G. The data thus illustrates both the problems in overemphasizing return and the usefulness of those techniques which explicitly take into account risk as well as return when constructing a portfolio.

CONCLUSION

We've seen in this chapter that we can use statistical techniques to determine stock groupings that are homogeneous; that is, stocks within the group tend to move together while the groupings tend to move independently of one another. In one sense this differing price action of groupings within the domestic stock market is analogous to the differing price behavior of national markets like the United States, Germany, Japan, and the United Kingdom, which we'll describe in Chapter 9. In another sense this finding indicates that there are powerful underlying economic forces giving rise to the differing market behavior of the groupings. We indicated that in a broad sense these underlying economic forces are growth-rate characteristics that differentiate growth stocks from the other three groupings and differential rates of inflation as measured by consumer, wholesale, and energy prices which give rise to the differentiated price behavior of stable, cyclical, and energy stocks.

The finding that stocks tend to perform as homogeneous groupings has several implications. First, the existence of such groupings directly indicates that a model such as the single-index model will be deficient with respect to portfolio selection as well as when it is used to measure the systematic risk of stocks. We analyzed these problems back in Chapter 2 and showed that augmenting the model with multiple indexes derived from homogeneous stock groupings allows one to appropriately describe the risk relationship among stocks and to generate portfolios with superior performance characteristics.

Homogeneous stock groupings are also applicable in active-passive strategies of investment management. We showed that returns accruing to a favored grouping at a particular time can be quite favorable and that for those with the capability of forecasting such group moves the potential rewards can be substantial. At the same time there are significant penalties associated with being in the wrong group at the wrong time, so that for those with little skill in this area the best solution would be to hedge the risk through a passive strategy. For those having some skill but desiring to hedge against estimation errors, we illustrated a framework based on the simplified portfolio selection techniques of Elton and Gruber for balancing risk against the potential reward from an active strategy of group rotation.

APPENDIX A DISCRIMINANT ANALYSIS AND FUNDAMENTAL VARIABLES

While the diagrams in the body of the chapter show that growth stocks differ significantly from nongrowth stocks with respect to sustainable growth and dividend yield variables, we can use a statistical technique known as *discriminant analysis* to provide a more powerful test of the usefulness of these variables for classifying companies into the appropriate groupings. Discriminant analysis is a statistical technique that allows observations (firms in this case) to be classified into appropriate a priori groups on the basis of a set of independent or predictor variables. Discriminant analysis is similar to regression analysis except that the dependent variable in discriminant analysis must be qualitative, such as growth or nongrowth. It has been employed in finance to distinguish bankrupt firms from nonbankrupt firms and to classify companies into different bond-rating groups.

For our purposes, discriminant analysis provides a way of partitioning the diagrams (Figures 8-6 and 8-7) into two zones: growth and nongrowth stocks. Figure 8-A1 illustrates this by superimposing a dashed line on Figure 8-6. The line represents the graphing of the discriminant function that partitions the data into two zones. Those stocks falling into the zone to the right of the line would be classified in the nongrowth category by the discriminant function, while those to the left of the line would be classified in the growth category.

Table 8-A1 shows the classification results of discriminant analysis using the fundamental variables of dividend yield and sustainable growth for the two periods of the test. It shows the number of actual growth or nongrowth firms over the 1961–1977

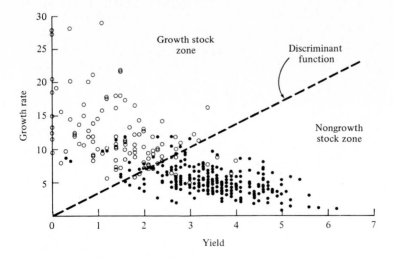

Figure 8-A1 Growth-yield characteristics (circles = growth; dots = nongrowth), 1961–1969.

Table 8-A1 Classification results for growth and nongrowth stocks

	Predicted based on fundamental variables			
	1961–1969		1970–1977	
Actual based on return behavior	Growth	Nongrowth	Growth	Nongrowth
Growth	89 (79.46%)	23	114 (91.94%)	10
Nongrowth	12	217 (94.76%)	20	210 (91.30%)
	89.74% overall		91.53% overall	

Source: James L. Farrell, Jr., George Pinches, and James Scott, "Growth Stock Fundamentals: Implications for Portfolio Management," unpublished paper, 1981.

period based on return behavior and the predicted growth or nongrowth firms based on the fundamental variables of sustainable growth and dividend yield. Note that the discriminant analysis model classified 89.74 percent of the firms into their return-based growth and nongrowth groups in the 1961–1969 period, whereas 91.53 percent of the firms were correctly classified in the 1970–1977 period. The models seemed to have worked well in classifying growth and nongrowth stocks except in the case of growth stocks in the 1961–1969 period.

APPENDIX B A SIMPLIFIED TECHNIQUE FOR DETERMINING OPTIMUM GROUP WEIGHTS

This appendix illustrates in detail the application of the Elton and Gruber technique to developing optimum weightings of groups in a portfolio. The inputs necessary to apply the technique are the following: (1) expected return to the groups; (2) sensitivity of the group return to the market as measured by the beta coefficient; (3) the residual, or nonmarket, risk of the four groups; (4) expected return of the market and variance of market return; and (5) the risk-free rate. Table 8-B1 shows the input data for the market and for four stock groups.

Note that we're using a 16 percent return for the market, which is close to what might currently be a consensus estimate for the market along with a risk-free return of 9 percent, which is more or less in line with the current underlying rate of inflation (9–10 percent). The return on the groups includes a market component of 16 percent and an additional increment or decrement, as the case may be, which was derived in the body of the chapter. The variance of the market, the beta coefficients of the groups with the market, and the residual risks of the groups were calculated with data from the more recent historical period, 1970–1977.

Table 8-B1 Risk-return data — market and stock groups

Stock group (1)	Market return, % (1)	Incremental return, % (2)	Total return R_k, % (1) + (2) = (3)	Risk-free rate R_f, % (4)	Excess return, % (3) − (4) = (5)	Beta (B) (6)	Nonmarket Var(e) (7)
Cyclical	16	+2.8	18.8	9	9.8	1.05	324
Energy	16	+1.4	17.4	9	8.4	0.90	225
Growth	16	−1.4	14.6	9	5.6	1.20	400
Stable	16	−2.8	13.2	9	4.2	0.90	225

Note: Variance of market = 324; standard deviation of market = 18 percent.

This process first involves establishing a cut-off rate so that we can determine those groups that will be included in the portfolio. We can begin to determine the cut-off rate by calculating the excess return (return less risk-free rate) for each of the groups, dividing by the market risk, and then ranking the groups from the highest return-risk ratio to the lowest. Column 1 of Table 8-B2 indicates that the cyclical group ranks first and the stable group last on this basis.

Once we've ranked securities, we derive the ratios shown in column 2 of Table 8-B2 and cumulate the sum as shown in column 3. We also calculate the ratio shown in column 4 for each of the groups and again cumulate the sum as shown in column 5. We then use this data to calculate a C_k value for each of the groups, shown in column 6.

The optimum C^* value is where the excess return-risk ratio of the group is less than the calculated C value. All groups with a return-risk ratio greater than this value would be included in the portfolio, while those with values less than the cut-off rate would be excluded. Note that in this case the excess return-risk ratios for the cyclical and energy groups are in excess of the cut-off value — that is, both exceed 6.48. As a result, these groups should be included in the optimum portfolio, while the growth and stable groups should be excluded.

Once the cut-off value has been calculated and the groups to be included in the portfolio determined, the next step is to determine their weighting in the portfolio. Defining w_k as the group weight in the portfolio, Z_k as a value to be calculated, and Z as the sum of the Z_k values, we can use the following formula to determine the group weights:

$$w_k = \frac{Z_k}{Z}$$

In this formula, the Z_k values are calculated using information provided previously:

$$Z_k = \frac{b_k}{\text{Var}(e_k)}\left[\left(\frac{R_k - R_F}{b_k}\right) - C^*\right]$$

In this case, the Z_k values for each of the groups to be included in the portfolio are

$$Z_{\text{cyclical}} = 1.05/324(9.3 - 6.48) = .00914$$
$$Z_{\text{energy}} = .9/225(9.3 - 6.48) = .01128$$

Table 8-B2 Determining optimum group weights

Stock group	$\dfrac{R_k - R_F}{B_k}$ (1)	$\dfrac{(R_k - R_F)B_k}{\text{Var}(e)}$ (2)	$\displaystyle\sum_{k=1}^{K} \dfrac{(R_k - R_F)B_k}{\text{Var}(e)}$ (3)	$\dfrac{B_k^2}{\text{Var}(e)}$ (4)	$\displaystyle\sum_{k=1}^{K} \dfrac{B_k^2}{\text{Var}(e)}$ (5)	$C_k = \dfrac{\text{Var}M[3]}{1 + [\text{Var}M(5)]}$ (6)
Cyclical	9.3	0.0318	0.0318	0.0034	0.0034	4.90
Energy	9.3	0.0336	0.0654	0.0036	0.0070	6.48
Growth	4.7	0.0168	0.0822	0.0036	0.0106	6.01
Stable	4.7	0.0168	0.0990	0.0036	0.0142	5.73

Once these Z_k values are determined, we simply sum them to obtain a value of $Z = .02042$. We next divide each Z_k by Z to obtain the optimum weight for each group. The following are the calculated weights for each group:

$$W_{\text{energy}} = .55$$

$$W_{\text{cyclical}} = .45$$

Before concluding, we should note that Elton and Gruber have developed simplified portfolio optimization techniques assuming differing underlying models of the correlation structure of stock returns, including the single-index and multi-index representations. For purposes of developing optimal group weights, the multi-index variation of the basic technique would be the most appropriate. Exposition of this variation is, however, more involved than warranted for our purposes, so we've illustrated the techniques assuming that the single-index model represents the underlying structure of returns. The reader should, however, be aware that the resulting weightings in the portfolio may be biased away from optimality because of the use of a less-than-appropriate variation of the technique.

PROBLEMS

1 Describe in general the distinguishing characteristics of growth, cyclical, stable, and energy stocks. Also indicate how the market behavior of these groups qualifies them as homogeneous.

2 Describe the opportunities that are available from a strategy of underweighting and overweighting the major stock groups. Also explain the risks that are involved in such a strategy.

3 Indicate some variables that distinguish growth stocks from other groupings as well as variables that distinguish the three categories of nongrowth stocks (cyclical, stable, and energy) from one another.

4 On average, stocks are expected to grow at a rate of 10.5 percent, and the current yield is 5.5 percent. A stock is growing at the rate of 30 percent per annum but currently pays no dividend. The P/E ratio for the average stock is 8, while for the growth stock it is 13. What is the expected duration of growth for the growth stock? Also, would the stock be undervalued or overvalued if your expectation for the period of superior growth is four years?

5 Assume that one has forecast a period of accelerating real growth along with a decline in the general rate of inflation as well as a decline in the rate of increase of wholesale and energy prices. Which groups would be benefited relatively and which would be affected less favorably? Also indicate the strategy for such an environment.

6 Assume that the expected return for growth stocks is 18 percent, for cyclical stocks 16 percent, for stable stocks 17 percent, and for energy stocks 14 percent, and that the risk characteristics are the same as those given in Appendix B to this chapter. Determine the optimum weighting of the groups in a portfolio.

7 Determine the superior and inferior portfolios from three with the following risk and return characteristics: (a) excess return of 7 percent and standard deviation of 18 percent; (b) excess return of 9 percent and standard deviation of 28 percent; and (c) excess return of 5 percent and standard deviation of 11 percent.

SELECTED REFERENCES

Arnott, R.: "Discussion of Cluster Analysis Project," paper presented at the fall 1979 meeting of the Institute for Quantitative Research in Finance, Vail, Colo.

Cohen, Kalman, and Jerry Pogue: "An Empirical Evaluation of Alternative Portfolio Selection Models," *Journal of Business,* April 1967, pp. 166–193.

Elton, Edwin J., and Martin J. Gruber: "Homogeneous Groups and the Testing of Economic Hypotheses," *Journal of Financial and Quantitative Analysis,* January 1970, pp. 581–602.

———: "Improved Forecasting through the Design of Homogeneous Groups," *Journal of Business,* October 1971, pp. 432–450.

———: "Estimating the Dependence Structure of Share Prices — Implications for Portfolio Selection," *Journal of Business,* December 1973, pp. 1203–1232.

Farrell, James L., Jr.: "Homogeneous Stocks Groupings: Implications for Portfolio Management," *Financial Analysts Journal,* May–June 1975, pp. 50–62.

———: "Analyzing Covariation of Return to Determine Homogeneous Stock Groupings," *Journal of Business,* April 1974, pp. 186–207.

———: "The Multi-Index Model and Practical Portfolio Analysis," *Financial Analysts Research Foundation,* Occasional Paper no. 4, 1976.

———, George Pinches, and James Scott: "Homogeneous Stock Groupings: Fundamental Determinants," unpublished paper, 1981.

Fogler, Russell, K. John, and J. Tipton: "Three Factors, Interest Rate Differentials and Stock Groups," *Journal of Finance,* May 1981, pp. 323–335.

Haugen, R., and D. Wichern: "The Elasticity of Financial Assets," *Journal of Finance,* September 1974, pp. 1229–1240.

Higgins, R. C.: "Growth, Dividend Policy and Capital Costs in the Electric Utility Industry," *Journal of Finance,* September 1974, pp. 1189–1201.

Holt, C. C.: "The Influence of Growth Duration on Share Prices," *Journal of Finance,* September 1962, pp. 465–475.

King, Benjamin: "Market and Industry Factors in Stock Price Behavior," *Journal of Business,* January 1966, pp. 139–190.

Litzenberger, R. H., and C. U. Rao: "Estimates of the Marginal Time Preference and Average Risk Aversion of Investors in Electric Utility Shares," *Bell Journal of Economics and Management Science,* Spring 1971, pp. 265–277.

Livingston, Miles: "Industry Movements of Common Stocks," *Journal of Finance,* June 1977, pp. 861–874.

Malkiel, B. G.: "Equity Yields, Growth, and the Structure of Share Prices," *American Economic Review,* December 1963, pp. 1004–1031.

Martin, J. D., and R. C. Klemkosky: "The Effect of Homogeneous Stock Groupings on Portfolio Risk," *Journal of Business,* July 1976, pp. 339–349.

Martin, John D., and Arthur J. Keown: "Interest Rates Sensitivity and Portfolio Risk," *Journal of Financial Quantitative Analysis,* June 1967, pp. 85–106.

Meyers, S. L.: "A Reexamination of Market and Industry Factors in Stock Price Behavior," *Journal of Business,* July 1976, pp. 695–705.

Moore, B. J.: "Equities, Capital Gains, and the Role of Finance in Accumulation," *American Economic Review,* December 1975, pp. 872–886.

Tobin, J.: "A General Equilibrium Approach to Monetary Theory," *Journal of Money Credit and Banking,* February 1969, pp. 15–29.

Treynor, Jack, and Fischer Black: "How to Use Security Analysis to Improve Performance," *Journal of Business,* January 1973, pp. 66–86.

NINE

INTERNATIONAL INVESTING

INTRODUCTION

This chapter is devoted to international equity investing and supplements the previous three chapters on domestic equity investing. Expanding the investment universe to include foreign equities should have a beneficial impact on portfolio performance because foreign equities provide an expanded set of assets that generally show a low degree of correlation with domestic (U. S.) assets. Augmenting the selection universe with these generally desirable (low correlation) assets expands the efficient frontier, thereby increasing the potential for constructing a portfolio that maximizes return at a given risk level.

While foreign investing is likely to be beneficial to overall performance, it differs from domestic investing in one major respect: security holdings will be denominated in several different currencies rather than one currency (U. S. dollars). Since international investing means holding securities denominated in a variety of currencies whose relative values may fluctuate, it involves a foreign exchange risk, that is, exposure to gain or loss on assets or liabilities denominated in another currency. This additional risk should thus be considered in determining the degree of commitment to international investing as well as the sort of strategy to be employed in executing the investment plan.

This chapter begins by describing the size and characteristics of the international equity market and the potential benefits to be derived from an international investment program. We'll then discuss the importance of the currency risk in international investing and establish a framework for analyzing the reasons for currency rate differentials and the fluctuations in these differentials over time. We'll then describe a passive strategy for investing in international markets and conclude with an active counterpart to the passive investment strategy.

239

SIZE AND CHARACTER OF THE INTERNATIONAL EQUITY MARKET

Table 9-1 shows the market values of the individual world equity markets (including the U. S. market) and their proportional representation in the total international equity market. Note that the total international equity market was $1835 billion as of the end of 1979. The U. S. (domestic) equity market represented 52 percent, or the largest proportion of the total, reflecting both the relative size of the U. S. economy and the fact that the U. S. capital market is the most highly developed in the world. Japan ranked second, while several European markets — the United Kingdom, West Germany, France, and Switzerland — as well as Australia also represented meaningful proportions of the world total. Other markets were generally less important in terms of representation in the world market portfolio.

Figures 9-1 and 9-2 show the average annual realized rate of return and standard deviation of return for several of the major international equity markets over two time

Table 9-1 World equity markets

	Capitalization, 12/31/79	
	In billions of U. S. dollars	As % of total
United Kingdom	$ 142.2	7.75
Germany	80.4	4.38
France	54.2	2.95
Spain	13.6	0.74
Switzerland	44.3	2.41
Netherlands	24.4	1.33
Italy	12.9	0.70
Sweden	10.4	0.57
Belgium/Luxembourg	13.4	0.73
Denmark	3.6	0.20
Norway	3.3	0.18
Austria	2.3	0.13
Total Europe	405.0	22.07
Japan	274.0	14.93
Hong Kong	23.3	1.27
Singapore	13.6	0.74
Australia	39.1	2.13
United States	960.2	52.33
Canada	98.0	5.34
South African gold mines	21.7	1.18
Total	$1834.9	100.00

Source: Capital International Perspective, I, 1980, Geneva.

(a)

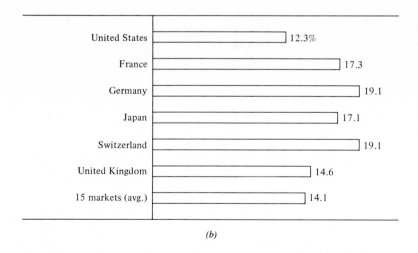

(b)

Figure 9-1 Rate of return (excluding dividends) and standard deviation, 1960–1969. (*a*) Rate of return (open bar = local currency, gray bar = dollars). (*b*) Standard deviation. *(Source: Joel R. Swanson, "Investing Internationally to Reduce Risk and Enhance Return," Morgan Guaranty Trust, 1980.)*

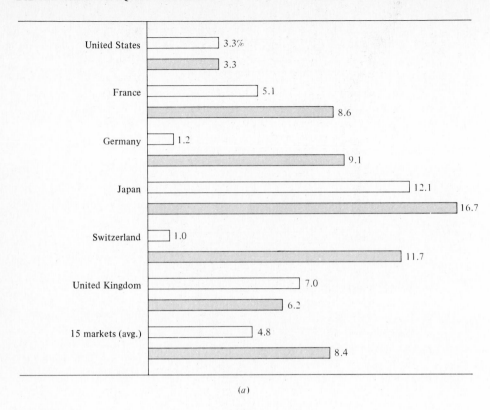

(a)

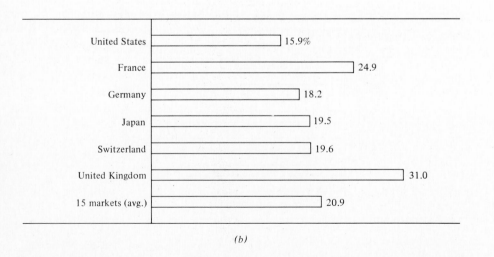

(b)

Figure 9-2 Total rate of return—compound annual rate, with dividends reinvested, 1970–1979. (a) Rate of return (open bar = local currency, gray bar = dollars). (b) Standard deviation. *(Source: Joel R. Swanson, "Investing Internationally to Reduce Risk and Enhance Return," Morgan Guaranty Trust, 1980.)*

periods, 1960–1969 and 1970–1979. The first period represents one of relatively favorable economic activity worldwide and fixed currency exchange rates. The second period represents a more difficult environment of energy shortages and high inflation as well as a change from fixed to flexible exchange rates. It's useful to separate the data into two subperiods in order to analyze how risk and return changed over the period and to assess what might be a normal operating environment in the future.

Note that the upper part of Figure 9-1 shows return (excluding dividends for lack of data) in both local currencies and dollars. Since foreign securities are denominated in local currency, returns are designated in local currency and must be converted to dollars at the prevailing exchange rate in order to be realized by the domestic (U. S.) investor. For example, returns earned on German securities need to be converted into dollars at the prevailing exchange rate of marks for dollars in order to be realized by the domestic (U. S.) investor.

Since exchange rates fluctuate, this conversion can result in an added gain or loss on returns earned in the foreign market. For example, suppose the rate of exchange for marks to dollars was $0.50 at the beginning of the year but changed to $0.525 by the end of the year. This would mean that the mark would have appreciated (dollar depreciated) relative to the dollar over the year resulting in a gain to a U. S. investor of 5 percent on currency over the year. This gain should be added to the return earned on the German market over the year; for example, if the return was 10 percent, the net return would be 15.5 percent.[1] Naturally, if there had been a currency loss, this should be subtracted from the return of 10 percent for the year.

Note in Figure 9-1 that returns stated in local currency and dollars were virtually identical, reflecting relatively stable worldwide economic conditions and fixed exchange rates. The only significant changes were in the U. K. market, where devaluations over the period resulted in losses for foreign investors, and in the German market, where upward revaluations resulted in currency gains. The U. S. market ranked somewhat above average in terms of return performance over the period but showed the least variability, as indicated by the standard deviations at the bottom of Figure 9-1. In terms of return per unit of risk (return divided by standard deviation) the United States would actually have ranked highest over the period.

In contrast to the earlier period, Figure 9-2 shows significant differences between returns earned in local currencies and dollars across practically all countries, reflecting the unstable economic conditions of the period along with the switch from fixed to flexible exchange rates. The U. S. market performed somewhat below average when measured in local currency; however, because of the generally declining value of the dollar (depreciating currency), U. S. investors in virtually all foreign markets would have made significant currency gains over the period. The net performance of the U. S. market relative to the foreign markets measured in dollars was about the poorest of all.

The bottom part of both Figures 9-1 and 9-2 show the standard deviation of return by countries over the periods 1960–1969 and 1970–1979. The variability in the latter period was essentially similar to that of the earlier period, with the exception of the U. K. market, which showed a significant increase between periods. Although the U. S.

[1] Denoting R_m as the market return and F_x as the currency change we derive the return as follows
$(1 + R_m)(1 + F_x) - 1 = (1.10)(1.05) - 1 = 15.5\%$.

standard deviation increased somewhat, the U. S. market still ranked as the least risky. The standard deviation across markets was virtually identical whether measured in local currency or dollars (data not shown), reflecting the fact that changes in currency values were generally independent of the return realized in the equity markets, thereby neither adding to or subtracting from variability in either period.

DIVERSIFICATION ADVANTAGES OF INTERNATIONAL INVESTMENT

While international investment would obviously have benefited domestic (U. S.) investors in a period like 1970–1979, a more fundamental reason for considering it is the favorable effects on portfolio diversification. This benefit derives from the opportunity that foreign markets offer in providing a wider array of assets (securities) with relatively low correlation. These can in turn be combined with domestic securities to generate a lower overall portfolio risk (standard deviation) than would be possible when investing exclusively in domestic assets.

This is, of course, the same principle from which the benefits of domestic diversification derive. Recall from Chapter 2 that the typical security in the U. S. equity market would have a correlation with a market index on the order of .5. This means there are some benefits to be derived from diversification as there is less than perfect correlation between securities, but that these benefits are limited because the correlation is significantly positive. We have noted that empirical studies show that diversification can reduce the variance, or standard deviation, of a portfolio by 43 percent to something on the order of 57 percent of the risk of a nondiversified (single-security) portfolio.

Table 9-2 shows the correlation between the returns of several major equity markets over the 1960–1969 and 1970–1979 periods. Note that the U. S. and Canadian markets showed a high degree of correlation, as might be expected from the high level of economic integration between the two countries. There was a significantly lower degree of correlation between the United States and the other countries during both periods. On average the correlation across countries was on the order of .31 in the initial period and .37 in the latter period, indicating opportunities for diversification.

Figure 9-3, which is similar to one used in Chapter 2 to illustrate the benefits of diversification, shows that it is possible to use this imperfect correlation among international markets to reduce the risk of a portfolio below the level that is possible when only dealing with domestic securities. Note that the lower line, which represents the possibility of international investing and hence diversification along with domestic investing, lies at a lower level over the full range of portfolio holdings than when diversification is limited exclusively to domestic investing. With international diversification the portfolio risk drops to 33 percent of the risk of a typical stock (undiversified portfolio), or about one-third less than the 57 percent that is possible with domestic diversification.

The potential of international diversification is likely to persist into the future, as the degree of correlation across international markets should remain relatively low. To begin with, many of the factors that affect stock values — such as tax laws, monetary

Table 9-2 Correlation of U. S. and key foreign markets, 1960–1969 and 1970–1979

Return excluding dividends, dollar basis

	Coefficient of correlation with U. S.	
	1960–1969	1970–1979
Canada	0.81	0.71
France	0.27	0.40
Germany	0.36	0.31
Japan	0.08	0.31
Switzerland	0.49	0.47
United Kingdom	0.29	0.46
15 markets (average)	0.31	0.37

Source: Joel R. Swanson, "Investing Internationally to Reduce Risk and Enhance Return," Morgan Guaranty Trust Co., 1980.

policy, and general political climate — are peculiar to the individual domestic economy. Furthermore, even factors that affect the world economy, such as the sudden increase in oil prices, can impact individual economies differently. These differences, which are the basic source of a lack of synchronization among markets, should persist into the future.

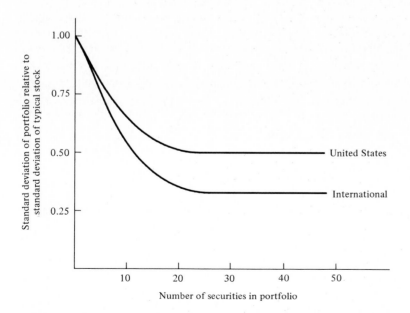

Figure 9-3 Risk reduction through national and international diversification. *(Source: B.H. Solnik, "Why Not Diversify Internationally Rather than Domestically?" Financial Analysts Journal, July–August 1974, pp. 48–54.)*

The data in Figure 9-4 further confirm that the degree of correlation among international markets is likely to remain low. The correlations across markets are broken down into several subperiods in the 1960–1979 period. The data show that correlations were high in the early 1960s, then declined and remained low in the middle and late 1960s, but rose again to the earlier levels in the latter part of the period. While correlations have varied over time, there does not appear to be any widespread trend toward greater correlation among the major equity markets. The most recent correlations appear to be a realistic, if not conservative, expectation for the future.[2]

MINIMUM RETURN REQUIRED FOR INTERNATIONAL INVESTING

Since international investing provides added diversification that is unavailable from domestic sources alone, it would be useful to determine the minimum return required in order to invest internationally. Alternatively, we could consider how low returns would have to be in order to prevent us from investing internationally. Presumably lower returns could be accepted from international investments than domestic investments because of the favorable impact these would have on reducing portfolio risk. The minimum return, or hurdle rate, in this context could be considered that which would give us the same risk-return trade-off as investing exclusively in domestic securities:

$$\text{Risk-return (international)} = \text{risk-return (domestic)}$$

Recall from our earlier analyses of the domestic equity market (Chapters 2 and 3) that the relevant risk of a security in a portfolio context is the contribution of that security to the portfolio risk. In effect it is the systematic risk and not the total risk of the security that is relevant in the portfolio context. This analysis should in turn be applicable in an international context, and hence we can say that the systematic risk is the relevant component to consider when structuring an internationally diversified portfolio.

[2] We should note that a continued trend toward greater economic integration among major nations could lead to increased correlation across international markets. It is, however, unlikely that the increased correlation resulting from such a potential trend would be sufficient to eliminate all the benefits of international diversification.

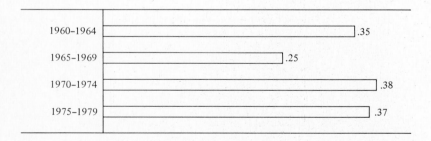

Figure 9-4 Correlation coefficients—U.S. market and average of fifteen foreign markets. *(Source: Joel R. Swanson, "Investing Internationally to Reduce Risk and Enhance Return," Morgan Guaranty Trust, 1980.)*

Table 9-3 shows risk-return data for several foreign equity markets along with data for the U. S. (domestic) market. The first three columns show risk data, including the standard deviation of return, the correlation with the U. S. market, and the beta of the foreign market with respect to the U. S. market. At any level of standard deviation or total risk, the beta will be high as the correlation between markets is high and, conversely, will be low as the correlation is low. For example, the U. K. market with a total risk more than twice that of the U. S. (33.3 percent versus 15.2 percent) but with a correlation of only .34 with the U. S. has a beta of .74 (refer to Chapter 2 for the formula for calculating beta). With respect to the standard deviation note that all the foreign markets show higher risk than the U. S. market; however, the correlations with the U. S. market are relatively low, resulting in lower systematic risk as measured by beta values that are less than the beta of 1 for the U. S. market.

Since the beta values are all lower than 1, a lower return would be required for investing in foreign equities than in U. S. equities. For example, with a beta of .74 the required return for investing in the U. K. market is 5.6 percent (.74 beta times 7.2 percent U. S. risk premium). The fourth column in the table shows these required returns under the presumption that the required risk premium (return less risk-free rate) for investing domestically (in the U. S. market) is 7.2 percent. These values are, as expected, lower than the required premium for investing in the U. S. market. It's thus possible to invest in international markets at the lower return derived in Table 9-3 and still maintain the same risk-reward ratio.

Based on the results in Figures 9-1 and 9-2, it might appear that these return targets would be easily exceeded. It would, however, be unwise to merely extrapolate that historic return experience. To begin with, at least part of the performance of foreign

Table 9-3 Risk and required return measures for foreign market portfolios from U. S. perspective

All figures estimated from data for 1975–1979

Country	Annualized standard deviation of returns (measured in U. S. dollars), %	Correlation with U. S. market (S&P 500)	Market-risk beta from U. S. perspective	Minimum risk premium from U. S. perspective, %*
France	22.3	0.32	0.47	3.6
Germany	16.7	0.38	0.42	3.2
Japan	18.8	0.36	0.45	3.4
Netherlands	24.2	0.50	0.80	6.1
Switzerland	22.6	0.45	0.67	5.1
United Kingdom	33.0	0.34	0.74	5.6
United States	15.2	1.00	1.00	7.2

*Risk premium = $beta_{US}$ × U. S. risk premium.

Source: D. R. Lessard, "International Investment Strategies: Conceptual and Empirical Foundations," paper presented at the Eleventh Congress of the European Federation of Financial Analysts Societies, The Hague, The Netherlands, October 1980.

markets can be traced to circumstances that are unlikely to be repeated — the postwar economic recovery of Europe, its subsequent boom resulting from the Common Market, and the economic phenomenon of Japan aided in part by a major increase in the degree of world economic integration. In addition, some of the performance advantage of foreign markets in the 1970–1979 period was due to currency gains that derived from the long downtrend in the value of the dollar. It's unlikely that such a trend would persist to provide continual gains on currency from foreign investing. The point of the previous analysis should be that foreign investing could be attractive even if historic experience does not repeat and that this investing could be justified even if the returns did not measure up to those available in the domestic market.

CURRENCY RISK

While international investing appears to be generally beneficial to portfolio performance, it entails the additional risk of currency fluctuations. Given this, one then asks whether these exchange risks are so large as to offset the benefits of international diversification. A related question is what, if any, special strategy should be followed to reduce the impact of the foreign exchange risk. We'll primarily deal with assessing the source and degree of exchange risks in this section and discuss later how the exchange risk is incorporated into active and passive strategies.

In assessing the causes of currency fluctuations we first need to differentiate between spot and forward exchange markets. The spot market is where currencies are exchanged immediately at the prevailing rate of exchange. The forward market is where traders buy and sell currency for delivery at a fixed future date but at a price that is set currently. Forward rates are typically quoted for delivery one month, three months, and six months forward; however, forward contracts can generally be arranged with most international banks for delivery at any specified date up to one year in the future. Contracts running beyond one year are also available but require special arrangements.

Table 9-4 shows the spot and forward rates of exchange for the U. S. dollar and the German mark (DM) and British pound (£) as of December 31, 1979. Note that the forward DM was more expensive than the spot DM. In technical terms the forward DM was selling at a premium relative to the spot DM, and the longer the contract, the higher the premium. In contrast, the forward pound was selling at a discount relative to the spot pound. The bottom part of the table shows the formula for calculating the premium or discount on forward exchange. Note that the six-month-forward premium on DM was 3 percent, while there was a discount of 0.5 percent on the six-month-forward pound.

FUNDAMENTAL DETERMINANTS OF EXCHANGE RATES

Figure 9-5 provides a graphic framework for evaluating fundamental determinants of changing exchange rates.[3] The figure shows that there is a four-way interrelationship

[3] Ian Giddy, "An Integrated Theory of Exchange Rate Equilibrium," *Journal of Financial and Quantitative Analysis,* December 1976, pp. 883–892, offers an excellent exposition of this analytical framework.

Table 9-4 Spot and forward exchange rates, 12/31/79

	Exchange rate	
	$/£	$/DM
Spot	2.2320	0.5799
One month forward	2.2280	0.5831
Three months forward	2.2211	0.5886
Six months forward	2.2215	0.5973

The percent premium or discount is calculated as

$$P = \frac{F - S}{S} \times \frac{12}{n} \times 100$$

S = spot rate
F = forward rate
n = number of months forward
where P = forward premium or discount (percent per annum)

For example, the forward premium on the DM six months forward was

$$P = \frac{.5973 - .5799}{.5799} \times \frac{12}{6} \times 100 = 3\% \text{ per annum}$$

A similar calculation for the six-month forward £ would show that $P = -.5\%$. Since the £ is selling at a discount, we would use the symbol D instead of the negative sign and indicate for the six-month forward £, $D = .5\%$.

---

among expected differences in inflation, differences in interest rates, expected changes in exchange rates, and forward exchange rates. These interrelationships are consistent, so that once any three are established, the fourth is then determined. Similarly, if any one of them is violated, at least one other must be violated.

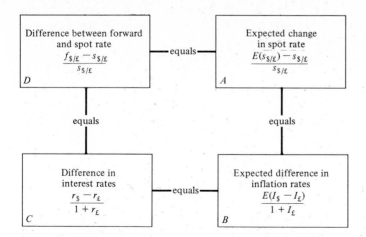

Figure 9-5 Inflation, interest rates, premiums, and exchange rates. *(Source: R. Brealey and S.C. Myers, Financial Planning and Strategy, New York: McGraw-Hill, 1980.)*

In Figure 9-5 the corners A to B indicate that the expected change in spot rates should be related to the expected difference in inflation rates in the two countries. To begin with, identical goods should trade at the same price even if they are traded in different markets. If there is a difference, those goods that can be bought more cheaply abroad will be imported, forcing down the price of the domestic product. Similarly, those goods that can be bought more cheaply in the United States will be exported, forcing down the price of the foreign product. In particular, the price of foreign goods when converted to dollars should be roughly the same as the price in the U. S. For example, for U. S. and U. K. goods we would have sterling price of the goods times the exchange rate ($/£) equals dollar price of the goods. Equivalently, the exchange rate ($/£) should equal dollar price of the goods divided by sterling price of the goods. If the price of sterling is always equal to the ratio of domestic prices, then any change in the ratio of domestic prices must be matched by a change in the price of sterling. For example, if inflation is 5 percent in the United States and 10 percent in the United Kingdom, then, in order to equalize the dollar price of goods in the two countries, the price of sterling must fall by $(.05 - .10)/1.10$ or about 5 percent.

This relationship is based on the purchasing power parity (PPP) theorem. The PPP has been tested empirically and one should be aware that the evidence may be sensitive to the countries, time periods, and price indexes that are selected for testing. Despite these difficulties, it seems reasonably clear from the evidence that over long time periods and during periods of hyperinflation (when monetary factors swamp real changes), PPP offers a fairly good description of exchange rate behavior. However, over shorter time periods, say, three to twelve months, it has not been uncommon to observe substantial exchange rate changes, say, 10 to 20 percent, which are unrelated to commodity price changes.

Corners B to C in Figure 9-5 indicate that differences in interest rates should be also related to differences in inflation rates. This relationship derives from the Fisher effect, which indicates that investors are interested in real rather than nominal returns. If this is so, then prices of securities or, alternatively, interest rates should adjust to provide the expected real return. We would in turn expect this to occur across different countries, so that there would be a tendency toward an equalization of real returns or real interest rates between countries. Differences in inflation rates would then account for the difference in nominal interest rates across countries. Empirical evidence on this relationship is limited and while we might expect that the real rate of interest would be equilibrated across countries over the longer term, we are also aware that there are impediments like exchange controls, government intervention in exchange markets, and taxes that can prevent this from occurring for extended periods.

The corners C to D in Figure 9-5 indicate that the difference in interest rates should be equal to the difference between forward and spot rates. This relationship is based on what is known as the *interest rate parity theorem* and is a very strong relationship since it is based on arbitrage. It must match the difference in interest rates, or else investors will be able to profit without bearing any risk. They could do this by borrowing in the country with the relatively low interest rate (including the cost of forward cover), investing in the money market in the country with the high rate, and removing the exchange risk by covering in the forward market.

For example, if interest rates were 10 percent in the United States, investing

$1 million would net $1.1 million at the end of the year. Presuming that the interest rate were 12 percent in the United Kingdom and the spot rate of exchange was $2/£, the investor could convert the $1 million to £500,000 and invest at the higher interest rate for a return of £560,000 at the end of the year. Since the future rate of exchange is uncertain, the investor can avoid risk (potential loss) by selling sterling forward at the prevailing forward rate, which in equilibrium should be $1.964/£. Converting the proceeds at this rate ($1.964 \times 560,000$) gives the same dollar proceeds of $1.1 million as investing directly in the United States. The gain on interest rates is offset by the loss on foreign exchange, as should be the case according to the analysis in Figure 9-5. Empirical tests in markets like Eurocurrency markets where such factors as exchange controls and tax considerations are not factors indicate that this relationship holds almost exactly. In other markets, the relationship will diverge as tax factors and potential exchange controls are more significant considerations.

Finally, from corners D and A at the top of the quadrilateral in the figure we expect the difference between forward and spot rates to be equal to the expected change in the spot rate. For example, a one-year-forward rate of $2/£ should mean that traders expect the spot rate in one year's time to be $2/£. If they expected it to be higher than this, no one would be willing to sell pounds at the forward rate; if they expected it to be lower, no one would be willing to buy at the forward rate. Alternatively, if forward rates differed from anticipated exchange rates, market participants would be induced to speculate on the difference between them, tending to move the forward rate toward the expected future spot rate. Empirical tests indicate that the forward rate is an unbiased estimate of future spot rates, that is, it consistently neither underestimates nor over-estimates future spot rates, and in this respect provides a good standard for assessing forecasting expertise.[4] We'll in fact use it as such when we discuss active approaches to managing an internationally diversified portfolio.

MANAGING CURRENCY RISKS

If the relationships just described held exactly, we'd expect that interest rates and security prices would reflect expected changes in exchange rates and currency would not represent a separate risk in international investing. We noted, however, that there is only a long-run tendency toward equilibrium and that real-world factors like taxes, exchange controls—both actual and potential—and transactions costs can further distort equilibrium. As a result, we would expect that exchange rates would diverge in the short run and would exhibit substantial unexpected fluctuations that investment managers need to consider in designing and implementing active and passive strategies of international investing.

In order to protect against currency risk, investors may hedge by borrowing or entering into forward currency contracts. These hedging strategies of course have a cost

[4] While the forward premium is an unbiased predictor of future exchange rate changes, it is a poor predictor in the sense that it explains only about 10 percent of the fluctuations in the future spot rate. This suggests that the bulk of the short-run exchange rate changes are dominated by unanticipated events and that the forward premium sits roughly in the middle of a wide distribution of exchange rate expectations. Alternatively, it implies that there is ample opportunity to apply forecasting techniques to attempt to explain this unaccounted-for exchange rate variation.

that may well outweigh the incremental risk reduction.[5] Alternatively, the investor might protect against currency risk by simply investing across many foreign markets. In this way, losses on weak currencies would tend to be offset by gains on strong currencies. Presumably, passive strategies that entail holding a broadly diversified portfolio of international securities would benefit from this risk-reducing effect over the short term, while over the long term, as markets tend toward equilibrium, passive investors would find their exposure to currency risk to be minimal.

On the other hand, investors following an active strategy that involves over-weighting in attractive countries or markets and underweighting in unattractive markets will by virtue of this activity become exposed to the currency risk, as the investor is taking a bet on the currency in addition to the market. This strategy in effect cancels the balancing-out effect of a passive, or world investing, strategy. Therefore, such investors should carefully consider the direction and magnitude of currency movements and incorporate these explicit forecasts into their assessment of the relative attrac-tiveness of the different markets. This would enable them to avoid undue penalties from possible currency risks and to capitalize on potential opportunities from an especially well-positioned currency.

A PASSIVE STRATEGY

As is the case with domestic investing, investors on the international market can pursue an active or passive strategy or combinations of these two alternative approaches. One way of investing passively is to create an international index fund, just as domestic investors following a totally passive strategy would attempt to replicate the market performance by investing in an index like the S&P 500. When investing internationally, the intent would be to replicate the performance of the world market rather than only a single domestic market. Ideally, one would want to obtain a representative index of the world market portfolio and invest in those companies according to their rela-tive weights.

There are, however, several major impediments to direct application of the U. S. index approach in the international arena. First, there is no index that investors gener-ally agree is representative of the world market portfolio, as is the case in the United States, where indexes like the S&P 500, NYSE, and Wilshire 5000, though perhaps flawed, are nevertheless deemed useful. Furthermore, many markets are dominated by only a handful of companies, while many other companies, though sizable, might be quite closely held and not readily marketable. Finally, there is probably a greater degree of mispricing in foreign markets than in the U. S. market, with the attendant difficulties for passive strategies and indexing.

A passive approach that seems practical and at the same time provides a direct way of obtaining many of the benefits of international diversification is one devised by Batterymarch. This approach focuses on the major world markets: Japan, the United

[5] Estimates are that the cost of such hedging for most major currencies is on the order of .5 to .7 percent per annum.

Kingdom, West Germany, France, Switzerland, and Australia. Gold-mining stocks are also included in the investment universe because of their inflation-hedging properties as well as the fact that they are a reasonably meaningful portion of the world market. These six countries and the gold-mining stocks represent 72.9 percent of the non-U. S.-Canadian world market, thus providing major representation of capitalization in the world market, while avoiding the difficulties inherent in operating across a multitude of smaller and perhaps less familiar markets.

In addition, the Batterymarch strategy entails investing only in the ten largest companies that dominate the market weighting within each of the six major equity markets.[6] This provides a list that is both representative and manageable; it eliminates the necessity of monitoring a large array of unfamiliar and less marketable securities. These companies would presumably also be the least likely to be inefficiently priced and hence the most suitable for use in a passive strategy.

Table 9-5 shows the weights of the seventy stocks in the portfolio grouped according to the seven major market categories. Each stock weighting represents its share of the total capitalization of the seventy companies in the universe. Note that the aggregate weighting of the companies within each major market is quite similar to the weighting in a broader index of international equities. The strategy appears, as intended, to provide a reasonable proxy for a world portfolio.

Table 9-6 on page 257 shows a simulation of the performance of this strategy over the 1971–1975 period compared with the performance of a broader market index. Note that the strategy tracks the performance of the market index reasonably well over the period and provides a total return that is close to that of the index; the simulated fund showed a correlation of .97 with the market index over the period. The results suggest that the strategy is a viable one for investing in international markets.

AN ACTIVE STRATEGY

An active strategy for investing internationally might be oriented to identifying relatively attractive and unattractive national markets. A market identified as attractive would be overweighted in the portfolio, while one judged unattractive would be underweighted or perhaps even eliminated entirely from the portfolio. Of course, a decision to actively manage a portfolio in this fashion presupposes some predictive capability, just as the decision to operate actively in the domestic equity market did.

Figure 9-6 shows the steps that an organization should follow in executing an active strategy. It first needs to develop explicit forecasts of the market return for each of the international markets of interest. Since active management means that an organization is implicitly taking a position either "long" or "short" in currency, there is also need to develop an explicit forecast of currency changes over the planning

---

[6] As of 1979, the top ten companies on average constituted approximately one-third of the market weighting of the markets in the six countries: Japan, United Kingdom, Germany, France, Switzerland, and Australia. The percentage ranged from a high of 63 percent in Switzerland to a low of 13 percent in Japan. This compares with the United States where the top ten companies represented 20 percent of the total capitalization of the market.

Table 9-5 International equity diversification — sample portfolio, 10/31/76

	As % of	
	Non-U. S. market	Batterymarch portfolio
Japan		
Toyota Motor		5.0
Nippon Steel		5.0
Matsushita Elec. Inds.		4.2
Nissan Motors		3.9
Sony		3.6
Hitachi		3.4
Tokyo Electric Power		3.4
Sumitomo Bank		3.1
Sanwa Bank		2.8
Mitsubishi Bank		2.8
	31.2	42.8
United Kingdom		
Shell T&T		4.1
British Petroleum		4.1
Imperial Chemical		3.4
BAT Industries		1.6
General Electric UK		1.4
Unilever		1.4
Marks and Spencer		1.2
Imperial Group		1.0
Beecham Group		0.9
Barclays Bank		0.9
	14.1	19.3
West Germany		
Siemens		2.4
Daimler-Benz		2.2
BASF		1.5
Bayer		1.5
Deutsche Bank		1.5
Hoechst		1.4
RWE		1.2
VEBA		1.0
Dresdner Bank		1.0
Thyssen Huette		0.8
	10.3	14.1
France		
Michelin		1.7
Aquitaine SNPA		1.6
St-Gobain P-A-M		1.2
Air Liquide		0.9
Pechiney-Ucine		0.8
Dassault Breguet		0.8
L'Oreal		0.8
Correfour		0.8
Francaise-Petroles		0.8
Moulinex		0.7
	6.0	9.0

Table 9-5 *(Continued)*

	As % of	
	Non-U. S. market	Batterymarch portfolio
Australia		
Broken Hill		1.6
Conzinco Rio Tinto		0.8
MIM Holdings		0.7
CSR		0.6
Hamersley		0.5
Myer Emporium		0.4
Bougainville Copper		0.4
Western Mining		0.3
Bank New South Wales		0.3
COMALCO		0.3
	4.8	6.6
Switzerland		
Nestle		0.9
Schweiz Bankverein		0.8
Schweiz Bankgesell		0.7
Hoffman LaRoche		0.7
Schweiz Kreditanstal		0.5
Ciba-Geigy		0.5
Sandoz		0.3
Oerlikon-Buharle		0.2
Aluminum Suisse		0.2
Brown Boveri		0.2
	4.2	5.8
Gold		
West Driefontein		1.6
Western Holdings		1.2
President Brand		0.8
Free State Geduld		0.7
Western Deep Levels		0.7
Blyvooruitzecht		0.5
President Steyn		0.5
	2.1	2.9
Total	72.9	100.0

Source: Batterymarch, Financial Management Corporation International Index Fund, case study prepared by Robert Vandell, Colgate Darden Graduate School of Business Administration, 1977.

period. The second step is to adjust these forecasts for the organization's predictive capability. The final step is to consider risk along with forecast return and generate an optimum portfolio.

In developing forecasts for the individual markets we can again use an approach like that used to generate forecasts of the domestic (U. S.) market. Recall from Chapter 7 that this first involved assessing the likely variability of market return by

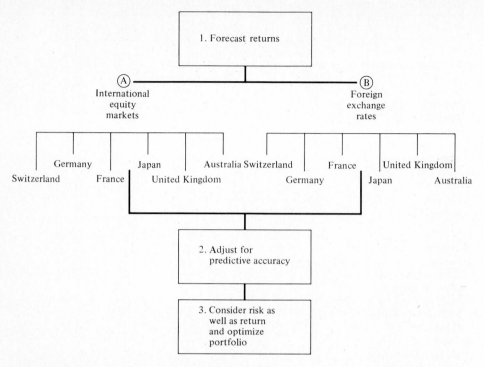

Figure 9-6 Executing an active international investment strategy.

using historical and/or projected estimates of the standard deviation of return. We would then assess the relative attractiveness of the market, using the five-way rating scheme we have been recommending throughout the book. The final step would be to adjust the implied return forecast for predictive capability. Again we have been recommending the information coefficient IC method for making this adjustment.[7]

Figure 9-7, prepared by a major international investment advisory organization, illustrates this procedure with a particular foreign market — the German market. Note that the standard deviation of return is 13.2 percent, the same experienced over the 1973–1978 period. For purposes of illustration we've assessed the market as attractive,

---

[7] This case is similar to the market timing illustration in Chapter 8, where we were attempting to assess divergences of the market from its long-term expected return. The process first involves rating the relative attractiveness of the market on a five-way scale — 1 being the most attractive and 5 the least. We then need to convert these ratings into units away from the mean by dividing the rating by the standard deviation of the rating distribution, which in this case is 1.25. For example, we convert a rating of 2, which is 1 rating unit from the mean, into $1 \div 1.25 = .8$ standard deviations from the mean.

Once we've converted the ratings into standard deviations from the mean, we then multiply these by the standard deviation of the return distribution, which in the case of the German market is 13.2 percent, and thereby obtain an equivalent return for each rating category. For example, when we multiply a rating of 2, which is .8 standard deviations from the mean by the 13.2 standard deviation of the return distribution, we obtain a return divergence of 10.6 percent. The final step is to adjust for predictive ability by multiplying by the assessed IC of .30. In this case, a 2 rating with a raw return divergence of 10.6 percent reduces to a divergence of 3.2 or an expected return of 13.9 percent.

Table 9-6 Actual and simulated performance of foreign markets

Annual returns, % change

	Adjusted for currency fluctuation					
	1971	1972	1973	1974	1975	Average
Foreign markets	29	27	−16	−24	33	7
Simulation	20	22	−13	−22	32	6

Source: Batterymarch, Financial Management Corporation International Index Fund, case study prepared by Robert Vandell, Colgate Darden Graduate School of Business Administration, 1977.

indicated by a rating of 2 on the five-way rating scale. The implied return of 21.3 percent needs to be adjusted, however, and in this case we're assessing predictive capability on the order of .30 for that purpose. The net result is a return forecast of 13.9 percent for the market.

As noted, it's also desirable to make an explicit forecast of the currency, in this case German marks, when undertaking an active international investment strategy. The procedure here would again be to estimate the likely future variability of the currency rate of exchange relative to the U. S. dollar. We could base this on historical and/or projected data on the standard deviation of currency exchange rates. We would then rate the attractiveness of the currency relative to the domestic (U. S.) currency on the same five-way rating scale. The final step would be to adjust the return forecast for the organization's predictive capability with respect to exchange rate changes.

Figure 9-8 illustrates the process using the exchange rate between U. S. dollars and German marks.[8] Note that the exchange rate for marks has shown a standard deviation of 9.5 percent over the 1973–1978 period — which we'll use as an estimate of the future variability. In addition, we're using the one-year forward rate as an estimate of the consensus expectation for the change in the spot rate over the period.[9] Since we've rated the currency as neutral, the consensus expectation becomes our forecast for the period. If we had rated the currency other than 3, we would have had to proceed as with the equity forecast by considering projected variability and adjusting for forecasting capability. Note that in this case we've assessed predictive capability on the order of .30,

[8] Converting the rating distribution to a return distribution and adjusting for predictive capability is similar to the procedure for the market forecast. First we convert the ratings into standard deviations from the mean by dividing them by the standard deviation of the rating distribution, which is 1.32. We can then multiply by the standard deviation of the currency, which is 9.5 percent, and obtain returns associated with the ratings. The final step is to adjust for the .30 predictive ability.

As an example, we'll rate the currency 1 for the coming year. This is 2 rating points or 1.52 standard deviations from the mean. When we multiply 1.52 by the 9.5 standard deviation of the currency distribution, we obtain a return divergence of 14.4. Multiplying again by the .30 IC, we obtain a divergence of 4.6 from that "forecast" by the forward rate, or a forecast return of 9.3 percent.

[9] We noted before that the forward rate provides an unbiased benchmark for evaluating forecasting capability. Using this benchmark, studies show that some commercially available forecasting services have the capability to improve on the forward rate forecast. This evidence indicates that active strategies incorporating exchange rate forecasts have opportunities for improving portfolio performance.

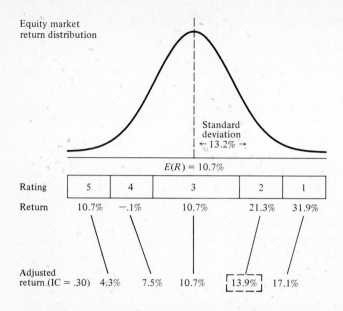

Equity market
return distribution

Standard
deviation
← 13.2% →

$E(R) = 10.7\%$

Rating	5	4	3	2	1
Return	10.7%	−.1%	10.7%	21.3%	31.9%

Adjusted
return (IC = .30) 4.3% 7.5% 10.7% 13.9% 17.1%

Figure 9-7 Equity return forecast—German market, Sept. 30, 1979. The expected return of 10.7 percent is an estimate of the consensus expectation for the German market. (It was derived in a manner similar to the way we've estimated the expected return in previous chapters and with respect to U.S. equities.)

which is the same as for equities but could differ with regard to currency versus equities as well as across countries.

Table 9-7 shows the results of the same sort of forecasting process for several major international markets, including the German market. It shows the forecasts for both currency and the equity market for each country along with the organization's estimated level of predictive capability as measured by the information coefficient.

Table 9-7 Return forecasts — currency, equity and total, 9/30/79

	Currency		Equity		
	IC	Forecast return, %	IC	Forecast return, %	Total return, %
United Kingdom	0.10	1.1	0.15	18.2	19.3
France	0.15	1.0	0.15	13.6 (−)	14.6
Germany	0.30	4.7	0.30	13.9 (+)	18.6
Switzerland	0.30	10.2	0.30	7.2	17.4
Hong Kong	0.30	0.0	0.10	19.4 (+)	19.4
Japan	0.15	6.1 (+)	0.15	10.8	16.9
Netherlands	0.15	1.8 (−)	0.15	11.6	13.4
Canada	0.15	1.3 (+)	0.15	15.8	17.1

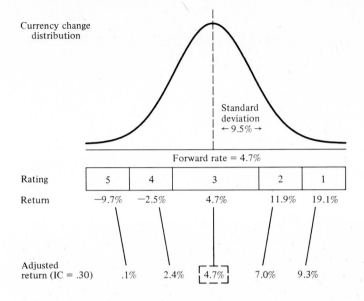

Forward rate = 4.7%

Rating	5	4	3	2	1

| Return | −9.7% | −2.5% | 4.7% | 11.9% | 19.1% |

Adjusted
return (IC = .30)   .1%   2.4%   4.7%   7.0%   9.3%

Figure 9-8 Currency change forecast — German market, Sept. 30, 1979. The forward rate is our estimate of the expected return for the currency over the year. It is based on our theoretical analysis in an earlier section of the fundamental determinants of differences in spot and forward exchange rates.

Note that the assessed level of predictive capability differs with respect to both the currency and equity forecasts as well as across countries. The pluses and minuses next to the forecast return indicate where the organization has made an other than neutral forecast — that is, a rating of other than a 3. The final column combines the currency and equity forecast to give a total expected return in each of the markets over the next year.

Note that the Hong Kong, U. K., and German markets rank high in terms of total return forecast for the period. The German and Hong Kong equity market were deemed to be of above-average attraction, while the German currency was forecast by consensus to be relatively strong over the period. On the other hand, the French and Dutch markets rank at the bottom in terms of forecast return; the French equity market is rated as unattractive, while the Dutch currency outlook is rated below average. Other markets show mixed patterns, with the equity market attractive but the currency unattractive, or vice versa. Hence these markets tend to rank in the middle with respect to total return over the forthcoming year.

OPTIMUM INTERNATIONAL PORTFOLIO

In order to develop an optimum portfolio structure we should consider risk as well as return, and the best way of doing this is within the framework of a portfolio optimization model such as we've discussed in Chapter 2. We would, of course, use the estimates developed in Table 9-7 as our projected return inputs. For purposes of the illustration we'll use historical standard deviation and covariance relationships over the 1973–1978 period as risk inputs.

Figure 9-9 shows an efficient frontier of portfolios generated by the optimization routine with the risk and return inputs already given.[10] It also shows the risk-return location of a currently held portfolio designated *CP* that was the object of the upgrading analysis. Note that the portfolio on the upper part of the efficient frontier offers a higher return at the same level of risk as the current alternative, while the portfolio on the lower part of the efficient frontier offers the same return at a lower level of risk. This dominance is the result of the presumed capability to forecast and hence generate greater return than is available to a passive investor, as well as the more explicit consideration of risk (covariance relationships) than is possible without formal optimization procedures.

Table 9-8 shows the weightings of the individual countries in both portfolios (equal risk and equal return) from the efficient frontier compared with the weightings in the current portfolio. Note that the optimum portfolio carries relatively heavy weightings in the high-return countries — the United Kingdom, Germany, and Hong Kong — but no weightings in France and the Netherlands. The German market is in a sense acting as a substitute for the French and Dutch markets, which are highly correlated with the

[10] Since the assets or, alternatively, countries to be considered for international diversification are unlikely to exceed fifteen (in this case there are eight), return, variance, and covariance inputs can be readily developed. As in the case of asset allocation, the full-covariance Markowitz model can and is generally employed in generating an efficient frontier of internationally diversified portfolios.

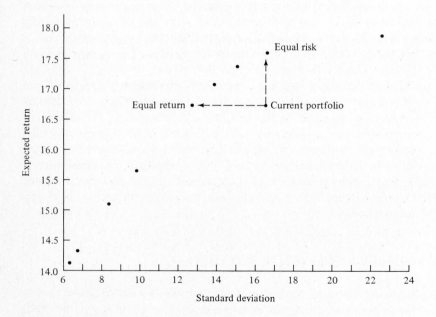

Figure 9-9 Efficient frontier and current portfolio, Sept. 30, 1979.

Table 9-8 International portfolio composition, %

	Current portfolio	Optimum equal risk	Optimum equal return
United Kingdom	33	20	33
France	12	0	0
Germany	9	41	39
Switzerland	2	2	2
Hong Kong	5	5	5
Japan	19	23	19
Netherlands	5	0	0
Canada	2	2	2
	87	93	100
Cash equivalent	13	7	—
Total	100	100	100
Expected return	16.75	17.65	16.71
Standard deviation	16.44	16.72	13.00

Note: The optimum equal-risk portfolio is one that has the same risk (approximately) as the current portfolio but, as shown in Figure 9-9, a higher return. Correspondingly, the equal-return portfolio is one that has the same return as the current portfolio but, as also shown in Figure 9-9, a lower risk. Both dominate the current portfolio.

German market but have significantly lower forecast returns. In fact the major divergence between the optimum and current portfolios is with respect to these three countries. A shift from the French and Dutch markets to the German market would improve prospective return and/or reduce risk as indicated by the statistics on the expected return and standard deviation of the three portfolios.

CONCLUSION

International investing expands the set of opportunities available to the investor and thereby offers the potential for generating a portfolio with a higher return per unit of risk. We have indicated that investors could attempt to capitalize on this potential through active or passive strategies of investing. If one chooses an active strategy of investing, there is need to consider explicitly the risk of fluctuating exchange rates as well as deal with the problem of forecasting returns for the foreign markets of interest. We illustrated a framework of analysis for explicit consideration of forecasting both foreign exchange rates and market returns.

While international investing appears to be generally beneficial, there are factors that represent potential obstacles and these should be considered in implementing strategies of international investing. These factors include formal barriers to international transactions such as exchange controls, double taxation of portfolio income for certain investors in particular countries, and restrictions on ownership of securities according to the nationality of the investor. In addition, there are informal barriers such as the difficulty of obtaining information about a market, differences in reporting practices that make international comparisons difficult, transactions costs, and markets that are generally less liquid than the U. S. market. Finally, investors should be aware of the generally remote yet extreme risk (in terms of consequences) of governmental confiscation or expropriation of foreign assets.

PROBLEMS

1 The spot rate for the German mark is currently .4055 per dollar, while the six-month forward rate is .4178 per dollar. Is the forward rate at a premium or discount? Calculate what it is.

2 Assume that the exchange rate of marks to dollars was $0.50 at the beginning of the year and $0.48 at the end of the year. Over the same period the return on German stocks had been 18 percent. What was the net return to the U. S. investor over the year?

3 Discuss why inclusion of foreign securities in a portfolio might be beneficial even if the expected return was less than expected from domestic securities.

4 Assume that the rate of interest is 9 percent in the United States and 12 percent in the United Kingdom, and that the spot rate of exchange is $2/£. Determine what the forward rate of exchange should be to ensure equilibrium.

5 Indicate the problems of conducting a totally passive international investment strategy and suggest a workable way around these problems.

6 Refer to Figure 9-8. Assume that the standard deviation of currency was 8 percent and that the organization deemed its IC to be .15. Determine the expected return on the currency when it is rated 1.

7 Indicate the essential elements of an active strategy of investing in international markets, and briefly describe the importance of each.

SELECTED REFERENCES

Agmon, Tamir: "Country Risk: The Significance of the Country Factor for Share Price Movements in the United Kingdom, Germany and Japan," *Journal of Business,* January 1973, pp. 24–32.

Bergstrom, Gary L.: "A New Route to Higher Returns and Lower Risks," *Journal of Portfolio Management,* Fall 1975, pp. 30–38.

Black, F.: "International Capital Market Equilibrium with Investment Barriers," *Journal of Financial Economics,* December 1974, pp. 337–352.

Giddy, Ian: "An Integrated Theory of Exchange Rate Equilibrium," *Journal of Financial and Quantitative Analysis,* December 1976, pp. 883–892.

Grubel, Herbert G.: "Internationally Diversified Portfolios: Welfare Gains and Capital Flows," *American Economic Review,* December 1968, pp. 1299–1314.

Joy, Maurice, Dan Panton, Frank Reilly, and Stanley Martin: "Co-Movements of International Equity Markets," *Financial Review,* Fall 1976, pp. 1–20.

Lessard, Donald F.: "World, Country and Industry Relationships in Equity Returns: Implications for Risk Reduction through International Diversification," *Financial Analysts Journal,* January–February 1976, pp. 31–38.

Levy, Haim, and Marshall Sarnat: "International Diversification of Investment Portfolios," *American Economic Review,* September 1970, pp. 668–675.

Logue, Dennis E., and Richard J. Rogolski: "Offshore Alphas: Should Diversification Begin at Home?" *Journal of Portfolio Management,* Winter 1979, pp. 5–10.

Makin, John: "Portfolio Theory and the Problem of Foreign Exchange Risk," *Journal of Finance,* May 1978, pp. 517–534.

Ripley, Duncan: "Systematic Elements in the Linkage of National Stock Market Indices," *Review of Economics and Statistics,* August 1973, pp. 356–361.

Solnik, B. H.: "Why Not Diversify Internationally Rather than Domestically?" *Financial Analysts Journal,* July–August 1974, pp. 48–54.

Subrahmanyam, Marti: "On the Optimality of International Capital Market Integration," *Journal of Financial Economics,* March 1975, pp. 3–28.

Swanson, Joel R.: "Investing Internationally to Reduce Risk and Enhance Return," Morgan Guaranty Trust Co., 1980.

THREE

MANAGING THE FIXED-INCOME PORTFOLIO AND THE USE OF OPTIONS

BOND ANALYSIS

INTRODUCTION

Recall from Chapter 7 that bonds have historically performed well relative to other asset classes during periods of deflation. This attribute as a hedge against deflationary periods derives from the fact that the income (coupons) to be received from bonds remains fixed while the capitalization rate for this income declines as the general level of interest rates falls during such a period. Correspondingly, depending on the quality of the issue, bonds generally are secure from the business and financial risks that impact common stocks so severely during a deflationary period.

Whereas bonds are expected to be superior performers during deflationary times, they are expected to turn in inferior performance during inflationary periods and perform less well than common stocks during periods of high growth in real economic activity. This again derives from the basic characteristic of bonds: income is fixed, and there is no opportunity to adjust these payments upward to defend against inflation or capitalize on the opportunity for improved growth that develops during periods of economic prosperity. Bonds might thus be regarded as having a primary role in a balanced portfolio as a hedge against the risk of deflation, and as such they should have a greater or lesser weighting in the portfolio depending on the assessed probability of deflation versus high inflation or favorable economic growth.

This chapter assumes that the investor has assessed the probability of occurrence for the various economic scenarios and that the asset allocation determination has been made to establish the appropriate weighting for bonds in the portfolio. Once this decision has been made, the problem then becomes one of managing the bond portion in such a way as to meet performance objectives for this portion of the portfolio. To achieve performance, the manager will focus on one or more of the three major components of return to the bond investment: coupon income, capital gain or loss, and interest earned on reinvestment of coupons, or interest-on-interest. For investors with a short horizon, or holding period, capital gains or losses are the prime consideration, while for investors with a long horizon the interest-on-interest component is the most critical. Whether the investor has a long- or short-term investment horizon, the prime factor that provides opportunities and at the same time creates risk is the shifting level and structure of interest rates. We'll begin by describing an active strategy for capitalizing on the opportunities presented by shifts in the level of interest rates. We'll then describe a passive strategy for hedging against adverse shifts in interest rates. We'll conclude by describing the risks and rewards of attempting to capitalize on the shifts in the structure of interest rates, especially with respect to the risk premium across sectors.

REALIZED AND EXPECTED BOND RETURN

Recall from Chapter 4 that the yield to maturity for a bond provides a measure of the expected return for a bond. For a bond selling at par, the yield to maturity is easily calculated as the coupon rate divided by the par value (generally 1000) of the bond. Furthermore, when interest rates and consequently the yield to maturity do not change over the life of the bond, then the realized return on the bond would be the same as the expected return. Correspondingly, the current yield (coupon rate divided by price) would represent the total return that is realized by the investor in this special circumstance.

Interest rates, however, change over time, which in turn leads to changes in the yield to maturity of bonds, whether short, intermediate, or long. Changes in the yield to maturity correspondingly lead to changes in the prices of bonds, with rising yields resulting in price declines and declining yields resulting in price increases. In this case the realized return of the bond over a holding period will not necessarily simply be measured by the coupon payment. There is need to include capital gains or losses resulting from these price changes when calculating the total return realized on a bond holding. The divergence between the yield to maturity of the bond at purchase and the realized return will increase as the fluctuation in interest rates is greater over the holding period.

In fact, for those investors engaging in active bond management, presumably with relatively short time horizons, the primary component of return is likely to be derived from the capital gain or loss realized over the holding period. The level of interest rates will in turn be the prime determinant of the price of bonds and hence of returns over any short holding period of, say, one to five years. Assessing the future trend of interest rates is thus likely to be a primary focus of analysis for those investors pursuing active strategies of bond portfolio management.

YIELD CURVE

The yield curve shown in Figure 10-1 provides a way of expressing the structure of yields on bonds of the same quality across the spectrum from short to intermediate to long maturity. Note that the vertical axis refers to the yield to maturity and that the horizontal axis represents the years to maturity, ranging from three months (short-term) to thirty years (longest term). The plots on the graph represent the yield to maturity of

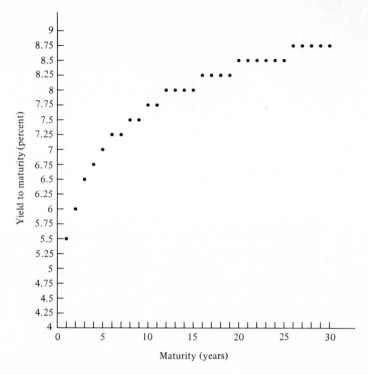

Figure 10-1 Yield curve.

individual bonds of the same quality — in this case, government bonds — differing only with respect to maturity. The curve fitted to the points is known as the *yield curve*.

The level of the curve is determined by the general level of interest rates and will be high when rates of interest are high and low when rates of interest are low. The shape of the curve is largely determined by what investors expect interest rates to be in the future and will vary in shape as investor expectations about rates change. (Appendix A to this chapter discusses the theory underlying the expectations determination of the yield curve.) These expectations, in turn, tend to change in line with the economy as it progresses through the economic cycle from recession to economic peak and back again to recession.

Figure 10-2 shows several typical shapes of the curve that are encountered over the course of the economic cycle. Curve T is upward-sloping, indicating that investors expect rates to be higher in the future than currently, and is typically the shape of the curve in the trough of the cycle. On the other hand, curve P is downward-sloping, indicating that investors expect rates to decline in the future, and is typical of the state of affairs at the peak of the cycle. The third case, labeled M, indicates that investors expect rates to be the same in the future as they are currently and might be typical of the state of affairs at the midpoint of the economic cycle.

While the curve varies in shape over time, generally in line with the economic cycle, it has over most periods been typically upward-sloping, as illustrated by curve

T in Figure 10-2. This is generally attributed to the risk aversion of investors in addition to their expectations about rates. In particular, it is generally presumed that investors require a premium return to invest in long-term rather than short-term bonds to compensate for the sacrifice in liquidity. Long-term bonds have greater capital risk — their prices vary the most with interest rate changes — than short-term bonds, which leads to lesser liquidity and the presumed need for a premium return. Recall that the Ibbotson and Sinquefeld data showed that long-term bonds provided an added return of approximately 1 percent (presumably a liquidity premium) over short-term bonds in the 1926–1978 period of analysis.[1]

AN ACTIVE BOND STRATEGY

In executing an active management strategy, investors can attempt to forecast the level and shape of the yield curve at the end of a particular forecasting horizon. This forecast yield curve then provides the structure of yields for short-term, intermediate-term, and long-term government bonds in the investor's bond portfolio at the horizon. Given the forecast structure of yields to maturity and the current yield structure, the investor can calculate the returns attributable to the bonds in the portfolio owing to the yield curve change. This is because we know current prices and can derive future prices from the projected yield curve; when the known coupon payments are included, we derive a total return.

For example, Figure 10-3 shows a yield curve at the beginning of the period — that is, current yield curve — and the forecast yield curve at the end of the year — a one-year forecast. Note that the forecast in this case calls for an upward shift in the curve, with

[1] Roger G. Ibbotson, and Rex A. Sinquefeld, *Stocks, Bonds, Bills, and Inflation: The Historical Record (1926–1978),* Financial Analysts Research Foundation, Charlottesville, Va., 1979.

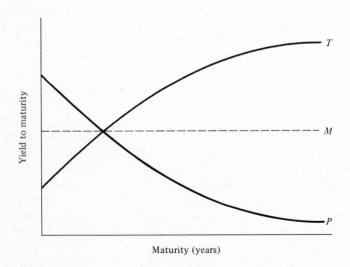

Figure 10-2 The yield curve and the economic cycle.

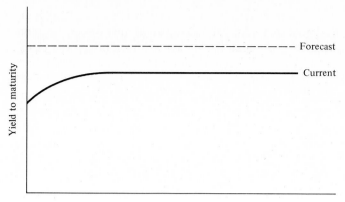

Maturity (years)

Maturity	Current yield to maturity	Yield shift (basis points)	Total return (percent)
1	6.00	132	2.95
2	7.10	119	2.05
3	7.10	107	1.37
4	7.10	99	.34
5	7.00	94	−.12
10	7.65	72	−.73
20	8.00	84	−4.02
30	7.90	82	−4.53

Figure 10-3 Current and forecast yield curve. (*Source: Gifford Fong Associates, Santa Monica, Calif.*)

the short end of the yield spectrum up by more than the long end of the bond spectrum. This means, of course, that yields across the whole spectrum of the bond universe would increase with a decline in prices of bonds accompanying the shifts in yields.

The table below the graph in Figure 10-3 shows specific data for the eight individual bonds in a hypothetical portfolio, ranging from a one-year treasury issue to a thirty-year government bond. The second column shows the yield on each of the bonds at the beginning of the period, while the third column shows the basis-point shift in yields on each at the end of the period.[2] These yields are uniformly higher, as is indicated by the upward shift in the yield curve. Prices of the bonds would, of course, all be lower at the end of the period than at the beginning. The resulting capital loss on the bonds, shown in the last column, is greater than the coupon rate in some cases, so that there would be a net loss on some bonds in the portfolio over the year.

SCENARIO FORECASTING

The previous example illustrated the forecasting of a single yield curve over a horizon of one year. In a sense, it presumes the ability to forecast precisely and ignores the

[2] A basis point is the same as .01 percent, so that 100 basis points equal 1 percent. Many investment professionals, especially in the bond area, commonly refer to basis point changes rather than percentage changes. For small percentage changes it is probably clearer to refer to basis points.

possibility of other sorts of yield curve shifts. In effect, forecasting a single yield curve focuses only on return and ignores risk. The scenario approach that we described with regard to asset allocation can also be usefully applied in this circumstance to provide a way of explicitly taking into account the risk in active bond management.

In applying the scenario approach to bond analysis, we can proceed similarly to the way described in Chapter 7. The investor would first develop mutually exclusive scenarios describing the shift in the yield curve over the forecasting horizon. The scenarios could vary between, say, three and seven, again depending on the preference of the forecaster. The investor would then assign probabilities to the occurrences of the scenarios, with the total assigned adding to 100 percent to assure consistency in the forecast. The final step would be to weigh the scenarios on the basis of these assigned probabilities and develop an expected return and standard deviation for each of the bonds in the portfolio.

Figure 10-4 shows a current yield curve along with yield curves associated with three hypothetical scenarios that are presumed to be possible at the end of a forecast horizon, which in this case is one year. Curve A reflects a further upward shift in the yield curve as credit demand and economic activity continue at a high level. It would be considered a pessimistic scenario as bond prices would be expected to fall. Curve C is the most optimistic scenario as it projects a decline in yield across the whole spectrum, especially in the short end, with the attendant rising prices. This would be

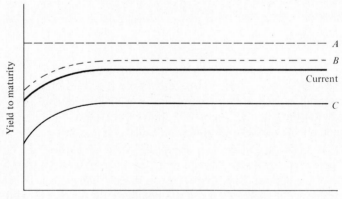

Maturity	Current yield to maturity	Yield shift–basis points scenario			Total return scenario			Composite return	Standard deviation
		A	B	C	A	B	C		
1	6.00	132	28	−146	2.95	3.32	3.96	3.41	.4
2	7.10	119	19	−119	2.05	3.33	5.18	3.52	1.3
3	7.10	107	18	−107	1.37	3.27	6.03	3.56	1.9
4	7.10	99	18	−97	.34	3.13	7.10	3.52	2.8
5	7.00	94	17	−87	−.12	3.01	7.41	3.57	3.3
10	7.65	72	15	−54	−.73	2.88	7.55	3.23	3.4
20	8.00	84	6	−48	−4.02	3.45	9.04	2.82	5.4
30	7.90	82	6	−41	−4.53	3.34	8.83	2.55	5.5

Figure 10-4 Current and forecast yield curves. *(Source: Gifford Fong Associates, Santa Monica, Calif.)*

associated with the entry into a recession and the consequent softening in credit demands. The third curve, *B*, is a more neutral scenario with bond prices expected to rise somewhat, but not excessively, as yields decline over the forthcoming year.

The table below the curves in Figure 10-4 shows the yield shift for each of the bonds in the portfolio associated with each of these yield curves, both current and forecast. It also shows the return over the one-year holding period for each of the bonds in the portfolio that is attributable to each of the forecast scenarios. For purposes of illustration we're assuming that each scenario has an equal probability of occurring, so that we can simply average the returns associated with each scenario to derive an expected or composite return for each of the bonds in the portfolio, as shown in the next to last column of the table. The last column of the table shows the standard deviation as a measure of the uncertainty of the expected return for each of the bonds.

Figure 10-5 provides a way of evaluating the trade-off between risk and return for bonds in the portfolio. The horizontal axis refers to the return associated with the pessimistic scenario, while the vertical axis refers to the more favorable return experience associated with the composite, or average, scenario. This is a two-dimensional return diagram on which one can plot the bonds in a portfolio and the return associated with each of two scenarios on the diagram.

As a matter of perspective, those securities plotting in the upper-left-hand area will do well in the composite scenario but perform poorly in the worst case, the pessimistic scenario. Conversely, those securities in the lower-right-hand area will do well in the pessimistic scenario but poorly in the case of the composite scenario. Those securities plotting in the upper-right-hand area will do well in either case. As a general rule, then, moving the portfolio holdings and weighting toward those holdings which are in the middle right region would appear to provide the best balance between risk and return for the portfolio.

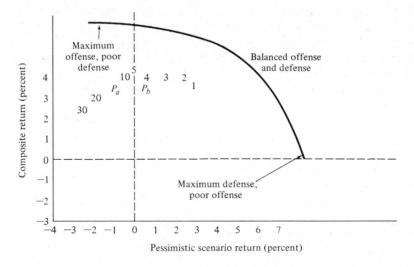

Figure 10-5 Risk-reward analysis. *(Source: Gifford Fong Associates, Santa Monica, Calif.)*

To illustrate this, in Figure 10-5 we've plotted the data for the eight bonds, designating each according to its maturity. We've also constructed a hypothetical portfolio giving equal weight to each of the eight bonds in the portfolio and plotted this as *PA*. As indicated, one can upgrade a portfolio by emphasizing those bonds which will perform relatively well in either scenario, while de-emphasizing those which will do poorly in one or the other scenario — that is, emphasizing those bonds in the middle right and de-emphasizing those at the extremes.

Note that bonds 1, 2, and 3 will do well in either scenario, while bonds 20 and 30 will do poorly in the pessimistic scenario, as they plot on the extreme left of the diagram. One might well consider eliminating bonds 20 and 30 to upgrade the portfolio. For purposes of illustration we've eliminated these two bonds and constructed a portfolio of the six remaining bonds, again weighted equally. Note that this portfolio, designated *PB,* plots farther to the right and higher on the diagram, indicating a more desirable portfolio than portfolio *PA.*

REINVESTMENT OF COUPON PAYMENTS

As has been noted, the investor pursuing an active strategy of bond management is primarily concerned with price changes of the bonds in the portfolio over the holding period. Price changes represent both potential opportunity and risk for active managers. At the same time, the passive manager, or one characterized as a buy-and-hold manager, is primarily concerned with coupon payments, as those are the primary source of return to this investor. The major risk for this investor derives from the need to reinvest these coupon payments, which are received twice a year, over the life of the bond at the same or higher yield to maturity as provided by the current structure of interest rates.

We can most easily illustrate this reinvestment rate risk, or inability to earn the same interest-on-interest as implied by the current interest rate structure, by means of the data shown in Table 10-1. The table shows that a five-year 9 percent bond will provide $450 of coupon income and $1000 of maturing principal over its five-year life; however, in order to achieve a compound growth rate of 9 percent in asset value over the five-year period, the original $1000 would have to reach a cumulative value of $1553; or an incremental dollar return of $553. This $103 gap in return has to be

Table 10-1 Realized return from a five-year 9% par bond over a five-year horizon

Reinvestment rate, %	Coupon income	Interest-on-interest	Total return	Realized compound yield, %
0	$450	$ 50	$450	7.57
7	450	78	528	8.66
8	450	90	540	8.83
9	450	103	553	9.00
10	450	116	566	9.17
11	450	129	579	9.35

Source: Martin Leibowitz, Salomon Brothers, New York, N. Y., October 1979.

Table 10-2 Magnitude of interest-on-interest to achieve compound yield of 9% from 9 percent par bonds of various maturities

Maturity in years	Total return	Interest-on-interest at 9% reinvestment rate	Interest-on-interest as % of total return
1	$ 92	$ 2	2.2
2	193	13	6.5
3	302	32	10.7
4	422	62	14.7
5	553	103	18.6
7	852	222	26.1
10	1,412	512	36.2
20	4,816	3,016	62.6
30	13,027	10,327	79.3

Source: Martin Leibowitz, Salomon Brothers, New York, N. Y., October 1979.

overcome through the accumulation of interest-on-interest. As Table 10-1 shows, this amount of interest-on-interest will be achieved when coupon reinvestment occurs at the same 9 percent rate as the bond's original yield to maturity. At lower reinvestment rates the interest-on-interest will be less than the amount required, and the growth in asset value will fall somewhat short of the required target value of $1553. Naturally, at higher reinvestment rates the cumulative value will be greater than required.

Table 10-2 shows that the magnitude of the reinvestment rate risk increases as the maturity of the bonds in the portfolio increases. In particular, it shows the percentage of the total return of the bond that is represented by interest-on-interest. Note that for a one-year bond the interest-on-interest component represents 2 percent of the total, while for the five-year bond used in Table 10-1 the interest-on-interest component represents close to 20 percent of the total return. For twenty-year bonds it represents 62.6 percent and for thirty-year bonds it represents 79.3 percent of the return, or the major component of total return. Interest-on-interest is thus a negligible to only moderate risk factor for shorter-term bonds, while for longer-term bonds it is the major risk consideration.

A PASSIVE STRATEGY

While the reinvestment rate risk constitutes a major problem in closely achieving any assured level of target return, there are ways of limiting this risk.[3] Using the same

---

[3] We should note that most bonds are issued with a call provision. This provision gives the issuing corporation the right to redeem the outstanding bonds at a specified price either immediately or after some future date (deferred call). The price is usually a few dollars more than par value and represents a premium to compensate for the privilege of the call; however, this feature presents a further problem to bond investors, because when interest rates decline, the issuing corporation will be inclined to call the existing bonds and refund with a new issue at the lower interest rates. The bondholder will then be faced with the problem of reinvesting the proceeds from the called bond at the lower prevailing interest rate. Moreover, even if the bonds are not called immediately, the existence of the call provision will limit the upside move in the bond to the call price, as investors will assume that the bonds will eventually be called.

Table 10-3 Realized return from a five-year 9% par bond over various horizons

Reinvestment rate and yield to maturity at horizon, %		Horizon period			
		1 year	3 years	4.13 years	5 years
	Coupon income	90	270	372	450
7	Capital gain	68	37	16	0
	Interest-on-interest	2	25	51	78
	Total return	160	331	439	528
	Realized compound yield	*15.43%*	*9.77%*	*9.00%*	*8.66%*
9	Capital gain	0	0	0	0
	Interest-on-interest	2	32	67	103
	Total return	92	302	439	553
	Realized compound yield	*9.00%*	*9.00%*	*9.00%*	*9.00%*
11	Capital gain	− 63	− 35	− 16	0
	Interest-on-interest	2	40	83	129
	Total return	29	275	439	579
	Realized compound yield	*2.89%*	*8.26%*	*9.00%*	*9.36%*

Source: Martin Leibowitz, Salomon Brothers, New York, N. Y., October 1979.

five-year 9 percent bond, Table 10-3 shows the total return and its components — coupon income, capital gain or loss, and interest-on-interest — earned over investment horizons ranging from one to five years. It shows these returns and components for three assumed interest rates: 7, 9, and 11 percent. The capital gains and losses as well as the interest-on-interest are calculated on the assumption that the interest rate moves immediately to the level shown in the rows after purchase of the bond at the beginning of the period. The bond prices are established and the reinvestments are at these same rates over the remainder of the period.

Note that when the interest rate declines to 7 percent the interest-on-interest component drops below the level that would have been earned if the rate had stayed at 9 percent. Offsetting this, however, is a capital gain that would be earned from the rise in prices attendant on the yield decline. For example, sale of the bond after year 3, when rates declined to 7 percent, would provide a capital gain of $37, which would more than offset the lower interest-on-interest earnings ($25 versus $32) that would have occurred if rates on bonds had remained at 9 percent. Conversely, when interest rates rise to 11 percent, the interest-on-interest earnings component would rise above the level that would have been earned at 9 percent. Counterbalancing this, however, would be a capital loss that would be incurred if the investor sold at the lower prices before maturity. If the investor held the bond to maturity, there would, of course, be no capital loss as the price would move to par. Under this circumstance the total return on the bond due to greater interest-on-interest earnings would have been greater by $26 ($129 less $103) than if the interest rate had remained at 9 percent.

Table 10-3 thus illustrates that lower interest rates lead to increased returns over the short term through price appreciation, while lower interest rates lead to reduced returns over the longer term through reduced interest-on-interest. For periods between the short term and the longer term, we find that the two conflicting forces provide some compensation for each other, with the one force (interest-on-interest) growing stronger and the other force (capital gains) growing weaker with time. As a matter of fact, we can see from the table that there is an intermediate point in the five-year horizon — 4.13 years — where the decrease in capital gain is precisely offset by interest-on-interest. Furthermore, it is the same point in terms of years whether interest rates decline to 7 percent, rise to 11 percent, or, of course, remain at 9 percent.

We should also note that 4.13 years represents the duration of the 9-percent coupon bond. Recall from Chapter 4 that duration is an average life based on the present value of each of the bond's cash flow payments, coupons as well as principal. For the hypothetical case of a pure discount bond — zero coupon bond — the duration will coincide with its maturity. Since zero coupon bonds have no cash flows prior to maturity, they are free from the problem of coupon reinvestment. A 4.13-year zero coupon bond priced to yield 9 percent would always provide the target return over its maturity period no matter how interest rates may change. Discount bonds would thus be ideal for achieving target rates of return, except that they exist primarily with maturities of less than one year.[4]

Fortunately, there is a technique known as *immunization* which allows one to immunize the portfolio against the "disease" of changing rates even when dealing with coupon bonds. It allows one to lock in a specific rate of return (as well as dollar return) over a specified time period. Immunization depends on the concept of duration for ensuring that the portfolio is structured in such a way that any capital losses (or gains) from interest rate changes will be offset by gains (or losses) on reinvested return. Duration allows this simply because a coupon bond with a given duration is similar mathematically to a zero coupon bond having a maturity equal to that of duration. For example, as shown in Table 10-3, a 9-percent target return over a 4.13-year period could be achieved by either a 4.13-year zero coupon discount bond with a 9-percent yield or a five-year 9-percent par bond, as both bonds have the same duration — 4.13 years.

Table 10-4 shows the duration of a zero coupon bond and a 9-percent coupon bond at maturities ranging from one year to thirty years. To achieve the objective of providing an assumed target return of 9 percent over a five-year period, we see that one should choose a bond having a duration of five years as opposed to a maturity of five years. To obtain a duration of five years in a 9-percent par bond, it turns out that one would need a maturity of around 6.3 years.[5] Table 10-5 shows how such a bond will indeed achieve the required growth in asset value to provide the guaranteed return of 9 percent compounded semiannually.

[4] We should note that J. C. Penney recently issued a long-term (twenty-year) bond that pays all interest and principal at maturity; it is a twenty-year discount bond. It is, however, too early to judge whether this is the beginning of a trend to issue this type of instrument. If it does in fact become a trend, then we would expect that immunization strategies would become less important.

[5] We can see from Table 10-4 that the period over which one can immunize is limited by the period of duration available on bonds. In this illustration, duration, even for 100-year bonds, is limited to under twelve years. Furthermore, the higher the rate level, the lower the duration will be, as we saw in Table 4-8 in Chapter 4. With interest rates at the current high levels of 13 percent and above, it's difficult to immunize for periods of more than five to eight years.

Table 10-4 Durations of zero and 9% coupon bonds with various years to maturity

Maturity in years	Duration in years	
	0%	9%
1	1	0.98
2	2	1.87
3	3	2.70
4	4	3.45
5	5	4.13
7	7	5.34
10	10	6.80
20	20	9.61
30	30	10.78
100	100	11.61

Source: Martin Leibowitz, Salomon Brothers, New York, N. Y., October 1979.

Before proceeding, we should note that in describing immunization, which can be characterized as a passive bond management strategy, we made several simplifying assumptions. The most significant of these concerns the special and simplified manner in which the yield curve shifts. Unfortunately, this special yield curve shift does not represent the many varieties of shifts that are encountered in practice. Immunizing against these other shifts requires many other refinements than we have discussed here, although the basic principles remain the same. Several commercial services and money management organizations have in fact applied the principles of immunization along with the refinements to solve practical problems of bond management.[6]

RISK PREMIUM

As noted in Chapter 1, government bonds are subject only to interest rate and purchasing power risk while corporates are subject not only to those risks but to business and financial risk as well. The yields on corporates are thus determined by these credit risks as well as the basic factors that are critical in determining the yield on "riskless" government bonds. The difference in yields on corporates to compensate for this added risk is known as a *risk premium*. It can be expressed as a yield spread, or difference, between the yield on corporates and the yield on relatively riskless government bonds.

---

[6] Gifford Fong Associates and Salomon Brothers have done extensive and innovative work in this area. Gifford Fong Associates offers money managers a computer package for executing an immunization strategy. Manufacturers Hanover, the first money management organization to offer an immunization product, is now managing close to $1 billion of investment according to this strategy.

Table 10-5 Realized return from 6-year, 4-month 9% par bond over a 5-year horizon

Reinvestment rate and yield to maturity at horizon	Coupon income	Capital gain	Interest on interest	Total $ return	Realized compound rate
7%	$450	$25	$78	$553	9.00%
8	450	13	90	553	9.00
9	450	0	103	553	9.00
10	450	−13	116	553	9.00
11	450	−26	129	553	9.00

Source: Martin Leibowitz, Salomon Brothers, New York, N. Y., October 1979.

Correspondingly, there is a spectrum of risk or quality differences within the corporate sector, as corporate bonds vary in exposure to business and financial risks. Investment rating services attempt to calibrate these quality differentials and to provide their opinions on the relative safety of corporate bonds. The two rating systems in general use are those of Moody's Investment Services and Standard & Poor's. The ratings, or ranks, assigned to corporate bonds under each of these systems are stratified as shown in Table 10-6.

Bond ratings are designed essentially to rank issues in order of the probability of default—that is, inability to meet interest or sinking-fund payments or repayment of principal. Thus AAA (or triple-A) bonds are those judged to have a negligible risk of default and therefore to be of highest quality. AA (or double-A) bonds are also of high quality but are judged not to be quite so free of default risk as triple-A bonds. Bonds rated A and BBB (Baa is Moody's designation) are generally referred to as medium-quality obligations, with the BBB possessing a higher risk of default than the A. Bonds not falling within the first four rating categories are believed to contain a considerable speculative element.

We can illustrate the difference in yields due to quality or risk differences by means of the data shown in Figure 10-6. This figure shows the yields on government bonds

Table 10-6 Corporate bond quality ratings

Moody's	Standard & Poor's	Quality designation
Aaa	AAA	Highest quality
Aa	AA	High quality
A	A	Upper medium grade
Baa	BBB	Medium grade
Ba	BB	Speculative elements
B	B	Speculative
Caa	CCC-CC	Default possible
Ca	C	Default, some recovery possible
C	DDD-D	Little recovery possible

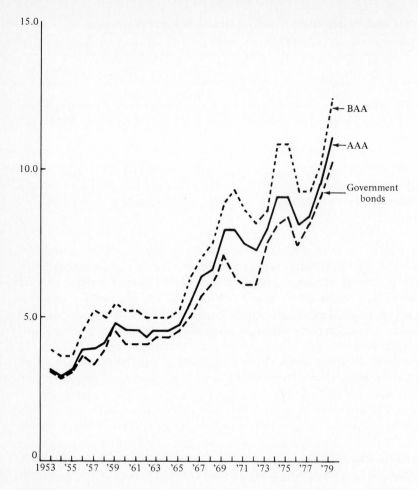

Figure 10-6 Yield spreads — treasuries and AAA and BAA corporates.

as well as AAA corporates and BAA corporates over the 1953–1979 period. The yield on governments represents the return on a riskless bond, while the yield on AAA corporates reflects business and financial risk as well. The BAA yield represents the return on a bond of investment quality subject to significantly greater credit risk than AAA corporates.

Note that AAA corporates provided a higher yield than governments as would be expected, with the difference or risk premium averaging around 50 basis points over the 1953–1979 period. Correspondingly, BAA corporates provided a yield that was consistently in excess of AAA corporate yield, averaging about 90 basis points for the full period. There was consistently a premium paid for credit risk both across as well as within security classes over the period.

Table 10-7 shows that the spread, or premium, fluctuated over the time period, seemingly in line with cyclical fluctuations in the economy. In particular, it appears that the spread was widest at the trough of an economic cycle — 1954, 1957, 1961,

1970–1971, and 1974–1975 — and narrowest at the peak. This would seem reasonable, given the fact that perceived credit risk and potential bankruptcy would be the greatest at the trough and the least severe at the peak of the economic cycle.

CREDIT QUALITY DETERMINANTS

There are essentially four fundamental financial factors that can be used in assessing the credit quality of corporations. The level and trend of fixed-charge coverage, which is the ratio of earnings available to pay interest (profits before income taxes) to fixed charges, is perhaps the prime measure of credit quality. In stable industries, earnings coverage of two or more times interest charges may be regarded as adequate, whereas in industries subject to wide fluctuations in earnings a coverage of three, four, or more

Table 10-7 Bond yield table, %

Year	AAA	BAA	20-year treasury bonds	Yield spread of AAA and treasuries	Yield spread of AAA and BAA
1953	3.13	3.74	2.89	0.24	0.61
1954	2.90	3.45	2.67	0.23	0.55
1955	3.15	3.62	2.98	0.17	0.47
1956	3.75	4.37	3.45	0.30	0.62
1957	3.81	5.03	3.38	0.43	1.22
1958	4.08	4.85	3.86	0.22	0.77
1959	4.58	5.28	4.33	0.25	0.70
1960	4.35	5.10	3.91	0,44	0.75
1961	4.42	5.10	4.07	0.35	0.68
1962	4.24	4.92	3.92	0.32	0.68
1963	4.35	4.85	4.19	0.16	0.50
1964	4.44	4.81	4.18	0.26	0.37
1965	4.68	5.02	4.50	0.18	0.34
1966	5.39	6.18	4.76	0.63	0.79
1967	6.19	6.93	5.59	0.60	0.74
1968	6.45	7.23	5.88	0.57	0.78
1969	7.72	8.65	6.91	0.81	0.93
1970	7.64	9.12	6.28	1.36	1.48
1971	7.25	8.38	6.00	1.25	1.13
1972	7.08	7.93	5.96	1.12	0.85
1973	7.68	8.48	7.29	0.39	0.80
1974	8.89	10.63	7.91	0.98	1.74
1975	8.79	10.56	8.23	0.56	1.77
1976	7.98	9.12	7.30	0.68	1.14
1977	8.19	8.99	7.87	0.32	0.80
1978	9.16	9.94	8.90	0.26	0.78
1979	10.74	12.06	10.18	0.56	1.32

Sources: "An Analytical Record of Yields and Yield Spreads," Salomon Brothers, New York, and Federal Reserve bulletins.

times may be required for a good rating. In industries sensitive to the business cycle, coverage of fixed charges under recession conditions is the significant ratio.

The second factor is the level of long-term debt in relation to equity, with debt measured by the amount shown on the balance sheet and the amount represented by off-balance-sheet obligations such as lease obligations. An analysis of the corporation's capital structure is in a sense a measure of asset coverage which supplements the measure of earnings coverage. Again, higher debt to equity ratios are appropriate for companies in stable industries than for those operating in industries more exposed to the cyclicality of the economy.

Third, there is the debtor's liquidity position, current and prospective. Some companies may appear to have satisfactory earnings and capital, yet the holders of their bonds or preferred stocks may not be sure that enough cash will be on hand to pay debts when they come due. One ratio that is particularly useful is that of net working capital to long-term debt. The reasoning here is that net working capital is the permanent portion of working capital and is appropriately financed with longer-term obligations — long-term debt — while equity, which is the only truly permanent source of capital, finances the other less "liquid" portion of corporate assets. Generally, a ratio of one is satisfactory for industrial companies.[7]

Finally, the size and competitive position of the company within its industry is important in assessing credit quality. Generally, there is good reason to have much greater confidence in the long-term continuity of companies that are of substantial size and competitive leaders in their industry. Although size alone does not guarantee a profitable level of operations, seasoned firms that are dominant in their industry naturally tend to be better able to withstand adversity.

We can best illustrate how differences in these factors affect the credit quality of corporate bonds by means of the data in Table 10-8 for two companies: Bristol-Myers and Control Data. The fundamental data shown are interest coverage, debt to total capitalization ratio, the net working capital to debt ratio as a measure of liquidity, and the return on assets as a measure of basic profitability. It also shows the industry affiliation of the company as well as the rating of the company's bonds by Moody's Investor Service.

[7] While the ratio is generally useful for industrial companies, the ratio of net working capital to long-term debt is not relevant for utilities, because of their small overall working-capital positions and large long-term debt financing.

Table 10-8 Comparative bond data

	Bristol-Myers	Control Data
Industry	Drugs	Office equipment
Rating	AAA	Baa
Long-term debt	$120 million	$165 million
Interest coverage	18.7 times	5.5 times
Debt/total capitalization	8%	9%
Net working capital/debt	7 times	2.4 times
Net income/total assets	17.9%	9.1%

Note that the Bristol-Myers bond is rated AAA, while the Control Data bond is rated BAA, indicating that the rating service views the Bristol-Myers bond as of significantly higher credit quality than the Control Data bond. The reasons for the difference in ratings can be fairly easily discerned from the fundamental credit factors. In particular, Bristol-Myers had a significantly higher fixed-charge coverage, a somewhat lower debt to total capital ratio, a better liquidity position as evidenced by a higher net working capital to debt ratio, and higher profitability. In addition, Bristol-Myers is a leading factor in its industry, while Control Data generally holds a secondary position in the field of office equipment.

IMPLICATIONS FOR BOND MANAGEMENT

The fact that there are differences in riskiness between corporates and governments and among corporates has some immediate implications for investment policy. In particular, the fact that there is a premium for risk means that an investor as a matter of policy might wish to earn that added return over time. Some investors, such as insurance companies, invest primarily in lesser-quality private placements in order to gain this added return. Generally this policy has been rewarding in generating added return, because these organizations have focused heavily on analyzing the creditworthiness of the enterprise. This expertise, along with a strategy of holding a broadly diversified list of these investments, has helped avoid undue exposure to bankruptcy risk, which might more than dissipate the added reward from the risk premium.

In addition, the fluctuating return spread between governments and corporates as well as between the risk classes in the corporate sector may present the manager with an opportunity to undertake a strategy generally referred to as *bond swapping*. In this case the manager would attempt to assess whether the spread at a point in time is abnormally wide or narrow. For example, the spread between corporates and governments had been 50 basis points, and if it were currently, say, 100 basis points, the manager might well consider switching from governments to corporates. Conversely, if the spread were only 25 basis points, then the manager might be inclined to switch from corporates to governments.

In either case the presumption would be that the abnormal spread, either too high or too low, would in time be corrected back to a more normal relationship. The movement back to a more normal relationship would in turn result in a superior performance on the part of the undervalued bond: the corporate bond if the spread had been too large or the government bond if the spread had been too narrow. Success in implementing this sort of strategy requires, however, an ability to judge whether spreads are in fact abnormally large or narrow. History provides a guide, but success ultimately depends on the judgment of the manager as historical relationships can change at the most inopportune times.[8]

[8] Homer and Leibowitz, in their *Inside the Yield Book*, would classify this type of swap as an *intermarket spread swap*. They also discuss three other types: (1) the substitution swap; (2) the rate-anticipation swap; and (3) the pure yield pick-up swap. The substitution swap is ideally an exchange of a bond for a perfect substitute. The rate-anticipation swap is oriented toward profiting from an anticipated movement in overall market rates. The pure yield pick-up swap is an attempt to simply pick up extra yield with little regard for interim price movements.

Finally, there is opportunity for investors to evaluate the creditworthiness of bonds within the corporate sector. While the services on balance provide reasonable evaluation of bond credit, there are instances of misclassification: the rating on an individual bond may be too high or too low. Analyses identifying these misclassifications would suggest sale of an overrated bond and purchase of an underrated bond. Correspondingly, there are instances when the rating of the bond lags behind the actual change in fortune of the company. Timely credit analysis can again aid in anticipating these changes and would suggest sale of a bond before a downgrading in the ratios and purchase before an upgrading in the ratios.

CONCLUSION

Just as in the equity market, bond investors can employ active or passive strategies to meet investment goals. Furthermore, the active strategies that bond investors can use to generate above-average returns are analogous to those available in the equity market. For example, interest rate forecasting might be considered similar to market timing in the equity market, sector selection is analogous to the strategy of group rotation, and credit analysis is somewhat similar to a stock selection. In this chapter we have outlined these three major strategies and described some techniques of analysis appropriate for each.

In addition we have illustrated the strategy known as immunization, which is a passive strategy for ensuring that minimum return targets are met over time. It's a viable investment strategy that is growing in use and spawning several variations on the basic theme that are also finding practical application. For example, one of these variations combines an active strategy of interest rate forecasting with the passive strategy of immunization to provide a hybrid active-passive strategy known as *contingent immunization*.

APPENDIX A THEORIES OF THE TERM STRUCTURE OF INTEREST RATES

There are at least three theoretical explanations for the changing shape of a yield curve. The theory that best explains the shape and most of the changes in shape is the *expectations hypothesis*. The curve in Figure 10-1 is an upward-sloping curve, with longer-term bonds offering higher yields than shorter-term bonds — the implication being that investors expect interest rates to rise. If rates rise, prices will fall. Since prices of long-term bonds will probably fall more than prices of short-term bonds, investors will prefer short-term bonds, other things being equal. But other things are not equal, since long-term bonds are offering higher yields than short-term bonds, just enough higher to offset the preference for short-term bonds.

This yield difference between long-term bonds and short-term bonds can thus be used as a measure of what investors apparently think is going to happen to interest rates. If a four-year bond, for example, is yielding 6.8 percent to maturity (as shown in Figure 10-1, back on page 269) and a five-year bond is yielding 7 percent, an investor with a five-year horizon can buy the five-year bond and hold it to maturity, or he can buy the four-year bond, hold it to maturity, and then buy a one-year bond and hold it to maturity. In the first case, $100 will grow to $100(1 + .07/2)^{10}$, since interest is paid semiannually and there are ten half-years to maturity. In the second case, $100 will grow to $100(1 + .068/2)^8$ by the end of four years. To make the two investments equivalent at the end of five years, the one-year bond will have to yield F, where

$$100(1 + .068/2)^8(1 + F) = 100(1 + .07/2)^{10}$$

$$F = .080 = 8.0 \text{ percent}$$

F is the forward one-year rate for four years in the future. It is the one-year rate that investors apparently expect will be available at the end of four years — "apparently" because that is what the four- and five-year bond yields imply. An investor who believes F will be less than 8 percent will buy five-year bonds rather than four-year bonds. If other investors agree, they will do the same, until four- and five-year yields have adjusted to a value of F that investors do expect.

Since the current yield curve represents equilibrium, in which there are buyers and sellers at all maturities but no stampede from one maturity to another, the yields on four-year bonds and five-year bonds can be used to deduce the expected forward rate F as shown above. Similarly, yields on three- and four-year bonds can be used to deduce the one-year forward rate expected to be available three years in the future. We can go right across the yield curve, computing the forward rates for one year, two years, or any number of years, for that matter. For the yield curve in Figure 10-1 we get a set of forward rates that looks like that shown in Figure 10-A1 (at the top of page 286). In Figure 10-A1 each point on the curve represents a one-year forward rate plotted at the particular point in time when that rate is expected to be available on a one-year instrument.

We should note, however, that the equation shown above for calculating F will work exactly only under special and somewhat unrealistic conditions. In particular, it ignores the existence of such factors as income taxes and other market imperfections like transactions costs and call features that are of importance in actual practice. Furthermore, it assumes that the bonds being analyzed are discount instruments, whereas we've seen that the bulk of the universe of bonds, at least the long-term variety, are coupon instruments. Finally, the equation ignores the fact that there may be a liquidity premium in the forward rate to compensate investors for the added risk of holding long-term bonds rather than short-term bonds. While incorporating these factors into the analysis makes it much harder to estimate F and construct the forward yield move, reasonably good estimates can nevertheless be made.

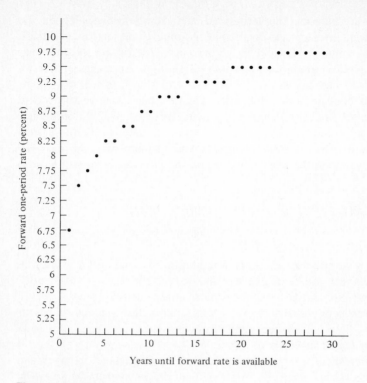

Figure 10-A1 Forward rate curve.

PROBLEMS

1 Discuss the role of the yield curve in active bond management and the reasons for its shape and change in shape over time.

2 Refer to Figure 10-4 (on page 272) and assume that the probabilities of the three scenarios are now 10 percent for A, 20 percent for B, and 70 percent for C. Using these weights, calculate the composite return and standard deviation for each of the bonds. Then plot those bonds on a risk-reward diagram like the one in Figure 10-5 (on page 273) and discuss the action that might be taken in order to improve the characteristics of the portfolio.

3 Discuss why the realized return on a bond may differ from the anticipated return as indicated by the yield to maturity.

4 Describe the kind of strategy that is available for ensuring that yield to maturity (promised return) is realized.

5 Compute the average yield spread between AAA and BAA corporate bonds from the data that appear in Table 10-7 (on page 281). Then presume that the spread is currently above that historical spread, and describe the sort of bond swap that might be undertaken and the risks that would be associated with that action.

6 Indicate the factors that bond analysts use in assessing the credit quality of bonds, and discuss how these impact the level of quality of the bond.

7 Assume that a bond is now rated A and your credit evaluation indicates that it should be rated AA. What opportunity does this present?

SELECTED REFERENCES

Altman, E.: "Financial Ratios, Discriminant Analysis and the Prediction of Corporate Bankruptcy," *Journal of Finance*, September 1968, pp. 589–609.

Ayres, H. F., and John Barry: "Dynamics of the Government Yield Curve," *Financial Analysts Journal*, May–June 1979, pp. 31–39.

Carlton, Willard T., and Ian A. Cooper: "Estimation and Uses of the Term Structure of Interest Rates," *Journal of Finance*, September 1976, pp. 1067–1083.

Curley, A., and R. Bear: *Investments*, Harper & Row, New York, 1979.

Eisenbeis, R. A., and R. B. Avery: *Discriminant Analysis and Classification Procedures: Theory and Applications*, D. C. Heath, Lexington, Mass., 1972.

Fama, E. F.: "Short-Term Interest Rates as Predictors of Inflation," *American Economic Review*, June 1975, pp. 269–282.

Feldstein, Martin, and Otto Eckstein: "The Fundamental Determinants of the Interest Rate," *Review of Economics and Statistics*, November 1970, pp. 422–430.

Fisher, Lawrence: "Determinants of Risk Premiums on Corporate Bonds," *Journal of Political Economy*, June 1959, pp. 217–237.

Brennan, Michael and Eduardo Schwartz: "Bond Pricing and Market Efficiency", *Financial Analysts Journal*, Sept.–Oct. 1982, pp. 49–56.

Fong, Gifford: "Bond Portfolio Analysis," Monograph 11, *Financial Analysts Research Foundation*, Charlottesville, Va., 1980.

Francis, J. C.: *Investments*, McGraw-Hill, New York, 1979.

Graham, Benjamin, David Dodd, and Sidney Cottle: *Security Analysis*, 4th ed., McGraw-Hill, New York, 1962.

Grier, Paul, and Steven Katz: "The Differential Effects of Bond Rating Changes among Industrial and Public Utility Bonds by Maturity," *Journal of Business*, April 1976, pp. 226–239.

Hickman, W. Braddock: *Corporate Bond Quality and Investor Experience*, National Bureau of Economic Research, New York, 1958.

Homer, Sidney, and M. L. Liebowitz: *Inside the Yield Book*, Prentice-Hall, Englewood Cliffs, N. J., 1972.

Hopewell, Michael H., and George G. Kaufman: "Bond Price Volatility and Term to Maturity: A Generalized Respecification," *American Economic Review*, September 1973, pp. 749–753.

Kessel, Reuben: "The Cyclical Behavior of the Term Structure of Interest Rates," Occasional Paper 91, National Bureau of Economic Research, New York, 1965.

Leibowitz, Martin: "The Horizon Annuity," *Financial Analysts Journal*, May–June 1979, pp. 68–74.

Macauley, F. R.: *The Movement of Interest Rates, Bond Yields and Stock Yields in the United States since 1856*. National Bureau of Economic Research, New York, 1938.

Malkiel, Burton: "Expectations, Bond Prices, and the Term Structure of Interest Rates," *Quarterly Journal of Economics*, May 1962, pp. 197–218.

McCulloch, J. Huston: "Measuring the Term Structure of Interest Rates," *Journal of Business*, January 1971, pp. 19–31.

Meiselman, D.: *The Term Structure of Interest Rates*, Prentice-Hall, Englewood Cliffs, N. J., 1962.

Modigliani, Franco, and Richard Sutch: "Debt Management and the Term Structure of Interest Rates: An Empirical Analysis of Recent Experience," *Journal of Political Economy*, August 1967 Supplement, pp. 569–589.

Pinches, George E., and Kent A. Mingo: "A Multivariate Analysis of Industrial Bond Ratings," *Journal of Finance*, March 1973, pp. 1–18.

Pinches, G. E.: "Factors Influencing Classification Results from Multiple Discriminant Analysis," *Journal of Business Research*, December 1980, pp. 429–456.

Pogue, Thomas F., and Robert M. Soldofsky: "What's in a Bond Rating?" *Journal of Financial and Quantitative Analysis,* June 1969, pp. 201–228.

Reilly, Frank: *Investment Analysis and Portfolio Management,* The Dryden Press, Hinsdale, Illinois, 1979.

Reilly, Frank, and Rupinder Sidlus: "The Many Uses of Bond Duration," *Financial Analysts Journal,* July–August 1980.

Sharpe, William F.: *Investments,* Prentice Hall, Englewood Cliffs, N. J., 1978, pp. 58–72.

ELEVEN

OPTIONS

INTRODUCTION

There are essentially three dimensions to managing the risk in a portfolio: (1) diversification, (2) changing the leverage in the portfolio, and (3) insurance. Diversification is the process of mixing risky securities together in a portfolio to reduce risk to its lowest level while holding the level of expected return constant. We described the notion underlying this process in Chapter 2, where we discussed portfolio analysis and described techniques of executing this in practice for different portfolio selection models. Changing the leverage in the portfolio can be accomplished by increasing or reducing the proportion of riskless fixed-income securities held in the portfolio, as was described in Chapter 3 as part of the analysis of the capital-market line and its relevance to capital-market theory. It was illustrated more broadly in practical application in Chapter 7, where we discussed the objectives and techniques of asset allocation. Insurance differs from these other two risk-changing procedures and can be accomplished by the employment of options in the process of portfolio management. The prime purpose of this chapter is to discuss this third method of risk management — insurance through the use of options.

Options have been used for centuries in a variety of business dealings, such as real estate, commodity purchases, and securities. In the United States, securities options have a tainted past as there were a number of abuses in the years immediately preceding the 1929 crash. Since their introduction by the Chicago Board Options Exchange (CBOE) in 1973, trading in options has expanded rapidly as the instruments have gained respectability and various types of investors have learned of their varied uses. Basically options have several unique properties that set them apart from other securities.

1. *Limited loss.* Losses are limited to the amount paid for the option while enjoying much of the profit potential of the underlying security position.

2. *High leverage potential.* Only a relatively small amount of money may be needed to obtain high profits.
3. *Limited life.* The option ceases to exist after the expiration date; long positions are considered a wasting of assets.

The chapter begins by defining an option and describing the two basic types of options: *calls* and *puts.* We'll then describe the differing patterns of returns provided by options and compare these with the patterns that are achievable when dealing with conventional securities: stocks and fixed-income securities. We'll indicate several ways of using options to provide this insurance function in managing portfolio risk. We'll conclude by discussing the basic factors that give value to options, as well as one formal model based on these factors that is generally used in the valuation of options.

SECURITY OPTIONS

In general terms we can say an option is an agreement conveying the right to buy or sell common stock at a later date for a specified price. This price is called the *exercise price,* more commonly referred to as the "striking" price. For the right to buy or sell common stock the buyer of the option pays the writer (seller) a price or premium for selling the option. We'll discuss in a later section of the chapter the methods of valuation for establishing this price or premium.

The most common forms of security options are puts and calls. A put gives the buyer the right to deliver (sell) to the writer a specified number of shares, generally 100, of a certain stock at any time on or before the expiration date of the option.[1] The buyer of a put profits and the writer loses if the market value of the stock falls below the striking price by an amount exceeding the premium. For example, if the price of the put is $5 and the exercise price is $60, the buyer would gain if the price of the stock were below $55 at expiration. A call provides the buyer with the opposite opportunity, the right to receive delivery of shares at any time within the option period at the striking price. The buyer of a call profits if the market value of the stock when the call is exercised exceeds the striking price by more than the premium.[2] For example, if the price of the call is $5 and the exercise price is $60, the buyer would gain if the price of the stock were above $65 at expiration.

Table 11-1 illustrates how the option process works with a put and a call for a single hypothetical stock. The table shows the current price of the stock, $60 per share, as well

---

[1] Options can be written to provide for exercise at any time prior to expiration or only at expiration. Those options which allow exercise at any time over the life of the option are known as American calls or puts. Options which allow exercise only at the date of expiration are known as European calls or puts. The added flexibility of American options gives them more value than European options. The American option, as the name would imply, is the predominant type traded on the U. S. markets.

[2] There are four other kinds of options which are a combination of puts and calls. A *straddle* is a combination of a put and call, giving the buyer the right to either buy or sell stock at the exercise price. If the price of the stock fluctuates sufficiently, the buyer may exercise both the put and call portions of the straddle. A *strip* is two puts and one call at the same exercise price for the same period. A *spread* consists of a put and a call option on the same security for the same time period at different exercise prices. A *strap* is two calls and one put at the same contracted exercise price for the same period. Evaluation of these more complex options is better left to a more specialized book.

as the exercise price of the put and call, also $60 for both options. The expiration date for the two options is January 1981, while the current date is July 1980, so that each has a term to expiration of six months. This means in the case of the call that the holder can buy the stock at $60 per share at any time over the six-month term to expiration, while in the case of the put it means that the holder can sell the stock for $60 per share at any time between July 1980 and January 1981.

For example, presume that the call is held to expiration, at which time the price of the stock was $70 per share. We could exercise the option at that time, buying the stock for $60 per share and then selling it for a market price of $70. This would yield a $10 gain per share as shown in the first column of Table 11-1 in the row labeled value at expiration or gross return on option. On the other hand, for a put the option is of some value as long as there is some chance that the stock price will move below the exercise price. For example, assume that we held the put to expiration, at which time the price of the stock was $50 per share. We could buy the stock at $50 per share and then exercise the option to realize a sale price of $60. This creates a $10 per share gain, which is shown in the second column of the table, again in the row labeled value at expiration or gross return on option.

The bottom part of Figure 11-1 shows the general formula for computing the return on a call at expiration. This formula says that the return on the call is simply the difference between the price of the stock — which for purposes of illustration was the price at expiration — and the striking price. Figure 11-1 also graphs the formulation and indicates that the higher the stock price is above the strike price ($60), the higher the profitability to the call. At the same time, when the stock price is below the strike price ($60), there is a constant zero return at all stock-price levels; in particular, the risk in the call is limited.

The bottom part of Figure 11-2 shows the general formula at expiration for computing the return on a put. This formula again says that the return on the put is simply the difference between the price of the stock at expiration and the striking price, which for purposes of illustration is $60 per share. Figure 11-2 also graphs the formula and

Table 11-1 Put and call valuation

	Call	Put
Current price of stock	$60	$60
Exercise price of option	$60	$60
Current date	July 1980	July 1980
Expiration date	Jan. 1981	Jan. 1981
Term to expiration	6 months	6 months
Price of stock at expiration	$70	$50
Value at expiration or gross return on option*	$10	$10
Price of option	$ 5	$ 5
Net return on option*	$ 5	$ 5

*These returns disregard commissions and the costs of tying up the dollar cost of the options. Adjustment for those costs would lower the returns from option strategies.

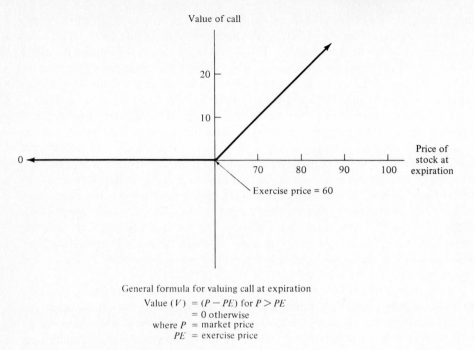

General formula for valuing call at expiration

Value $(V) = (P - PE)$ for $P > PE$
$= 0$ otherwise

where P = market price
PE = exercise price

Figure 11-1 Value of a call at expiration.

indicates that the lower the price is below the strike price of $60, the higher the value of the put. At the same time, when the stock price is above the strike price ($60), there is a constant zero return at all stock-price levels. As in the case of calls, the risk on puts is limited, the difference being that the risk protection is in the opposite direction.

The previous calculations and graphs illustrate gross returns to puts and calls at expiration. To compute the net return on the option, we simply subtract the price, or cost, of the option from the gross return.[3] If a call option expires when the stock is below the striking price, the result is a net loss rather than a zero return, whereas if a put option expires when the stock price is above the strike price, the result is also a net loss rather than a zero return. Adjustments for the cost of the option also lower profitability at all levels of return. It effectively raises the break-even price for the buyer of the call and lowers the break-even price for the buyer of the put. Commissions and the cost of tying up the dollar cost of the options would have a similar effect.

Figures 11-3 and 11-4 illustrate this for calls and puts, respectively, by super-imposing a dashed line on the graphs to indicate the cost of the option and the resulting net return to the strategies. Note that the cost of the option shifts the curve down by a constant amount — the price of the option. This cost increment results in a higher break-even price for the option; in the case of the call it is now $65 per share, while

[3] To calculate the relative return on the option, we divide the net return by the investment base, which in this case is the price, or cost, of the option. As noted before, we'll discuss the factors giving value to options and describe a model for determining their value based on these factors in the final part of this chapter.

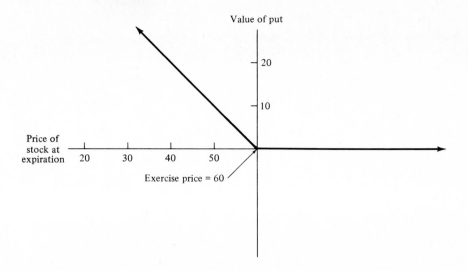

General formula for valuing put at expiration
$$Value\ (V) = (PE - P) \text{ for } P < PE$$
$$= 0 \text{ otherwise}$$
$$where\ P = \text{market price}$$
$$PE = \text{exercise price}$$

Figure 11-2 Value of a put at expiration.

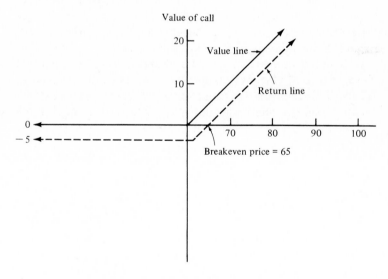

General formula for determining net return of call
$$Return\ (R) = V - \phi \text{ (option price)}$$
$$R = V - 5 \text{ or } (P - 60) - 5 \quad P > 60$$
$$- 5 \quad P \leqslant 60$$

Figure 11-3 Net return to the call.

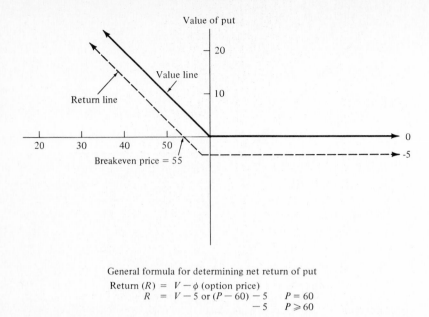

General formula for determining net return of put

$$\text{Return } (R) = V - \phi \text{ (option price)}$$
$$R = V - 5 \text{ or } (P - 60) - 5 \qquad P = 60$$
$$\phantom{R = V - 5 \text{ or } (P - 60)} - 5 \qquad P \geqslant 60$$

Figure 11-4 Net return to the put.

in the case of the put it is $55 per share. The maximum loss in both cases is $5 per share, or the cost of the option. The net profit, as derived in Table 11-1, becomes $5 for both the put and call. The bottom parts of the Figures 11-3 and 11-4 give the general formula for deriving the net return to the option strategies.

In practice, trading in options generally takes place through one of the organized exchanges — the Chicago Board of Options (CBOE); the American Stock Exchange; the Philadelphia, Baltimore, Washington Exchange; or the Pacific Stock Exchange. Options for a stock listed on an exchange come due at specific times throughout the year — January, April, July, and October — and each option has a fixed striking price. Variation in the value of a listed option as the price of the underlying stock changes is reflected in the level of the quoted premium, rising as the stock price increases and falling as the stock price declines.

Organized options exchanges offer several significant advantages to investors. First, options contracts on these exchanges are standardized and simple. In addition, the exchange acts as an intermediary so that the contracts are not between specific buyers and sellers but are the obligations of the exchange. Finally, the exchange promotes a more efficient market by quickly providing information on prices, volume, and other attributes of an option and making it widely available.

As a result of these factors, the listed options market has a liquidity that an unlisted, or over-the-counter, market would not, and trading in options can generally take place continuously over the life of most listed options. The availability of an actively traded options market thus allows an option holder the choice of either exercising his option at expiration or selling it in the market prior to expiration. Correspondingly, the writer of an option on a stock that is now selling above its exercise price may wish to close out this position by going into the open market and purchasing the same option contract. The purchase of the option then cancels out the position.

PATTERNS OF RETURNS

As indicated before, the primary attraction of options is that they allow investors to obtain a pattern of returns that would be unattainable when dealing exclusively with the more conventional sort of securities.[4] To illustrate this, we'll compare the returns on options — calls and puts — with those attainable from investing in stocks and bonds. We'll show these patterns for both long and short positions in the different securities, relying heavily on the same sort of graphs used in Figures 11-1 to 11-4 to compare the patterns of return. These graphs are useful both for illustrating an individual strategy and for comparing strategies.[5] For example, any two strategies can be compared at any stock price by transferring the profit-loss line from one graph to the other or by preparing a new graph and superimposing both strategies on that graph.

To facilitate the illustration, we'll make the same assumptions about the securities under analysis shown in Table 11-2. The table shows four securities: short-term bond, common stock, a put option, and a call option. Note that the assumptions about the hypothetical stock are the same as we used in the previous section. Also, the character- istics of the put and call that are written against the stock are the same with respect to the striking price and term to expiration. The only significant difference is that we've initially assumed that the price of the put and the call is $5 each. This additional assumption mainly has the effect of changing the gross return display to a net return display for the graph of the option strategies.

In the analysis we have ignored other factors such as dividends, commission costs,

[4] There are other securities that are options or have optionlike features. For example, a *warrant* is a call option issued by the firm whose stock serves as the underlying security. A major difference between warrants and options is the limitation on the number of warrants outstanding. A specific number of warrants of a particular type will be issued; the total cannot easily be increased and typically will be reduced as the warrants are exercised. An option, however, can be created whenever two parties wish to create one; therefore, the number of outstanding options is not fixed. Options are thus more suitable for providing the function of risk transfer or insurance that we are primarily concerned with in this book. For this reason we'll not devote much space to discussing warrants and other optionlike securities.

[5] Their disadvantage lies in the fact that they describe position values (or net values) only at expiration, and not at intermediate times prior to expiration.

Table 11-2 Stock, bond, and option data

	Stock	Bond	Call	Put
Current price	60	95	5	5
Exercise price	—	—	60	60
Term to expiration	—	6 months	6 months	6 months
Price at termination	Variable	100	Variable	Variable

taxes, interest, or opportunity costs that can affect the profit and loss to the different strategies. These can be important in the actual execution of an option strategy and should be understood and evaluated accordingly; however, for our purposes, fully considering those factors would unnecessarily complicate the analysis. (Several excellent books and articles listed in the reference section to this chapter provide perspective on the impact of those factors in managing options programs.)

Figure 11-5 shows the profit and loss associated with the different strategies — both conventional and option-related. They all indicate the return that would be earned on the particular security at differing price levels of the hypothetical stock at the end of the assumed six-month holding period for the security. The lines showing the pattern of returns essentially give a notion of how the return of the security responds to changes in the price of the hypothetical stock.

Figure 11-5a shows the profits associated with investing in the short-term fixed-income instrument. Note that the return pattern is a horizontal straight line. Variations in the price of the stock have no effect on the return of this security, as the return of $5 is certain, at least nominally, over the six-month holding period. Figure 11-5b illustrates a short position in the bond which would correspond to borrowing. Note that the returns are opposite those of the long position, that is, there is a net cost of $5 at all levels of the stock price.

Figure 11-5c shows the pattern of returns associated with purchasing and holding the stock long, while Figure 11-5d shows the pattern associated with selling the stock short.[6] When the stock is held long, the profits increase directly in line with increases in the stock price, while losses increase directly with decreases in the stock price. For example, the buyer of a stock at $60 would realize a $10 profit if the stock went to $70 and a $10 loss if it dropped to $50. Conversely, when the stock is sold short, profit increases with decreases in the stock price and losses accrue when the price increases. For example, a short seller of stock at $60 would realize a profit of $10 if the stock dropped to $50 and a loss of $10 if it increased to $70. The diagonal lines in the two charts show similar patterns, except that the long position for the stock is upward-sloping while the short position is downward-sloping. The long buyer's gain is the short seller's loss and vice versa.

Figure 11-5e, showing the pattern associated with purchasing a call, is identical to Figure 11-3. The position here can be most usefully compared with the position of a long holder of the stock. Note first that the buyer of the call derives a greater percentage gain on his investment when the stock price rises than the long holder of the stock. For

---

[6] A short sale occurs when one person sells a second person securities the first person does not own. Short sellers sell a security short because they expect its price to fall and want to profit from that price fall. So the short seller sells a security he or she does not own to a second party, who takes a long position in the security; the long buyer expects the price to rise. Thus, a short sale requires a short seller who is bearish and a long buyer who is bullish about the same stock at the same time. The short seller borrows the shares of stock to be sold from a third party in order to make delivery on the short sale. Then the short seller waits for the price of the security to fall so that he can purchase it at the lower price he expects and can repay the third party for the shares he borrowed. If the price of the security does fall, the short seller profits by the difference between the price he has paid for the shares given to the third party and the price at which he earlier sold the shares to the long buyer, less any commission costs. Therefore, apart from the commission costs taken out of the transaction, the short seller's profit equals the long buyer's loss, or vice versa, if the security's price rises after the short sale.

example, when the stock rises to $70, the buyer derives a net profit of $5 ($10 gross gain less the $5 cost of the call), for a 100 percent gain versus a 17 percent gain for the long holder of the stock. The call buyer has greater leverage than the long holder of the stock. At the same time, the loss to the call buyer is limited to the $5 price of the call, whereas the loss to the long holder is the $60 price of the stock, which is higher than the call price. The call buyer will, however, suffer a total loss even in the event that the stock price remains even (at $60) over the period, whereas the stockholder will break even.

Figure 11-5*f,* showing the pattern associated with purchasing a put, is identical to Figure 11-4. The position here can be most usefully compared with the position of a short seller of the stock. Note first that the buyer of the put derives a greater percentage gain on his investment when the stock price declines than the short seller of the stock. For example, when the stock declines to $50, the buyer of the put derives a net profit of $5 ($10 gross gain less the $5 cost of the put) for a 100 percent gain versus a 17 percent gain for the short seller of the stock. Again, the buyer of the option, in this case a put, has greater leverage than the short seller of the stock. At the same time, the loss to the buyer of the put is limited to the price of the put, whereas the loss to the short seller is unlimited, since stock prices can only go to zero on the downside but are theoretically unlimited on the upside. As in the case of the call buyer, the put buyer will suffer a total loss even if the stock price remains even (at $60) over the period, whereas the short seller will essentially break even.

Figure 11-5*g* shows the pattern associated with selling a call, and Figure 11-5*h* shows the pattern associated with selling a put. Note that the seller of the call derives a fixed profit — the call premium — as long as the stock price remains below the exercise price, but can suffer unlimited losses when the price rises above the exercise price. In this case the profit is the $5 premium for the call, so that a loss accrues when the price rises above $65. Conversely, the seller of the put earns a fixed profit as long as the stock price remains above the striking price, but can suffer losses to the extent that the price of the stock declines below the exercise price. In this case the profit is the $5 premium for the put, so that a loss accrues when the price declines below $55. In the case of the call seller note that the risk position is similar to that of a short seller of stock, while for the seller of the put the risk position is similar to that of a purchaser of stock. In both cases the reward is the option premium, or the price of the call or put, as the case may be.

As noted before, options allow the investor to attain patterns of return that are unavailable from the more conventional ways of investing. It should be fairly evident that the return patterns attainable from the conventional stock and bond strategies shown in panels *a, b, c,* and *d* contrast sharply with those attainable from the option strategies shown in panels *e, f, g,* and *h*. The differing patterns associated with option strategies can in turn be combined with conventional strategies to obtain more desirable risk-return combinations for the portfolio than would be available when only conventional approaches are used. Furthermore, strategies like selling puts or calls, which would seemingly appear unattractive when used alone, become attractive for certain purposes when used in combination.

Given the differing patterns of returns available from conventional and option-related strategies and the many ways of combining these patterns, there are innumerable

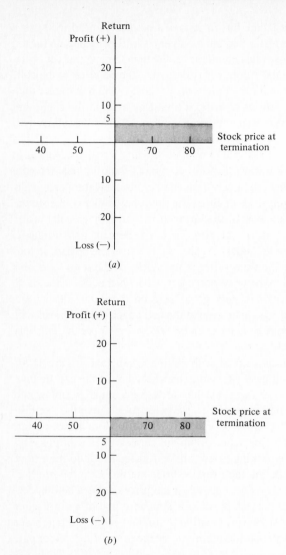

Figure 11-5 Profit and loss from various strategies. (*a*) Buy a short-term bond. (*b*) Sell the bond short (borrow).

portfolio strategies, but we'll focus on only a few of them, as discussing all or even many of the available combinations would be beyond the scope of this book. More importantly, we'll focus on those that have been accepted as prudent in a fiduciary sense and are either being implemented currently or will be in the near future. Three of the available strategies are particularly relevant: (1) protective put — buy the stock and buy a put; (2) covered call writing — own the stock and sell a call; and (3) artificial convertible bond — buy bonds and buy calls.

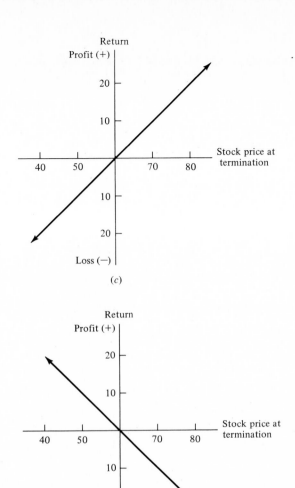

Figure 11-5 *(Continued)* (c) Purchase the stock. (d) Sell the stock short.

PROTECTIVE PUT

Figure 11-6 illustrates the protective put strategy, in which case the investor holds the stock long and at the same time purchases a put on the stock. The resulting graph is, in effect, a combination of Figure 11-5c, showing the results of purchasing a stock, and Figure 11-5f, showing the results of purchasing a put. The graph shows that the long holder of the stock participates fully in the upward movement of the stock. For example, the investor earns a $5 net profit (gross gain less cost of the put) when the stock goes to $70, a $15 net profit when it goes to $80, and so on. The investor's return

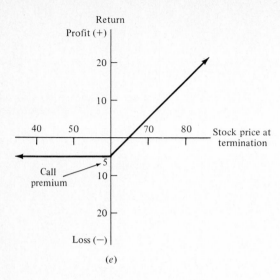

(e)

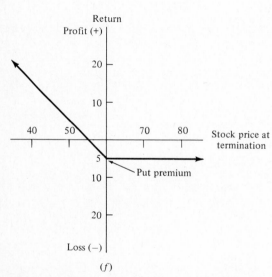

(f)

Figure 11-5 *(Continued)* *(e)* Buy a call. *(f)* Purchase a put.

opportunity is unaltered, but the investor has limited the downside risk on the stock to the exercise price of the put, in this case $60. The net loss, even in the event of a decline below $60, would be the $5 cost of the put. The use of the put has in effect truncated the return distribution.[7]

[7] Note that this compound action results in a position that is equivalent to outright purchase of a call, as can be seen by comparing this chart to Figure 11-5f. This ability to obtain equivalent positions indirectly implies, in turn, that within limits the put price should be linked to the corresponding call price. In particular, puts and calls should be priced equivalently; there should be what is known as put and call parity.

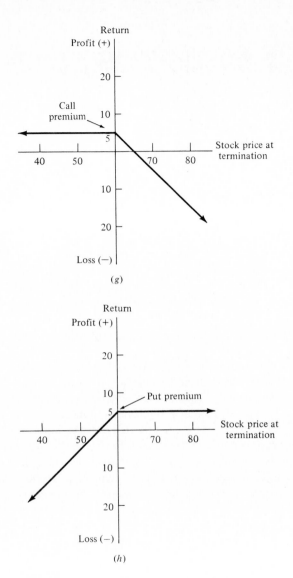

Figure 11-5 *(Continued)* *(g)* Sell a call. *(h)* Sell a put.

The strategy would be especially desirable to investors particularly concerned with protecting against downside fluctuations in stocks. This could be especially important for, say, a fire and casualty insurance company which needs to maintain a certain level of policyholder surplus to sustain its underwriting. Reductions in the value of the investment portfolio — particularly the stock portion — would directly translate into a reduction in the surplus account and lead to an impairment of the ability of the company to operate effectively. Use of the protective put in this instance would help the company

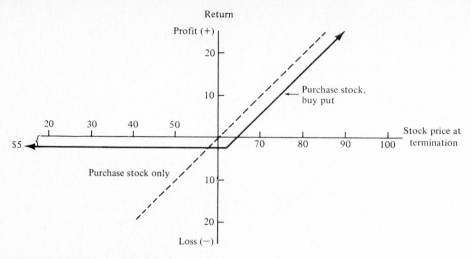

Figure 11-6 Protective put strategy.

insure against having to sell stocks at an inopportune time to avoid impairing the surplus account.

The protective put could also be a useful instrument of insurance for those pursuing an active equity strategy of group rotation. Recall from Chapter 8 that group rotation entails an overweighting or underweighting of the major stock groups — growth, cyclical, stable, and energy — in order to take advantage of any perceived attractiveness or unattractiveness of a particular stock group. This process of underweighting or overweighting the grouping in turn exposes the portfolio to risk that cannot be offset by merely adding more securities to the portfolio — that is, diversification. The risk, however, could be hedged by means of a protective put. For example, a possible adverse performance caused by an extreme overweighting in a group such as energy stocks could be hedged by purchasing protective puts on this component of the portfolio. Of course, this protection has a cost, which in this case is the price of the put. Over time this cost of insurance will penalize the return on the portfolio, reducing it by the amount of this cost. The investor needs to assess whether the insurance is worth the cost, which clearly appears to be the case for a fire and casualty insurance company. Whatever the decision it's clear that the availability of the put gives any potential investor greater latitude in tailoring his portfolio strategy.

COVERED CALL WRITING

Figure 11-7 illustrates the strategy of covered call writing. It shows that the investor in this case holds the stock long and at the same time sells (or writes) a call on the stock. The resulting graph is in effect a combination of Figure 11-5c, showing the results of purchasing a stock, and Figure 11-5g, showing the results of selling a call. The use of the call again truncates the return distribution, but in this case puts a ceiling on the upside potential of the stock. The seller of the call in this instance is exposed to the downside movements of the stock but not to the unlimited risk associated with selling the call outright where the risk position is similar to that of a short seller of the stock.

This strategy might appeal to an investor who had a negative outlook on the market at a particular time. Outright sale of the stock might incur transactions costs that are unacceptable or might be prohibited entirely for legal or institutional reasons. Selling covered calls provides a partial hedge against a negative market scenario. The investor at least earns the premium income from selling the option, which could be, say, 5–10 percent of the value of the portfolio on average. This incremental return provides some offset against downside risk.

Again this insurance has a cost. In this case it is the foregone opportunity to capitalize on strong upward movements in the stock or the market in general. When the stock moves above the striking price, it will be called away from the writer and the incremental return above the call premium would go to the buyer of the call. Persistent selling of call options over time would almost certainly result in a loss (opportunity cost) of this portion of the return distribution. Risk has been reduced, but again so has return.

ARTIFICIAL CONVERTIBLES

Figure 11-8 shows the strategy of creating an artificial convertible bond.[8] The investor in this case buys a short-term fixed-income security, such as treasury bills or commercial paper, and at the same time buys a call on the stock. The resulting graph is in effect a combination of Figure 11-5a, showing the results of purchasing a short-term fixed-income security, and Figure 11-5e, showing the results of buying a call. The call allows the investor to participate in the favorable fortunes of the stock (price movement above the $60 exercise price), while the fixed-income security provides a certain income. This income in turn offsets the cost of the call or can alternatively be viewed as providing protection against downside risk, which would be a complete loss if the stock remains below the exercise price.

This strategy would appeal to those who wish to participate in the equity market but are concerned with controlling their exposure to the risk associated with stocks.

[8] Convertible bonds are hybrid securities. They are similar to other bonds in the sense that they promise a stream of interest payments, maturity or par value, and other features typical of fixed-income securities. But they differ in one very important respect: convertible securities can be exchanged for common stock at a predetermined exchange ratio at the option of the investor. The conversion feature thus provides an opportunity to share in any appreciation in the price of the underlying common stock.

A convertible bond is for practical purposes a bond with nondetachable warrants plus the restriction that only the bond is usable to pay the exercise price. If the bond were not callable, the value of this package of one bond and several latent warrants would equal the value of a straight noncallable bond plus that of the warrants. However, most convertible bonds are callable and thus involve a double option: the holder has an option to convert the bond to stock, and the issuing corporation has an option to buy the bond. To further complicate the situation, the greater the value of a bond, the smaller will be the risk of default, and—other things being equal—the higher a corporation's stock price, the lower the risk that it will default on outstanding bonds.

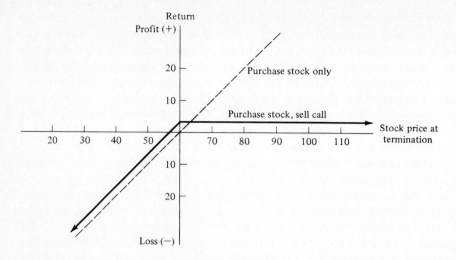

Figure 11-7 Covered call writing strategy.

Hybrid securities like convertibles provide this opportunity, as they can be viewed as a bond with options or warrants attached that provide a call on the equity of the company. Investors can manufacture the same opportunity, albeit one with a generally shorter time horizon, by combining call buying with fixed-income investment, as we've just illustrated. Here the investor gets the downside protection of a less risky instrument—the bond—and at the same time reaps some of the benefits of stock ownership through the call.

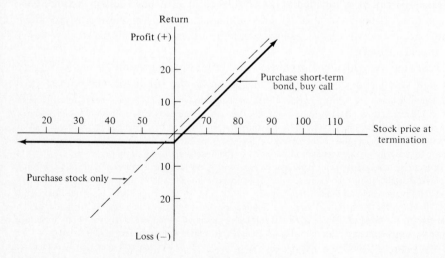

Figure 11-8 Artificial convertible bond strategy.

Again this downside protection, or insurance, has its cost. In this case it is the foregone opportunity to participate fully in the favorable fortunes of the company. The fixed-income portion of the package is by definition fixed and will not appreciate when the stock price moves up. The only opportunity to participate is through the call, and investors executing this strategy would typically commit a minor portion of funds to calls compared with the commitment to fixed-income securities. In fact, proponents of this strategy suggest a commitment on the order of 90 percent of the total to fixed income securities and 10 percent to calls.

The three examples of combining option strategies with conventional methods of investing all illustrate the additional latitude that options provide in allowing an investor to tailor a particular strategy to his needs or risk-return preferences. Note also that the insurance provided by the option strategies has a cost in terms of reducing return or at least altering the return distribution. Options and combined strategies do not offer the proverbial "free lunch." The only way that investors can use options to earn above-average risk-adjusted returns is by identifying mispriced options. The following section is thus devoted to developing insights into the valuation of options, to help both identify undervalued options and avoid incurring too great an option cost, which would dissipate the benefits of the strategy.

OPTION VALUATION

In the analysis so far we have assumed that the current price of the stock was the same as the exercise price of the stock and that any valuation of the option was with respect to the expiration date. We'll now discuss valuation in a more general context which will enable us to consider the appropriate value of the option at any time before expiration as well as at expiration. Also, we'll consider how the value of the option varies as the price of the stock varies both above and below the exercise price prior to expiration. Analyzing this in a more general context means in turn that we need a different, yet essentially similar, option valuation diagram than the one we've been discussing so far.

Figure 11-9 shows a diagram that is more suitable for appraising the value of an option both before and at expiration. The horizontal axis is much the same as in the previous diagrams except that the stock prices are broken into three separate zones: (1) out of the money where the stock price is below the exercise price; (2) at the money or close to the exercise price; and (3) in the money where the stock price is above the exercise price. The vertical axis refers to the value of the call rather than the profit and loss associated with the strategy, as was the case in the previous diagrams.

Note that the solid line running along the horizontal axis below the exercise price and bisecting the angle above the exercise price is identical to the line used in the previous diagrams to depict the profits and losses at expiration associated with the strategy of purchasing a call. This line might alternatively be thought of as a lower bound—a minimum economic value for an option. At prices of the stock above the exercise price the option would have value as depicted by the diagrams and calculated in the usual fashion (it is the area under the 45° line between the exercise price and

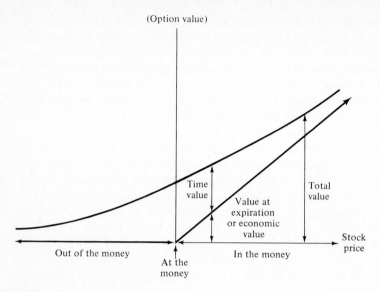

Figure 11-9 Value of the option.

the ending stock price). Below the exercise price the option would have zero value at termination.

Prior to expiration, however, the option will have value in excess of this baseline economic value, which we will refer to as the time value of the option. The way this value varies around the exercise price of the option is illustrated by the curved line in Figure 11-9. Note that the value of the option is at the maximum when the price of the stock is at the exercise price. This excess, or time value decreases when the price of the stock moves away from the exercise price in either direction.

Table 11-3 illustrates this notion of the time value of options by showing the economic value of the option, the time value of the option, and the total value of the option, which is the sum of the time value and economic value of the option. It shows these values again for a six-month option on a hypothetical stock with an exercise price and current price of $60. These values were calculated at prices above, below, and at the exercise price using the Black-Scholes option valuation formula, which will be described later in this chapter.

In Table 11-3 note that the value of the option increases as the price of the stock is higher, reaching its highest value of $23.80 at the high stock price of $80. When the stock price is at or below the exercise of $60, the option has no economic value; however, it has some value—time value—reflecting the probability of the stock moving above the exercise price before expiration. For example, when the stock is at $50, the option has a time value of $1.97, which represents its total value—that is, it has no economic value. When the stock is above the exercise price of $60, the option has both economic value and time value. As the stock price increases, economic value becomes the predominant component of total value. For example, at the high price of

$80 the economic value is $20 ($80 current price less $60 exercise price) and the time value is $3.80.

Table 11-3 also indicates, as we've noted before, that the time value of the option is at a maximum when the stock is at the exercise price and lower when the stock is above or below the exercise price. For example, at the $80 high price the time value of $3.80 is only slightly more than one-half the value at the exercise price of $60, while at a price of $50 the time value of $1.97 is less than one-third the value at the exercise price. The time value is smaller at lower prices because there is less chance of a profit on the call — that is, greater chance of total loss. At higher prices the option becomes more like the stock in terms of variance, beta, and capital investment; thus there is less reason to pay a premium over its economic value.[9]

FACTORS AFFECTING VALUE OF OPTIONS

Three prime factors influence the value of an option — that is, the level of the time value curve on the diagram. These are (1) the expected variance in price or return of the underlying stock, (2) the time remaining to expiration of the option contract, and (3) the level of interest rates. In addition, the relationship between the market price and exercise price of the stock is important because it determines whether the option is in the money and therefore has economic value or it is out of the money and has only time value. Finally, dividends on the underlying stock can also influence the value of the option, but since this factor is generally of only secondary importance, we'll focus mainly on the influence of the three primary factors of valuation.[10]

We can begin analyzing how the variance in price of the underlying stock influences the value of the option by referring to the two diagrams in Figure 11-10. The diagrams compare the payoffs at expiration of two options with the same exercise price and the same stock price. The only difference is that the price of stock *B* at its option's expiration date is harder to predict than the price of stock *A* at its option's expiration date. The probability distributions superimposed on the diagrams illustrate the greater

[9] It should be noted that stock itself might be considered an option on the stock value: the exercise price is zero and the expiration date is infinite. Of course, this option would not maintain any premium over the stock itself. This might be attributed to the fact that the option is "deep in the money."

[10] Listed options do not receive the dividends accruing to the stock over the holding period. This makes the stock more attractive relative to the options, at least in this sense. To take advantage of this, the investor may want to execute or sell the option prior to the ex dividend date.

Table 11-3 Option values

Stock price	Economic value	Time value	Total value
40	0	0.22	0.22
50	0	1.97	1.97
60	0	6.86	6.86
70	10	4.58	14.58
80	20	3.80	23.80

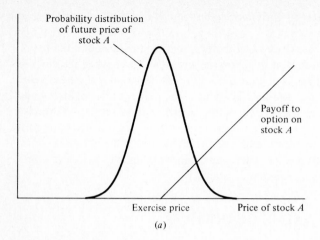

(a)

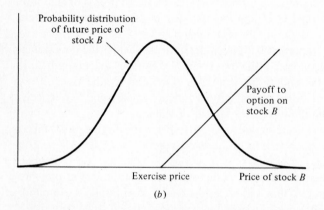

(b)

Figure 11-10 Stock price distribution and option payoff. (a) Payoff to call option on stock A. (b) Payoff to call option on stock B.

uncertainty associated with stock B than with stock A, since stock B is seen to have a wider distribution, or variance, than stock A.[11]

Note that in both cases there is a 50 percent probability that the stock price will decline below the exercise price, thereby making the option worthless; however, when the stock price rises above the exercise price, there is a greater probability that stock B will have a greater value than stock A. The option on stock B correspondingly has greater probability of a higher final payoff than the option on stock A. Since the probability of a zero payoff is the same for the two stocks, the option on stock B should be worth more than that on stock A.

[11] Actually, the lognormal distribution is more commonly used to portray the distribution of stock price changes. For clarity of exposition we've simply used the normal distribution.

Figure 11-11a shows how the greater underlying variability of the stock affects the time value of the option. Note that the value line of an option on a stock with greater variability will be at a higher level than that of an option on a stock with lower variability. The upper line might be considered the value of the option on stock B, while the lower line is the value of the option on stock A. Note that when the variance of the stock is zero, as it would be at expiration, then the value of the option should correspond to the baseline economic value—that is, the time value will be zero.

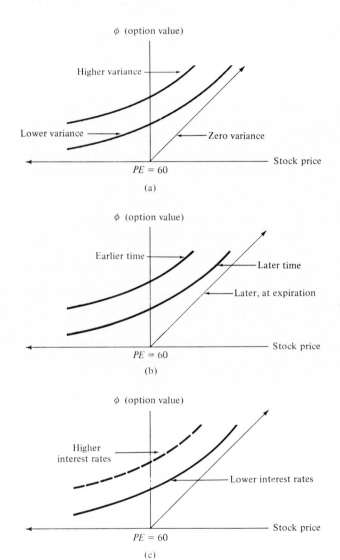

Figure 11-11 Factors affecting time value of an option. (a) Variance. (b) Time. (c) Interest rates.

The principle illustrated in Figure 11-11 is that the greater the expected variance of price changes for a stock, then the higher should be the option value from that stock. For example, a comparison of two companies with approximately the same current stock prices and with six-month options at the same exercise price showed that the option of the more risky oil and gas exploration company, Mesa Petroleum, sold at $3.75, whereas the option on the more stable company, Bankamerica, sold at $2. This is because investors would expect Mesa Petroleum to trade over a wider range (have higher variance) over any period of time than Bankamerica. Observation of the values of options over time bears out that options on higher-risk stocks persistently tend to have greater value than those on lower-risk stocks. This again derives from the fact that the variance of return of the stock is a prime determinant of the value of the option.[12]

The second important factor in determining the value of an option is the time remaining to expiration of the option. It seems reasonable that the longer the life of the option, then the greater should be the opportunity for the price of the stock to move into the favorable region of the distribution — that is, into the area above the exercise price. Analytically we know that the variance of the distribution of returns, or price changes, will increase with time. In fact, the standard deviation increases with the square root of time, so that a stock with a standard deviation of return of 5 percent over a three-month period would be expected to have a standard deviation of 10 percent over the full year, or four-quarter period (standard deviation of 5 percent times the square root of four quarters). In effect, this increased variance due to the lengthening of the time horizon gives added value to the option. Conversely, the maturing of the option automatically reduces the value of the option. Figure 11-11b shows that over time the curve shifts down as the variance becomes smaller, until at expiration it lies on the baseline as we previously noted it should.

The third major factor determining the value of an option is the level of interest rates. Higher interest rates would lead to greater values for the options, while lower interest rates would lead to lower values. We can justify this in two ways. First, investors can obtain leverage in stock investment by borrowing (establishing a margin account) or by purchasing calls, and in this sense the two techniques can be considered competitive investment strategies. When interest rates rise, the cost of the margin account increases, making this technique relatively less attractive than the call strategy. Investors would presumably be attracted to the use of calls, thereby driving their prices up. Second, we noted that a strategy of buying fixed-income securities (treasury bills) and calls is equivalent to creating an artificial convertible security. This quasi-equity security can be considered an alternative, or competitive instrument, to the stock. At higher interest rates more can be earned on the treasury bill portion of the "convertible" package. This makes the overall approach relatively more attractive and should lead to greater demand for calls with the attendant upward pressure on call prices. Figure 11-11c shows the effect on the option value curve: the curve will be at a higher level at higher interest rates and a lower level at lower interest rates.

[12] Later in the chapter we'll see that estimating the variability of the underlying security is perhaps the most critical input to determining the appropriate value of an option. Assume for the moment that the standard deviation estimate is a "given." We'll discuss ways of developing this estimate in the final section of this chapter.

HEDGE RATIO

The data in Table 11-4 help illustrate the significance of the shape of the option value curve, again using our hypothetical stock as it ranges in price from $40 to $80 per share. Column 1 shows the stock price, and Column 2 the values of the option at that price, which are the same as those given in Table 11-3. Column 3 shows the slope of the option value curve at the particular price level; this slope is also known as the *hedge ratio*. The slope will change with the price level. As the price of the stock increases more and more above the exercise price, the slope will approach 1 (a 45° angle). As the price of the stock declines below the exercise price, the slope of the curve approaches zero (a horizontal line). Note that in this case the slope is .65 at the exercise price of $60 and .96 at the highest price of $80.

For ease of interpretation Column 4 shows the reciprocal of the slope. It gives the number of short-call options needed to neutralize a long position in the stock. Correspondingly, it represents the number of long-call options that will neutralize a short position in the stock. Note that when the stock price is $50 it would take 3.12 short calls to neutralize a position in the stock. Also note that the ratio decreases as the stock price increases, so that at $80 per share only 1.04 calls will be needed to neutralize a position in the stock.

Using these hedge ratios, one can then ensure that gains (losses) on long positions are offset exactly by losses (gains) on short positions, so that the investor's beginning and ending positions are identical. Figure 11-12 on p. 313 more specifically illustrates how this process of hedging eliminates investment risk. The diagram is a plotting of the option values against the stock price as it ranges from $40 to $80. It shows the value of the option at the exercise price of $60 and allows us to assess how the value of the option changes as the stock price varies around the exercise price.

Note that the value of the call option rises or falls by $0.65 when the stock price changes by $1. Recall from Table 11-4 that the reciprocal of the hedge ratio at the exercise price of $60 is 1.54 to 1, indicating that investors can protect themselves against the stock price change by selling 1.54 call options for $6.86 each. In this instance, when the stock price declines by $1 to $59, the investor gains $1 on the short position in the options; it is now possible for the investor to repurchase the 1.54 call

Table 11-4 Option curve data

Stock price (1)	Option value (2)	Slope, or hedge ratio (3)	Calls to neutralize stock (4)
$40	$ 0.22	0.06	16.67
50	1.97	0.32	3.12
60	6.86	0.65	1.54
70	14.58	0.87	1.15
80	23.80	0.96	1.04

options for $1 less than they were sold, as each option has declined by $0.65 with the fall in the stock price. Correspondingly, when the stock rises by $1 to $61, the investor gains $1 on the stock position but loses $1 on the short position in the options. In this case the cost of repurchasing the 1.54 options is $1 more than they were sold, as each has risen by $0.65.

For any sufficiently small change in the stock price the relationship between the stock and option price change is effectively linear; however, for larger changes the relationship is curved, so that gains and losses will not be perfectly offsetting. For example, as shown in Figure 11-12, when the stock price rises to $70, there will be a gain of $10 on the long position in the stock but a loss of $11.89 on the short position in the options. Similarly, if the price falls to $50, there will be a loss of $10 on the long position in the stock but a gain of only $7.53 on the short position in the options. The hedge ratio is thus a valid indicator only for small changes in price and for short intervals of time.[13]

THE BLACK-SCHOLES OPTION VALUATION MODEL

The operation of hedging and the hedge ratio are critical notions of the Black-Scholes option valuation model. The model is based on the fact that it is possible, given a number of assumptions, to set up a perfectly hedged position consisting of a long position in an underlying stock and a short position in options on that stock, or a long position in the option and a short position in the stock. By "perfectly hedged" Black and Scholes mean that over a stock price interval close to the current price any profit resulting from an instantaneous increase in the price of the stock would be exactly offset by an instantaneous loss on the option position, or vice versa.[14]

The Black-Scholes formula is developed from the principle that options can completely eliminate market risk from a stock portfolio. Black and Scholes postulate that the ratio of options to stock in this hedged position is constantly modified, at no commission cost, in order to offset gains or losses on the stock by losses or gains on the options. Because the position is theoretically riskless, we would expect the hedge to earn the risk-free rate, somewhat analogous to the assumption invoked in deriving the capital-asset pricing model (CAPM). Given that the risk-free hedge should earn the risk-free rate, this implies that the option premium at which the hedge yields a return equal to the risk-free short-term interest rate is the fair value of the option. If the price of the option is greater or less than fair value, the return from a risk-free hedged position could be different from the risk-free interest rate. Since this is inconsistent with equilibrium, we would expect the option price to adjust toward fair value.

Using this notion, Black-Scholes derived an explicit formula for determining the price of the option. The formula is

$$V = P[N(d_1)] - E[e^{-rt}][N(d_2)]$$

[13] It should be noted that it would be difficult to maintain a neutral position over time since all factors, including time, are changing.

[14] Black-Scholes assumption that one can instantly and continuously rebalance means that the relationship between the stock price and option value is effectively linear, so that gains and losses are exactly offsetting.

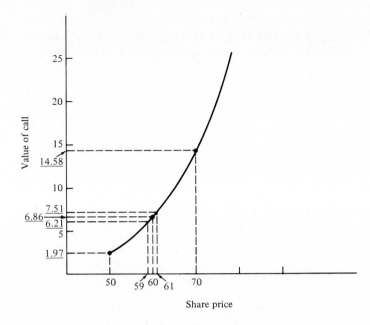

Figure 11-12 Stock price and value of call option.

where V = market value of option
P = current market price of underlying stock
$N(d_1)$ = cumulative density function of d_1, as defined below
E = exercise price of call option
r = "risk-free" interest rate
t = time remaining before expiration, in years, (e.g., 180 days = .5)
$N(d_2)$ = cumulative density function of d_2, as defined below

$$d_1 = \left[\frac{\ln(P/E) + (r + .5S^2)t}{S\sqrt{t}} \right]$$

$$d_2 = \left[\frac{\ln(P/E) + (r - .5S^2)t}{S\sqrt{t}} \right]$$

$\ln(P/E)$ = natural logarithm of P/E
S = standard deviation of annual rate of return on the underlying stock

Although the formula appears quite forbidding, using it is fairly direct. The major inputs are: (1) current stock price P, (2) exercise price E, (3) time to maturity t, (4) market interest rate r, and (5) standard deviation of annual price changes S. The first three inputs are readily observable from current market quotations or are known items of data. The market interest rate must be estimated, but it can be established fairly easily. One obvious source is the rate on prime commercial paper quoted daily in *The Wall Street Journal* for different maturities ranging from 30, 60, and 90 to 240 days.

One should use the rate for the maturity that corresponds to the term of the option. The other estimated input, the standard deviation of the stock price change, is more difficult to estimate, and errors can have a significant impact on the established option value.

There are several techniques for estimating the variability of the stock price. One might use historically derived values of the standard deviation of price changes of the stock as an estimate of the standard deviation to be generated in the future. The time period of the measurements becomes important in this regard: too long a period may result in the inclusion of irrelevant observations, and too short a period may exclude valuable information and not be representative. Some recommend the most recent six months' or year's trading data as the best measurement interval with the use of histori-cal data.

An alternative way to estimate the variability of a stock is the option valuation formula. Rather than using the formula to assess the proper price of an option, one can observe the current price of an option and deduce the standard deviation of the stock price as implied by the formula. Calculating and averaging the implied deviation over a series of past periods may provide a more accurate assessment of the basic variability of the stock than a straightforward averaging of past values. In either case it may be necessary to adjust these historically derived values for possible future changes in the variability of the stock price. Here one would want to examine those underlying factors which are basic determinants of the riskiness of securities: (1) interest rate risk, (2) purchasing power risk, (3) business risk, and (4) financial risk. If the exposure of the stock to these factors is changing, the historically derived variability estimate should be adjusted to reflect this. For example, if the company is now financing more heavily with debt, its exposure to financial risk and expected future variability would be greater than in the past.

VALUATING AN OPTION

To illustrate use of the Black-Scholes option valuation, or pricing, formula,[15] we can use the following inputs for a hypothetical option: $P = 60$; $E = 60$; $r = .12$ (the rate on 180-day prime commercial paper); $t = 6$ months $- .5$ year; and $S = .3$. Given these inputs, we can begin by calculating values for d_1 and d_2.

$$d_1 = \frac{\ln(60/60) + [.12 + 1/2(.09)](.5)}{.3\sqrt{.5}} = .389$$

$$d_2 = \frac{\ln(60/60) + [.12 - 1/2(.09)](.5)}{.3\sqrt{.5}} = .177$$

[15] Mark Rubinstein, "How to Use the Option Pricing Formula," Salomon Brothers Center, New York University, Working Paper 115, May 1977. In this paper Rubinstein outlined the programming steps for mounting the formula on a hand calculator such as the HP-65. He also gave a listing of a computer program written in APL that would be suitable for use on a minicomputer. Some calculators, such as the TI-59, have prepackaged programs for calculating option values. Naturally, availability of these programs speeds up the calculation of option values considerably.

Using a table for the cumulative normal distribution, we then compute

$$N(d_1) = N(.389) = .651$$
$$N(d_2) = N(.177) = .563$$

The value of the call is then computed as

$$V = 60(.651) - 60[e^{-.12(.5)}](.563) = 6.86$$

To assess whether the call option was undervalued or overvalued, we could compare this calculated value to the market price of the call. For example, an actual market price of, say, $5 for the call would indicate that the call is undervalued, and an investor might take advantage of this by directly buying the call. Alternatively, the investor could be protected against adverse stock price changes by buying the call and selling the stock short. As you remember from a previous section, this action can provide a riskless hedge. According to the Black-Scholes valuation model, the appropriate hedge ratio to use for this purpose is given by $N(d_1)$, or in this case .651. This means that for every call option purchased, .651 shares of stock should be sold short, or alternatively, for every share of stock sold short, 1.54 calls should be purchased.

While the Black-Scholes model is theoretically elegant, we should note before concluding that there are some concerns regarding practical application of the model. To begin with, we should be concerned with the realism of the basic assumption of being able to set up a riskless hedge by rebalancing continuously and instantaneously. In actual practice there are transactions costs that would impede the continuous process of buying and selling securities; these costs could eventually dissipate any investment return. In addition, while price changes are generally small over a short interval, there are occasions when the price change can be quite sizable. Finally, the assumption of a risk-free rate is unrealistic.

With respect to the actual estimate of option values, we should emphasize the importance of developing appropriate inputs to the model, because differences in the estimates — interest rate and standard deviation — can affect the calculated value of the option significantly. Table 11-5 illustrates this by showing calculated values for options with different interest rate and standard deviation inputs to the Black-Scholes formulation.

Table 11-5 Option values as a function of interest rates and standard deviation

Interest rate	Standard deviation		
	0.20	0.30	0.40
0.10	4.97	6.54	8.15
0.12	5.32	6.86	8.44
0.14	5.69	7.19	8.45

Note, for example, that using a 10 percent interest rate, rather than a 12 percent interest rate as in our previous example, provides an option value of $6.54, or 5 percent lower than in the prior calculation. Alternatively, using an estimated standard deviation of .40, which is 33 percent greater than the original estimate of .30, provides an option value of $8.44, or 23 percent greater than in our previous example. The sensitivity of option values to variations in these inputs, especially the standard deviation, emphasizes that the avoidance of input errors should be a prime consideration in using the model.

CONCLUSION

Most options activity is linked to other investment decisions or positions, because the use of options allows one to alter the return distribution of the underlying position(s); different strategies may be used to reduce risk or boost leverage and returns. Of particular interest are those strategies which provide the portfolio manager with the insurance capability mentioned in the introduction to this chapter. The purest insurance play is the protective put, where the minimum value of the underlying stock is guaranteed over the life of the option. By comparison, covered call writing provides limited insurance through the proceeds of selling the upside potential of the underlying stock.

Given the right market price for the option, these strategies would be desirable for any investor (free puts would be coveted by all investors). Thus the big question always is, Does the option price warrant the use of these or other strategies? Some insight might be provided by theoretical valuation models, such as Black-Scholes formula. One must be wary, however, of the limitations of the model as well as of the need to provide suitable inputs, particularly variance estimates for the underlying stock. In the final analysis one must decide whether the market price of the option justifies a strategy, given the risk preference of the portfolio manager.

PROBLEMS

1 Assume that an investor has purchased a call option and a put option, each at a price of $3, with an exercise price of $27. Determine the value and net profit of each if the stock sells at
  (a) $35,
  (b) $27, and
  (c) $22 at expiration.
Also determine the net profit on the combined position under each terminal stock price.

2 Assume that a bond yields 10 percent, a stock sells at $20, and a call and put on the stock each sell at $3 and have an exercise price of $20. Graph the profit and loss from the following strategies:
  (a) buying the bond
  (b) selling the bond short (borrowing)
  (c) buying the stock
  (d) selling the stock short
  (e) buying the call
  (f) selling the call
  (g) buying the put
  (h) selling the put

3 Describe several ways that options may be used to serve an insurance function in a portfolio context, and indicate the cost of this insurance.

4 Discuss and show graphically how one would undertake a protective put strategy. Also explain under what conditions the strategy would be most appropriate.

5 Show graphically the effect on the value of an option of
  (a) an increase in the variability of the underlying stock
  (b) a reduction in the maturity of the option from six months to three months
  (c) an increase in interest rates from 10 percent to 12 percent.

6 The hedge ratio for a particular stock is .333. Evaluation shows that the option is overvalued. What action should be taken to earn a risk-free profit?

7 Assume that a stock is selling at $30 and has an exercise price of $40, a maturity of three months, and a standard deviation of .50 and that the current interest rate is 15 percent. Calculate the value of the option, and indicate the hedge ratio.

SELECTED REFERENCES

Black, Fischer. "Fact and Fantasy in the Use of Options," *Financial Analysts Journal,* July–August 1975, pp. 36–72.

———, and Myron Scholes: "The Pricing of Options and Corporate Liabilities," *Journal of Political Economy,* May–June 1973, pp. 637–654.

Boness, A. James: "Elements of a Theory of Stock-Option Value," *Journal of Political Economy,* April 1964, pp. 163–175.

Brigham, Eugene F.: "An Analysis of Convertible Debentures: Theory and Some Empirical Evidence," *Journal of Finance,* March 1966, pp. 35–54.

Cootner, Paul (ed.): *The Random Character of Stock Market Prices,* M. I. T. Press, Cambridge, Mass., 1964.

Cox, John C., Stephen Ross, and Mark Rubinstein: "Option Pricing: A Simplified Approach," *Journal of Financial Economics,* September 1979, pp. 229–263.

Gastineau, Gary: *The Stock Options Manual,* McGraw-Hill, New York, 1979.

Kassouf, Sheen T.: "Option Pricing: Theory and Practice," The Institute for Quantitative Research and Finance, Spring 1977 Seminar, Palm Springs, Calif.

Leland, Hayne, and Mark Rubinstein: "Replicating Options with Positions in Stock and Cash," *Financial Analysts Journal,* July–August 1981, pp. 63–72.

Malkiel, Burton G., and Richard E. Quandt: *Strategies and Rational Decisions in the Securities Options Market,* M. I. T. Press, Cambridge, Mass., 1969.

Merton, Robert C.: "Theory of Rational Option Pricing," *Bell Journal of Economics and Management Science,* Spring 1973, pp. 141–183.

Merton, Robert C., Myron S. Scholes, and Mathew L. Gladstein: "A Simulation of the Returns and Risk of Alternative Option Portfolio Investment Strategies," *Journal of Business,* April 1978, pp. 183–242.

Pozen, Robert C.: "The Purchase of Protective Puts by Financial Institutions," *Financial Analysts Journal,* July–August 1978, pp. 47–60.

Sharpe, William F.: *Investments,* Prentice-Hall, Englewood Cliffs, N. J., 1978.

Shelton, John P.: "The Relation of the Price of a Warrant to the Price of Its Associated Stock," *Financial Analysts Journal,* May–June 1967, pp. 143–151, July–August 1967, pp. 88–99.

Smith, Clifford W.: "Option Pricing," *Journal of Financial Economics,* January–March 1976, pp. 3–51.

Stoll, Hans R.: "The Relationship between Put and Call Option Prices," *Journal of Finance,* December 1969, pp. 801–824.

PORTFOLIO EVALUATION

TWELVE

EVALUATING PORTFOLIO PERFORMANCE

INTRODUCTION

The ultimate objective of an investment process is to accomplish the investment goals established by the investor. Performance evaluation aims not only at assessing the success of the investment process in achieving the overall investment goals but also at diagnosing the contribution of the individual elements that have made possible achievement of the overall goal. In turn the performance evaluation should provide a feedback mechanism enabling the organization to emphasize those aspects of the process which are productive and downplay, or reconstitute, those which have failed to contribute to the investment goal.

This chapter is concerned with performance evaluation. We'll begin by describing the investment needs of a hypothetical pension fund and illustrate the sort of investment goals that the fund might establish. Then we'll indicate the three major aspects of the investment process that should be evaluated: (1) asset allocation, (2) weighting shifts across asset classes, and (3) security selection within asset classes. With respect to evaluating security selection we'll discuss two general methods of evaluation: (1) comparison against asset-class indexes as well as against comparable managers within the asset class and (2) risk-adjusted performance comparisons that derive from the portfolio theory and capital-market theory described in Chapters 2 and 3. We'll conclude by illustrating how the different aspects of performance can be compared simultaneously.

SETTING INVESTMENT GOALS

Since achieving investment goals is the basic aim of the investment process, an explicit statement of these goals is a critical step in the evaluation of the process. It will perhaps be best to illustrate the goal-setting process by using a hypothetical pension fund, as investors in pension funds are confronted with as wide an array of investment problems as any other investors.

Table 12-1 shows the characteristics of our hypothetical pension fund. Note that the fund has a total asset value of $500 million, which approximates the size of a moderately large pension fund. The plan has a goal of earning a real return of 4 percent on assets; that is, the nominal return on assets, less the inflation rate, should be 4 percent. Since the market cycle is typically about five years, as is its planning period, the fund has a goal of earning this 4 percent return over any rolling five-year period. It expects to meet or exceed this goal at least two-thirds of the time. Alternatively, the acceptable risk in not reaching this goal is a short-fall of one-third the time.[1]

The fund includes in its eligible list of assets both domestic and international equities. Among the eligible foreign national markets are Japan, the United Kingdom, and Germany. The fund has established a size limitation on securities of no less than $200 million in market capitalization to avoid the proliferation of an excessive number of individual small holdings. Corporate and government bonds, but not municipal bonds or preferred stocks, are eligible in the fund's investment universe. The fund — as is the case with pension plans in general — is not subject to tax, so that tax-exempt securities are not of interest. Short-term obligations — treasury bills and commercial paper — are also eligible for purchase and serve as a reserve.

Table 12-1 also shows the asset allocation for the plan, which provides the most likely opportunity to meet the goal at the least risk. Note that the plan has a normal

[1] An alternative way of expressing this is to say that the objective of a pension fund is to return at least as much as the actuarial rate. Another example of an investment objective for an institutional investor is that of an endowment fund with a goal of providing sufficient capital or income to meet the needs of the sponsoring organization.

Table 12-1 Setting goals for an investment fund

Fund type:	Pension fund
Fund value:	$500 million
Return goal:	4% real return
Planning period:	5 years
Risk of loss:	$\frac{1}{3}$ probability of not earning the return

Eligible assets and desired allocation:

Asset	Normal position, %	Allowable divergence, %
Domestic equities	60	±15
International equities	15	± 5
Japan	5	
United Kingdom	5	
Germany	5	
Fixed income	25	±10
Long-term	20	
Short-term	5	

allocation of 60 percent domestic stocks, 15 percent international equities, and 25 percent fixed-income securities. These normal allocations provide the best opportunity for earning the objective return at the least risk over the longer term, again defined as the five-year planning period. The plan allows, however, the allocation to diverge from the normal allocations with the following ranges: ±15 percent for domestic stocks, ±5 percent for international equities, and ±10 percent for fixed-income securities.

We'll assume that the fund sponsor assumes responsibilities in setting the longer-term allocation as well as in advising when and to what extent to shift the weights in the major asset classes. In managing the assets within the major asset classes, we'll assume that the fund uses outside professional money management organizations: (1) a management organization for domestic equities and (2) an international investment specialist for international equities. We'll also assume that the fund uses the bond management division of a major financial institution to oversee the fixed-income portion of the fund.[2]

Table 12-2 illustrates the three major aspects of evaluating the performance of this hypothetical fund. First, we would want to determine whether our overall asset distribution (allocation) was effective in meeting the longer-term real rate of return objectives. Second, we would want to assess the productivity of any changes in the weightings of the asset allocation from its longer-run target; that is, we need to determine the incremental gain or loss from weighting the various asset classes differently than for the longer-run objective. Finally, we would want to analyze whether the managers of the differing asset categories — domestic equities, international equities, and fixed-income securities — were performing relatively better or worse than the appropriate benchmarks for the category.

LONG-TERM GOALS: ASSET ALLOCATION

In an inflationary environment many plan sponsors have come to state their longer-term goals in terms of a real return on investment — that is, nominal return less inflation rate. This is in keeping with the necessity for pension plan assets to be sufficient to meet future pension liabilities, which will generally incorporate the rate of inflation experi-

[2] In managing pension assets, corporations vary in operating procedures, from managing the whole process internally — in-house management — to complete delegation of asset allocation, differential weighting, and security selection to an outside manager. The example here is a hybrid situation and may be illustrative of the typical sponsor-management relationship for pension funds.

Table 12-2 Appraising fund performance

---

1. Long-term goals: Evaluating the efficacy of the asset allocation
2. Appraising asset mix changes
3. Evaluating the performance of managers within major asset categories

---

enced over the period. Generally, pension sponsors seem to be targeting this real return at the 4 percent level. The prime determinant of whether the plan will meet the real-return target at minimum risk over an intermediate to longer period of time — say, five to twenty years — is the effectiveness of the asset allocation.

Recall from Chapters 1 and 7 that the various asset classes behave differently over differing economic episodes. In particular, we noted that bonds perform well during periods of deflation or disinflation but suffer adverse effects during periods of inflation. Treasury bills provide returns in line with the rate of inflation which have generally served as a hedge against inflation, especially in the postwar period. Common stocks perform most favorably during periods of strong real economic growth, but they show a mixed pattern as a hedge against inflation, especially over shorter periods. International equities might be expected to provide some protection against inflation, but they are subject to other political and economic risks. The objective of an asset allocation is to blend assets together so as to hedge against adverse economic changes (reduce risk) and, at the same time, provide the greatest opportunity for achieving longer-term rate of return.

Table 12-3 shows the returns earned on the various asset classes along with the rate of inflation experienced over the 1976–1980 period, allowing us to assess the real return earned on these assets over the period. Note that domestic common stocks showed high returns that were in excess of the 8.9 percent rate of inflation over the period. International equities also showed strong returns, especially in the early part of the period, and exceeded the rate of inflation for the overall period. Treasury bills tracked the annual rate of inflation and essentially showed returns about in line with the rate of inflation over the period. Finally, long-term bonds — as might be expected during a period of accelerating inflation — were unable to provide returns to offset the rate of inflation, showing a net real loss of 5 percent over the period (3.9 percent nominal return less 8.9 percent inflation rate).

Table 12-3 Rate of return — asset classes and portfolio allocation, 1976–1980

	Asset allocation weight	1976	1977	1978	1979	1980	Annual average
Domestic stocks (S&P 500)	0.60	23.9	− 7.2	6.6	18.6	32.4	14.1
International equities							
Germany	0.05	6.7	25.7	27.0	− 2.1	− 9.0	8.7
Japan	0.05	25.7	15.9	53.3	−11.8	30.2	20.7
United Kingdom	0.05	−12.4	58.0	14.7	22.2	41.1	22.3
Fixed-income							
Long-term bonds	0.20	19.6	3.2	0.4	− 2.1	− 0.3	3.9
Treasury bills	0.05	5.1	5.1	7.2	10.1	11.6	7.7
Consumer Price Index		4.8	6.8	9.0	11.3	12.4	8.9
Return to portfolio allocation		19.5	1.6	9.2	11.7	23.1	12.7
Real return		14.7	− 5.2	0.2	0.4	10.7	3.8

Source: Intersec Research, Inc., Greenwich, Conn.

Table 12-3 also shows the year-by-year return and average annual return over the full five-year period for a portfolio with an asset allocation in line with that of Table 12-1. Over the full five-year period the asset allocation resulted in an average annual return of 12.7 percent exceeding the 8.9 percent inflation rate and providing a real return of 3.8 percent, which was essentially in line with the objective of 4 percent. At the same time the return over the period was relatively stable, as the real return was positive in four of the five years. The asset allocation for the hypothetical portfolio was appropriate for meeting the longer-term objective of the pension fund.[3]

APPRAISING ASSET-MIX CHANGES

A second dimension to analyze in appraising the performance of a fund is to assess the productivity of any changes in the weighting of the assets from the longer-run-target asset allocation. In particular, we would be interested in assessing to what extent the fund has shifted classes, from the longer-term target weightings and then measure the effect of those shifts on performance. For example, if the fund had been overweighted in international equities and underweighted in domestic equities over the period, we would measure to what extent this had impacted performance relative to the mainte- nance of a position in line with the longer-term target.

To implement this, we first compare the return earned on the asset class to the return earned on the portfolio, assuming no change in the weighting from its longer- term target weighting. We would then simply multiply the differential return or loss on the asset class from that earned on the portfolio by the weighting divergence of the asset class. For example, if the manager had determined that long-term bonds were relatively attractive in a particular year and therefore overweighted bonds in the portfolio by, say, 5 percentage points, we would multiply the 5 percentage points by the relative gain or loss in long-term bonds. If bonds had earned a higher return during the year than the overall portfolio, there would have been an overall gain to the weighting decision. On the other hand, if bonds had earned a lower return (shown losses) relative to the overall portfolio, there would have been a weighting loss.

Table 12-4 shows the longer-term target weights for the hypothetical fund along with the actual weightings in these components and allows us to evaluate the re- weighting decisions of the fund year by year over the 1976–1980 performance period. Note that the fund overweighted domestic equities in 1976 and again in 1980 but underweighted this asset class in 1977 and 1978. Within the international asset class, the fund overweighted German equities in 1977, overweighted Japanese equities in 1978, and underweighted U. K. equities in 1976 and overweighted these equities in 1979. The fund held the weighting in the fixed-income class in line with the longer-term allocation, with the exception of a decision to underweight long-term bonds in 1980.

---

[3] One should be cautious in drawing firm conclusions about the success or failure of one's asset allocation. Over periods as short as a year and even a period as long as five years, the overall market environment for the asset classes will be a prime factor in determining achievement of the target return. During some periods the market environment may be such that it is impossible to meet the target—say, during a period of severe deflation. Any assessment should thus be made not only against the target return but also with the market environment in mind.

Table 12-4 Target and actual fund weightings, 1976–1980 (%)

Asset class	Target weight	Actual weight				
		1976	1977	1978	1979	1980
Domestic stocks	60	65	55	55	60	65
International equities						
Germany	5	5	10	5	5	5
Japan	5	5	5	10	—	5
United Kingdom	5	—	5	5	10	5
Fixed-income securities						
Long-term bond	20	20	20	20	20	15
Treasury bills	5	5	5	5	5	5

Table 12-5 shows the return added by these weighting decisions. Note that the weighting decisions in 1976 — overweighting domestic equities and underweighting U. K. equities in the international sector — added 1.8 percent to overall performance; underweighting domestic equities and overweighting German equities added 1.6 percent in 1977; underweighting domestic stocks and overweighting Japanese securities added 2.3 percent to performance in 1978; overweighting U. K. securities and underweighting Japanese securities added 1.7 percent to performance in 1979; and overweighting domestic stocks and underweighting long-term bonds added 1.6 percent to performance in 1980. The fund thus showed a favorable performance with respect to weighting decisions on both an overall and year-by-year basis.

EVALUATING ASSET-CLASS MANAGERS

The third dimension to performance evaluation is assessment of the success of managers within individual asset classes: domestic equity, international equities, and fixed-income securities. In making this comparison we are essentially trying to evaluate the ability of the manager or managers to make individual security and industry selections. There are three types of comparisons: (1) with a market index, such as the S&P 500, when evaluating the domestic equity manager; (2) with the performance of others specializing in the management of securities within the asset class; and (3) evaluation based on measurements of risk-adjusted return derived from the risk-return framework discussed in Chapters 2 and 3.

Table 12-6 illustrates how one might use market indexes to evaluate the performance of asset-class managers. It shows the year-by-year and cumulative rate of return over the full 1976–1980 period for the asset-class market indexes. It also shows returns for hypothetical managers within each of the classes.[4] Returns in excess of the

[4] The performance of domestic equities is actually measured by the returns attributable to the implementation of the stock selection strategy described in Chapter 6. Measurement of the performance of the international equities manager is strictly hypothetical, while that of the bond manager is the actual performance of the Manufacturer's Hanover Trust Company bond-management department.

Table 12-5 Performance attributable to nonstandard weighting, 1976–1980 (%)

Asset class	Incremental return				
	1976	1977	1978	1979	1980
Domestic stocks	0.2	0.4	0.1	—	0.5
International equities					
Germany	—	1.2	—	—	—
Japan	—	—	2.2	1.2	—
United Kingdom	1.6	—	—	0.5	—
Fixed-income securities					
Long-term bonds	—	—	—	—	1.1
Treasury bills	—	—	—	—	—
Total	1.8	1.6	2.3	1.7	1.6

market index benchmark would be considered indicative of above-average performance, while returns below the index would be considered indicative of below-average performance.

Note that the domestic-equity manager provided superior return in each of the five years and for the overall period an above-average return of 5.1 percent. The

Table 12-6 Asset-class manager performance, 1976–1980 (%)

Asset class	1976	1977	1978	1979	1980	Annual average
Domestic stocks						
Market index	23.9	− 7.2	6.6	18.6	32.4	14.1
Manager	33.7	− 2.7	13.6	21.4	34.2	19.2
Performance increment	9.8	4.5	7.0	2.8	1.8	5.1
International equities						
German market index	6.7	25.7	27.0	− 2.1	− 9.0	8.7
Manager	9.0	25.0	31.0	− 1.0	−13.0	9.0
Performance increment	2.3	− 0.7	4.0	1.1	− 4.0	0.3
Japan market index	25.7	15.9	53.3	−11.8	30.2	20.7
Manager	26.5	13.2	55.6	−13.2	32.7	20.8
Performance increment	0.8	− 2.7	2.3	− 1.4	2.5	0.1
U. K. market index	− 12.4	58.0	14.7	22.2	41.1	22.3
Manager	− 15.3	55.0	17.3	24.0	37.5	20.9
Performance increment	− 2.9	− 3.0	2.6	1.8	− 3.6	− 1.4
Fixed-income securities						
Long-term bond index	19.6	3.2	0.4	− 2.1	− 0.3	3.9
Manager	17.7	3.4	3.1	6.2	8.0	7.6
Performance increment	− 1.9	0.2	2.7	8.3	8.3	3.7

international-equity manager outperformed the Japanese and German equity indexes for the overall period but earned a slightly below-average return against the U. K. index. The fixed-income manager provided superior return in four of the five years and outperformed the fixed-income index by 3.7 percent over the full period. On the basis of comparison with the market indexes the individual asset managers appear to have delivered superior performance.

Furthermore, it's useful to compare the performance of individual managers against the performance of other managers within a particular asset class. For example, we would compare the fixed-income manager to other managers specialized in managing fixed-income securities. In this regard we would need to ensure that the managers in the comparison are in fact primarily engaged in the management of securities within the particular asset class; that is, we should make sure that the fixed-income managers are focused on fixed-income securities, that the domestic-equity managers are predominantly engaged in managing domestic equities, and that the international-equity managers are primarily concerned with managing international equities.

In making the comparison the usual method is to array the managers within an asset class from the one providing the highest return to the one providing the lowest return over a performance period, and then to display the distribution as illustrated in Figure 12-1. This figure shows the return distribution for domestic-equity managers and fixed-income managers for the five-year period ending with 1980. It shows the median return earned by the universe of managers and a breakdown of the distribution into quartiles of manager performance. It also shows the ranking within the fund-manager distribution of the pertinent indexes — the S&P 500 and the Lehman Brothers — Kuhn Loeb bond index.

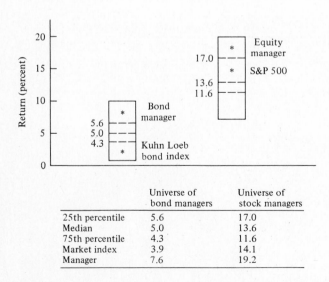

	Universe of bond managers	Universe of stock managers
25th percentile	5.6	17.0
Median	5.0	13.6
75th percentile	4.3	11.6
Market index	3.9	14.1
Manager	7.6	19.2

Figure 12-1 Relative performance — bond and equity managers, 1976–1980. (*Sources: Frank Russell Company, Tacoma, Wash., and A. G. Becker Company, Chicago.*)

Note that the median fixed-income manager would have outperformed the bond index, while the median stock manager performed about in line with the stock market index over this period. There was, however, a wide dispersion around these average returns, especially in the case of the stock managers; this comparison is useful for placing the manager's performance in perspective. As for our hypothetical managers, we can see that the performance of the bond manager was well into the first quartile of performance, as was the stock manager with respect to other domestic equity managers. The performance of both managers would therefore have been rated above average according to this measure.

RISK-ADJUSTED PERFORMANCE

The previous two comparisons, though providing a useful perspective on performance, are based only on rate of return. Since the differential return earned by a manager may be due to a difference in the exposure to risk from that of the index or typical manager, there would be merit in attempting to adjust the return for any differences in risk exposure. For this purpose there are essentially three major methods of assessing risk-adjusted performance: (1) return per unit of risk, (2) differential return, and (3) components of performance.[5] These methods are interrelated and evolve out of the risk-return theory described in Chapters 2 and 3.

Return per Unit of Risk

The first of the risk-adjusted performance measures is the type that assesses the performance of a fund in terms of return per unit of risk. The technique is to relate the absolute level of realized return to the level of risk incurred, to develop a relative measure for ranking fund performance. According to this method, funds that provide the highest return per unit of risk would be judged as having performed best, while those providing the lowest return per unit of risk would be judged as the poorest performers. Low-return funds would rank better than high-return funds on this basis if the risk incurred in earning the return was sufficiently lower for the low-return funds than the high-return funds.

Figure 12-2 is a risk-return diagram showing why return per unit of risk is an appropriate standard for judging performance. Note that the vertical axis represents return and the horizontal axis represents risk, but for this purpose we interpret them as representing either the standard deviation or beta coefficient. The diagram shows the plots for three funds designated A, M, and Z, where fund M represents the market fund (say, the S&P 500) and funds A and Z are hypothetical funds.

Note that fund Z provides the highest absolute return, while fund A provides the lowest return and fund M an intermediate return. Fund A, however, ranks highest in

[5] While the risk-adjusted measures to be discussed are highly plausible, they have limitations — not the least of which is that to some extent risk in the mind of the investor remains subjective and difficult to quantify. Furthermore, all are based on the single-index formulation which we've seen is not representative of the underlying return-generating process. This may result in a bias in the assessed risk-adjusted performance.

terms of return per unit of risk, fund Z lowest, and fund M at an intermediate level. Assuming that an investor could borrow or lend freely at the risk-free rate R_F, the investor could attain any point along the line from R_F through the plot of fund A. Investors should prefer line R_FA to the other two formed by borrowing and lending and investing in funds M and Z, because line R_FA provides a higher return at all levels of risk than R_FM, which in turn dominates line R_FZ.

There are two alternative, yet similar, methods of measuring return per unit of risk: (1) the reward to variability ratio developed by William Sharpe and appropriately referred to as the Sharpe ratio,[6] and (2) the reward to volatility ratio developed by Jack Treynor and fittingly referred to as the Treynor ratio.[7] The Sharpe ratio is simply the ratio of the reward, defined as the realized portfolio return R_p in excess of the risk-free rate R_F, to the variability of return as measured by the standard deviation of return S_p; that is, $R_p - R_F/S_p$. The Treynor ratio is the ratio of the reward, also defined as the realized portfolio return R_p in excess of the risk free rate R_F, to the volatility of return as measured instead by the portfolio beta B_p; that is, the ratio $R_p - R_F/B_p$.

The two performance ratios thus differ only inasmuch as one measures total risk by the standard deviation while the other measures market risk by the portfolio beta. Recall from the discussion in Chapter 3 that the standard deviation as a measure of total risk is appropriate when evaluating the risk-return relationship for well-diversified portfolios. On the other hand, when evaluating less than fully diversified portfolios or individual stocks, the relevant measure of risk is the beta coefficient (also described in Chapter 3).

The appropriate return per unit of risk measure to use will, in turn, depend on one's view of the risk that is relevant for the purpose of evaluation. When the portfolio being

[6] William F. Sharpe, "Mutual Fund Performance," *Journal of Business*, January 1966, pp. 119–138.
[7] Jack L. Treynor, "How to Rate Management of Investment Funds," *Harvard Business Review*, January–February 1965, pp. 63–70.

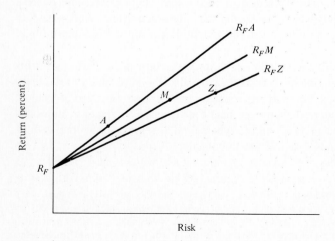

Figure 12-2 Risk-return relationship: market portfolio and two hypothetical portfolios.

evaluated comprises the total or predominant representation in the particular asset class, the total variability of return measured by the standard deviation should be the relevant risk measure. On the other hand, for some investors the portfolio being evaluated is only one component of the investor's representation in the asset class — as, for example, where major pension plan sponsors use several different managers within an asset class.[8] For those investors employing a multimanager strategy, the beta coefficient is the appropriate measure of risk.

Table 12-7 illustrates the calculation of the two measures of return per unit of risk for the two hypothetical funds, A and Z, along with the market fund as a benchmark for comparison. Note that the market fund provided a .333 return per unit of standard deviation and exceeded the .250 return provided by fund Z, but it was below the .400 provided by fund A. According to the reward to volatility ratio, the market fund provided a return per unit of risk of 7, which again exceeded the 6 for fund Z but was below the 9 derived from fund A. Using either measure, the ranking of the funds was identical: fund A the best, fund Z the worst, and the market fund an intermediate performer.

In fact, the ranking according to both measures — reward to variability and reward to volatility — will be identical when the funds under consideration are perfectly diversified or, for all practical purposes, when the funds are highly diversified. The rankings of the two measures will diverge, however, when the funds being appraised are less highly diversified.[9] For example, a poorly diversified fund that ranks highly on the reward to volatility ratio compared with another fund that is highly diversified will rank less favorably — and may, in fact, rank lower on the basis of the reward to variability ratio. This is because the less diversified fund will show relatively greater risk when using the standard deviation than the better diversified fund. As noted before, the appropriate measure of risk-adjusted performance depends on whether the fund constitutes the investor's total representation in the asset class or is only one of the investor's many funds.

[8] The trend during the 1970s was for pension funds to employ several asset class managers, especially in managing the equity portion of the fund. This was partly induced by the ERISA legislation and the desire to diversify risk. It was also motivated by a desire to capitalize on the special capabilities of different "style" of managers, such as the growth-stock specialist, undervalued-asset manager, and small-capitalization growth-stock specialist.

[9] Note that the hypothetical funds, though not perfectly diversified, are sufficiently highly diversified, so that the relative ranking does not change as the measurement standard differs.

Table 12-7 Calculation of risk per unit of return ratios
Market fund and two hypothetical funds

Fund	Return R_p, %	Risk-free rate R_F, %	Excess return $R_p - R_F$, %	Standard deviation S_p, %	Sharpe ratio $R_p - R_F / S_p$	Beta B_p	Treynor ratio $R_p - R_F / B_p$
A	8	2	6	15	0.400	0.67	9
M	9	2	7	21	0.333	1.00	7
Z	10	2	8	32	0.250	1.33	6

Differential Return

A second category of risk-adjusted performance measures is the type referred to as differential return measures. The underlying objective of this technique is to calculate the return that should be expected for the fund, given the realized risk of the fund, and to compare that with the return actually realized over the period. In making this comparison it is assumed that the investor has a passive or naive alternative of merely buying the market portfolio and adjusting for the appropriate level of risk by borrowing or lending at the risk-free rate. Given this assumption, the most commonly used method of determining the expected fund return at a given level of risk is the following formula:

$$R_p = R_F + (R_M - R_F)B_p \qquad (1)$$

Note that this formula is the same in form as the formula for the security market line (SML), with the difference that the variables are expressed in terms of realized returns and risk rather than ex ante variables, as would be appropriate for the SML.[10] The equation is graphically represented as line $R_F M$ in Figure 12-3. Also shown are the two hypothetical funds, A and Z, from the previous section, to illustrate the use of the equation for performance evaluation.

To evaluate the performance of fund A we would insert the appropriate variables from Table 12-7 into the formula

$$R_p = 2 + .67(9 - 2)$$
$$= 6.7$$

With this data, fund A would have been expected to earn 6.7 percent over the period, whereas it actually earned 8 percent as indicated in Table 12-7, thus providing a differential, or risk-adjusted, return of 1.3 percent. This difference is represented graphically as the distance $A = A_M$ in Figure 12-3.

Similarly, we can evaluate the performance of fund Z by also inserting the appropriate variables from Table 12-7 into the formula

$$R_p = 2 + 1.33(9 - 2)$$
$$R_p = 11.3$$

Given this data, fund Z would have been expected to earn 11.3 percent over the period, whereas the fund actually earned 10 percent as indicated in Table 12-7, thus providing a differential, or risk-adjusted, return of -1.3 percent. This difference is represented graphically as the distance $Z=Z_M$ in Figure 12-3.

This measure of risk-adjusted return, developed by Michael Jensen, is sometimes referred to as the Jensen measure.[11] In addition to this method of calculating differential return, Jensen also developed a means of determining whether the differential return could have occurred by chance or whether it is significantly different from zero in a

---

[10] An alternative way to determine differential return is to use the standard deviation as the measure of risk and the formulation of the capital-market line (CML). The return adjustment by way of the security market line (SML) is more commonly used, but it is not necessarily a better measure.

[11] Michael C. Jensen, "The Performance of Mutual Funds in the Period 1945–1964," *Journal of Finance*, May 1968, pp. 389–416.

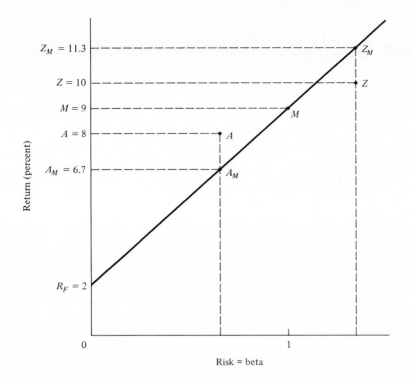

Figure 12-3 Differential return: funds A and Z.

statistical sense. This is possible because, in practice, the Jensen measure is ordinarily derived by running a regression of monthly or quarterly returns of the fund being evaluated against the return of a market index over the relevant performance period. The regression equation usually takes the following form:

$$R_p - R_F = A_p + B_p(R_M - R_F) + e \qquad (2)$$

Note that the regression equation is the same as the previous equation except that an intercept (alpha) term and an error term e have been added. The error term allows us to assess how well the regression equation fits the data—a low error indicating a well-defined relationship and a high error indicating a poorly defined relationship. The intercept term measures the extent to which the fund under evaluation gave an above-average or a below-average performance—a negative value indicating below-average performance and a positive value above-average performance.

The alpha value can in turn be tested by statistical methods for its degree of significance from a value of zero. The measure for this is the t value, which is merely the alpha value divided by the error of the regression. When the alpha value is high and the error in the regression is low, the t value will be high, and when the alpha value is low and regression error high, the t value will be low. A t value in excess of 2 is strongly indicative that the performance, either positive or negative, is highly significant in a statistical sense; that is, there is a small probability that the performance results from chance. For the two hypothetical funds, the t value of $+2.5$ for fund A indicated that the performance was above average and significantly so in a statistical sense, while the t value of -1.0 for fund Z indicated that its below-average performance could have occurred by chance.

COMPARISON OF PERFORMANCE MEASURES

Table 12-8 demonstrates the calculation of risk-adjusted returns for the three-year period 1978–1980 for a sample of seventeen mutual funds, as well as for the S&P 500, which is the benchmark for the comparison. The mutual funds include all those with assets over $500 million, with eight classified as having an investment objective of growth (G) and the other nine classified as having an investment objective of growth with income (IG). The data is thus generally representative of the investment behavior of large all-stock mutual funds over this performance period.

Note that the table shows the excess returns earned by the funds as well as the standard deviations and betas of the funds over the three-year period. It also gives the R^2 of the fund as a measure of the degree of diversification. The last three columns show the ratios of reward to variability, the ratios of reward to volatility, and the differential returns of the funds. The numbers in parentheses show the ranking of the individual funds according to each of the three risk-adjusted return measures.

Note that the realized excess return of the funds ranges between 6.4 and 22.9 percent, with an average of 11 percent, which was above that of the S&P 500 for the period. The betas of the funds range between .89 and 1.27, with an average of 1.06, slightly greater than that of the market as represented by the S&P 500. Note that the R^2 of the funds are all less than 1, averaging around .92 and thereby indicating that the funds are less than perfectly diversified. As a result, the riskiness of the funds is relatively larger when measured by the standard deviation than by the beta coefficient. Over the period the average standard deviation of the funds is 18.1 percent, 1.12 times the 16.1 percent standard deviation of the market.

The performance of the individual funds is consistent for alternative measures, as can be seen by the fact that the performance ranking of the funds is fairly similar with respect to all three measures. This is not surprising given the fact that we're evaluating large relatively well-diversified funds; that is, the riskiness of the funds differs little whether evaluated on the basis of standard deviation or market risk. By comparison with the overall market, the funds did better than the market over the period. Using the reward to variability ratio, ten of the seventeen funds have a better ratio than the market, while the reward to volatility ratio shows ten of the seventeen funds giving better risk-adjusted performances than the market. On the basis of differential return, ten funds show a positive return, with four funds having t values in excess of 2, thereby indicating a statistically significant performance according to this measure.[12]

---

[12] Mutual funds as a group obviously did quite well over this period; however, the period of evaluation is so short that it would not be appropriate to draw firm conclusions about the relative superiority or inferiority of the funds.

Table 12-8 Comparison of risk-adjusted performance measures for large all-stock mutual funds with the S&P 500, 1978–1980

	Excess return	Standard deviation	Beta	R^2	Sharpe ratio	Treynor ratio	Differential return
Affiliated (IG)	7.7	16.9	1.02	95	0.46 (12)	7.55 (12)	− 0.2 (12)
Chemical (G)	11.3	16.6	0.99	93	0.68 (7)	11.41 (7)	3.4 (7)
Dreyfus (IG)	11.6	18.1	1.07	92	0.64 (8)	10.84 (8)	2.6 (14)
Fidelity Fund (IG)	7.8	17.5	1.05	94	0.45 (13)	7.43 (13)	− 0.4 (14)
Fidelity Trend (G)	9.7	22.5	1.31	89	0.43 (14)	7.40 (14)	− 1.0 (16)
Investment Company of America (IG)	7.4	18.3	1.06	89	0.40 (16)	6.98 (16)	− 0.8 (15)
Investors Stock (IG)	4.5	16.1	0.94	89	0.28 (18)	7.79 (18)	− 2.4 (18)
Massachusetts Investors Growth Stock (G)	15.4	18.2	1.09	94	0.85 (3)	14.13 (3)	5.7 (3)
Massachusetts Investors Trust (IG)	9.0	17.9	1.09	97	0.50 (10)	8.26 (10)	0.4 (10)
National Investors Corp. (G)	12.9	20.4	1.22	94	0.64 (9)	10.57 (9)	2.4 (9)
Pioneer (IG)	12.3	17.6	1.04	92	0.70 (6)	11.83 (6)	3.6 (6)
Price Rowe Growth Stock (G)	6.4	17.9	1.04	93	0.36 (17)	6.15 (17)	− 1.5 (17)
Putnam Growth Fund (G)	12.5	14.6	0.89	96	0.86 (4)	14.04 (4)	5.2 (4)
Putnam Investors Fund (IG)	14.8	17.6	1.04	92	0.84 (2)	14.23 (2)	5.5 (2)
Technology Fund (G)	22.9	21.6	1.27	91	1.06 (1)	18.03 (1)	10.5 (1)
Templeton Growth Fund (G)	13.0	18.2	1.02	82	0.73 (5)	12.94 (5)	4.4 (5)
Windsor Fund (IG)	6.9	16.9	0.94	80	0.41 (15)	7.34 (15)	− 0.2 (13)
S&P 500	7.8	16.1	1.00	100	.48 (11)	7.80 (11)	0.0 (11)

Source: Computer Directions Advisor, Silver Spring, Md.

COMPONENTS OF INVESTMENT PERFORMANCE

The measures of risk-adjusted performance discussed in the previous section are primarily oriented to an analysis of the overall performance of a fund. For some purposes it will be useful to develop a more refined breakdown and assess the components, or sources, of performance. Eugene Fama has provided an analytical framework that elaborates on the three previously discussed risk-adjusted return methods and allows a more detailed breakdown of a fund's performance.[13] We'll conclude this section on risk-adjusted performance analysis by discussing Fama's approach.

Figure 12-4 is a risk-return diagram from the Fama study illustrating that framework of performance analysis. The vertical axis, as is usual, refers to return, while the horizontal axis shows risk measured in terms of both beta coefficient and standard deviation of return. Use of these two risk measures allows us to evaluate the performance of the fund both in terms of market risk and total risk. The diagonal line plotted on the diagram is the equation of the security market line (SML), using same data from Table 12-7 in the previous section — that is, a market return R_M of 9 percent and a risk-free rate R_f of 2 percent. It again provides the benchmark for assessing whether the realized return is more or less than commensurate with the risk incurred.

[13] Eugene Fama, "Components of Investment Performance," *Journal of Finance,* June 1972, pp. 551–567.

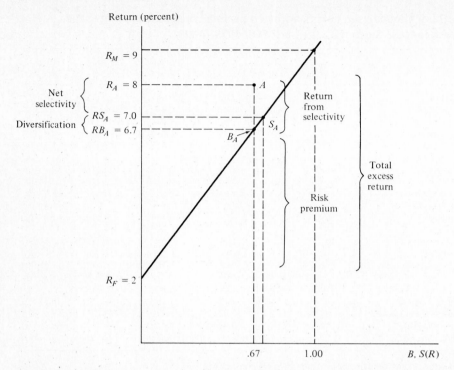

Figure 12-4 Decomposition of performance. *(Source: Eugene F. Fama, "Components of Investment Performance," Journal of Finance, June 1972, pp. 551–567.)*

For purposes of illustration, the data for the realized return (R_A = 8 percent) and market risk (B_A = .67) on hypothetical fund A, also shown in Table 12-7, are plotted on the diagram and designated point A. The diagram shows that at the fund's market-risk level B_A it would have been expected to earn the return RB_A = 6.7 percent. This expected return is composed of a risk-free component of 2 percent, shown as the distance from the baseline to R_f, and a risk premium of 4.7 percent, shown as the distance R_F to RB_A. The fund actually earned a return of 8 percent, which was 1.3 percent greater than expected, shown as the distance RB_A = R_A. We can designate this incremental return as the return to selectivity. Using this framework, we can then examine the overall performance of the fund in terms of selectivity and the return from assuming risk:

$$\text{Overall performance} = \text{selectivity} + \text{risk}$$
$$R_A - R_F = (R_A - RB_A) + (RB_A - R_F) \qquad (3)$$
$$8 - 2 = (8 - 6.7) + (6.7 - 2)$$
$$6 = 1.3 + 4.7$$

In striving to achieve above average returns, managers will generally have to forgo some diversification that will have its cost in additional portfolio risk. We can use this framework to determine the added expected return that would compensate for this additional diversification risk. We do this by first using the capital market line (CML) equation to determine the return commensurate with the incurred risk as measured by the standard deviation of return. Again using data from Table 12-7 for the standard deviation of the market (S_M) of 21 percent and the standard deviation of the fund (S_A) of 15 percent, along with the same risk-free rate and market return as used previously, we can determine the expected return for the fund (RS_A) as follows:

$$RS_A = R_F + (R_M - R_F)(S_A/S_M) \qquad (4)$$
$$= 2 + (9 - 2)(15/21)$$
$$= 7$$

The difference between this return of 7 percent and the expected return when considering only the market risk RB_A of 6.7 percent is the added return for diversification $RS_A - RB_A$—in this case $7 - 6.7 = 0.3$ percent, or the distance between RB_A and RS_A in the diagram. The net selectivity of the fund then becomes the overall selectivity less whatever penalty or added return is needed to compensate for the diversification risk. The diagram shows that the net selectivity of the fund is the distance $R_A = RS_A$. In terms of formulation the net selectivity can be shown as

$$\text{Net selectivity} = (R_A - RB_A) - (RS_A - RB_A) \qquad (5)$$
$$= (8 - 6.7) - (7 - 6.7)$$
$$= 1.3 - 0.3$$
$$= 1$$

Because the diversification measure is always nonnegative, net selectivity will always be equal to or less than selectivity.[14] The two will be equal only when the portfolio is completely diversified, as would be indicated by a coefficient of determination R^2 with the market of 1. By comparing the R^2 of funds, one can obtain a quick indication of the degree of diversification risk incurred by a fund. Funds with a high R^2 of, say, .95 and above have relatively little diversification risk, while funds with a relatively low R^2 of, say, .90 and below have a relatively large diversification risk.

To conclude this section, we can use the Fama framework for components of performance to evaluate the mutual funds shown in Table 12-9. These are the same funds that we used in previous comparisons of risk-adjusted performance. Note that for each fund's overall performance the table breaks down into the component due to selectivity and the component due to risk. It further shows the expected return from diversification and from that derives the net selectivity of the fund.

Note that all the funds, as would be expected, are less than perfectly diversified, with an R^2 of less than 1, and as a result require added return to compensate for the diversification risk. The required return ranges from 0.2 to 0.9 percent, with an average of 0.4 percent for the sample of funds. After adjusting for the diversification risk, the funds showed, on average, a net return to selectivity of 1.8 percent with a high of 9.9 percent and a low of -2.9 percent, compared with an average gross return to

[14] The Fama framework of analysis allows further and more elaborate comparisons. For our purposes the one dealing with stock selectivity is most pertinent.

Table 12-9 Components of performance for large all-stock mutual funds (%), 1978–1980

	Total excess return	Risk premium	Return from selectivity	Diversification	Net selectivity
Affiliated (IG)	7.7	7.9	− 0.2	0.2	−0.4
Chemical (G)	11.3	7.9	3.4	0.2	3.2
Dreyfus (IG)	11.6	9.0	2.6	0.5	1.9
Fidelity Fund (IG)	7.8	8.2	− 0.4	0.3	−0.7
Fidelity Trend (G)	9.7	8.7	1.0	0.7	0.3
Investment Company of America (IG)	7.4	8.2	− 0.8	0.6	−1.4
Investors Stock (IG)	4.5	6.9	− 2.4	0.5	−2.9
Massachusetts Investors Growth Stock (G)	15.4	9.7	5.7	0.3	5.4
Massachusetts Investors Trust (IG)	9.0	8.6	0.4	0.2	0.2
National Investors Corp. (G)	12.9	10.5	2.4	0.4	2.0
Pioneer (IG)	12.3	8.7	3.6	0.4	3.2
Price Rowe Growth Stock (G)	6.4	7.9	− 1.5	0.3	−1.8
Putnam Growth Fund (G)	12.5	7.3	5.2	0.2	5.0
Putnam Investors Fund (IG)	14.8	9.9	5.5	0.4	5.1
Technology Fund (G)	22.9	12.4	10.5	0.6	9.9
Templeton Growth Fund (G)	13.2	8.8	4.4	0.8	3.6
Windsor Fund (IG)	6.9	7.1	− 0.2	0.9	−1.2
S&P 500	7.8	7.8	0	0	0

Source: Computer Directions Advisor, Silver Spring, Md.

selectivity of 2.2 percent, with a low of −2.4 percent and a high of 10.5 percent. The appropriate yardstick of performance — gross or net selectivity — will of course depend on whether the investor evaluates the performance of the fund manager as a single or multiple manager.

CONCLUSION

It's useful to conclude this chapter on performance evaluation by consolidating the three aspects of performance — asset allocation, weighting shifts across asset classes, and security selection within asset classes — into an overall performance evaluation for our hypothetical pension fund. Comparing these three aspects simultaneously allows us to determine the relative effectiveness of the individual components of the investment process. In addition, it allows us to assess the effectiveness of the process toward achieving the fund's overall investment goal of earning a real return at or exceeding the target return of 4 percent.

Table 12-10 shows the performance of the three main components of the investment process along with the net effect of these three individual aspects on the overall fund

Table 12-10 Aggregate performance evaluation, 1976–1980

Activity	Five-year average
Asset allocation	12.7
Weighting	2.1
Selectivity	3.5
Aggregate performance	18.3
Consumer Price Index	8.9
Real return	9.4
Target return	4.0
Performance increment	5.4

performance over the 1976–1980 period. Note that the table shows a building-up of performance, beginning with the basic asset allocation, then weighting, and finally security selection. The fourth line shows the net effect on the fund's return from all these activities, while the bottom line shows how the aggregate performance relates to the fund's goal of earning a 4 percent real return.

Note that all three components contributed to performance. The basic asset allocation essentially resulted in a return sufficient to meet the minimum target, as was previously indicated in this chapter. Weighting added an increment of 2.1 percent to return, and selectivity added another 3.5 percent. Each of the investment activities was thus productive, and the overall endeavor resulted in a return well in excess of the 4 percent target. The performance evaluation of this hypothetical fund implies that it is productive and under control.

PROBLEMS

1 Indicate and describe the three major aspects of performance that one should assess in evaluating fund performance.

2 Referring to Table 12-3, determine the year-by-year and five-year average return assuming the following asset allocation:
    (1) domestic equities, 55 percent
    (2) German equities, 10 percent
    (3) Japanese equities, 10 percent
    (4) U. K. equities, 5 percent
    (5) long-term bonds, 15 percent
    (6) treasury bills, 5 percent

3 Using Tables 12-4 and 12-5, determine the year-by-year return to weighting assuming the following changes:
    (1) U. K. equities overweighted by 5 percent and treasury bills underweighted by 5 percent in 1976
    (2) domestic equities overweighted by 5 percent and Japanese equities underweighted by 5 percent in 1977
    (3) domestic equities overweighted by 5 percent and long-term bonds underweighted by 5 percent in 1978
    (4) Japanese equities overweighted by 5 percent and treasury bills underweighted by 5 percent in 1979
    (5) long-term bonds overweighted by 5 percent and U. K. stocks underweighted by 5 percent in 1980

4 Contrast performance evaluation based on index comparisons to that based on comparison to other peer groups (e.g., bonds versus bonds).

5 Refer to Table 12-7, and assume that all the data is the same except that fund *A* earned a return of 5 percent and fund *Z* earned 12 percent. Calculate the Sharpe ratio and Treynor ratio, and rank the performance of the three funds, including market.

6 Assume again that fund *A* earned 5 percent and fund *Z* earned 12 percent. Calculate the differential return for the two funds, using the same risk data and market data as before.

7 Using the Fama framework of performance components, determine the selectivity, diversification return required, and net selectivity for fund *Z*. Use the data from Table 12-7 as inputs.

SELECTED REFERENCES

Bank Administration Institute: *Measuring the Investment Performance of Pension Funds,* Park Ridge, Ill., 1968.

Dietz, P. O.: *Pension Funds: Measuring Performance,* The Free Press, New York, 1966.

————, H. R. Fogler, and D. J. Hardy: "The Challenge of Analyzing Bond Portfolio Returns," *Journal of Portfolio Management,* Spring 1980, pp. 53–58.

Elton, Edwin, and Martin Gruber: *Modern Portfolio Theory and Investment Analysis,* Wiley, New York, 1981.

Fama, Eugene: "Components of Investment Performance," *Journal of Finance,* June 1972, pp. 551–567.

Jensen, Michael C.: "The Performance of Mutual Funds in the Period 1945–1964, *Journal of Finance,* May 1968, pp. 389–416.

Lorie, James, and Mary Hamilton: *The Stock Market: Theories and Evidence,* Irwin, Homewood, Ill., 1973.

Martin, John, Arthur Keown, and James L. Farrell: "Do Fund Objectives Affect Diversification Policies?" *Journal of Portfolio Management,* Winter 1982, pp. 19–28

Reilly, Frank: *Investment Analysis and Portfolio Management,* Dryden Press, Hinsdale, Ill., 1979.

Roll, Richard: "Performance Evaluation and Benchmark Errors," *Journal of Portfolio Management,* Summer 1980, pp. 12–20.

Rosenberg, B.: "A Critique of Performance Measurement," paper presented at Spring 1980 Seminar of the Institute for Quantitative Research in Finance, Napa, Calif.

Sharpe, W. F.: "Mutual Fund Performance," *Journal of Business,* January 1966, pp. 119–138.

Treynor, J. L.: "How to Rate Management of Investment Funds," *Harvard Business Review,* January–February, 1965, pp. 63–75.

Williams, Arthur: *Managing Your Investment Manager,* Dow-Jones–Irwin, New York, 1980.

Williamson, Peter: "Performance Measurement," in Edward Altman (ed.): *The Financial Handbook,* Wiley, New York, 1980.

ANSWERS TO END-OF-CHAPTER PROBLEMS

Presented here are the answers to those end-of-chapter problems that require numerical calculations. For the most part, only the final answers are given. They should serve as a guide to whether or not one is "on the right track." Not presented are the answers to those problems that involve verbal discussion.

Chapter 1

1. 20 percent
2. 9.5 percent market weighted; 17.5 percent equal weighted
3. 26.7 percent
4. −22.2 percent; −.7 percent compound
5. 67 percent^2 covariance; +1 correlation
7. 3.1 percent; 86.9 at 12 percent inflation; 94.3 at 3 percent inflation

Chapter 2

1. .16 expected return; .2575 variance of return
2. 20 percent; 13 percent; 8 percent; 7 percent; 6 percent
3. 31125 and 319600 Markowitz model; 752 and 2402 single-index model; 760 and 2410 multi-index model
4. 1.11
5. 15.7 percent expected return; 482 percent^2 variance of return
6. 15.3 percent expected return; 405 percent^2 variance of return

Chapter 3

1. All earn 5 percent; 3.5 percent to lender; 2 percent to all-equity investor; .5 percent loss to borrower
2. 16 percent
4. 13.2 percent security J; 16.8 percent security K
6. $48.21

Chapter 4

1. (a) 8 percent; (b) 16.8 percent; (c) 3.8 percent
2. 4-year is $1067 at 8 percent and $938 at 12 percent for a price decline of 12.1 percent; 7-year is 1106 at 8 percent and $907 at 12 percent for a price decline of 18 percent
3. 4 years; 3.4 years; 2.2 years; 13.5 years; 15.7 years
4. .37 percent; .29 percent; .17 percent; 1.25 percent; 1.41 percent
5. 8 times
6. 7.7 times
7. (a) -22 percent; (b) -7 percent

Chapter 5

1. 14.9 percent rate of return; $6.38 EPS; 5 percent sustainable growth
2. 9.2 percent
3. $39.46 price
4. (a) 14.6 percent; (b) 17.7 percent
5. $31
6. 19 percent
7. 15 percent Raychem; 20 percent Great Lakes; 10 percent Emery; 31 percent ACF; 24 percent Gulf

Chapter 6

4. .26 combined IC
5. 3.5 percent (1); 1.7 percent (2); 0 percent (3); -1.7 percent (4); -3.5 percent (5)

Chapter 7

4. 1.1; 1.4 assuming equal probability
5. 6.0 percent (1); 3.0 percent (2); 0 percent (3); -3.0 percent (4); -6.0 percent (5)
6. 1.43

Chapter 8

4. 4.3 years; overvalued
6. .63 (stable); .24 (growth); .13 (cyclical)
7. (a) inferior; (b) inferior; (c) superior

Chapter 9

1. Premium; 6.1 percent per annum
2. 13.3 percent
3. $2.05/£
6. 6.5 percent

Chapter 10

2. Composite return: 3.72 percent (1); 4.50 percent (2); 5.01 percent (3); 5.63 percent (4); 5.78 percent (5); 5.80 percent (10); 6.62 percent (20); 6.40 percent (30)

Chapter 11

1. (*a*) $8 call, zero put, $2 net profit; (*b*) zero call, zero put, $6 net loss; (*c*) zero call, $5 put, $1 net loss
2. Sell 3 calls short and purchase one share of stock
3. $4.69; .61 hedge ratio

Chapter 12

2. 19.0 percent (1976); 3.8 percent (1977); 12.7 percent (1978); 10.8 percent (1979); 22.7 percent (1980); 13.2 percent (avg)
3. −2.3 percent (1976); −1.1 percent (1977); −.2 percent (1978); −1.3 percent (1979); −.3 percent (1980)
5. Sharpe ratio and rank: .20(3) fund *A*; .33(1) fund *M*; .31(2) fund *Z*. Treynor ratio and rank: 4.5(3) fund *A*; 7.0(2) fund *M*; 7.5(1) fund *Z*
6. −1.7 percent fund *A*; .7 percent fund *Z*
7. −1.3 percent selectivity; 1.4 percent diversification; −2.7 percent net selectivity

Table B-1 Compound sum of $1

Period	1%	2%	3%	4%	5%	6%	7%	8%	9%	10%	12%
1	1.010	1.020	1.030	1.040	1.050	1.060	1.070	1.080	1.090	1.100	1.120
2	1.020	1.040	1.061	1.082	1.103	1.124	1.145	1.166	1.188	1.210	1.254
3	1.030	1.061	1.093	1.125	1.158	1.191	1.225	1.260	1.295	1.331	1.405
4	1.041	1.082	1.126	1.170	1.216	1.262	1.311	1.360	1.412	1.464	1.574
5	1.051	1.104	1.159	1.217	1.276	1.338	1.403	1.469	1.539	1.611	1.762
6	1.062	1.126	1.194	1.265	1.340	1.419	1.501	1.587	1.677	1.772	1.974
7	1.072	1.149	1.230	1.316	1.407	1.504	1.606	1.714	1.828	1.949	2.211
8	1.083	1.172	1.267	1.369	1.477	1.594	1.718	1.851	1.993	2.144	2.476
9	1.094	1.195	1.305	1.423	1.551	1.689	1.838	1.999	2.172	2.358	2.773
10	1.105	1.219	1.344	1.480	1.629	1.791	1.967	2.159	2.367	2.594	3.106
11	1.116	1.243	1.384	1.539	1.710	1.898	2.105	2.332	2.580	2.853	3.479
12	1.127	1.268	1.426	1.601	1.796	2.012	2.252	2.518	2.813	3.138	3.896
13	1.138	1.294	1.469	1.665	1.886	2.133	2.410	2.720	3.066	3.452	4.363
14	1.149	1.319	1.513	1.732	1.980	2.261	2.579	2.937	3.342	3.797	4.887
15	1.161	1.346	1.558	1.801	2.079	2.397	2.759	3.172	3.642	4.177	5.474
16	1.173	1.373	1.605	1.873	2.183	2.540	2.952	3.426	3.970	4.595	6.130
17	1.184	1.400	1.653	1.948	2.292	2.693	3.159	3.700	4.328	5.054	6.866
18	1.196	1.428	1.702	2.026	2.407	2.854	3.380	3.996	4.717	5.560	7.690
19	1.208	1.457	1.754	2.107	2.527	3.026	3.617	4.316	5.142	6.116	8.613
20	1.220	1.486	1.806	2.191	2.653	3.207	3.870	4.661	5.604	6.727	9.646
25	1.282	1.641	2.094	2.666	3.386	4.292	5.427	6.848	8.623	10.835	17.000
30	1.348	1.811	2.427	3.243	4.322	5.743	7.612	10.063	13.268	17.449	29.960

Period	14%	16%	18%	20%	25%	30%	40%	50%
1	1.140	1.160	1.180	1.200	1.250	1.300	1.400	1.500
2	1.300	1.346	1.392	1.440	1.563	1.690	1.960	2.250
3	1.482	1.561	1.643	1.728	1.953	2.197	2.744	3.375
4	1.689	1.811	1.939	2.074	2.441	2.856	3.842	5.063
5	1.925	2.100	2.288	2.488	3.052	3.713	5.378	7.594
6	2.195	2.436	2.700	2.986	3.815	4.827	7.530	11.391
7	2.502	2.826	3.185	3.583	4.768	6.275	10.541	17.086
8	2.853	3.278	3.759	4.300	5.960	8.157	14.758	25.629
9	3.252	3.803	4.435	5.160	7.451	10.604	20.661	38.443
10	3.707	4.411	5.234	6.192	9.313	13.786	28.925	57.665
11	4.226	5.117	6.176	7.430	11.642	17.922	40.496	86.498
12	4.818	5.936	7.288	8.916	14.552	23.298	56.694	129.746
13	5.492	6.886	8.599	10.699	18.190	30.288	79.371	194.620
14	6.261	7.988	10.147	12.839	22.737	39.374	111.120	291.929
15	7.138	9.266	11.974	15.407	28.422	51.186	155.568	437.894
16	8.137	10.748	14.129	18.488	35.527	66.542	217.795	656.841
17	9.276	12.468	16.672	22.186	44.409	86.504	304.913	985.261
18	10.575	14.463	19.673	26.623	55.511	112.455	426.879	1,477.892
19	12.056	16.777	23.214	31.948	69.389	146.192	597.630	2,216.838
20	13.743	19.461	27.393	38.338	86.736	190.050	836.683	3,325.257
25	26.462	40.874	62.669	95.396	264.698	705.641	4,499.880	25,251.168
30	50.950	85.850	143.371	237.376	807.794	2,619.996	24,201.432	191,751.059

Table B-2 Sum of an annuity of $1 for *n* periods

Period	1%	2%	3%	4%	5%	6%	7%	8%
1	1.000	1.000	1.000	1.000	1.000	1.000	1.000	1.000
2	2.010	2.020	2.030	2.040	2.050	2.060	2.070	2.080
3	3.030	3.060	3.091	3.122	3.153	3.184	3.215	3.246
4	4.060	4.122	4.184	4.246	4.310	4.375	4.440	4.506
5	5.101	5.204	5.309	5.416	5.526	5.637	5.751	5.867
6	6.152	6.308	6.468	6.633	6.802	6.975	7.153	7.336
7	7.214	7.434	7.662	7.898	8.142	8.394	8.654	8.923
8	8.286	8.583	8.892	9.214	9.549	9.897	10.260	10.637
9	9.369	9.755	10.159	10.583	11.027	11.491	11.978	12.488
10	10.462	10.950	11.464	12.006	12.578	13.181	13.816	14.487
11	11.567	12.169	12.808	13.486	14.207	14.972	15.784	16.645
12	12.683	13.412	14.192	15.026	15.917	16.870	17.888	18.977
13	13.809	14.680	15.618	16.627	17.713	18.882	20.141	21.495
14	14.947	15.974	17.086	18.292	19.599	21.015	22.550	24.215
15	16.097	17.293	18.599	20.024	21.579	23.276	25.129	27.152
16	17.258	18.639	20.157	21.825	23.657	25.673	27.888	30.324
17	18.430	20.012	21.762	23.698	25.840	28.213	30.840	33.750
18	19.615	21.412	23.414	25.645	28.132	30.906	33.999	37.450
19	20.811	22.841	25.117	27.671	30.539	33.760	37.379	41.446
20	22.019	24.297	26.870	29.778	33.066	36.786	40.995	45.762
25	28.243	32.030	36.459	41.646	47.727	54.865	63.249	73.106
30	34.785	40.568	47.575	56.085	66.439	79.058	94.461	113.283

Period	9%	10%	12%	14%	16%	18%	20%
1	1.000	1.000	1.000	1.000	1.000	1.000	1.000
2	2.090	2.100	2.120	2.140	2.160	2.180	2.200
3	3.278	3.310	3.374	3.440	3.506	3.572	3.640
4	4.573	4.641	4.779	4.921	5.066	5.215	5.368
5	5.985	6.105	6.353	6.610	6.877	7.154	7.442
6	7.523	7.716	8.115	8.536	8.977	9.442	9.930
7	9.200	9.487	10.089	10.730	11.414	12.142	12.916
8	11.028	11.436	12.300	13.233	14.240	15.327	16.499
9	13.021	13.579	14.776	16.085	17.519	19.086	20.799
10	15.193	15.937	17.549	19.337	21.321	23.521	25.959
11	17.560	18.531	20.655	23.045	25.733	28.755	32.150
12	20.141	21.384	24.133	27.271	30.850	34.931	39.581
13	22.953	24.523	28.029	32.089	36.786	42.219	48.497
14	26.019	27.975	32.393	37.581	43.672	50.818	59.196
15	29.361	31.772	37.280	43.842	51.660	60.965	72.035
16	33.003	35.950	42.753	50.980	60.925	72.939	87.442
17	36.974	40.545	48.884	59.118	71.673	87.068	105.931
18	41.301	45.599	55.750	68.394	84.141	103.740	128.117
19	46.018	51.159	63.440	78.969	98.603	123.414	154.740
20	51.160	57.275	72.052	91.025	115.380	146.628	186.688
25	84.701	98.347	133.334	181.871	249.214	342.603	471.981
30	136.308	164.494	241.333	356.787	530.312	790.948	1,181.882

Period	25%	30%	40%	50%
1	1.000	1.000	1.000	1.000
2	2.250	2.300	2.400	2.500
3	3.813	3.990	4.360	4.750
4	5.766	6.187	7.104	8.125
5	8.207	9.043	10.946	13.187
6	11.259	12.756	16.324	20.781
7	15.073	17.583	23.853	32.172
8	19.842	23.858	34.395	49.258
9	25.802	32.015	49.153	74.887
10	33.253	42.619	69.814	113.330
11	42.566	56.405	98.739	170.995
12	54.208	74.327	139.235	257.493
13	68.760	97.625	195.929	387.239
14	86.949	127.913	275.300	581.859
15	109.687	167.286	386.420	873.788
16	138.109	218.472	541.988	1,311.682
17	173.636	285.014	759.784	1,968.523
18	218.045	371.518	1,064.697	2,953.784
19	273.556	483.973	1,491.576	4,431.676
20	342.945	630.165	2,089.206	6,648.513
25	1,054.791	2,348.803	11,247.199	50,500.337
30	3,227.174	8,729.985	60,501.081	383,500.118

Table B-3 Present value of $1

Period	1%	2%	3%	4%	5%	6%	7%	8%	9%	10%
1	0.990	0.980	0.971	0.962	0.952	0.943	0.935	0.926	0.917	0.909
2	0.980	0.961	0.943	0.925	0.907	0.890	0.873	0.857	0.842	0.826
3	0.971	0.942	0.915	0.889	0.864	0.840	0.816	0.794	0.772	0.751
4	0.961	0.924	0.888	0.855	0.823	0.792	0.763	0.735	0.708	0.683
5	0.951	0.906	0.863	0.822	0.784	0.747	0.713	0.681	0.650	0.621
6	0.942	0.888	0.837	0.790	0.746	0.705	0.666	0.630	0.596	0.564
7	0.933	0.871	0.813	0.760	0.711	0.665	0.623	0.583	0.547	0.513
8	0.923	0.853	0.789	0.731	0.677	0.627	0.582	0.540	0.502	0.467
9	0.914	0.837	0.766	0.703	0.645	0.592	0.544	0.500	0.460	0.424
10	0.905	0.820	0.744	0.676	0.614	0.558	0.508	0.463	0.422	0.386
11	0.896	0.804	0.722	0.650	0.585	0.527	0.475	0.429	0.388	0.350
12	0.887	0.788	0.701	0.625	0.557	0.497	0.444	0.397	0.356	0.319
13	0.879	0.773	0.681	0.601	0.530	0.469	0.415	0.368	0.326	0.290
14	0.870	0.758	0.661	0.577	0.505	0.442	0.388	0.340	0.299	0.263
15	0.861	0.743	0.642	0.555	0.481	0.417	0.362	0.315	0.275	0.239
16	0.853	0.728	0.623	0.534	0.458	0.394	0.339	0.292	0.252	0.218
17	0.844	0.714	0.605	0.513	0.436	0.371	0.317	0.270	0.231	0.198
18	0.836	0.700	0.587	0.494	0.416	0.350	0.296	0.250	0.212	0.180
19	0.828	0.686	0.570	0.475	0.396	0.331	0.277	0.232	0.194	0.164
20	0.820	0.673	0.554	0.456	0.377	0.312	0.258	0.215	0.178	0.149
25	0.780	0.610	0.478	0.375	0.295	0.233	0.184	0.146	0.116	0.092
30	0.742	0.552	0.412	0.308	0.231	0.174	0.131	0.099	0.075	0.057

Period	12%	14%	16%	18%	20%	25%	30%	40%	50%
1	0.893	0.877	0.862	0.847	0.833	0.800	0.769	0.714	0.667
2	0.797	0.769	0.743	0.718	0.694	0.640	0.592	0.510	0.444
3	0.712	0.675	0.641	0.609	0.579	0.512	0.455	0.364	0.296
4	0.636	0.592	0.552	0.516	0.482	0.410	0.350	0.260	0.198
5	0.567	0.519	0.476	0.437	0.402	0.328	0.269	0.186	0.132
6	0.507	0.456	0.410	0.370	0.335	0.262	0.207	0.133	0.088
7	0.452	0.400	0.354	0.314	0.279	0.210	0.159	0.095	0.059
8	0.404	0.351	0.305	0.266	0.233	0.168	0.123	0.068	0.039
9	0.361	0.308	0.263	0.225	0.194	0.134	0.094	0.048	0.026
10	0.322	0.270	0.227	0.191	0.162	0.107	0.073	0.035	0.017
11	0.287	0.237	0.195	0.162	0.135	0.086	0.056	0.025	0.012
12	0.257	0.208	0.168	0.137	0.112	0.069	0.043	0.018	0.008
13	0.229	0.182	0.145	0.116	0.093	0.055	0.033	0.013	0.005
14	0.205	0.160	0.125	0.099	0.078	0.044	0.025	0.009	0.003
15	0.183	0.140	0.108	0.084	0.065	0.035	0.020	0.006	0.002
16	0.163	0.123	0.093	0.071	0.054	0.028	0.015	0.005	0.002
17	0.146	0.108	0.080	0.060	0.045	0.023	0.012	0.003	0.001
18	0.130	0.095	0.069	0.051	0.038	0.018	0.009	0.002	0.001
19	0.116	0.083	0.060	0.043	0.031	0.014	0.007	0.002	0.000
20	0.104	0.073	0.051	0.037	0.026	0.012	0.005	0.001	0.000
25	0.059	0.038	0.024	0.016	0.010	0.004	0.001	0.000	0.000
30	0.033	0.020	0.012	0.007	0.004	0.001	0.000	0.000	0.000

Table B-4 Present value of an annuity of $1

Period	1%	2%	3%	4%	5%	6%	7%	8%	9%
1	0.990	0.980	0.971	0.962	0.952	0.943	0.935	0.926	0.917
2	1.970	1.942	1.913	1.886	1.859	1.833	1.808	1.783	1.759
3	2.941	2.884	2.829	2.775	2.723	2.673	2.624	2.577	2.531
4	3.902	3.808	3.717	3.630	3.546	3.465	3.387	3.312	3.240
5	4.853	4.713	4.580	4.452	4.329	4.212	4.100	3.993	3.890
6	5.795	5.601	5.417	5.242	5.076	4.917	4.767	4.623	4.486
7	6.728	6.472	6.230	6.002	5.786	5.582	5.389	5.206	5.033
8	7.652	7.325	7.020	6.733	6.463	6.210	5.971	5.747	5.535
9	8.566	8.162	7.786	7.435	7.108	6.802	6.515	6.247	5.995
10	9.471	8.983	8.530	8.111	7.722	7.360	7.024	6.710	6.418
11	10.368	9.787	9.253	8.760	8.306	7.887	7.499	7.139	6.805
12	11.255	10.575	9.954	9.385	8.863	8.384	7.943	7.536	7.161
13	12.134	11.348	10.635	9.986	9.394	8.853	8.358	7.904	7.487
14	13.004	12.106	11.296	10.563	9.899	9.295	8.745	8.244	7.786
15	13.865	12.849	11.938	11.118	10.380	9.712	9.108	8.559	8.061
16	14.718	13.578	12.561	11.652	10.838	10.106	9.447	8.851	8.313
17	15.562	14.292	13.166	12.166	11.274	10.477	9.763	9.122	8.544
18	16.398	14.992	13.754	12.659	11.690	10.828	10.059	9.372	8.756
19	17.226	15.678	14.324	13.134	12.085	11.158	10.336	9.604	8.950
20	18.046	16.351	14.877	13.590	12.462	11.470	10.594	9.818	9.129
25	22.023	19.523	17.413	15.622	14.094	12.783	11.654	10.675	9.823
30	25.808	22.396	19.600	17.292	15.372	13.765	12.409	11.258	10.274

Period	10%	12%	14%	16%	18%	20%	25%	30%	40%	50%
1	0.909	0.893	0.877	0.862	0.847	0.833	0.800	0.769	0.714	0.667
2	1.736	1.690	1.647	1.605	1.566	1.528	1.440	1.361	1.224	1.111
3	2.487	2.402	2.322	2.246	2.174	2.106	1.952	1.816	1.589	1.407
4	3.170	3.037	2.914	2.798	2.690	2.589	2.362	2.166	1.849	1.605
5	3.791	3.605	3.433	3.274	3.127	2.991	2.689	2.436	2.035	1.737
6	4.355	4.111	3.889	3.685	3.498	3.326	2.951	2.643	2.168	1.824
7	4.868	4.564	4.288	4.039	3.812	3.605	3.161	2.802	2.263	1.883
8	5.335	4.968	4.639	4.344	4.078	3.837	3.329	2.925	2.331	1.922
9	5.759	5.328	4.946	4.607	4.303	4.031	3.463	3.019	2.379	1.948
10	6.145	5.650	5.216	4.833	4.494	4.192	3.571	3.092	2.414	1.965
11	6.495	5.938	5.453	5.029	4.656	4.327	3.656	3.147	2.438	1.977
12	6.814	6.194	5.660	5.197	4.793	4.439	3.725	3.190	2.456	1.985
13	7.103	6.424	5.842	5.342	4.910	4.533	3.780	3.223	2.469	1.990
14	7.367	6.628	6.002	5.468	5.008	4.611	3.824	3.249	2.478	1.993
15	7.606	6.811	6.142	5.575	5.092	4.675	3.859	3.268	2.484	1.995
16	7.824	6.974	6.265	5.668	5.162	4.730	3.887	3.283	2.489	1.997
17	8.022	7.120	6.373	5.749	5.222	4.775	3.910	3.295	2.492	1.998
18	8.201	7.250	6.467	5.818	5.273	4.812	3.928	3.304	2.494	1.999
19	8.365	7.366	6.550	5.877	5.316	4.843	3.942	3.311	2.496	1.999
20	8.514	7.469	6.623	5.929	5.353	4.870	3.954	3.316	2.497	1.999
25	9.077	7.843	6.873	6.097	5.467	4.948	3.985	3.329	2.499	2.000
30	9.427	8.055	7.003	6.177	5.517	4.979	3.995	3.332	2.500	2.000

INDEX